A History of
English Food

Clarissa Dickson Wright

A History of English Food

BOOKS

Published by Random House Books 2011

2 4 6 8 10 9 7 5 3 1

Copyright © Clarissa Dickson Wright 2011

First published in Great Britain in 2011 by
Random House Books
Random House, 20 Vauxhall Bridge Road,
London SW1V 2SA

www.randomhouse.co.uk

Addresses for companies within The Random House Group Limited can be found at:
www.randomhouse.co.uk/offices.htm

The Random House Group Limited Reg. No. 954009

A CIP catalogue record for this book is available from the British Library

ISBN 9781905211852

The Random House Group Limited supports The Forest Stewardship Council (FSC®), the
leading international forest certification organisation. Our books carrying the FSC label are
printed on FSC® certified paper. FSC is the only forest certification scheme endorsed by
the leading environmental organisations, including Greenpeace. Our paper procurement
policy can be found at www.randomhouse.co.uk/environment

Text designed by Dinah Drazin

Typeset by Palimpsest Book Production Limited
Falkirk, Stirlingshire

Printed and bound in Great Britain by
Clays Ltd, St Ives plc

Excerpt from *French Provincial Cooking* by Elizabeth David (copyright © Elizabeth David),
reproduced by kind permission of the author's estate

Excerpt from *The Road To Wigan Pier* by George Orwell (copyright © George Orwell, 1937)
reprinted by permission of Bill Hamilton as the Literary Executor of the Estate
of the Late Sonia Brownell Orwell and Secker & Warburg Ltd.

The publisher has made all reasonable effort to contact copyright holders for permission
and apologises for any omissions or errors in the form of credits given.
Corrections may be made to future reprints.

To my father, who taught me how and where to look things up and how to join the facts up laterally

Contents

Introduction

This is the book I always knew I would write some day. Over my sixty-four years, two of my great passions have been food and history. So when, in 2006, Nigel Wilcockson of Random House clicked his fingers, I jumped and the book was born. There was something of a hiatus when I fell ill with pleurisy and complications set in, but last autumn I was able to return to the task.

England is unique: a small island with a history of European holdings and foreign empires, of waves of invasions and immigration. English food is an amalgam of all these experiences. At times the results have been very exciting, at others dull and pedestrian. Things have never stayed static: every generation has made its contribution, and just as certain foods have come into fashion, others have disappeared. Today, we no longer yearn for swan or heron, and country folk no longer subsist on badger or seal. On the other hand, I suspect many of our ancestors would be horrified by our addiction to the duller reaches of fast food.

Food tells us so much about the nature of society at a particular point in time, whether royalty, the urban and rural poor, or the merchant class who have played such a vital role in English history (I'm intrigued, for example, by the fact that the Puritans among them were instrumental in banning

Christmas plum pudding after the Civil War, though they other-wise ate well). Food also tells us about individuals. For me, the picture I have of Queen Victoria's boiled egg sitting in its gold egg cup with its gold spoon helps to humanise her, just as her passion for puddings does. Dr Johnson's vast daily intake of tea may not explain his other secret vice – you will have to go to Lichfield to find out about that – but it does help to explain that nose and that complexion.

Throughout the book like a silver thread runs my other great passion: field sports, an important means of providing food and controlling pests and vermin.

A professor of nutrition at Strathclyde University remarked recently that we have no idea how soon we will need to be self-sufficient. I hope, therefore, that while our food continues to evolve, we will increasingly produce our own ingredients and show the same flexibility and ingenuity that our ancestors did.

And I do hope that as you read the book, you will come to share my admiration for our forebears and will want to try some of the dishes that they prepared and loved. At the same time I hope that I may be able to shatter a few firmly held beliefs and drop in a few surprises.

Eat well and enjoy the book.

Clarissa Dickson Wright
20 July 2011

Acknowledgements

I would like to thank my publisher, Nigel Wilcockson, who conceived and commissioned this book and was a tower of strength throughout. I would also like to extend my gratitude to my friend and agent Heather Holden-Brown, who always believed it would be finished; to Isabel Rutherford, for her excellent research; to Pauline Dinsdale, who valiantly typed it all up; and to Suzannah, my cranial osteopath, without whose ministrations I might never have made it.

Sometime between 1320 and 1340 Geoffrey Luttrell, who owned substantial estates in Lincolnshire, commissioned a psalter whose magnificent illuminations provide fascinating glimpses of contemporary everyday life. Here sheep are being tended by two shepherds, one of them playing a double pipe. The rather diminutive nature of the sheep is partly due to artistic licence and partly due to the fact that medieval sheep were much smaller than the ones we know today.

CHAPTER I

Bacon and New-laid Eggs
The Medieval Larder

A history of English food could very well start in Anglo-Saxon times, or possibly the Roman period, or arguably even earlier, but I have elected to begin my journey in the mid twelfth century. The date may seem a little arbitrary, but I think the 1150s and 1160s were a significant moment in our culinary history, for they were the decades that started to see major developments in what we ate and the way we ate it. And there were two simple reasons for this: peace and wealth. This was a time of relative tranquillity: Henry Fitz-Empress's enthronement as Henry II in 1154 ended years of civil war between his mother Matilda, only surviving daughter of Henry I, and her cousin Stephen. As for wealth, Henry ruled an empire that included Normandy and Anjou as well as England. Moreover, England at this time was governed by dynamic and stylish people: Henry's reign wasn't without its problems, but he had all the energy and intelligence you could wish for in a ruler and he was married to one of the most stylish and influential women ever to have lived – the beautiful Eleanor of Aquitaine, who also happened to be the richest woman in Europe.

England during this period was, of course, a feudal country. Loyalty was to your lord, not to your country. Tenure of property descended in established order from the Crown (who owned all the land), through the great nobles to the minor lords and knights, and down eventually to the peasants who worked the land and turned out to fight for their landlords as and when required. Everyone derived seisin, or possession of land, from someone else, and it was in the interests of the overlord to ensure that his labour was housed and fed. At the same time the power of community created an interdependence where everyone had their place and had to pull their weight for the good of all. This meant that the basics of life were generally provided. Ariadne, a thirteen-year-old friend of mine, once asked me what homeless people ate at this time, and it struck me that the homeless didn't really exist then. Yes, there were outlaws who lived in the forest for various reasons, mostly to do with evading the law (hence their name), but even they tended to band together to make life easier. The fact is that labour was a valuable asset, not to be wasted or starved. This became even more the case in the mid fourteenth century when over a third of the population was wiped out by the Black Death.

To an extent, the Church stood apart from this feudal culture. Its primary allegiance was to the Pope, not to the king, and it wielded huge power, holding dominion over people's souls and with the power of anathema and excommunication that could refuse baptism, marriage, absolution of sins and funeral rights, and consign men to hell. Yet it was also deeply embedded in society, providing home and food not just for monks and friars but many lay brothers. It was, moreover, a substantial employer. As we will see later, once the Church's control was shattered by the Reformation, homelessness erupted.

Another group that lay a little outside feudal society was that of the steadily growing livery companies and guilds of the nation's cities, which controlled the governance of trades, from goldsmiths to butchers and street cleaners. They too, however, had responsibility for employment and so for the individual's welfare. Towns and cities at this time were small affairs. Of the 2 million people who lived in England at the time the Domesday Book was compiled in the late eleventh century, perhaps only 10 per cent could describe themselves as urban dwellers. Winchester, the second largest city in the country, had a population of probably no more than 6,000. Norwich, York and Lincoln contained perhaps 5,000 inhabitants each. As for London, described proudly by William FitzStephen in the late 1170s as 'head and shoulders' above other cities in the world, this could boast around 10,000 citizens – a handful less than the population of, say, Cranleigh in Surrey today. Nevertheless, towns and cities continued to expand throughout the Middle Ages to become major centres of trade and wealth.

I will talk about the ways in which the national diet developed during Henry II's reign a little later. For the moment, let's focus on the basics: the staple fare that people in medieval England would have had access to. For most, that meant only what could be grown or reared locally and what happened to be in season. Opportunities to buy food from further afield would have been few and far between – and well outside the budget of most. For the wealthy, things were a little different. The king and the great lords would move around the country from estate to estate so as not to devour all the provisions in one place. Their households, from the highest born to the lowliest scullions, would move with them, so being assured of their next meal. It must have been quite a sight: up to several hundred people making their way along the inadequate roads to the next place of sojourn, their ox carts creaking with everything needed for the journey – carpets, wall hangings, cooking pots – under cloths waxed against the rain and secured with rope. Nevertheless, the basic building blocks of their diet, like everyone else's, were seasonal, except where food could be preserved by salting, drying and preserving in fat, oil or wine.

Much reliance was placed on the living larder – after all, food was much fresher if you kept it alive until the last moment, rather as they do in Far Eastern markets today. Many of the animals used for food were indigenous, but the Normans were responsible for some important additions. Indeed, their powerful impact on the food of this country can be traced through language: the names of the various animals that were eaten were transformed at the moment of death and preparation for the table from Old English to Norman French, a bullock becoming beef, a sheep becoming mutton, pig becoming pork, a deer, venison, and so on.

Rabbits are a case in point. We know that the Romans certainly reared them for food, but while they brought the brown hare to Britain for sport in the form of coursing, if they introduced the rabbit as well no traces of this have remained and the animals must have died out with their departure. The Normans, however, reintroduced them, keeping them in warrens or artificial burrows. They did not become wild until, possibly, the sixteenth century. We know a lot about the Normans' relationship with coneys, as the animals were called. Rabbits were a luxury and the keepers of the king's warrens were great lords. Initially the animals were reared in tiled courtyards so that they bred above ground, but later artificial burrows were built by raising large mounds of earth, known as pillow mounds. These were situated on poor ground – an excellent way of utilising such locations. The rabbits were kept within a designated area protected by a palisade or stone walls, and were harvested by men with nets and ferrets. The last working warrens in England remained in use until the mid twentieth century, and the one at Thetford in East Anglia covered a square mile. I once talked to a lovely man called Basil whose father had been head keeper at Kingsclere in Berkshire, which had a large working warren. He told me that when he was a child they would import buck rabbits from East Anglia to improve the breeding stock, a practice that must have dated back to medieval times.

The walls that enclosed the warrens were there not only to keep the rabbits in but to keep the poachers out: coneys were a valuable asset, the price per beast being around 3d (perhaps £6 or so in today's money). Poaching was prevalent and not limited just to the peasantry. There is a court record of proceedings in Blythburgh in 1182 where three Augustinian friars were prosecuted for poaching with specially trained greyhounds and were fined 46s 8d. This was regarded – shock horror – as an indication of the deterioration of church morals: the friars were acting with their prior's approval.

The optimum eating age for rabbits was three months. This was not just because they were beautifully tender but because, by one of those fictions beloved of the medieval world, they were not designated as meat at that age and so could be eaten on fish days (more of which later). They were eaten seethed (stewed) with galingale (galangal, a type of ginger) and verjuice (apple or wine vinegar) or, if older, were roasted or made into pies. They also supplied fur (I have a hat made from such fur, and it is very warm and soft), and a very good quality glue could be made from their bones. Such glue is still used today by workers with gold leaf. Nowadays we bury tons of wild rabbit a year and import farmed rabbit from China and rabbit glue from Germany. Madness? Yes!

Pigeons also formed part of the living larder and the country is still littered with dovecotes, most of them sadly no longer in use. Only lords of the manor and others of rank, along with churches and monastic properties, were allowed to own *pigeonniers*, as the lofts were called. These were usually built of stone and were circular in form. The birds lived and nested on stone platforms arranged around the building. Most had a central laddered pole on a swivel known as a potence, which allowed for harvesting and cleaning. Many were closed in, with shutters that were opened at certain times to allow the birds to go out and feed on the stubble fields, berries or whatever was thought suitable; for the rest of the time they were fed on peas. Some of the bigger lofts may have held up to 1,000 birds. Fine examples of disused lofts remain, two particularly good ones being in Dunster in Somerset and another at nearby Compton Martin. The latter, which stands in the churchyard and was intended for use by the parish priest, is unusual in that it is square.

The medieval household harvested the squabs (young pigeons) that had not yet flown the nest. In Italy they still rear a species of pigeon that produces a very large squab, and I would imagine a similar type was reared in pigeon lofts in medieval times. As usual, nothing was wasted. The guano such lofts produced was a useful fertiliser for the fields and potagers (vegetable gardens), and the feathers were used for stuffing mattresses, comforters and pillows. Pigeons when kept in captivity always return to their own lofts if allowed to fly free, the recognition of which led to the development of the carrier pigeon as a means of communication.

Deer parks were also important. In the Middle Ages all deer, whether red, fallow or roe, belonged to the Crown and to have a private deer park you generally needed a royal licence, although there is considerable evidence for unlicensed parks (as long as they were well away from royal hunting domains, the rules don't seem to have been strictly enforced). Only the largest of parks were used for hunting deer – Sutton Park in Birmingham, one of the largest enclosed parks in Europe and associated at one point with the bishopric of Exeter, was one such. The smaller ones simply kept the deer for the table. Probably one of the last contemporary examples of a working deer park is Richmond Park in London, where 300 red and 350 fallow deer roam in their separate herds over its green expanse throughout the year. The stags fight each other and breed with the does, and the calves are born as they have been for centuries, all with very little trouble to the rangers. Every November and February the park is closed early for a few days while the deer are culled. The meat is then distributed to grace-and-favour recipients and the rest sold through the local butcher.

In the Middle Ages the deer would have been taken at various times throughout the year, whenever it was in season according to the various forest laws that had come into force shortly after the Conquest (the first forest laws being passed in William the Conqueror's time). Today quite a lot of farmed fresh venison is available, produced in a similar way if on a more intensive basis, its sale still governed by the game laws. As with other animals in medieval times, nothing was wasted. Because deer were kept enclosed, their antlers were easily collected when they dropped each year. Known as hartshorn, these antlers were one of the few sources of ammonia available. Deer bone was a good source of gelatine, while the skin provided buckskin – a supple, tough leather suitable for clothing. Buckskin breeches are still worn today. Umble pie, a term which has given us the expression 'to eat humble pie', was the beaters' or huntsmen's perk when a deer was killed. The umbles were what is now called the fry or offal – the kidneys, liver, lights (lungs), heart, testicles and parts of the tripe. These were the perishable parts of the beast which needed to be eaten almost immediately, either in a pie or possibly in a haggis, which was a dish found throughout England and not just a perquisite of Scotland. Incidentally, because venison is a lean meat it is better suited to the human digestion than beef: this no doubt helps to explain why venison featured so heavily in the diets of our ancestors.

Also crucial to the living larder were the stew (or fish) ponds. As much for the practical reason of preserving animal stocks as for religious beliefs, the Church decreed that over and above the forty days of Lent, every Friday and Saturday were to be fish days – flesh-free days of abstinence. Lent coincides with the season when ruminants are giving birth and suckling their young and the poultry are just starting to lay, so it's completely understandable why the powers that be were anxious to avoid

8

meat-eating then. There was also a health angle to a fish diet at this time of year. Most people in medieval times would probably have come out of winter suffering slightly from scurvy, a condition that could be cured not just by eating green stuff but by consuming fish. Monastic orders were particularly strict about keeping to a meat-free diet except on certain holy days, and it was probably the monks who developed the idea of 'farming' fish so that they would always be readily available. Fish stews, or ponds, were dug in a rectangular shape on or near a spring and usually with a nearby stream channelling through them. This ensured not only that the ponds were self-cleansing and oxygenated, but that the fish were not reared in muddy water, which might taint the flavour of their flesh. The sides of the pool were banked up to allow a moderate depth of water. Some households had separate pools for different types of fish, with areas set aside for breeding.

Edible freshwater fish such as carp and pike were the most popular. An order, for example, survives from the reign of Henry III (1216–72), Eleanor and Henry II's grandson, for a purchase of 600 luce, or pike as we know them, 100 of which were assigned for delivery to the fish ponds at the Palace of Westminster. Pike were an expensive luxury: by the end of the thirteenth century a large pike cost 6s 8d, the price of two pigs. Recipes of the time also mention other freshwater fish, such as roach, perch, tench and dace, and presumably, though it is not specifically named, zander (pike perch) was also used. It was a social nicety that the higher you ranked in the Order of Precedence, the larger the fish you were served. Bishop Grosseteste (c. 1170–1253), the great Bishop of Lincoln, is recorded as having once reprimanded his servants for having transgressed the rules of etiquette by giving the Earl of Gloucester a smaller fish than himself. Apparently the earl was rather surprised by the bishop's reprimand: he knew the bishop was of low birth and therefore assumed that he would not know the correct way to behave. Given that the bishop may well have been educated at Oxford and Paris universities and had been Chancellor of Oxford University as well as bishop of a major diocese, this says a lot about the arrogance and snobbery displayed by a Norman to someone who had come from a poor Saxon family. The Church offered the easiest way for an intelligent lad to rise on the social ladder.

Eels were another staple and popular fish. Every mill race held eel traps, and dabbing for eels with a piece of rotten meat on a hook was a popular sport as well as a way of supplying the table. There is a scene in Günter Grass's *The Tin Drum* where a horse's head is used for this method of fishing: ideal in times of war when there would have been a lot of dead horses around. Eels were particularly prevalent in the Fens, which at this time was a pretty wild and trackless country, rich in fish and wildfowl. Before the drainage of the Fens was begun in earnest in the seventeenth century, tens of thousands of eels (known as Fenman's gold) were caught and supplied to the University of Cambridge, the great city of Lincoln and elsewhere. Some idea of their value can be gauged from the fact that the Barnach stone for the 'Ship of the Fens', Ely Cathedral (Ely means 'eel region'), was bought from Benedictine monks in Northamptonshire in the eleventh century in exchange for the supplying of 8,000 eels a year for a fixed period of time, the details of which are now lost to us. In the same period, some Cambridgeshire people actually appear to have paid their taxes in eels. Eels had another use, too. Eelskin could be cured and dried to produce a strong supple leather used to make wedding rings, shoes, satchels and belts. Twenty years ago there was a fad for eelskin wallets until it was discovered that their thinness was such that credit cards were very susceptible to any magnetic forces that might be lurking. End of fad.

Even in recent times eels six foot long, calculated as being sixty years old, have been taken from the Fens, so imagine what they might have harvested in the Middle Ages. All eels were merchantable, and the Fens were not the only source. One of the main exports of Cornwall, a rich county in the Middle Ages, were conger eels dried and sold to Europe to feed their days of abstinence. Eels could be prepared in various ways: salted, smoked or dried. They have gone out of fashion in my lifetime, but when I was a child every London fishmonger had a live eel tank, and along the Hammersmith Mall I remember rough boys fishing for eels and selling them to customers in pubs to take home for tea. Today most eels caught are sent to Holland for smoking, though a limited number are smoked in England, mostly in Somerset. Elvers, young eels, are a valuable commodity, and most are sold to Spain or Japan or are reared into fully grown eels in areas such as Lough Neagh.

Obviously it was not just freshwater fish that fed the nation. Sea fish of all types were sold widely in coastal areas. One of the great staples – as it was to remain for many centuries to come – was the herring. It was a cheap fish selling at around ten pence per hundred (in fact, this would have been the curious medieval measurement for fish of a long hundred, which was actually six score, in other words 120; I am not sure of the rationale behind this, but it may have allowed for spoilage).

This was at a time when a labourer would have earned between one and three pennies a day or their equivalent in kind. Yarmouth was the main centre of the herring industry and dealt in both white herrings (salted but not smoked) and red herrings (more about preservation than pleasure, these are heavily salted, then dried, then smoked). Red herrings are still produced but are only popular now in Africa and the West Indies, and in the days before the potato existed to balance their flavour in a meal, they must have been really quite unpleasant.

Bloaters were also popular (kippers came along a little later). A bloater is hot-smoked in the round rather than split, and as it is not gutted it does not keep anywhere near as long as a cold-smoked split kipper. The name, incidentally, comes ultimately from an Old Norse word meaning 'soaked' or 'wet' – perhaps because herrings cured in this way are plumper than those that have been completely dried. There is a belief that bloaters are a Victorian invention (bloater paste was popular in Victorian times, when glass jars became cheaply available), but references in the Countess of Leicester's household accounts indicate that something very akin to a bloater was sold in the thirteenth century. The records also show that the countess's household at Odiham Castle consumed between 400 and 1,000 herrings a day during Lent 1265. Easter must have seemed a long way off!

Bloaters are still cured at Yarmouth and the Cley Smokehouse nearby, though they are not so popular outside the area. As for fresh herrings, these were a luxury for people who lived away from the coast, even for the king. East Carlton had an obligation to deliver twenty-four herring pies to the monarch each year from the first herring shoals. Each pie had to contain a minimum number of herrings and to be seasoned with ginger, pepper and cinnamon. Supplying pies to the monarch was a feature of the Middle Ages; the city of Gloucester, for example, sent a large lamprey pie to the Crown annually until well into the nineteenth century. Lampreys are not much eaten in modern England, but having tasted one I have to say that it was so delicious I can see why Henry I died of eating a surfeit of them. They are a type of sucker fish that prey on salmon – very popular in Portugal, but now only used for fishing bait in England.

Salmon was another commonplace fish through most of English history. So many salmon came up the rivers that the apprentice boys of the main cities sometimes rioted in protest at the amount of the fish they were fed by their employers, and legislation prevented employers from feeding salmon to their servants more than three times a week. Salmon was salted for keeping and also hot-smoked, which would have made it last a bit longer. But for the most part it was potted in some way. Potting under fat, oil or wine in sealed jars was an effective method of storing food and, provided the air was excluded by the potting covering, was remarkably successful in keeping food unspoiled for a surprisingly long time.

As for other seafood, contemporary household accounts list John Dory, mackerel, mullet, flounder, plaice, sole, whelks, crayfish and crabs. Cod were commonly dried and salted. At the more exotic end, whale, porpoise and sturgeon were particularly prized. Whale and sturgeon were reserved for the king, although in the case of whale, as long as the king received the head and the queen the tail, the pieces in between could be distributed elsewhere. A barrel of whale meat cost thirty shillings: it was clearly something of a luxury. No doubt the whales in question were usually those that had swum ashore and become stranded. Seal is also recorded as being eaten, and in coastal regions would have been a useful supplement to the diet of the poorer elements of the population. Seal, I should tell you, is disgusting, but falls within the medieval taste for oily, fishy flavours, which we'll explore later.

Back on land, a common component of the living larder was poultry. Chickens were kept in some quantity, eggs being a major part of the English diet, and they were always killed fresh for the table. Capons (castrated cocks), fatter and more tender than ordinary chickens, were also popular. It is difficult to find capons in England today as rearers have taken to relying on chemical castration, which was once (in my opinion, rightly) prohibited, but they are well worth looking for and are still readily available in France.

As for geese, these were a regular feature of the diet and each manor would have had a gooseherd to look after flocks of them. Of all livestock, geese add weight most easily from the smallest amount of food: they are the most efficient of feeders. Moreover, their feathers were used to stuff beds or to flight the arrows that were so crucial to England's success in the European wars of the period. Goose fat was used in cooking and even to grease axles. Up until the Second World War, country people would rub their bodies with goose grease and sew themselves into their long johns to endure the winter cold.

But perhaps the ultimate multi-purpose animal was the sheep, as the following somewhat modernised version of a thirteenth-century verse makes abundantly clear:

Of the sheep is cast away nothing,
His horns for notches – to ashes goeth his bones,
To Lordes great profit goeth his entire dung,
His tallow also serveth plastres, more than one.
For harp strings his ropes serve everyone,
Of whose head boiled whole and all
There cometh a jelly, and ointment full Royal.
For ache of bones and also for bruises
It is remedy that doeth ease quickly
Causing men's stark points to recure,
It doeth sinews again restore to life.
Black sheep's wool, with fresh oil of olive,
The men at armes, with charms, they prove it good
And at straight need, they can well staunch blood.

It's perhaps worth elaborating on some of this. In the old breeds
of sheep both sexes have horns, and the rough, ridged material
was perfect for the notches over which the bow string was
hooked on an archer's bow. Sheep were folded at night to manure
the lord of the manor's field, and shepherds were told to look
out for barren patches on which to place the animals; they were
then enclosed by woven wooden hurdles, the action of their
own sharp hooves tramping the dung into the field. The tallow
the poem refers to was burnt as a cheap source of light, and
the lanolin obtained from the wool must have been particularly
useful in the rough and tumble and achingly cold world of the
twelfth and thirteenth centuries. It is still in use. A clean piece
of fleece over a wound will help it heal, and patients who are
laid on a fresh fleece are less likely to get bedsores. The tallow
'plastres' referred to in the verse reflect the original meaning of

the word plaster: a medicinal substance spread on a bandage.

Sheep's wool had long been an important commodity in England when the Normans arrived, but wool as an industry was really developed by the Cistercian order of monks, who spread to England from France in the early twelfth century. Convinced that traditional monasticism had become lax, the Cistercians, or White Monks, broke away from the Benedictines, adopting a more austere life in abbeys often built in remote places. These happened to be better suited to the raising of sheep, and the Cistercians then practised selective breeding, improving the wool crop from the old breeds and, by better feeding, enhancing the size and breeding productivity of their flocks. Their success made the order very rich indeed, as the ruins of Rievaulx and other abbeys indicate – ironic given that it was an order that initially prided itself on poverty and simplicity. By Eleanor and Henry's time, wool was becoming an important component of the nation's wealth, much of it being sent to Flanders for processing into cloth that was then sold all over Europe. Incidentally, although the Cistercians did much to improve the quality of sheep, the animal remained much smaller than its modern descendants; as late as the early eighteenth century a sheep wasn't much bulkier than a Labrador dog.

In addition to the wool, the meat of the sheep was also important. The English tend to think of themselves as a nation of beef eaters. In fact, mutton eaters would be more historically correct. Sheep would have been surrendered to the table when they were four or five years old and their wool production was starting to drop. In the thirteenth century they might have fetched between 6d and 10d at this point. Much of the meat would inevitably have been salted down, and having eaten Macon, which is mutton ham, I can tell you that salted sheep is not something to rush home for. Having said that, I have eaten the fresh meat of a five-year-old blackface sheep – the sort of animal our medieval ancestors would have recognised – and it was very good indeed.

Cattle were as adaptable as sheep in medieval husbandry. Dairy animals were there to produce milk for butter or cheese and would have been eaten only when their yield started to drop; moreover, what we would think of as a beef animal had the double purpose of being a working or draught animal that could pull heavy loads. There is an old adage, 'A year to grow, two years to plough and a year to fatten'. The beef medieval people would have eaten would have been a maturer, denser meat than we are used to today. I have always longed to try it. The muscle acquired from a working ox would have broken down over the fattening year and provided wonderful fat covering and marbling. Given the amount of brewing that took place, the odds are that the animals would have been fed a little drained mash from time to time. Kobe beef, that excessively expensive Japanese beef, was originally obtained from ex-plough animals whose muscles were broken down by mash from sake production and by massage. I'd like to think our beef might have had a not dissimilar flavour.

Venues today that sell mock medieval feasts, and indeed television programmes that recreate great baronial halls, suggest that the Middle Ages were nothing but a continuous round of massively over-the-top banquets involving enormous joints of meat. Don't believe it. Medieval kitchens were designed for pragmatism and efficiency. Given the time it takes to carve a large roast, and not forgetting the fact that most meat was salted down as soon as it was killed, it seems highly unlikely that great spits of meat were being eaten by Sheriff of Nottingham types on a daily basis. Many cattle, in fact, were killed at a particular time of the year – Michaelmas, at the end of September – when they had enjoyed the benefits of summer feed and were at their fattest and in the best condition. Obviously there were ox roasts on occasion to celebrate some special event – the coming of age or marriage of an heir, for example – but these were designed to feed a whole estate over a day-long party and were the exception rather than the rule.

Much of the milk from cows went to make cheese, a great staple in medieval times, in part because it kept well. Andrew Boorde, the sixteenth-century physician and writer, records that cheese fell into four distinct types: 'harde', 'softe', 'grene' and 'spermyse'. Grene meant new and not heavily pressed, so that some of the whey remained. It was rather in the nature of today's Cheshire or Caerphilly, ready within a few weeks or so of pressing and binding. Spermyse was made from curds and was largely used for tarts and pies, sometimes flavoured with juice extruded from herbs; the modern-day Sage Derby is probably the only remaining example of this. Softe was cheese made from whey (the leftover curds being eaten by the poor). Harde cheese was probably made with skimmed milk and its main advantage was undoubtedly that it kept: it could help a castle to resist a siege or a ship endure a long voyage.

Some parts of the country inevitably had better grazing land than others and so could produce better cheese. The rich pasture lands of the west coast, running from Lancashire down to Somerset, with their consistent seam of salt, would probably,

as now, have produced the most varied and best cheeses; Leicestershire would have come next. The household records of the
Countess of Leicester show that she bought cheese by the 'poise'
or 'wey' – a vague measure that varied from fourteen to twenty
stone. The cellars of a castle would have provided perfect storage
conditions. The fourteenth-century Goodman of Paris in his
household book gives instructions for choosing cheese which
hold just as true today. I have judged at the Nantwich cheese
festival in Cheshire (even in the Middle Ages, Nantwich was
regarded as an important centre of the cheese industry), and
the judges might well carry his words on their clipboards:

> Not white as snow, like fair Helen,
> Nor moist like tearful Magdalen,
> Not like Argus, full of eyes,
> But heavy, like a bull of prize,
> Well resisting a thumb pressed in,
> And let it have a scaly skin,
> Eyeless, and tearless, in colour not white,
> Scaly, resisting and weighing not light

It's amazing, isn't it, the level of knowledge he expects from his
readers: such classical and biblical references in a twenty-first-
century book would fly over the head of most readers!

The dairy was the preserve of women. (I have tried and failed
over the years to find out whether the sterner orders of monks
trained men for this chore, though I suspect that the answer is
probably yes.) The choice of women might have been due to the
need to multitask in the dairy, or because the labour involved
was not as physically demanding as other agricultural work. That

said, milking is certainly not as easy as it looks. The dairymaid would have had to hobble the cow, seat herself on her three-legged stool and milk into her bucket by hand. She would also have had to know the individual idiosyncrasies of each animal: the kicker, the head-butter and the animal that doesn't willingly let down her milk. And she would have had to look out for infections, mastitis or sore udders. Once she'd finished milking, she would have taken the pail of milk to the main dairy building, strained it to remove any impurities and left it to stand in shallow earthenware dishes for the cream to rise – one day for single cream and two days for double cream. The cream would then be skimmed from the top of the dish and either sent to the kitchen or churned for butter. If the milk was to be used for cheese it would be poured into large containers and rennet would be added. The rennet might come from a piece of dried intestine from a veal calf or possibly from the seed head of a milk thistle (so named for obvious reasons), or even from a cardoon if one was available. The juice of the small, yellow-flowered plant known as Our Lady's Bedstraw was also regularly used, so called because it was supposed to have been among the herbs in the Christ child's manger in Bethlehem. Women would add it to the straw used to stuff their mattresses, possibly because of superstitious connections with fertility but more likely because it had properties as a fleabane. The juice not only acts as an effective rennet but also helps to colour the cheese a good yellow. In medieval times it was also used as a dye, but the roots were too small to make it commercially effective.

Once the curds were set and well combed they were drained and set into a mould to be pressed. Few medieval cheese presses have survived, but their design lasted for many centuries to come: a smooth, coopered barrel-type construction with holes drilled in the sides to allow the whey to drain out. A fitted board would be placed on top and then weights added to put pressure on the cheese. If you go to Blanchland in Northumberland, you will find the remains of an ancient cheese press in the centre of the town: a bollard formed the base, and grooves and a spout carried off the drained liquid. The whey was, for the most part, drained off and fed to the pigs. Once the curds were well pressed they would be wrapped in a muslin cloth and set to mature.

What the cows ate was said to influence the flavour of the cheese. The particular flavour of spring Wensleydale, for example, was attributed to the cattle grazing in limestone meadows. There are only fleeting references to blue cheese in the Middle Ages, but as it is quite hard to exclude mould from cheese, quite a lot would have been blued. I remember once coming across a rather unpleasant cheese made from skimmed milk which was blued by having an uncleaned horse harness dragged through it. This was probably a type of hard cheese familiar to medieval times and certainly the blue did give it an improved flavour, if only marginally. Another rather nasty type of cheese, probably only eaten by the very poor, was made from whey and buttermilk.

Milk was also, of course, made into butter. Some would have been spread on bread, but butter was also the main fat used in the more delicate forms of cooking. Medieval cooks used a lot of pastry, and while raised pies would have been made with lard, and coffyns (pastry boxes) made simply with flour and water, flans, cheesecakes and puff pastry would all have called for butter. The commonest vessel for making it would have been a barrel with a plunger for the dairymaid to work up and down until the butter took. Once the butter set it was scraped out of the churn, leaving the buttermilk to be poured off and kept for drinking; with its slightly tart flavour it was a popular drink and was also used in baking. Salt was always added to butter, both for taste and for preservation, and during the summer period it was packed into earthenware crocks which were sealed and stored for use in the winter months. Regulations were quite strict: no animal could be milked or suckled for some weeks after Lady Day (25 March), as this rule allowed them to build up their strength for the winter months.

Sheep and goats also provided milk that could be turned into butter and cheese, but then, as now, the principal dairy animal was the cow. There was little of the specialised breeding that was to come later. In medieval times you would have seen an animal much like the Dexter: an all-purpose cow providing milk and meat, economic in the utilisation of food and amenable to handle.

The other large domestic animal was the pig, provider not just of pork but of bacon and ham as well. When people ask me, as they often do, 'what did the poor eat in the past?' the answer is bacon. Every village probably kept a boar and virtually every cottager would have owned pigs. They are a perfect low-maintenance food animal that could be turned out into the woods with the other village pigs under the watchful eye of the swineherd. Villagers had rights of pannage, meaning that they could allow their pigs to feed on the beech mast and the acorns that fell to the forest floor. This helped to keep the woodland floor clear of brambles and general undergrowth, letting the light in and aiding the growth of young trees. There were problems in areas that surrounded the royal hunting preserves, for it is difficult to keep a determined pig from roaming, but common law back then was shaped by the common people.

The medieval pig looked much more like the wild boar from which it was descended than our modern pigs. Illustrations in psalters of the time show a lean, rangy animal, smaller than the pigs we know but perfectly suited to its lifestyle. A sow farrows twice a year and with the old breeds that probably meant five or six piglets, of which the cottager might sell or barter two or three for extra income. One of the suckling pigs that was farrowed in the New Year would be sacrificed to provide fresh meat after the depredations of winter, but the main season for killing pigs was the autumn, after they had gorged themselves on acorns and windfall fruit. The process would probably have been staggered, so that the villagers could share the perishable bits around and build up their own fat and condition for the winter ahead. As for the boar, having peformed his duty he would be killed and his head might well be beautifully dressed and paraded as the centrepiece of a Michaelmas feast. I am proud to be a member of the Guild of Butchers, who each year still parade a dressed boar's head through the streets of London from Smithfield to the Mansion House to present to the lord mayor – something they have done since 1343. Health and safety regulations require that the processed head these days is a facsimile made of papier mâché and paint, but the real one is also still delivered.

When I was a child we would help to kill my father's pigs, joining in the labour of scalding the pig and scraping the bristles off, mixing the blood with oatmeal and vinegar for black pudding, washing the tripe for chitterlings and sausages, butchering the carcass and sending off cuts for curing and smoking. Once a professional slaughterer would have gone round the villages to kill the animals, and the medieval villager would have salted and smoked his own, hanging the pieces up high in the cooler part of the smoke hole. The adage has always been that everything is eaten of the pig except the squeak.

In towns the pigs did a splendid job of keeping the streets clear of the garbage, sewage and other mess that might otherwise have led to disease. St Anthony's pigs, wearing a bell round their neck with the badge of the saint, were a feature of thirteenth-century London and were allowed to scavenge at will. Cockney slang reduced the name to 'Tantony pigs'. The Hospital of St Anthony had the right to go to Smithfield market and take for their own those pigs that were too scrawny to be sold. These animals cleaned up the various London market sites and the streets, and when they had reached a suitable weight they were either sold or butchered, and the benefits went to the hospital and its school. When I was young, pigs did the same job in the villages of Malaya and the Far East, and very efficiently. There was a risk of tapeworm, but that was overcome by proper cooking.

It is a constant source of joy to me to think that all those European wars England won, all those great cathedrals and castles that were built and all the conquests of the wider world that were secured were done on a diet of bacon and eggs. And yet health pundits today condemn the country's oldest national dish!

What else did the poor eat? Well, one thing they didn't eat, except *in extremis*, was horse meat. I was once told that this abstention came about because of a decision made by King Alfred way back in the ninth century. The story goes that he was trying to raise a nucleus of heavy horses for his cavalry and the farmers on whose land they were placed kept eating his breeding stock, so he got Aethelred, his Archbishop of Canterbury, to anathematise the eating of horse meat. I'm not sure about that, but I do find the religious dimension of the story intriguing, and wonder whether the real reason why horse-eating might have been discouraged was because the Church associated it with paganism. Ultimately, the truth of the matter is lost in the mists of time. There is no doubt, though, that while, thanks to French influence, horses were eaten in Scotland on occasion, the English have long tended to avoid horse meat.

Otherwise, I suspect the answer is that the poor would have eaten anything they could get their hands on, probably cooking it in a large cauldron suspended over a domestic fire. And 'anything' might even include something like badger. In fact, badger was a regular part of the rural diet until protected by law in 1973, and a ham off a big brock would have kept a family going for some time. West Country pubs of my childhood had badger hams on the bar rather as a Spanish tapas bar has a *jamón ibérico*. Badger meat tastes rather like young wild boar and would have gone well in the stew pot with roots dug from the hedgerow, some greens, a bit of wild celery and sage. Though I have not tasted badger for many years, the dish is one that comes unbidden to my head.

Another ingredient in the cottager's menu, depending on where he lived, would have been beaver tail. Trapping a beaver and selling its pelt to the castle would have been a nice earner, and its tail would have provided a good supper. In *The Hungry Cyclist* Tom Kevill-Davies talks of modern-day Native North Americans eating beaver tail, which is a firm white meat, and he even gives a recipe.

The main staple of the medieval diet was bread: comforting, filling and simple to make. The lord of the manor owned the mill, and the miller paid him a fee known as 'thirlage': a levy on the corn ground for the customer. The Middle Ages was a great time for building watermills – simple enough in principle but involving complex construction that was a real test of skill, particularly bearing in mind the limited tools available. A mill race was dug and water from the river diverted along it. The mill itself stood between the river and the race, and the mill wheel was lowered into the race. The pressure of the water on the paddles turned the wheel, which, by dint of a series of cogs, turned the millstones. The corn was fed into a hopper and then between the stones, which ground it to flour. Manorial dictates prohibited the grinding of corn at home. It all had to go to the lord's mill, and hand querns (contraptions which were used for grinding corn) were illegal: if a villager or farmer was found with one on his premises the quern was confiscated and a heavy fine imposed. As for the miller, he was a well-off member of the community and charged well for his business.

We get a good sense of the sheer number of watermills in medieval times from the Domesday Book, which was compiled by bureaucrats after the Norman Conquest of 1066, so that they could assess the taxes they could impose. A typical example is the mill near Barton Stacey in Hampshire. Standing on a tributary of the River Test and not far from the confluence of the two, it is in a perfect position for controlling water flow.

In fact, there may have been a mill there since Roman times; there was certainly one when the Domesday Book was put together. Not all medieval mills had such perfect locations, however, and flooding was a real danger.

Working mills still exist, and it is worth visiting one to see what a clever invention they were; at the same time you could also buy some stoneground flour. Once when I had a catering venture we bought all our flour from the old mill at Ford and Etal: it was perfect for baking. In medieval times wheat was the commonest grain in the southern shires, but on poorer ground it yielded pride of place to barley, rye or oats, all of which could also be used for making bread. Most medieval bread would have contained a lot of wholemeal. However, for the finer flour which went to make the white manchet loved by the gentry, the flour would have been passed through sieves known as bolters and sold at a higher price. Corn if properly dried would keep well from one year to the next in a specialist granary raised on mushroom-shaped pillars to keep out rats and would be taken to the mill for grinding as needed. Its price varied wildly according to the state of the harvest. In the early 1260s, for example, a quart of wheat cost anywhere between 3s 8d and 8s.

The baking of bread was taken very seriously, and by the late thirteenth century there was an Assize of Bread which dictated all aspects of commercial bread production. The Assize specified how many loaves were to be made from a quarter of grain and how much a baker could charge per loaf. It is difficult to get any real accuracy from medieval records, and it's clear in any case that weights could vary from time to time and place to place (even such factors as the quality of the harvest and the dryness of the grain played a part in this). But the basic aim of the Assize was clear: to try to ensure that there was a strict relationship between the price of wheat and the price of bread, with variations allowed according to the fineness of the flour used in the loaf.

Five types of bread are listed in the Assize. Wastel was the finest. Simnel bread was twice baked and more biscuity in texture than wastel. Cocket loaves came in two sizes, the larger one being made of less expensive flour (wholemeal was far and away the commonest in use). Treet was made from wheat that was not bolted – that is, sieved through a cloth – at all. What is described as common wheat was probably the sweeping of the mill, and a farthing loaf in this category weighed as much as 'two great cocket'. It was probably pretty horrible but provided the sort of roughage today's health pundits tell us to eat.

As the existence of the Assize of Bread suggests, there was plenty of room for dishonesty on the part of the baker and, if you were caught, the penalties could be severe. A dishonest baker could be fined, condemned to a spell in the stocks or even be flogged through the streets behind a cart while the populace threw muck, rotten fruit and the odd dead cat. The latter two penalties also required that the defective loaf be tied round his neck so that his crime was identified. One cunning baker is recorded as having added so much yeast to his dough that, in the words of the court, 'what he was selling was not bread but air'.

Manor houses, castles and towns would have had their own bake houses with dome-shaped ovens constructed of brick. A fire of sticks would be lit within the oven to heat the bricks to a given temperature, the embers would then be scraped out and

28

the bread put in to bake. The baker's skill was to determine the correct temperature of the oven and the length of baking time required because, of course, to open the oven early was to let the heat escape. Knowing the eccentricities of your oven was vital. I have baked in one such oven in a *casa colonica* in Italy (in fact it was the occasion on which I first met Jennifer Paterson, who came across to ask me what I was doing). It wasn't an easy skill to acquire, but the results were very satisfying.

Cottagers or villagers who did not have access to a bake house would have had to cook loaves over their own fires on a flat bakestone, a sliver of stone or other material strong enough not to break from the heat of the fire. Stones which had been exposed to and smoothed by water were considered the best. Cakes would have been baked in the same way. Many will know the story of how King Alfred, hiding from the Vikings, burnt the cakes and was berated by the woman who was sheltering him. We're not talking here about Black Forest gateaux or Victoria sponges but barley bannock, or possibly an oatcake or a drop scone. Bakestone cookery continued down the following centuries until supplanted by iron griddles. It is still possible to buy a bakestone, so if you have an open fire you can try it for yourself. It is an interesting experiment loved by children.

A large, wealthy household could use up to forty-five bushels of grain a month when the lord was home with his full retinue. It's interesting to note that in the de Montfort household in the thirteenth century the hunting dogs and greyhounds were fed three quarters of grain over a ten-day period while the dole given to the poor over the same period amounted to only one quarter! The poor did, however, also get thirteen gallons of beer in that same time.

Establishments on the de Montfort scale or somewhere like the Hospital of St Cross and Almshouses of Noble Poverty at Winchester would have had to produce huge quantities of loaves a day. The bakers therefore faced a considerable challenge, and with great ingenuity they rose to it by developing a machine that allowed the kneading of dough with the feet, the baker's assistant using a board placed over a trough.

One of the great mysteries about the medieval dining hall to my mind is the use of trenchers of bread at table. A trencher was a square of bread, probably two days old, placed in front of each diner. Portions of each dish would then be served directly on to it. Yet this was an era that had wooden, earthenware and pewter dishes, and we know for a fact that pottage, or thick soup, was served in hall in bowls. Trenchers can hardly have been satisfactory: they must have made the tablecloth dirty, particularly if food slopped off them, and if they became too messy during the meal they had to be replaced. They may have saved on the washing up, but not on the laundry. The one thing that can be said for them is that at the end of the meal they were all gathered up and given to the poor.

A peculiar assumption among some historians is that people didn't eat vegetables in medieval times. True, there was not the variety that later overseas exploration has given us, but I know that when I was a child, countrywomen went out into the hedgerows to collect edible green stuff – sorrel, Good King Henry or fat hen, to name just a few – and it is likely that an age that identified a small wayside flower as a rennet would have known what was edible. All the alliums – onions, scallions, garlic and leeks – were certainly eaten on a regular basis, and we know that as early as 1237 a covenant was made between London merchants and those of Nesle, Corbie and Amiens providing free entry into the country for their onions and garlic. Although this pact was tied into the supply of woad for use by the dyers, it does at least show there was a demand.

Parsnips were among the most commonplace everyday vegetable (when fed to dairy cows they were thought to improve the cream content of the milk). Carrots followed closely behind, though in medieval times they would have been purple, yellow, white or red; orange carrots didn't make an appearance until Tudor times. Beetroots were also eaten. Before potatoes became popular centuries later, peas and beans of all sorts both fresh and dried were eaten on an almost daily basis. What a flatulent age it must have been! In the thirteenth century, Bartholomew the Englishman expresses a great dislike of beans, of which as a friar he must have had to eat a large quantity. He says that they are damned by Pythagoras and remarks, 'by oft use the wits are dulled and they cause many dreams'. Bartholomew notwithstanding, they were an important food and a good source of protein. Dried peas were cooked as pease pudding; the old adage 'pease pudding hot, pease pudding cold, pease pudding in the pot nine days old' shows how often this dish was probably served. Curiously, as I have discovered for myself, pease pudding does improve in flavour with keeping. Medieval recipes for pease pudding dictate that eggs be beaten into the mixture to enrich it. As for lentils, we know that puy lentils were imported from France; in Sussex in my childhood they were called Nantiles, a term derived from the labelling on the sacks.

Herbs were an essential part of medieval life, not just for cooking but for medicinal purposes, and a great range of them was available: the thirteenth-century expert on growing herbs and vegetables, John of Garland, for example, gives a long list that includes sage, parsley, dittany, hyssop, borage, leek, garlic and onions among many others. Gardens were much loved by the medieval gentry, and they would have contained herbs as well as flowers. Any surplus herbs and vegetables would have been sold in nearby markets. The 3rd Earl of Lincoln, for example, had a large establishment in London with a fish pond (records show the purchase of frogs, eels and small fish to feed the pike), and employed a head gardener and several under-gardeners. After feeding his household, he sold the surplus produce to the London markets.

Along with herbs, we also find that mustard was used – not finely ground, but more like a grain mustard. We are told that a wedding party of forty people required two quarts of mustard, and one fifteenth-century household is recorded as having got through 84 pounds of mustard seed in a year. Mustard greens, a delicious green vegetable, were also eaten.

Part of the reason for the later popular belief that medieval people didn't eat vegetables and fruit is that details of what was served are not often mentioned in surviving records. That, I suspect, was simply because they were taken for granted. It all rather reminds me of my mother's dinner-party book, which recorded what dishes she fed visiting guests so that she didn't serve them the same dish on their next visit, but made no reference to the vegetables because she would have served what-ever was in season at the time. Even leaving that aside, there's a simple practical reason why I'm confident that medieval people ate fruit and vegetables. If they hadn't, they would have suffered from scurvy, from which ultimately they would have died. I'm sure that most medieval people experienced a touch of winter scurvy, but as soon as the green stuff started sprouting they would have scoured the hedgerows for anti-scorbutics. It wasn't until Tudor times that a certain suspicion of vegetables and fruit developed, and even then only when they were served in their raw form ('Beware of green sallets & rawe fruytes for they wyll make your souerayne seke [your lord sick]', warned the author of *The Boke of Keruynge* ('The Book of Carving') in the early sixteenth century).

Pears, a good scource of vitamin C and native to England, were the commonest fruit, followed by their cousins the apple, but there are also contemporary mentions of cherries, plums and quinces. A fairly wide range of fruits and nuts were also eaten, but little mention is ever made of them except in recipes as they were invariably gathered from the wild. Strawberries, where mentioned, would have been *fraise de bois*, wood strawberries.

Where there are gardens and crops there are bees, and these were similarly an important part of the medieval scene. They had been cultivated by people in England for centuries: the Romans had brought their own bees to Britain, where they interbred with the native British breed, and we know that the Anglo-Saxons were avid bee-keepers. This is scarcely surprising. In the days before sugar was widely available, honey was the main source of sweetener; it was used not only in cooking but also in the brewing of ale and mead. Medieval hives or skips were generally plaited either from willow twigs or from straw, and they were quite small by modern standards. I suspect that that might have led to continual swarming, and it reminds me of the old rhyme:

A swarm of bees in May is worth a load of hay;
A swarm of bees in June is worth a silver spoon;
A swarm of bees in July isn't worth a fly.

When bees start a new hive they have to recreate the wax cell structure for storing honey or raising grubs, leaving the wax to be harvested from the old hive. The movement of the swarm and its re-establishment in a new hive was therefore important for ensuring a constant supply of wax. Beeswax was invaluable. It was used not only to make candles but also to waterproof cloth, which could then be used to protect comestibles from the damp, rather like a tarpaulin, and as an early form of macintosh for travellers and workers (even today, waxed jackets are typical outdoor countrywear). Thread was waxed to make it stronger and eggs were coated in wax to preserve them. Honey fairs, selling both wax and honey, were held at different times of the year. England actually produced so much honey that it was able to export it; however, because so many of the months in England are quite dark, and because there were few alternatives for lighting at that time, it didn't export wax.

Most people would have kept bees on a sort of cottage-industry scale. It was the monasteries that made a major business of it. A number of treatises on bee-keeping were written, the most notable being that by Bartholomew the Englishman. One of the nuggets of information he proffers is that puffballs can be used for smoking bees when taking the honey: apparently the fungus gives out a soporific smoke which lulls the insects and allows the taking. If nothing else, this does show that this rather tasteless mushroom has its uses (it could also be used in tinderboxes since in its dried form it catches fire very easily). Incidentally, if you ever feel compelled to eat a puffball, it is best to fry it in bacon fat. Another useful piece of advice from medieval times is that as bees don't move during rain or thunderstorms, the keeper could stop them swarming while he prepared a new hive by sprinkling water and beating pans to simulate a tempest; he could then scatter the new interior with sweet-smelling herbs beloved of bees to attract them into it.

Honey was seldom sold in the comb. As the wax was valuable, the comb would be broken into pieces, put into a deep linen sack, hung up and left to drip. These drips were considered the purest and finest honey. The sack was then placed before a fire, where the warmed honey ran out freely. This was considered second quality. Finally the sack was pressed, possibly in a cheese press. Sometimes the honey was drained though clean straw to purify it, and the straw then pressed into bundles to make excellent fire lighters. Next the empty comb was placed into water and the temperature raised until the wax floated to the surface. Once this wax set solid, the dross was scraped off, and the wax was remelted and poured into moulds of regulated size according to usage.

I have mentioned that honey was important to the production of mead, but it's clear that as the centuries went by, mead started to decline in popularity. Wine would have been the drink consumed at court and in some manorial circles (but even then only among those who sat above the salt, of which more shortly). For others the normal drink was, increasingly, ale. Milk was for children, and water was simply unsafe: wells were likely to be corrupted by sewage draining into them. Ale, for which the water had been boiled, was therefore by far the safest bet. This was not beer as we understand it today. Hops were not used in English brewing until the fifteenth century.

Ale, though, was wonderfully flexible: it could be made from virtually any grain that the brewer had to hand and could be flavoured with anything from oak bark to garlic to ginger. Large individual households had their own brewhouses, towns might well have had commercial breweries, and villages had their alewives.

I remember that the village of Berwick in East Sussex preserved a remnant of the alewife tradition into modern times. The Cricketers was not a pub as we know it but the front room of a cottage on the village green. A trestle table stood at the back of the room, cutting it off from the kitchen, in which stood a barrel of beer. In summer the barrel was covered with wet cloths to keep it cool, and beer was drawn off into jugs as needed and poured into the tankards of eager customers. The Cricketers was run by two old sisters who gave me a withering look on the occasion I asked if they had any gin. True, they didn't brew their own beer, what they sold wasn't ale, and they didn't hoist a gorse bush outside to show when they had broached a barrel, but the basic set-up differed very little from the medieval version. Health and safety regulations and brewery pressure have long since closed down the Cricketers. To my mind that is a great pity, but I am glad to have seen the last flowering of a very old rural tradition.

In order to produce ale you have to malt grain. Today only barley is used for most brewing, but in the Middle Ages they used what was available, so the grain may have been part wheat and part barley and may even on occasion have had oats mixed in with it. Malting requires the sprouting of grain and therefore needs both heat and water. This leads to the danger of fire, so malting houses tended, where possible, to be underground. You can still see the remains of some in Nottingham, a town with an old brewing tradition where the soft sandstone could easily be dug out, and a number of English castles still retain their old malting and brewhouses. Where water was not readily to hand it was drawn up by horse-driven pumps, and a great deal of ingenuity went into their design. The whole process of malting could occupy the rest of this book, but I will leave it to Walter of Bibbesworth, writing in the thirteenth century (though here in a Victorian translation), to tell you all that you and the brewer need to know about malting grain and brewing:

> Then steep your barley in a vat
> Large and broad, take care of that,
> When you shall have steeped your grain,
> And the water let out drain,
> Take it to an upper floor
> If you've swept it clean before.
> There couch, and let your barley dwell
> Till it germinates full well.
> Malt now you shall call the grain
> Corn it ne'er shall be again.
> Stir the malt then with your hand
> In heaps or rows now let it stand,
> On a tray then you should take it
> To a kiln to dry and bake it,
> The tray and eke [also] a basket light
> Will serve to spread the malt aright.
> When your malt is ground in mill
> And of hot water has drank its fill
> And skill has changed the wort to ale
> Then to see you shall not fail.

The price of ale was as strictly controlled as that of bread, and the Assize of Ale, which came into force at the same time as the Assize of Bread, worked on a similar sliding scale: the rate was lowered or raised according to the price of grain but averaged out at about a penny for three or four gallons, the equal of around eight pints.

There is ample evidence even in medieval times of the English penchant for heavy drinking – for example a rather charming reference relating to the Hospital of St Cross and Almshouses of Noble Poverty at Winchester, which tells us that at Christmas the inmates were allowed as much ale as they could drink while daylight lasted. I'm sure they started early. One manorial tenant's Christmas feast records that the tenants should have more firewood and two candles and that they should sit and drink for as long past daylight as the candles burnt consecutively should last. Alewives were well paid. The Countess of Leicester while in the castle at Odiham hired an alewife from Banbury (a town noted for its brewing) and paid her five shillings for the winter brewing, with an extra eighteen pence for her travel expenses (a journey of some thirty-five miles).

When Henry II married Eleanor she brought to the marriage large areas of the best wine districts in France. The English gentry had long imported wine and we even grew our own grapes. In fact, the Romans had established a wine industry as far north as Lincolnshire, and the practice had continued after they left. Vineyards pop up in the Domesday Book and in 1290 one vineyard at Ledbury belonging to Bishop Swinfield produced seven pipes of white wine and a tun of verjuice (a sour juice obtained from unripe grapes) in one year, while the Earl of Cornwall's vineyard at Isleworth produced three tuns and one pipe. A tun was a measure of 252 gallons, subdivided into 63 sesters of 4 gallons each. When it came to wine from abroad, some of the most favoured tipples came from Poitou. As for Bordeaux, Henry and Eleanor's son John, who lost many of his holdings in France to Philip Augustus in the early thirteenth century, set up a special trade agreement with merchants that included an exemption on export taxes for all ships sailing from the port.

So greatly did the wine trade grow that French vineyards were even planted on land previously used for cereal production. Everything was focused on the profits from the English wine trade. In fact Gascony grew so many vines that it became heavily dependent on England for grain. Medieval wine didn't keep, barely lasting the year, so when the harvest was pressed in September the race was on to ship it as early as possible in October before the autumn gales set in. The rush to ship reminds me of that hideous con of the 1970s and 1980s when Beaujolais nouveau (barely drinkable) was rushed to England as though we were in for a major treat. In the Middle Ages, large fleets of a great variety of ships set out from Bordeaux after the annual autumn wine-making, seeking premium prices. A second fleet set out in the spring, aiming to arrive before Easter. This time the wine had had time to be racked, allowing the lees to settle fully before the wine was drawn off.

Large quantities were shipped. In Christmas week 1246, for example, the Cinque Port of Winchelsea alone unloaded 465 tuns of wine. So great was the wine trade that the tun barrels that occupied forty cubic feet of a ship's hold became the internationally accepted measure of a ship's capacity; to this day we define ships in terms of tonnage (for which, read tunnage).

England imported millions of gallons of wine a year – a third of all its import trade. This was most agreeable to the king, who levied a 'prise' of one cask from every ship carrying ten or more casks, and two casks where the cargo was twenty casks or more. (In time this was turned into a duty of two shillings on every tun and became known as 'butlerage' because it was paid to the king's chief butler.) The best wine would have been reserved for the high table at court. The rest would have been distributed among the royal castles.

Offloading your wine at a major port was one thing, but the barrels then had to be distributed around the country. Some might have been shipped on smaller vessels to other smaller ports, but most would have travelled by road – not very good roads at that time, especially in winter. Major magnates and vintners would have had their own ox carts, but others would have had to hire a carter at a rate of appoximately 1d a day per tun. The allocation of wine for each member of the household who qualified was approximately a quart a day. The quality was pretty variable. Peter of Blois, a French poet and diplomat who visited Henry II's court, wrote:

> The wine is turned sour and mouldy: thick, greasy, stale, flat and smacking of pitch. I have sometimes seen even great lords served with wine so muddy that a man must needs close his eyes and clench his teeth, wry-[sour] mouthed and shuddering, and filtering the stuff rather than drinking.

It would be inappropriate, however, to conclude a survey of the medieval larder with wine drinkers at the top of the social scale. When we think of the Middle Ages, we may conjure up images of palaces, castles and cathedrals, but these were for the very few. The vast majority of English people were poor agricultural workers, living in small one- or two-roomed cottages. They had allotments for their vegetables, their own field strips for crops, perhaps a pig or two to provide bacon, ham and lard, some chickens for eggs, and a cow or goat for milk and cheese. In good times, their diet was certainly sufficient. In bad times, life could be grim, and it's scarcely surprising that life expectancy in medieval England was probably only about thirty years (though that figure takes into account the high levels of infant mortality). That said, it would be misleading to assume that the ordinary people of medieval England were frail and rickety. If you have ever handled a longbow – that key English weapon in medieval warfare – you will know that you need considerable strength to draw back the string. The battles of Crécy and Agincourt would scarcely have been won had they been fought by soldiers from a destitute nation.

A woodcut from Caxton's second edition of Chaucer's *Canterbury Tales* (c. 1483). The pilgrims gather together for a meal on their way to Thomas à Becket's shrine in Canterbury Cathedral. Quite what food is on offer here is hard to discern, but it seems to include a boar's head, and the flagon on the left presumably contains ale.

CHAPTER 2

Eastern Spices and Baked Venison

The High Middle Ages

I t is tempting to assume that because travel in the Middle Ages was fraught with difficulties and dangers, England stood isolated on the periphery of Europe and was little influenced by what happened elsewhere. Tempting, but very wrong. In fact, as we've already seen, the Norman Conquest created strong ties between England and the Continent, and these were reinforced by the marriage on 18 May 1152 of Henry II and Eleanor of Aquitaine at Poitiers Cathedral, when he was nineteen and she was thirty. Henry already held land in France – he was Count of Anjou and Duke of Normandy – but Eleanor was Duchess of Aquitaine and Countess of Poitou in her own right and owned virtually all the land between the Loire and the Pyrenees. She had previously been married to the worthy and pious Louis VII of France, a young man heavily under the influence of two misogynists: Bernard, Abbot of Clairvaux (later canonised), and Abbot Suger, an aesthete who lived in a tiny cell and wore a hair shirt. The two men had indoctrinated Louis with the Catholic belief that marriage was only for the procreation of children, so while the naive young man longed for Eleanor, he didn't visit her bed very often and initially only one daughter was born to them.

Unsurprisingly, the marriage was not exactly a success. Eleanor may well have had an affair with Henry II's father, Count Geoffrey of Anjou, and may also have committed adultery with her uncle, King Raymond of Sicily, with whom she stayed for quite some time. Eventually, her inability to produce a son caused real tensions and the marriage was annulled on the technical grounds of consanguinity. Eleanor clearly wasn't upset by the outcome. Considering that Louis's options were to retire her to a nunnery, have her executed for adultery or even have her quietly murdered – in all of which events he could have kept her estates – it says a lot for Eleanor's personality that she got her way. Now she married Henry, a man much more suited to her dynamic personality: he was energetic, intelligent, well educated, beautifully mannered – and lusty, fathering eight children, five of whom were boys.

Eleanor was an extraordinary woman. She set up the first refuge for battered women from every walk of life at Fontevrault Abbey, and her support and development of the art of courtly love probably ameliorated the lot of many wives – you don't bash your lady on the head if you are pining for her favours. Eleanor is also said to have introduced the mulberry tree to her French estates to establish the French silk industry (unlikely, I suspect) and to have introduced the damask rose (later the symbol of the Lancastrian and Yorkist houses, which led, of course, to the merged Tudor rose) to her new homeland. In addition, as we have seen, her marriage to Henry II helped to promote the wine trade. But Eleanor also did something else that had a major impact on English food. She went on Crusade.

It is perhaps difficult for us to comprehend the furore that the Crusades caused in medieval Europe. At a time when the Church used the fear of hellfire to control the behaviour of their flock, the chance of obtaining a 'get out of hell free' card by embarking on expeditions to rescue the Holy Land from the infidel sent people wild with enthusiasm. They rushed to take the cross. Those who didn't were pilloried and on some occasions even lynched. The only comparison I can think of in modern times was the rush to join up in the First World War and the white feathers given to those who didn't.

Eleanor's first husband Louis enthusiastically took the cross, and, since it was clear that he was going to be away for several years, Eleanor accompanied him. She spent time in Outremer, as the Crusader areas of the Holy Land were known, visiting Acre and Jerusalem. While there she inevitably encountered the food and, more particularly, the spices of the East. And my belief is that Eleanor and her ladies then helped to introduce spices to England, her celebrity encouraging their swift adoption, rather as Princess Diana's hairstyles inspired imitation in our own time. Pedants will say there is no evidence to support my theory. True, but neither is there any to disprove it. I wonder if in 900 years there will be any concrete evidence of how in the twentieth century olive oil went from being sold for external use only to an everyday commodity supposedly better for health than England's own native butter!

Whatever the precise truth of the matter, there is no doubt that the Crusades had a huge impact on English culture. On the military front, the men who went on Crusade brought back falcons and falconers, and they learnt from the Saracens how to improve their chain mail and weaponry. On the domestic front, they brought back beautiful textiles and handicrafts. A handful of spices, such as pepper and ginger, had been known in England for a while, but their popularity seems to have grown hugely at this time. Others, such as cinnamon and nutmeg, were new arrivals in the twelfth century, and it's hard not to believe that Eleanor had a part in popularising them.

Dishes with a hint of the Middle East soon made an appearance. Hindle Wakes, a capon stuffed with dried fruit, lemon rind and blood, could possibly be an example (it certainly first appeared in England in medieval times). The North Staffordshire oatcake, so different from any other oatcake, seems to me very reminiscent of a Middle Eastern flatbread. Mint sauce with lamb is, I am sure, our last real and regularly cooked connection with the Crusades. Interestingly, there are mentions of Saracens settling in northern England after the Crusades (for example in Staffordshire) and various Victorian writers were convinced that the northern populations of their day included both those with long Viking bones and fair hair and shorter people with darker hair; dried fruit is commonly used in dishes in those regions, just as it has been in Middle Eastern food for centuries. Documentary evidence, mainly in the form of the household books of the day, confirms the arrival of spices in the twelfth century. They also feature largely in the only cookery book to have come down to us from this early period, *The Forme of Cury*, produced in around 1390 by the cooks of the household of King Richard II, Eleanor's great-great-great-great-grandson.

The spice trade was an elaborate international spider's web. It gathered ingredients from the Malabar coast and to a lesser extent from the Spice Islands of the Moluccas. These were then shipped to ports such as Aden in the Middle East. From there they made their way overland by camel train towards the Mediterranean. By the fourteenth century the trade from there on was largely in the hands of the Venetians and their galleys, but in Eleanor's day they would have come across country to the markets of Champagne.

It's often said that medieval dishes used large quantities of spices to disguise the taste of rotten meat. I cannot understand this strange idea that people would ever have considered eating putrid food or that if they did it wouldn't have killed them any less surely than it would us today. It seems far more likely that spices helped to mask the salt used to preserve food, and that the reason why they were used in quantities that can seem excessive to us is that, in the days before airtight containers, they would have lost their flavour fairly quickly in transport and so needed to be used in bulk to make an impact. Incidentally, another method employed by medieval cooks to deal with the salt in meat was to suspend a bag of split peas or oats in the cauldron in which the meat was boiled so as to absorb some of the salt. The peas or oats would then be served with the other dishes. Dried beans were treated in the same way.

Spices were very expensive in the twelfth century and consequently used only in the richest households. One of the most widely employed was pepper. Bartholomew the Englishman, with an ignorance of spices typical of the age, wrote that pepper grew in the southern parts of the Caucasus and that in order to pick it in woods infested with serpents the natives set fire to the woods, thereby turning the naturally white pepper black. As you will know, pepper is black when the unskinned berry is dried in the sun, and white when the berry is skinned before drying. Its importance is demonstrated by the fact that a Guild of Pepperers was established in 1180. Later the guild became responsible for aspects of weights and measures, and in 1328 became known as the Grossarii (i.e. people dealing with measures by the 'gross'), hence our word 'grocer'. A peppercorn rent, which has come to mean a purely nominal price, was quite the contrary in medieval times, when a pound of pepper involved a substantial investment. Dowries were paid in pepper, and in Germany there are even records of whole towns paying rents in it.

Along with what we think of as pepper, Ethiopian pepper (also known as Grains of Paradise), Cubeb pepper and long pepper from China were also imported. All of these would have been pounded in a pestle and mortar – in big households a very large one indeed. I once saw for sale a large, very old and much-used pestle made out of a tree trunk; sadly it was at a time when I had spent all my money on gin, and I have long regretted not making it mine.

Ginger was another popular spice in the medieval kitchen. It came in two varieties, columbine and string, of which the latter was more prized and expensive. Prices were pretty steep, which may partly explain why the related and generally cheaper galangal was often preferred in medieval recipes. Manuscripts that contain advice on buying ginger still survive, advising the would-be purchaser to look for heavy pieces that are not dry or woody – good advice today. One luxury use for ginger was to make gingerbread, a confection that, over time, proved to be very popular in England ('An I had but one penny in the world, thou shouldst have it to buy gingerbread,' the clown Costard says in Shakespeare's *Love's Labour's Lost*). Ginger also made its way into medicine, where it was considered to have both warming and opiate properties. In fact, many herbs and spices played an important part in medieval medicine, their properties thought to aid and balance the four body humours of black bile, yellow bile, phlegm and blood. (Cooking techniques also sought to achieve a balance; hence, for example, the reason why beef – considered a 'dry' meat – was so often boiled.)

Cinnamon was also regularly imported (the Countess of Leicester (1215–75), King John's daughter, bought the spice in quantities of six pounds at a time, which is an awful lot of cinnamon). Bartholomew the Englishman helpfully tells us that it was to be found in the nests of the phoenix, which had to be shot down with lead arrows and its nests set fire to before the spice could be gathered. Cloves, too, were favoured, though used in much smaller quantities. So far as other spices and herbs were concerned, most could be grown domestically. Cumin (used in large quantities for cooking with chicken), coriander and fennel were all grown in herb gardens. Saffron, which later Crusaders brought back and which is derived from the saffron crocus, thrived in such places as Saffron Walden (hence the name of the town), although a lot was imported from Spain. It takes 70,000 flowers to make one pound of saffron from the stamen of the autumn saffron crocus, and the cost then, as now, was considerable. However, as the cooks among you will know, a little saffron goes a very long way.

Early cookery manuscripts throw up one slight mystery and

one surprise. The mystery concerns the use of 'mace'. Food writers and historians have understandably tended to assume that this must refer to the lacy 'aril' on a nutmeg, but it was clearly used in such quantities that I have my doubts, even though we know that, thanks to the Crusades, nutmeg was around in England at this time. However, we also know that in the ninth century the emperor Charlemagne is recorded as having grown a herb called mace in his gardens at Aachen. I suspect that this herb tasted similar to the spice and so gave its name to it.

The surprise – for me, not least, when I was cooking from *The Forme of Cury* – is that in addition to making extensive use of spices, medieval cooks also used a lot of sugar (widely regarded as a spice at the time). It's been commonly believed that sugar didn't arrive in Europe until Tudor or even Elizabethan times, and yet here it is in a fourteenth-century manuscript. In fact, it turns out that cane sugar had been produced in the Arab world for several centuries by the time the Crusaders came across it, and its sweetness rapidly caught on with them. The Venetians soon monopolised the trade and by the late fourteenth century, around the time of *The Forme of Cury*, we find references to both loaf sugar and powdered white sugar. It certainly wasn't cheap. Loaf sugar cost anywhere between one shilling and two shillings a pound in the thirteenth and fourteenth centuries (a kitchen servant at that time might hope to earn four shillings a year).

Curiously, sugar was also regarded as having beneficial medical properties. King Edward I's son Henry (1268–74), a sickly boy who suffered from a bad chest, was prescribed liberal quantities of it, both as barley sugar and the more exotic concoctions of rose and violet sugar, by his physician Hugh of Evesham. To no avail: all the sugar and all the votive candles, not to mention the thirteen widows of Guildford who prayed all night for his health, couldn't keep him from an early death. One can't help wondering whether infant diabetes was to blame.

If you were rich enough, you bought a lot of sugar and spices. We know, for example, that Edward I spent the enormous sum of £1,600 on these luxuries in one year (bear in mind that an entire castle in Edward I's reign might cost £15,000 to build). Given the lamentable quality of so much of the wine on offer at this time it is not surprising that it was served sweetened and spiced with honey, pepper, ginger and, of course, sugar. One particularly elaborate version was fennel wine with added liquorice, which was supposed to increase sexual urges and prevent leprosy – the one is about as likely as the other, I suspect.

To get a sense of how all these new ingredients were used, it's worth spending a little time looking at *The Forme of Cury* in more detail, though to do so we have to leap forward 200 years from Eleanor's time to the end of the fourteenth century. I have been privileged to see the original, which is housed in the British Library, and it is a remarkable manuscript. It describes itself as a collection of recipes (*cury* means 'cook') from the master cooks of the court of King Richard II (note the use of the word 'cooks', not 'chefs'). It is not strictly a book but a scroll of vellum strips sewn together, handwritten presumably by clerks (then, as now, most cooks didn't really write). The language is English, for this is an age when English had gained the upper hand over Norman French and Englishness was becoming fashionable. It was first published in 1780 by a printer and bookseller called Samuel Pegge at the behest of Gustavus Brander, curator of the British Museum. Earlier, Lord Stafford had presented it to Elizabeth I; presumably some subsequent monarch presented it to the museum.

What shines through is the imagination and sophistication of the recipes. Nowhere are the crude large roasts and joints so beloved of Hollywood; this was food that would grace any restaurant, and it was rather better than most. The food is spicy, with a complex mixture of flavours. Almonds were used as a thickener, the nuts being blanched in boiling water, peeled, dried and then ground into powder – all very labour intensive. (Large quantities of almonds were used, some households buying 40 pounds at a time.) Sauces were also thickened with bread; our own bread sauce flavoured with cloves and onion is very reminiscent of what would have been popular then. In addition, there is a clear taste for the blending of sweet and sour, no doubt because it was either balancing heavily salted meat, or flavouring freshwater fish, which can be quite bland.

Look at this recipe for something called a 'colde brewet', which I have taken the liberty of translating from *The Forme of Cury*:

Take almonds and grind them. Take two parts of wine and a measure of vinegar and cook the almonds in this. Take aniseed sugar and a few sprigs of green fennel shoots; add this to the almond mixture powder, with some ginger and cloves, and add some whole blades of mace. Chop the meat of some kid and some chicken quite small and cook them. When cooked, transfer to a clean dish, season with salt and pepper and serve it cold.

This is actually a very good sort of cold soup. Also delicious is 'egurdouce of fysshe' (sweet and sour fish). For this you take roach, tench and sole, cut them into pieces and fry them in oil. You then make a syrup with equal quantities of wine and vinegar. Cook together chopped onions, raisins, currants and sultanas. Add a few powdered spices (precisely which ones are not specified, so you can make your own selection). Pour all this over the fish and serve – the best sweet and sour fish you will ever eat.

It's also worth pointing out that at this time many dishes would have been served in pastry. Indeed, there were considerably more varieties of pastry than we have today, some made with butter (like our puff pastry), some made with lard (like our own raised pies), and some simply a flour and water coffyn (or box), not designed for eating but simply as a serving vessel for the food. Bread was served on the side to help you mop up sauce and also to give you something to wipe your spoon on before you dipped it into the common serving dish.

The recipes, then, are quite complicated, and it was also common for dishes to be served in a spectacular way. The Middle Ages was mad for colour in hangings, in stained glass – and in food. Brawn, usually made with boar meat (preferably wild), might be gilded with gold and silver foil. Dishes would be coloured with mulberries or blackberries or even beetroot. Colour might also come from the yellow of saffron or grated hard-boiled egg yolks or the green of herbs freshly chopped in at the last minute. Tables might have an elaborate nef in pride of place – an ornament in the shape of a ship and made from precious metals, which would hold salt, spices and other things.

All this seems highly appropriate for the reign of a man like Richard II. He was a man who liked splendour. His greatest remaining creation is Westminster Hall with its amazing oak hammer-beam roof. Today the Hall has been relegated to the security entrance to the House of Commons, but none of its grandeur has been reduced by that. His sense of self-worth and his place at the forefront of Englishmen is displayed in the magnificent Wilton Diptych, now in the National Gallery. Richard carried it with him as the focus of his personal shrine, and it shows him backed by two English kings and saints, Edward the Confessor and King Edmund the Martyr, kneeling to the Virgin and Christ child, who appear before a rank of beautiful angels all wearing Richard's personal badge of the white hart. The Christ child is offering Richard a banner of the cross of St George, and recent restoration has revealed that at the top of the staff supporting the banner is a tiny map of England.

Richard's love of splendour, display and elegance extended to the dining hall. He is, for example, credited with the introduction of the table napkin. Before this invention, diners wiped their fingers on the tablecloth or washed them in a bowl and then dried them on a towel proffered by their squire. Even without Richard's direct influence, however, strict conventions governed the way in which meals for the great and the good were served. The diners in hall ate in messes of four, and food was served accordingly in dishes containing four portions (a tradition that long persisted in the dining halls of the Inns of Court and various Oxbridge colleges). There was not, however, a single dish per course: the medieval dinner was more like a Chinese meal where a variety of dishes make up a course. Sweet and savoury were served alongside each other and frequently appeared together in the same dish. It is probable that the diner didn't eat from all the dishes and made do with those nearest to him. Different rules applied to the high table, and the food above the salt (for which see overleaf) would have been of a better quality – something people have complained about since the time of the Roman poet Martial.

People of highest rank sat on only one side of the table, the other side being occupied by the servers and carvers. Each of these diners had their own personal attendants. Young men from the families of the gentry went away from home to be pages in the households of other families; a placement to a lord above you in the feudal scale could lead to all sorts of profitable connections, land tenancies and possibly even an advantageous marriage. Along with learning such skills as the use of weaponry, the young page would be trained in the art of waiting on his lord. He learnt to offer a ewer of warm water, in which soothing herbs had been infused, so that his lord could wash his hands, and he would then hand him a towel. He would also fill his lord's cup when he was thirsty. In the Middle Ages, drinking vessels were not left on the table but proffered on demand and returned to the buffet when finished with. It must have been rather like receiving the attentions of a sommelier in a smart restaurant who tends the diners' wine and water glasses and sulks if you fill your own glass should he prove tardy.

As the attendant became more experienced in his duties, he would be trained in the art of carving and seasoning of dishes. Again smart hotels still offer a similar service, practising the art of flambé and guéridon service: a chafing dish may be placed on the trolley to keep the dish warm and either, as in the case of crêpe Suzette or steak Diane, the food is cooked or reheated at table, or, if you are having a Dover sole or some such dish, it will be deftly taken off the bone and transferred to your plate. This is just how it would have been in the theatre that was the medieval dining hall. The carver had a collection of different knives, some with broad flat blades for transferring the meat to the trencher (forks did not make an appearance until the early seventeenth century). He began by removing the crust from a loaf and cutting a trencher, which he then placed in front of the diner, sprinkling it with a little salt taken from the great salt. Salt was, for obvious reasons, a much-valued – and expensive – commodity. The great salt would have been a rather large, dramatic object of silver or silver gilt, designed to be both functional and an adornment for the table. To sit 'above the salt' was a sign of social prestige.

The dishes were brought to the high table by the server (or sewer), who tasted a small portion to prove that it wasn't poisoned (a practice that continued at the court of the Russian tsar until the late nineteenth century). The carver then carved and seasoned each dish, placing it on the diner's trencher. I assume that the diner indicated which of the dishes he wanted. There was a lot of sending titbits from the high table to diners elsewhere in the hall, and these presumably were carried by the server. Interestingly, the chafing dishes for reheating food resembled almost exactly mini West Indian coalpots which are still used in households today. They would have contained a hot piece of charcoal or maybe even a hot coal.

In the days before 1980s New Wave American food crushed the conventions of which ingredients were served with which, every type of meat or fish had its own prescribed accompaniments: horseradish with beef, mint sauce with lamb, gammon with parsley sauce, and so on. The foundations of this were laid in the Middle Ages, and the medieval carver would have had to memorise all of them. He would also have known precisely which carving technique should be used for each dish. A coney, or rabbit, was 'unlaced' and sprinkled either with ginger and vinegar or with mustard and sugar. Venison was 'broken' and served with cinnamon and sugar. Meat was cut from a joint of venison in a long strip: the carver left a kind of handle at the top and cut the remainder of the piece up its length into three or four strips; the diner then took the meat by the handle and nibbled the long strips.

All sorts of game birds graced the table, and similar rules governed the way they were served. Bittern (which I am told by an old keeper who had eaten it in his youth tastes like lean beef) was 'unjointed' and served with camelyne sauce (essentially, wine, vinegar and/or verjuice and bread, flavoured with spices; the name may have come from the fact that the sauce is camel-coloured). Beaver tail, which counted as fish, was served with frumenty (made from husked wheat boiled in milk or almond milk, sometimes with sugar) or pease pudding. The spices the carver sprinkled were kept in a locked casket, often of silver gilt, with separate compartments for each spice, which would have been ground beforehand.

We must remember that dining was not just for the service of food but also provided entertainment in the days before television. On high days, birds such as swans and peacocks would, when cooked, be covered by a skin of the feathers of the species, the swan with its neck erect and the peacock displaying its tail. Dowels would have been inserted into the neck or tail feathers to keep them upright. One rather charming story about an early-medieval Duke of Savoy tells of how he disliked swan but liked the display it offered so he instructed his cook to place the swan skin over a cooked goose, something that must have been the cause of some surprise.

I have eaten swan twice, once at an Elizabethan banquet and once in Ireland in a stew. I can't say that I enjoyed it: it was very fishy, rather stringy and reminiscent of moorhen, which I also dislike. Swans were nevertheless an important feature of the medieval diet, their value underlined by the fact that in the Middle Ages they were deemed to belong to the Crown. Those on the Thames are still owned by the sovereign or by the Dyers' and Vintners' companies, and the ceremony of Swan Upping, which involves notching swans' beaks to identify their owners, still takes place every year. Swan eggs were also eaten, simmered for twenty minutes and then left in hot water for a further twenty minutes. (Swans, like many other birds, will continue to lay if the eggs are taken early from the nest. Personally I wouldn't want to face an angry nesting swan.) Heron had a similar status as a popular but rather exotic bird. I have never eaten heron, but I gather that it's much like swan. There was obviously something about the taste that appealed to medieval palates, but that thankfully no longer does.

After the main courses came the sweet (possibly wafers – which would have been like a sweet waffle – or tarts or fritters), and then the tables were drawn back to the wall, the diners moved to benches, and jugglers, minstrels and possibly strolling players formed the entertainment. At Richard II's court, Chaucer would have been on hand to read from his work, and the drink would have flowed. Obviously quicker, simpler meals would have been served on working days, possibly on a running basis between certain times as they are in the Inns of Court today. In winter, though, when outside work finished with the fading of daylight, there would have been time to spare. After each course was served, the trenchers and any food left over were taken out to be distributed to the poor.

All these conventions and traditions would have been second nature to the aristocracy of Richard II's time, but this was also a period when we begin to see greater social mobility and the growth of new classes of society who would have dined in a similar if not necessarily so lavish a way. And we can tell this partly because the late fourteenth century sees the beginning of etiquette guides – good indicators, as in Victorian times, that people were making their way in society and anxious to know how to behave. These guides tell the diner, among other things, not to fart at table, not to spit out bones or gristle into the shared dish, not to put their elbows on the table and to tear rather than cut their bread. All the stuff you would expect the aristocrat to have learnt during his years serving as a gentleman's squire or a young lady to have learnt from her governess.

A satirical portrait of this sort of social climber appears in Chaucer's *Canterbury Tales*, where the Prioress, Madame Eglantine, is depicted as a rather blood-thirsty anti-Semitic bigot who speaks French in the manner of Stratford-atte-Bowe not of Paris and is obsessed with lady-like manners. Chaucer, with his usual wit and irony, portrays her vividly, taking time to describe her perfect table manners:

At mete [table manners] well ytaught was she with alle;
She leet no morsel from hir lippes falle,
Ne wette hir fyngres in hir sauce depe;
Wel koude she carie a morsel and wel kepe
That no drope ne fille [no drop fell] upon hire brest.
In curteisie was set ful muchel hir lest [she deeply desired to
    behave in a refined manner].
Hir over-lippe wyped she so clene
That in her coppe [cup] ther was no ferthyng [speck] sene
Of grece, whan she dronken hadde hir draughte.

Chaucer himself came from a family that was on the up. He was the son of a wealthy vintner, but his grandfather had been a Suffolk publican.

A key event in Richard II's life also confirms the rise of these new social classes. Men of the Plantagenet dynasty tended to fall into one of two categories. Some were macho warriors who delighted in war, like Richard's father the Black Prince, who died before coming to the throne but proved his valour at the Battle of Poitiers, or his grandfather Edward III. Others were like Richard: somewhat wimpy, very cultivated and sybaritic. Henry III, for example, was easily moved to tears and obsessed with installing lavatories in his palaces at a time when not that much emphasis was placed on personal hygiene. However, in an event that defined the early years of Richard's reign he actually showed considerable personal courage. At the age of fourteen, in 1381, he rode out to confront the leaders of the Peasants' Revolt – a brave move given that they had already killed the Archbishop of London and the Lord Chancellor. At a second meeting at Smithfield, the lord mayor, who was in

Richard's retinue, pulled one of the leaders, Wat Tyler, from his horse and stabbed him to death with a dagger which is still on display in Fishmongers' Hall. Things were turning nasty but Richard spoke to the mob, saying, 'I am your Captain and will lead you,' and persuaded them to go home.

Two points stand out in this story to my mind. Firstly that the common man had by now worked up enough resolve to revolt against his lot. Secondly that Richard's escort at the meeting at Smithfield was not some earl or duke but the lord mayor, a City tradesman. The previous decades had seen a huge growth in trade and international finance, and consequently the beginnings of international banking. Literacy and numeracy were spreading. This was therefore the era when the livery companies that had been formed to regulate the trades within the major cities of the kingdom and especially the City of London really began to thrive. The guilds were granted royal charters to safeguard their rights to dictate how the members would qualify.

The men who formed these guilds had money, power and growing social importance. Where once the Crown had looked to the Church for money or loans, or to the Jewish community (until their expulsion from England in 1290), it now came to depend ever more heavily on the guilds and the merchant class generally. Henry Fitz-Ailwyn de Londonestone, the first Lord Mayor of London, had persuaded Richard I to replace the royal official who ruled the City with himself and future guild members in exchange for loans for his Crusade, and from there on the City guilds stepped in, enlarging their rights and powers in exchange for hard cash. Such men had an important impact on the eating habits of the country.

And not only as consumers of food. Many of the guilds inevitably dealt with its production. I am, for example, a member of the Butchers' Guild, which has regulated the meat trade since the fourteenth century. In order to become a member of the guild and a freeman of the City of London a butcher would have had to serve a seven-year apprenticeship with an existing member, and then a further year with his master as a journeyman, before being permitted to join the guild and progress within it to being a liveryman, a member of the company court, an alderman and possibly, ultimately, lord mayor. (To this day you cannot become lord mayor unless you are a member of a livery company.) The food guilds – the Butchers', the Fishmongers', the Bakers' and of course the Guild of Cooks (established in 1482 from an amalgam of earlier companies) – not only dealt with employment regulations but also the quality of the products sold. We have records of butchers being prosecuted for tying extra fat on to joints of meat with string and thereby fraudulently extracting a higher price, a practice that is commonplace today. They also regulated the great London markets of Smithfield, Billingsgate and Covent Garden.

Smithfield still stands within the City of London, owned today by the Corporation of the City of London. It ceased being a shambles (that is, a place where livestock is brought and killed) only in Victorian times. The markets of Billingsgate and Covent Garden occupied their original sites well into my lifetime. (Covent Garden, incidentally, had begun its life as the Garden of the Convent of St Peter's, Westminster. Surplus fruit and flowers were sold off by the monks and the market progressed from there.) Smithfield today is, to my mind, a shadow of its former self, but I can still recall its hustle and bustle, the great carcasses hanging in the open and the bumerees (the old name for the market porters) stopping for no one, as our director on *Two Fat Ladies* learnt to her cost when she placed her camera where I told her not to.

As the guilds became more powerful, there was a distinct improvement in the quality and safety of food on offer. The markets became an increasingly important source of meat for households in the later Middle Ages, but for the royal and wealthy the forests continued to be a rich source of game, and hunting remained a passion. Richard II himself, though effete in war, was devoted to the chase, and it's significant that his private badge should have been the white hart and that he had a favourite greyhound, called Mathe. One of the major acts of his reign, in fact, was to strengthen the already draconian game laws. Ever since the Norman Conquest, game in the form of deer or boar had been the preserve of the king and the gentry, while the royal forests had been for the king's exclusive use unless he chose to license rights to his friends as a gift or for money. No dog belonging to anyone of ordinary origins and over a certain size was allowed in the forest unless it had three claws removed from its front paws so that it could not attack a deer. Any poacher caught might have his testicles or fingers removed, and he might even suffer the death penalty if he stole the king's deer.

Poaching, by the way, was not just confined to commoners. A long-running case brought against William Ferrers, Earl of Derby, charged that between 1216 and 1222 he had taken 1,000 deer from the king's preserves – an average of over 100 deer a year. Nor was poaching the only way of getting your hands on a deer. Sometimes a wounded deer would escape the hounds but die later, to be quietly taken home to a nearby cottage; even the risk of selling its skin was worth the small sum it would bring. We know from the records of manorial courts that the cottagers poached with snares and pits lined with pointed sticks, and I expect any deer that strayed into a cottage garden was quickly and surreptitiously dispatched and bundled into the cooking pot. Deer are highly destructive: they eat crops and they damage trees by stripping and eating the bark, so quite apart from being a valuable food source there is good reason to control them.

It is an indication of how valued hunting was in the medieval world that among the clauses in Magna Carta and in the Charter of the Forests (1217) that sought to guarantee a man's right to be judged only by a jury of his peers or not to be deprived of the tools of his trade was one opening up the royal forests and another relaxing the penalties for hunting therein. Over time, penalties were mitigated to fines or imprisonment, probably because the depredations of the Black Death made labour more valuable, and royal forests started to be sold off to raise much-needed cash (Richard I sold land to help finance his Crusade and pay his ransom when he was captured by Duke Leopold; his successors continued the practice). Richard II, however, reinforced the game laws not only on royal preserves but throughout the country. He cut back on poaching with dogs and placed restrictions on who could even own a dog. The legislation hit the poorer people most but it also further upset the nobles, who were already at odds with the king.

As William Ferrers' illegal activities show, hunting (or, in his case, poaching) provided a valuable source of food. But hunting was also a social occasion. Lords, clerics and even women were devoted to the chase. In the thirteenth century Eleanor of England used to visit with a pack of fifty hunting dogs, which her hosts were required to feed. It helped that she was Henry III's sister. Chaucer, too, was a keen huntsman, and anyone who has ever hunted will identify with the words of the narrator of *The Book of the Duchess*, who hearing the clamour of the meet, and of hounds and horses gathering in the courtyard, exclaims:

> Anon-right, whan I herde that,
> How that they wolde on hunting goon [wanted to go hunting],
> I was right glad, and up anoon;
> I took my hors, and forth I wente
> Out of my chambre; I never stente [stopped]
> Til I com to the feld withoute [outside].

He goes on to describe the excitement and breathless momentum of the deer hunt, the running of the hounds and in this case the escape of the hart. A greyhound can achieve speeds of forty miles an hour or more, so breathless is probably an understatement. English hounds had been sought after since Roman times, and if you go to the National Coursing Club stand at any game fair or country show you will see hunting dogs among those assembled – wolfhounds, for example, grey-hounds, and deerhounds, whose manner of dealing with deer is to knock them off their feet. A medieval manuscript in the Pierpont Morgan Library in America shows a deer being pursued by greyhounds and a mounted field, but I suspect that a mixed pack was frequently used.

Wild boar were another popular quarry. The boar was a

dangerous beast. If it got past the boar spear it would gore the hunter, often fatally, but then this was an age that valued courage. Boar hounds were a distinct breed, probably rather like young fit mastiffs. Hunting certainly had its impact on boar numbers, but I suspect that their ultimate demise had an awful lot to do with the gradual destruction of England's forests. Having seen the damage boar did one night when I was visiting a friend in Italy, I suspect they were, hunting apart, not much missed. That said, boar is quite delicious and would have been a great treat when served in hall.

The other popular form of hunting was falconry, another area of life to be transformed by the Crusaders' contact with the East. The desert Arabs had perfected the art, and when the Crusaders returned from the Middle East they brought both hawks and falconers back with them and set up mews for their birds. In the days before the shotgun it would have been virtually impossible to bring down a heron or even a pheasant with a bow and arrow, so these lethal birds of prey were invaluable hunters and much treasured by their owners. Some idea of the importance of falconry to the life of the nation is given by the sheer number of words and phrases that have come into the language from the sport. 'Fair exchange is no robbery', for example, is a reference to coaxing the bird off its prey with an offer of a scrap of meat; riding peg a back (piggyback), according to some, describes the way in which a hawk was carried on a peg behind the saddle. It was a sport of some formality which rather disguises the amount of effort involved in training a hawk. Everyone hawked, and the sumptuary laws that sought to regulate consumption and dictated every aspect of social life specified which birds could be carried by which section of society, from an eagle by an emperor to a buzzard by a bishop and a little kestrel by a lady.

Within decades of Richard II's murder in 1400 (ironically, for a man who loved fine dining, he was starved to death in Pontefract Castle), England was plunged into further unrest in the form of the Wars of the Roses. The world of food, however, remained largely untouched, except for two significant developments. The first was that, for the wealthy, dining in hall with the household started to become a rarer event. More and more the lord and lady and their special guests took to dining in a separate and often specially built chamber. Since the thirteenth century they had had a separate solar to which they retired to sleep or have a bit of privacy, but privacy was generally something that was in rather short supply: the populace lived, ate, slept, fornicated and indeed probably were born and died in some communal area in full sight of others. In the course of the fifteenth century, however, the ruling class started to withdraw into private spaces. Part of the reason may have been that, as fires in houses became more sophisticated, they welcomed the chance for a private one and the warmth it offered. In this respect, at least, medieval cooks had a certain advantage: they may have had to work very hard, but they kept warm and had an opportunity to eat well.

The other development was that of breakfast. Until the mid fifteenth century, dinner – the main meal of the day – was often served as early as 10 a.m. (particularly in grand establishments where there might be so many people to feed that two sittings were necessary). Many people therefore would have eaten only a bit of bread and cheese and drunk a mug of small beer to break their fast. True, there is evidence that Edward I used to eat substantial breakfasts back in the thirteenth century, but this may have owed something to his travels fighting the Scots and Welsh, which rather precluded dinner. By the late Middle Ages, however, the meal was becoming rather more substantial, and by the early sixteenth century records from the Northumberland household accounts show that on flesh days they ate a breakfast that consisted of boiled beef and mutton, bread, butter and beer, salt fish and buttered eggs, and – on fish days – salt fish, smoked and pickled herring, sprats and bread. Possibly all of these were served cold, although I expect the salt fish, sprats and eggs were cooked, probably in the butter.

Dinner, however, remained the main meal of the day. As it was served when there was the most natural light, its precise timing therefore varied a little with the seasons. Poorer people would have gone home for it after a morning's labour or, during harvest time, might well have consumed it in the fields; those attached to grand establishments would gather in the great hall, their placement dictated by their social standing. On high days and holidays, dinner would be a substantial meal with entertainment laid on; on ordinary days, it would be a fairly swift affair. Either way it would be followed a few hours later by a light supper of perhaps bread and cheese, a slice of cold pie or cold bacon and ale. And to get an idea of what one of the grander late-medieval dinners could look like, here's a slightly edited one from John Russell's *Book of Nurture* from around 1460. It is an upper-class meal, but by this time could as easily have been eaten by, say, a well-to-do landowner as by one of the gentry.

A dynere of flesche

First Course
Brawn of boar with mustard
Pottage of herbs, spice and wine
Beef, mutton, pheasant and swan with chawdron [a sauce made
from chopped liver and entrails boiled with blood, bread, wine,
vinegar, pepper, cloves and ginger]
Capon, pork, baked venison, 'leche lombard', 'fruture
viaunt' ['leche' involves pork, eggs, currants and spices boiled
in a bladder and served with a sauce; a 'fruture' is a meat fritter]

A subtlety [usually some sort of novelty decorated dish; in this
case, the text specifies that an inter-course prayer should be recited]

Second Course
Pottage, blancmange of meat
Roast venison, kid, faun or rabbit
Bustard, stork, crane, peacock in its skin, heron or bittern,
served with bread
Partridge, woodcock, plover, egret, suckling rabbit
Great birds, larks and bream
Dowcetts [small custards], 'payne puff' [puff pastry used as a
casing], amber jelly, poached fritters

A subtlety

Third Course
Cream of almonds, 'mameny' [almond cream]
Roasted curlew, snipe, quail, sparrow, house martin

Perch in jelly, crayfish, 'pety perueis' [possibly fish pie]
Baked quinces, 'leche dugard', sage fritters

A subtlety

Blaunderelle [white apples] or pippins, caraway comfits
Wafers with hippocras [wine spiced with ginger, cinnamon
honey, long pepper (chinese pepper) and rue]

Some of the dishes speak for themselves; others may seem rather
alien to us. To give an idea what medieval dishes were like, here
are four from *A Forme of Cury*, as rewritten by me.

Blancmange: Soak your rice in water overnight and next day
wash it clean (rice would, of course, have been imported). Add
it to some almond milk and cook it till it is done. Take some
finely chopped, cooked chicken and add it to the cooked rice,
return to the heat, stir well but keep the mixture stiff. Be careful
it doesn't burn. Add sugar and slivers of almonds fried in butter
and serve it forth. [In other words, this blancmange is not the
milk jelly given to Victorian invalids but the sort that you would
get in an Iranian restaurant today. It's very much a legacy of
the Crusades.]

Tartlettes: Cut up some pork and boil it, mix it with saffron,
eggs, currants, spices such as cinnamon and mace, and some
salt. Roll out some pastry and dot spoonfuls of the mixture on
to it, making each one up into a little separate parcel. Boil the
tartlettes and then serve in a pork broth.

Petty Puant: Take a marrow, hollow it out and cut it into pieces. Add powdered ginger, egg yolks, minced dates, raisins and currants. Add the ingredients to a pastry case and cook until done.

Tostee: Mix wine and honey together and simmer, then add ginger, pepper and salt. Spread on toast with some sliced candied ginger.

Tarte de Bry: Mash some brie and eggs together, add some sugar, saffron and ginger and bake in pastry.

The addition of rue to wine (which is still done in parts of Europe) offers an interesting little insight into one of the more uncomfortable aspects of medieval life. One of the chores of the yeoman usher and grooms of the hall was to turn the dogs out every morning; the animals would stay out until after supper time. However, they then slept alongside people in the hall. Rue was popular as a strewing herb among the rushes to repel the fleas.

If the menu in the *Book of Nurture* seems grand, it was nothing compared with the great feasts that marked special occasions. The one held in 1466 to celebrate the inauguration of George Neville as Archbishop of York, for example, involved 2,000 guests, not to mention the various officers of the feast and servants, who had to be fed as well. The Nevilles were one of the most powerful families in the land. The head of the family, the Earl of Warwick and Salisbury, known as the King-maker, was also a Knight of the Garter, the Captain of Calais and the Constable of Dover Castle and owned huge estates all around the country. He had married his daughters into the Yorkist royal family and personally led his troops into battle on their behalf. Having obtained the honour of an archbishopric for his younger brother, he was out to impress. The ingredients for the inaugural banquet are mind-blowing in their variety and quantity: 1,000 sheep, 2,000 suckling pigs, 500 deer, 4,000 rabbits, 200 pheasants, 4,000 pigeons, 400 swans, 400 herons, 2,000 chickens, 1,000 capons and 2,000 geese. The fish course included 608 bream and pike and 12 porpoises and seals. Baked goods included 4,000 cold and 1,500 hot venison pasties. Then there were 1,000 jellies, 3,000 cold custard tarts and 2,000 hot, and further cold, tarts. The drink flowed, with 300 tuns of wine, 300 tuns of ale and 1 pipe of hippocras. Fifty-seven cooks and 115 kitchen staff worked on the feast.

In attendance was the fourteen-year-old Richard, Duke of Gloucester, the future Richard III, who was attached to the earl's household. I can't imagine any of the guests that day could have guessed that in less than twenty years the Battle of Bosworth would see the end of the Middle Ages, the death of Richard, and his niece Elizabeth married to the enemy to establish the credentials of the last Lancastrian claimant, Henry, Earl of Richmond, who became King Henry VII and the founder of the Tudor dynasty. At any rate, it was certainly some feast.

How on earth did they cook all this? The large medieval kitchen was a complicated affair. It might, as at Gainsborough Old Hall in Lincolnshire, have two fires, perhaps one to support the spits on which joints were roasted, the other for the more complicated dishes. There was a large cauldron constantly in use for simmering the salted meat before it was cut up for different dishes. This would probably have been tended by a very lowly kitchen apprentice whose role it was to change the water when necessary, retrieve the bags of peas and so on, and also retrieve the meat with a ladle or a pronged fork when cooked. A separate pastry area would have been laid out at the north wall – you need a cool environment for pastry. This would have been the domain of the patissierre, just as in a modern restaurant kitchen. In the middle there would have been a rostrum for the head cook's chair, with preparation tables all around that he could keep an eye on.

They would have largely used wood for fuel. Those of you who, like me, have a wood fire will know that different woods burn hotter than others, some spit and some give a long slow burn. Medieval cooks knew a lot about wood in all its various categories. Bowls for keeping meat or mixing were always made of sycamore: its close grain ensured it didn't harbour germs. Bowls of willow wood were ideal for keeping liquid marinades. Ash was ideal for a kitchen fire as well as for tool handles. The light-coloured woods of beech and lime were used for dairy work and butter tubs. Birch twigs could sometimes be laid in the bottom of cooking pots and the meat placed on top when making soups and stews to stop it from sticking. Oak was crucial for medieval buildings, but oak chips played their part in cooking: they were perfect for smoking. An old story claims that the chippings from the building of York Minster were so plentiful that they were the origin of the particularly delicate smoking of York hams.

On great estates the cooks would probably have specified to the steward what type of firewood they required, and the requests were then conveyed to the officer of the woodyard. On smaller properties or in towns, wood was purchased from a purveyor, a woodmonger. Regulations covered the size of firewood on sale: billets, for example, were usually coppiced poles or branches about three feet four inches long. Anything that was too small to qualify as a log was split into kindling sticks for the bread oven.

Villagers had rights to gather dead and fallen wood by hook or by crook, that is, with a billhook or a shepherd's crook, which had the advantage to the landowner of clearing away the debris. Landowners who owned woodland had a valuable asset, and large quantities of wood were sent to London by boat, especially from the Kentish and Sussex Wealds. Forests and woods were carefully managed, trees being coppiced so that once the tree had received its first cutting, it was encouraged to resprout from the base. By dint of careful pruning, long straight shoots would be sent up which could be harvested every six years or so (less in the case of birch) for carrying poles and handles for implements.

Wood was also burnt in low-oxygen conditions to make charcoal, critical in the production of weaponry and armour. I can remember as a child the charcoal burners who lived in the woods. The grubby, nomadic style of living in bothies by the kilns – earthen mounds that needed constant watching – seemed a romantic but undoubtedly uncomfortable existence. Charcoal (as you who barbecue will know) is an excellent cooking medium, but expensive. You can still see examples of stoves built for charcoal use. The one at Hampton Court, though it was constructed in Tudor times, is a very good specimen, with layers of brick-built hobs bringing the cooking platform nearer to or further from the heat.

In peat areas the villages had rights of turbary allowing them to cut peat for their own use, and this, though hard work, would have provided a constant source of fuel. In rural Ireland peat was cut and burnt regularly in my lifetime. The increased use of wood for carbon production, however, created something of an energy crisis in the late fourteenth century. Woodland was diminishing and couldn't be replaced fast enough. A search for substitutes led to the beginnings of coal mining. Initially, seacoal from the Northumbrian cliffs was burnt, easy to collect if the cliff had given way and the coal had fallen to the beach or sea below. I have burnt Northumbrian seacoal and because the sea has washed away the dust it is an excellent fuel, burning steadily with a clean flame and perfect for cooking. Cooking over such a fire makes everything taste like lapsang souchong tea. I remember reading one Robin Hood legend that claimed he was originally a coal miner from Wakefield. At the time, that must have seemed a rather exotic, new-fangled job.

PALATIVM REGIVM IN ANGLIÆ REGNO APPELLATVM NONCIVTZ,
Hoc est nusquam simile.

Nonsuch Palace, the epitome of Tudor extravagance, was begun by Henry VIII in 1538 and, until its demolition in the 1680s, was reckoned to be even grander than Hampton Court. This detail from a 1582 engraving (based on an earlier drawing) may show Elizabeth I visiting it on one of her royal progresses – excursions that provided the queen with an excuse both to keep an eye on the great and the good and to eat them out of house and home. She was not that keen on coach travel (a recent innovation), complaining once that she had been 'knocked about' when one was 'driven a little too fast'.

CHAPTER 3

Marzipan and New World Turkeys

The Tudor Kitchen

T he last years of the Middle Ages were dominated by the Wars of the Roses: the struggle between the Yorkists and Lancastrians that brought about a change of ruling dynasty and the devastation of England's leading families. I remember being taught that the marquesses left in England after the Battle of Bosworth in 1485 would have been able to sit on one horse – largely because there was only one left. It's an exaggeration, but it's certainly the case that many of the great names of the Middle Ages – the Beauforts, Cliffords, Herberts, Howards, Nevilles and Percys – were decimated in the decades of struggle that culminated in Bosworth.

And there were royal losers, too: the devout and cultured Henry VI, for example, who founded King's College, Cambridge and Eton College, and who spent much of his later life imprisoned in the Tower, where he died (he may have been smothered); and his son by Margaret of Anjou, Edward, who died at the

Battle of Tewkesbury. The winners were the Tudor dynasty, and it is the matriarchal head of that dynasty, Margaret Beaufort, mother of the new king Henry VII, who has an important if indirect place in the history of English food: among her many other claims to fame (she was, for example, the foundress of two Cambridge colleges) she was a champion of printing.

Not only was Margaret the patron of the founder of English printing, William Caxton, but she was also associated with Wynkyn de Worde, who worked with Caxton and then took over his printing press when he died in 1492. There is a certain irony here. Margaret was a deeply conventional Catholic and very conservative; printing, on the other hand, made possible the dissemination of Protestant tracts and so helped to promote the Reformation. Wynkyn's publications were generally rather less controversial, including poetry and romances and books on grammar and religion. But his most important work from our point of view is *The Boke of Keruynge* ('The Book of Carving'), printed in Fleet Street at the sign of the Sun in the year of our Lord 1508. This was among the first household books to be published and it gives us a very clear idea of what people in the early sixteenth century ate and also how they lived. It's particularly useful to us because, rather like the medieval guides I have already mentioned, it was almost certainly intended to educate the new rich, who did not know exactly how they should behave. This means that it includes a wealth of detail that we might not otherwise know about: those already used to a certain type of living don't need to be told about it; those who aspire to a certain type of living want to know everything.

The book is aimed at butlers and panters (who were in charge of the pantry) and contains useful but, you would have thought, often fairly basic information for the nouveau riche and their servants. The butler is told, for example, that he must have three pantry knives: one to square trencher loaves, another to be a 'chyppere' (presumably used on bread which is slightly stale) and a third sharp one to make smooth trenchers. 'Chyppe [cut] your souerayne's [lord's] brede hote, and all other brede let it be a daye olde' is another injunction, a further suggestion being that household bread for those who sit below the salt should actually be three days old, and trencher bread four days old. Trencher bread should not be cut on the slant, to ensure that food can be put on it.

The butler is also told to keep the salt white and dry; the planer, which is for serving the salt out of the salt cellar and made of ivory, should be two inches broad and three inches long; and the salt cellar lid (generally of silver or silver gilt) should not touch the salt (to avoid the danger of corrosion). Tablecloths, towels and napkins must be kept clean and folded in a chest or hung upon a pole.

Very precise rules govern the setting out of the table. First the table must be cleaned with a dishcloth. Then the tablecloth must be properly arranged so that it is straight and does not hang over one side more than the other. It's clear from the book that the tablecloths are to be laid in layers so that when one course is finished and the table cleared, one cloth can be removed to reveal a clean one underneath. Napkins (introduced, if you recall, by Richard II) must be laid separately for each diner – certainly for those diners above the salt. The bread that is laid for eating (as opposed to the trenchers) must be covered with napkins, as must the spoons (properly cleaned) and knives (properly polished), cups and dishes, and everything must be placed precisely, as must the salt. Again we're back to messes of four, with each person in the mess having a loaf of bread to themselves (these would have been manchet loaves, the size, I suppose, of large rolls). The server is told that he must convey all the soups, meats and sauces from the board, or side table, to the table, and every day liaise with the cook to find out which dishes are to be served and how best they are to be preserved and carved. The instructions finish with, 'then serue ye forth the table mannerly, that every man may speke your curtesy.' I suspect it's just as difficult today to train serving staff in all these traditions of service, cleanliness, politeness and efficiency as it was presumably for the inhabitants of Tudor England.

To my mind, one of the most charming passages in *The Boke of Keruynge* is the one that deals more generally with proper conduct on the part of servants – in this case the chamberlain of the house. The chamberlain is told that he must be clean and diligent in the execution of his duties, with his hair combed. He must assume responsibility for laying out his lord's clothes (a clean shirt, breeches, petty coat and doublet), brushing his lord's hose – or breeches – both within and without and ensuring that his lord's shoes and slippers are properly cleaned and polished. In the morning, when his lord is about to rise from his bed, the chamberlain must warm his shirt by the fire, set the lord's chair close to it, with a cushion for his back and one under his feet. He must warm the petty coat (a garment worn under a coat or doublet), the doublet and the stomacher (decorative cloth worn over the stomach and chest), and help his lord on with his hose, shoes and slippers, lace up his doublet, lay a cloth around his neck and comb his hair. He must have a basin, a ewer with warm water and a towel for his lord to wash his hands. Then, kneeling, he must ask his lord which robe he wishes to put on for the day, bring it to him, help him into it, do up the girdle and make sure that he goes to church or to chapel in a mannerly and well-ordered fashion.

Having seen to it that the lord has his prayer book and anything else he may need, including his 'carpets' (thick fabric, rather like a bedspread) and cushions for chapel, the chamberlain must then draw back the bed-curtains, pull back the bedclothes, beat the bolster and make sure that there are no crumbs or mess on the blankets and the sheets. If there are, he must put clean sheets on the bed and make it up. Then he must remove the towel and the basin and lay carpets and cushions around the bed and on the window seat, making sure that a good fire is burning brightly. The chamberlain must also check that the house of easement (that is, the lavatory) is sweet and clean and that the privy boards are covered with a green cloth and a cushion.

When the time comes for his lord to go to bed again, he must be provided with a ewer, a basin and a towel, his gown must be removed and a mantle given him to keep him from the cold. Having put him to bed and drawn the bed-curtains around him, the chamberlain's final duties of the day are to drive out any cats and dogs, make sure there is a basin and a urinal set by the lord's bed, 'than take your leaue mannerly that your souerayne may take his rest meryly'. There then follows a list of the social pecking order, from those of the blood royal down to knights with small livelihoods.

Along with instructions on how to run the household, *The Boke of Keruynge* contains fascinating insights into the food that would have been served, what the popular likes and dislikes were, and what to do if your lord overindulged. Butlers and panters are expected to have, as appropriate to the season, butter, cheese, apples (including small apples called pippin), pears, nuts, plums, grapes, dates, figs and raisins, green ginger and compote of quince, not to mention strawberries (those would be wild strawberries), purple-berries (which were a type of loganberry), and caraway seeds in confets, that is, made into little sweetmeats with sugar. Fruit is regarded as good when it is cooked, as are such foodstuffs as tansy (a fritter often flavoured with the herb tansy), root vegetables and gruel made with beef and mutton.

On the other hand, the panter is told to beware of green salads and raw fruits or, at least, not to serve them in any quantity that will make his lord sick; to avoid such meats 'as wyll set your tethe on edge' – in other words, meat that is not fresh; and if an antidote to all this is required, to serve almonds, hard cheese and Romney wine. There is a great warning to beware of milk, cream and junket, as they will 'close the mawe' (gullet) and make your lord sick; if this happens he must eat hard cheese as it will keep his stomach open and purge away all sorts of poisons. If your lord is suffering from an upset stomach due to over-fermented drink (which I rather suspect means consuming too much of it), he is advised to eat a raw apple: 'abstynence is to be praysed whan god therewith is pleased'.

A list of the correct names that apply to the carving of each ingredient makes one realise just how varied the diet was at this time; they are rather reminiscent of medieval venery – or hunting – terms, such as 'a murder of crows', 'a paddling of ducks', 'a sett of badgers' and 'a parliament of rooks' in their matching of a precise technical term to a particular animal. Among the many included are:

Breke that deer

Lesche that brawne

Rere that goose

Lyft that swanne

Sauce that apon

Spoyle that henne

Frusshe that chekyn

Unbrace that mallarde

Unlace that coney

Dysmembre that heron

Dysplaye that crane

Dysfygure that pecocke

Unjoint that bytture [bittern]

Untache that curlewe

Alaye that fesande [pheasant]

Wynge that partryche

Thye all maner of small byrdes

Tyere that egge

Chyne that salmon

Strynge that lampraye

Culpon that troute

Transsene that ele

Traunche that sturgyon

Undertraunch that purpos

Tayme that crabbe

Barbe that lopster

As these 'goodly terms' imply, serving was a complex art. The server had to remove any salt crust, any sinews, any fat or any raw meat from the red meats. He also had to remember to touch venison not with his hand but only with the knife, cutting it into twelve slices and then putting it on to the frumenty (coarse boiled wheat which was very much a staple of those days, and which formed a sort of thick porridge upon which the meat was laid). The same rules applied to bacon, beef and mutton, which, we are told, were better served with pease pudding. Remember that we're still not in the age of the potato, so the staples of the time would have been pease pottage, pease pudding, frumenty, boiled barley or various other pulses.

The server is told that in the case of 'fawne' – that is, young deer, kid and lamb – he is to lay the kidney in front of his lord and then lift up the shoulder and give his lord a rib. With rabbit, the server is told to lay it on its back, cut away the vents between the hind-legs, break the camel bone (presumably the chest bone), then cut away the fillets, lay the rabbit on its womb (presumably its front), chine the two sides and serve. Baked meats that have been cooked in a coffyn (pastry case) are to be removed from it and placed in front of the diner, pieces then being cut from the cold coffyns and served to the diners.

When it comes to game birds and poultry, the carver is advised to take them by the pinion and, with the forepart of the knife, lift up the wings and mince the meat into the syrup – by which I imagine he means sauce – and again to beware of raw skin and sinew. Some birds require very particular attention. In the case of goose, teal, mallard and swan, for example, the carver is to remove the legs, then the wings and lay the body in the middle or on another platter. The appendages are served around the breast. The legs are served with the feet still attached (whether this was to make them easy to lift to eat, or to show that the fowl was young, I'm not quite sure, although to this day, the Chinese, the French and indeed I myself find the feet of poultry very edible indeed).

Swan required particularly careful attention and was generally served with what was known as a 'chawdron'. This would have been a black sauce that involved soaking bread in some of the broth that the giblets had been cooked in, straining it with some of the blood of the swan, a little piece of the liver and some red wine to make it thin enough, then adding spices such as cinnamon, ginger, pepper, salt and sugar and boiling until the mixture was thick. Swans were not always served in their plumage: sometimes the neck would be boned out and stuffed with the offal of the swan, bread and various other goodies, rather like a sort of blood pudding, and then served on the side with the swan.

There are also instructions for serving small birds such as quail,

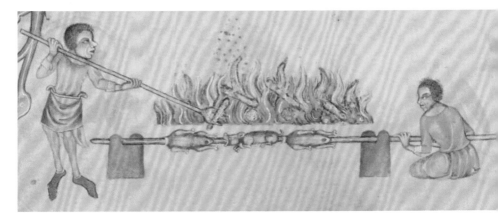

Roasting meat Meat was often boiled, but spit-roasting was popular, too. This illustration from the Luttrell Psalter shows two rather intimidating-looking cooks roasting pork.

A medieval kitchen Gainsborough Old Hall in Lincolnshire dates from the latter half of the fifteenth century. By this time, fireplaces with chimneys – as opposed to open fires – were commonplace in the houses and castles of the wealthy. The kitchens at Gainsborough include a pantry and buttery, with servants' quarters above.

Wine from abroad Although there were vineyards in medieval and Tudor England, an increasing quantity of wine was imported. The wine shown here being measured is being shipped from France.

Spices from afar A cinnamon merchant, as depicted in a fifteenth-century manuscript. Spices were a valuable commodity and feature constantly in medieval cookery. The origins of the more exotic of them, such as cinnamon, were the subject of endless speculation – one suggestion was that cinnamon came from the nest of the phoenix.

Hunting A fourteenth-century illumination of King John pursuing a stag, his hounds apparently oblivious to the rabbits that they are leaping over. Hunting was a royal obsession for many centuries and royal forests were protected by draconian laws.

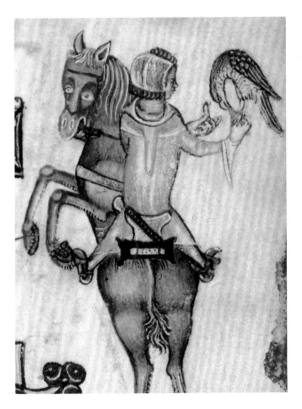

Hawking A mounted man with a hawk, as depicted in the early-fourteenth-century Luttrell Psalter. According to the Book of St Albans there were strict rules governing which bird of prey could be owned by what rank of person: an eagle for an emperor, a sparrowhawk for a priest, and a kestrel for a knave.

Milling A watermill with, upstream, fish nets and an eel trap, an illumination from the Luttrell Psalter. There were thousands of watermills in England by the time of the Domesday Book in the late eleventh century. Windmills came later: the first unambiguous reference to one is at Weedley in Yorkshire in 1185; rented at 8 shillings a year, it belonged to the Knights Templar.

Milking Until Georgian times no real distinction was made between dairy and meat cattle. Cows, such as the one in this fourteenth-century manuscript, would have been butchered and eaten once their milk production started to drop.

Ploughing An illumination from the fourteenth-century Luttrell Psalter. The type of plough shown here being pulled by oxen would have had a vertical coulter that cut in to the soil, a horizontal share that cut the ground at the bottom of the furrow, and a mouldboard that helped steer the plough and turn the soil over, creating a characteristic ridge and furrow. Horses were also used to pull ploughs once horseshoes became common after the ninth century.

Harvesting An eleventh-century illumination of farm workers with scythes. Note the whetstones for sharpening the blade's edge.

'The properties of bees are wonderful, noble and worthy' Bartholomew the Englishman's view reflects the high value placed on honey in medieval times as a food in its own right, as a sweetener and as an invaluable source of wax. This illustration of bees flying in and out of a beehive comes from an early-thirteenth-century bestiary, probably from Durham.

'By a big fire he sat, roasting a swine great and fat' The words are by the fourteenth-century writer Robert Mannyng; the illustration comes from the Queen Mary Psalter, which was produced in the same century and which once belonged to Mary Tudor, whose emblem of a pomegranate appears on the binding. It accompanies December in the section on the months of the year and depicts one man killing a pig with the back of an axe, and another cutting open a pig that has been suspended by the hind legs.

Baking bread Bread was a major feature of the medieval diet, and its production was carefully regulated. The thirteenth-century Assize of Bread sought to control quality and price, not always successfully.

Medieval tableware The items shown here all date from the late thirteenth and early fourteenth centuries. The tall jars at the back were made in London; the jug with the human face, the drinking vessel in the foreground and the condiment dish on the right come from Kingston-upon-Thames in Surrey; while the jug with striped decoration on the right was made near Chelmsford in Essex. The jug in the centre, with its painted shields, is from the Saintes region of France and probably came to London via the wine trade with Bordeaux.

Fine dining Sir Geoffrey Luttrell (1276–1345) dining with his wife Agnes and others, including, possibly, Sir Geoffrey's chaplain, Robert of Wilford (one of the Dominicans seated on the left). Knives and spoons are in evidence here, but not forks, which were not used in England until the early seventeenth century.

Rich living Medieval and Tudor dining could be a magnificent affair, and the Burghley Nef, made in France in the 1520s, shows just how magnificent. Nefs are table ornaments in the form of a ship. They were usually designed to hold such things as salt and napkins.

sparrow, lark, martins, pigeons, swallows and thrush. One is reminded of those rather sinister pâtés that one used to get in France made with small birds with the feet sticking out of the pâté to let you know which particular bird they were made of.

As in medieval times, there is a strong sense of what should be served with what. The carver is told that mustard should accompany pork, bacon, mutton or brawn (which seems to have been a commonplace dish in those days). Verjuice (liquid obtained from sour, unripe fruit) is good with chickens and capons. Ribs of beef should be accompanied by garlic, mustard, pepper, verjuice or ginger sauce. Ginger sauce is good with lamb, pork and fawn; mustard and sugar with pheasant, partridge and coney. A gamelyne sauce should accompany heron ('heronsewe'), egrit, plover and crane. Gamelyne, camelyne or camelyn (spelling wanders around rather a lot at this time) was a popular sweet and sour sauce, involving wine and vinegar flavoured with cinnamon, to which such things as walnuts and breadcrumbs might be added. Curlews should be served with salt, sugar and water, and the same for lapwing, lark, quail, martin, venison and snipe. Sparrows and thrushes should be served with salt and cinnamon.

Having talked about how to serve particular foods, the instructions then move on to deal with the various annual religious feasts in the year. England at this time was still a Catholic country and the Church controlled what was eaten when. Along with the forty days of Lent and various key festivals, the four weeks of Advent leading up to Christmas was an important period of fasting, and Fridays and Saturdays were fast days.

Such occasions were rigorously enforced and punishments in the form of fines, imprisonment and stocks doled out on a fairly regular basis. The tradition continued even after Henry VIII's break with Rome – and, indeed, after his death. In 1548, when Henry's Protestant son Edward VI had come to the throne, Archbishop Cranmer issued a proclamation ordering abstention from meat during Lent. He was careful not to suggest that this had anything to do with popish tradition:

> . . . for all days and all meats be of one and equal purity, cleanness and holiness, that we should in them, and by them, live to the glory of God and at all times, and for all meats, give thanks unto him, of the which none can defile us at any time, or make us unclean, being Christian men, to whom all things be holy and pure, so that they be not used in disobedience and vice.

Nevertheless:

> . . . his majesty hath allowed and approved the days and times before accustomed to be continued and still observed here in this church of England; both that men should on those days abstain and forbear their pleasures, and the meats wherein they have more delight, to the intent to subdue their bodies unto the soul and spirit; unto the which to exort and move men is the office of a good and godly head and ruler; and also for worldly and civil policy certain days in the year to spare flesh, and use fish, for the benefit of the commonwealth and profit of his majesty's realm; whereof many be fishers, and men using that trade of living unto the which this realm on every part environed with the seas, and so plentiful of fresh waters, doth easily minister occasion; to the great sustenance of this his highness's people: so that hereby both the nourishment of the land might be increased by saving flesh, and specially at the spring time, when Lent doth commonly fall,

and when the most common and plenteous breeding of flesh is; and also, divers of his loving subjects have good livings, and get great riches thereby, in uttering and selling such meats as the sea and fresh water doth minister unto us; and this his majesty's realm hath more plenty of ships, boats, crays, and other vessels, by reason of those which by hope of lucre do follow that trade of living.

Note the blend of the religious and the practical there.

There were exceptions to the rules. Sick and pregnant women were excused from fasting, as were soldiers in any garrison whose commander had authorised them to eat meat or any person who obtained a licence from the king to do so. You could also obtain a dispensation from your bishop – if you paid for it. Erasmus, the noted scholar, obtained a dispensation from fasting on the grounds that he couldn't face it. However, if you broke the law you could be fined or imprisoned, during which time you would not be given any meat to eat, not to mention that you would also incur the king's indignation. For the second and any subsequent offences the penalty was increased. Cranmer's proclamation applied only to the eating of meat, and not to 'white meats' such as butter, cheese and eggs. It is clear, though, that fines and imprisonment had less impact than the hellfire previously threatened by the Catholic Church. Right through the Tudor era, in fact, long after the Act of Supremacy which had made Henry VIII head of the Church of England, laws were passed, imposing fines and imprisonment for breaches of the rules. There are even records of spies being sent out to check whether butchers had been selling meat to people who did not have a dispensation to eat it during the Lent and Advent periods.

Fast days made feast days welcome, and the first great feast of the year came on Easter Day. On this occasion *The Boke of Keruynge* stipulates the serving of a calf, 'soden' (presumably boiled or poached) and blessed, and also boiled eggs with green (herb) sauce. These would be set on the high table, the lord distributing them to those around him. A root vegetable soup would follow, and then various main dishes, including capons coloured with saffron, pigeon served in a pie and other meat served as tarts, 'chewettes' (small pies containing chopped livers, hard-boiled eggs and ginger) and 'flawnes' (flans). At supper time on Easter Day, mutton and veal in broth, chicken with bacon, veal, roast pigeons, lamb, and roasted kids', lambs' and pigs' feet sauced with vinegar and parsley would be served.

The next two great feasts after Easter discussed in *The Boke of Keruynge* are Pentecost and the feast of St John the Baptist at midsummer. Meat again was served, along with various game birds, including swan, which seems to have been something of a feature of the feast of St John the Baptist. Lighter dishes are also recommended, such as little 'pestelles', which I should imagine were minced patties of pork, served with a 'green' (in other words, herb) sauce.

Once we move from Michaelmas to 'Chrystynmasse' all sorts of game make an appearance – not just swans but also pheasants, herons, teals, widgeons, mallards, partridges, woodcocks, plovers, bitterns and curlews – not to mention deer and rabbits, and the roosters that seem to have been such a part of Michaelmas tradition. Some very specific instructions follow. Any birds that live on the water and eat fish, for example, have to be carefully cleaned with fresh water so that there is no smell of fish or 'corruption' on them. As for such field and wood birds as pheasants, peacocks, partridge, woodcock and curlew, they must have their heads removed, 'for they ete in theyre degrees foule thynges as wormes, todes and other suche'.

Given the importance of fish on days of abstinence, it is not surprising to find a mass of instructions dealing with them, including a guide to what sort of meal should be served on these days. Inevitably it is very fishy indeed. The first course consists of mussels, minnows in some sort of stew, porpoise, salmon, pike, gurnard, baked lampreys, and herring served with sugar. The second course is white jelly (some form of blancmange, presumably) and red dates in 'confetes' (little sweets) served with conger eel, salmon, turbot, halibut, trout, seal, mullet, eels, lampreys and roast tench in jelly. The third course is sturgeon, bream and perch, served together in a jelly of some sort. Then there is salmon and whelks served with apples and pears roasted with sugar candy, and figs, raisins and dates with minced ginger, wafers and hippocras. It's a rather one-themed meal.

The way in which fish should be served is complicated and involved. Salt porpoise or seal has to be cut in the same way as venison. Baked herring, on the other hand, has to be laid whole before the lord on a trencher, while white herring (presumably salted or pickled herring) has to have its bones removed before being served with mustard. The skin and bones of eels and lampreys are removed and the fish are then served with vinegar and powdered sugar. When it comes to crab:

> . . . breke hym a-sonder in to a dysshe, make the shelle clene, & put in the stuffe agayne, tempre it with vynegre & pouder, than couer it with brede, and sende it to the kytchyn to hete than set it to your souerayne, and breke the great clawes, and laye them in a disshe.

And so on and on with everything from gurnard and bream to sole, trout and shrimps. Preparing such dishes at the table quickly must have been an extraordinarily difficult feat.

It's not just that the serving instructions are complicated; so, too, are some of the recipes. One for lampreys, for example, proposes that they should be baked in a pie, and that when the pie is opened, the filling, which is described as the galantine (at this time, galantine meant the jellied juices of fish), should be served on thinly sliced white bread and then dressed with red wine and powdered cinnamon, while the lamprey meat should be cut from the bone, minced and then served with the galantine with more salt and wine. The taste for sweet and sour we saw in medieval times remains in evidence in many recipes here. Typical is one for salmon and seal which suggests that they should be prepared in white jelly with a cream of almonds, dates in confit (encased in sugar) and quinces in syrup. (Incidentally, it's worth bearing in mind just how important the fishing industry was to English fortunes at this time. Not only did it supply the country with food, but it also provided sailors for the navy that Henry VIII was busily building. These sailors also manned the ships that helped to open up the world through exploration in the course of the sixteenth century.)

Fortunately for Tudor drinkers, the laws that required periodic abstention from meat did not extend to drink. After all, the marriage feast at Cana had demonstrated that our Lord approved of drinking. Wine, a feature of fine dining since the time of Eleanor of Aquitaine, therefore remains very much in evidence in *The Boke of Keruynge*. But what is striking at that time is that it comes from all over the place, not just from France. Alongside inevitable references to clarets from Bordeaux and other French wines are ones to 'Rhenish' (from the Rhine area of Germany), 'Bastarde' (a red wine from Tuscany which utilised a grape now much used in California and Australia), 'Capryke' (from southern Italy) and wines from the Levant. Some have particular historical resonances for us. References to Portuguese wine, for example, remind us that England had had close ties with Portugal since the fourteenth century when John of Gaunt married his daughter into the Portuguese royal family. Malmsey, a sweet white wine from the Canaries, brings to mind the drowning of Richard III's brother George, Duke of Clarence, in a butt of malmsey wine in 1478: a suitable death for an alcoholic, perhaps. In 1577 the writer William Harrison calculated that some eighty types of wine were available in England.

Wine could be served in various ways. Vernage, a sweet wine from Crete, could be served hot 'against the cold winter'. Hippocras, which we have come across before, is still spiced with ginger, pepper, and grains of Paradise, cinnamon and sugar, but is now also heated and then strained through five or six bags, or bladders, to refine it. Finally, as *The Boke of Keruynge* stipulates, 'than put your ypocras in to a close vessell, and keep the dregs for cooking. Kepe the receyte for it wyll serue for sewes, than serue your souerayne with wafers and ypocras.' Hippocras prepared in this way would probably have been served once the great and the good had withdrawn to a more private room where they could listen to music or poetry and consume their dessert course – glacé fruits, wafers and such sweetmeats as dates. This continued a tendency, which we've noticed in later medieval times, for greater privacy for those who usually sat above the salt in hall, except on special occasions.

Wine remained relatively expensive during the Tudor period. In 1532 an Act was passed fixing the maximum price at which Gascon and Guienne or any other French wine could be sold at eighteen pence a gallon. The price for malmsey, sack and other sweet wines was to be held at twelve pence a gallon. Ale, on the other hand, was a lot cheaper and, not surprisingly, retained the popularity it had had in medieval times. Andrew Boorde strongly approved of it: 'Ale for an Englysshe man,' he said, 'is a naturall drinke.' He was rather less enthusiastic about beer, still a relatively new beverage at this period and associated very much with Holland:

Bere is made of malte, of hoppes, and water; it is the naturall drynke for a Dutche man, and nowe of late dayes it is moche used in Englande to the detryment of many Englysshe people; specyally it kylleth them the which be troubled with the colycke [colic], and the stone [kidney- or gallstone], and the strangulion [inflammation of the throat] for the drynke is a colde drynke; yet it doth make a man fat, and doth inflate the bely, as it doth appere by the Dutche men's faces and belyes.

Beer, however, made its way into English affections, though at this time mostly in the south. The price of both ale and beer was regulated.

Englishmen liked their ale – or beer – and most were ashamed to drink anything else. Sometimes this had disastrous consequences. When, for example, the English troops sent by Henry VIII to Fuenterrabía in northern Spain to assist Henry's father-in-law, King Ferdinand, ran out of beer and had to switch to wine they all fell apart and eventually mutinied. The Marquess of Dorset was forced to bring them home to face a furious

Henry. The marquess then had to grovel to the Spanish ambassador in Henry's presence; by this time he was so weak that his knees gave out and he had to be allowed to stand.

The mutiny remained in the memory of the military hierarchy and when thirty years later in 1542 a campaign against Scotland was being planned, it was considered of major importance that the army should not run short of beer. Orders were issued to sheriffs and gentlemen in the north of England to be at Newcastle with their tenants, ready to march for Scotland on 2 October. But the ships coming from London with the beer did not arrive and the march was put off to 7 October. When the beer still had not arrived, the march was put off again to 11 October. When it did finally arrive there was rather too little of it. The Duke of Norfolk, who was in command of the invasion, wrote to Henry VIII explaining that there would only be enough beer for a six-day campaign in Scotland, even if he rationed the men to two pots of beer a day, which he feared might cause trouble in any event. Norfolk had no alternative but to march with his men to Berwick and lead them across the border on 12 October, but either the quartermasters were mistaken in their arithmetic or the soldiers drank more than their allotted ration, for Norfolk soon realised that the beer would run out after only four days. There was virtually no resistance from the Scots, but the shortage of beer forced Norfolk to retreat back into England.

The Scots, not realising the reason for the retreat, were so emboldened that they invaded England and were led straight into the bog at Solway Moss where they suffered one of the largest defeats in British history, with only a handful of them managing to get back across the border. When the English went on to invade Scotland a couple of years later, they organised the beer supply rather more effectively. With plenty of provisions at Leith, they went on to attack Edinburgh and spent several days burning the city and the palace at Holyrood.

Even the nobility drank more ale than wine: on ordinary days at court, dukes and duchesses were provided with one gallon of ale at breakfast, dinner and supper every day. The early Tudors did, however, help to popularise one particular wine as an indirect consequence of their dynastic ambitions. Henry VII made good matches for his children, marrying one daughter into Scotland to keep the old enemy across the border at bay, and his other daughter to the king of France. More significantly, he married his oldest son, Prince Arthur, to Catherine, the daughter of Ferdinand and Isabella, the Spanish rulers who had expelled the heretic Moors from Spain and had sent Columbus off to discover the New World. When Arthur died in 1502, Henry VII did not return Catherine of Aragon to her parents but immediately entered into negotiations to marry her off to his second son, Prince Henry, then lost enthusiasm for the idea and left the poor woman in limbo at Durham House with a very stingy allowance. Eventually, though, the marriage was arranged. Catherine was six years older than Henry, but for most of the twenty-four years during which they were married, they were happy: the young couple were good-looking and enjoyed music and dancing. Had Catherine been able to bear Henry one or more sons, it is probable that theirs would have been a fairy-tale story.

In these early days the influence of Spain was very noticeable indeed, and one consequence of this was that sack became the new and fashionable drink. Sack is sherry, which was exported from Jerez in Spain. It began an English love affair with sherry that continues to this day.

The Spanish influence didn't just stop there when it came to food and drink. Catherine had been rather short of money during her widowhood. Anxious to remedy this, Henry went out of his way to please her. He brought her oranges and he also planted salad gardens for her: the Spanish were among the few in Europe actually to like salads and raw vegetables. He also helped to popularise the sweet potato, which, thanks to the Spanish exploration that had led to the opening up of the New World, had arrived in Europe a few years before and had started to be grown fairly extensively in the south of Spain. Henry was very fond of cubed sweet potato that had been candied in sugar and so turned into sweetmeats.

The whole of this early Tudor period, in fact, sees a gradual opening up of trade routes and the introduction of new foods. English and foreign merchants would attend the great national and international fairs in London and in Cambridgeshire and would come by sea from Holland, Scandinavia, North Germany and other such parts.

Some indication of how relatively quickly journeys could be made is given by records of a rapid and dramatic mission undertaken in 1511 by Cardinal Wolsey, at this time a rising junior official in Henry VIII's service. The king was at his palace in Richmond on the outskirts of London and ordered Wolsey to go to the court of the Holy Roman Emperor Maximilian, at that time staying at Gravelines in Flanders. Henry impressed on Wolsey the urgency of the mission, so Wolsey left Richmond at noon, rode to London, took a barge to Gravesend, arrived at Gravesend after a three-hour journey, rode through the night to Dover and, as the wind was good, crossed to Calais in three or four hours before riding to Gravelines, reaching the emperor's court on the evening of the second day. The next morning he had his audience and left by noon with Maximilian's reply to Henry. He was in Calais by nightfall, crossed the Channel and on the morning of the fourth day was in Dover by 10 a.m. and at the court of Richmond by that night. When the king saw Wolsey the next morning, ninety-six hours after he'd ordered him to go, he reprimanded him for not having left already and was favourably impressed when Wolsey explained that he'd already been and returned.

Perhaps the most dramatic food arrival on the scene in the early Tudor period was the turkey, a native of Central America. It came to Europe presumably via Spain, and by the reign of Henry VIII was to be found on English tables. A Yorkshire man, William Strickland, who reared turkeys, actually had a white turkey and a black wattle as his coat of arms. The Tudors would have roasted their turkeys on a spit over an open fire. It sounds wonderful, but I was once given a turkey that had been running around on a hill all summer and believe me, you wouldn't have wanted to roast it – it would have been as tough as old boots. Henry VIII may well have been the first monarch to have eaten turkey during his Christmas revels, but he wouldn't have eaten it roasted as we think of it; it's more likely that he would have had it poached in wine, say, or served in a pie. The English name of the bird, incidentally, shows how confused people were about where it came from. The French weren't much better: they called it *le coque d'Inde* (later shortened to *dinde* or *dindon*), or the cock of the Indies, presumably because the birds came into Marseilles, just as the spices of the East did.

We know that turkeys were quite commonplace in England by 1542 because Archbishop Cranmer, in his efforts to restrain the gluttony of the clergy, issued an order in the Convocation of Canterbury that included 'turkeycock' in his list of what could or couldn't be eaten on particular days. I have to say that the prohibitions don't sound particularly onerous. Archbishops, it was stated, were to be served no more than six different dishes of meat or fish, with four different dishes as a second course; bishops five dishes of meat or fish and three as a second course; archdeacons and deans four of meat or fish, and two as a second course; and the lower clergy with three of meat or fish, and two as a second course – that is to say, only two out of, for example, custard tarts, fritters, cheese, apples or pears. Archbishops were only allowed three partridges in one dish and all lower ranks of the clergy, including bishops, only two partridges. Archbishops were allowed to eat six blackbirds in one dish, bishops four and the clergy below the rank of bishop three. 'It was also provided,' the order goes on, 'that whatsoever is spared by the cutting of the old superfluity, should yet be provided and spent in plain meats for the relieving of the poor.'

The order was apparently scrapped after two or three months when, 'by the disusing of certain wilful persons, it came to the old excess'. In any event it would have been virtually impossible to enforce, so it is not surprising that it was withdrawn after only a few months. The inclusion of turkey in these lists of dishes, though, is significant and other evidence also suggests how widespread turkeys swiftly became in England at this time. Their popularity may well have contributed to a gradual loss of interest in swans as a food. Up until now swans had not only been gathered from the wild but also farmed – at Chesil Beach in Dorset, for example, the Benedictines kept a swannery of about 1,500 swans. This, along with other monastic swanneries, would have disappeared when the monasteries were suppressed in the

1530s, but it's interesting that new ones didn't spring up to take their place. Tastes were clearly changing. Sir William Petre of Ingatestone in Essex, a keen aficionado of poultry rearing, is recorded as having turkeys running around in his fowl yard, along with the more commonplace birds such as chickens and geese. Guineafowl from Africa are also recorded at this period.

At a time when trade routes abroad were opening up, some improvements were being made to the transport system of England. They certainly needed to be. It was over a thousand years since the Romans had gone, and nobody had really built any roads since. Subsequent civil strife had not helped their upkeep. In fact, it's difficult to believe how few roads there were in medieval times. Only three long-distance roads were kept in any sort of state of repair: the Great North Road, which ran from London to Berwick and across the border into Scotland; Watling Street, which ran from Dover via London to Chester and Wroxeter, and was used by travellers going to Ireland; and the Great West Road from London to Bristol and beyond.

Only a handful of main roads existed in England north of York. One ran into Scotland from Newcastle by Otterburn and across the Cheviots via Kelso; this was the shortest way to Edinburgh but very dangerous for travellers because border bandits would rob and kill anybody who travelled along it, given half a chance. Two roads went from east to west, one from York via Catterick Bridge to Penrith, and one running from Newcastle to Carlisle via Hexham and Haltwhistle along the Tyne. The other road out of York went to the port of Scarborough, from which the Scandinavian trade was carried on.

This was an important trade in the north of England and led in Tudor times to the Muscovy Company and trade with Russia.

Henry VII did much to improve the roads, but most people moved very little distance from home. Such roads as existed tended to be those between towns, enabling people to take their produce to market, although, as the poem says, 'It was the English drunkard built the rolling English road': the old roads between towns wound all over the place, probably following original cattle tracks. Where there were no towns, there were no highways, only tracks leading to the farms and villages. Virtually all the people travelling on the roads were going to or returning from the market, mostly on foot. As the old rhyme puts it:

> What is the way to London town?
> One foot up and the other foot down,
> That is the way to London town.

Some would be driving stock animals from the countryside to the town to be killed there. Some might be rich enough to afford a horse. If you didn't own one you could hire one, but the expense was well beyond the pockets of most. And, of course, there were carts to carry the various commodities, such as fruit and vegetables, butter and cheese, though, with few ways of preserving food for any length of time, these would have been taken the shortest possible distance to the nearest town.

The majority of the population, then, rarely left their parishes. It is difficult to believe today, with international travel being so much a part of everyday life, that even in my own lifetime there were many people who never left the place where they were born, married locally and were buried in their local churchyard. In medieval and early Tudor times, the only people to make long-distance journeys were couriers on royal business, students going to and from the universities of Oxford and Cambridge, and pilgrims going to the great shrines around the country: Our Lady of Walsingham in Norfolk, Thomas à Becket in Canterbury, and so on.

The diet of the working man consequently remained much as it had been in medieval times. There are signs, though, of an improvement in the overall standards of living. Houses were starting to be better constructed – even stone was being used more widely as a building material. That said, most would have been constructed of lath and plaster smeared with dung on the outside to keep flies away. They might also have had a lime-ash floor. I've seen such a floor in a cottage on an estate where I once worked. Nobody knew what it was made of until part of it was taken up and analysed, but it was smooth and easy to clean and looked rather like one of those composite floors that now cost a lot of money. It, however, had lasted for 500 years or so.

Some sense of the disparity between the diet of the rich and the poor is given by a Venetian nobleman who visited England at the turn of the sixteenth century. Having stated that the English have a tendency to get a bit above themselves ('they think that there are no other men than themselves, and no other world but England'), he goes on to say:

> Besides which the English being great epicures, and very avaricious by nature, indulge in the most delicate fare themselves and give their household the coarsest bread, and beer, and cold meat baked on Sunday for the week, which, however, they allow them in great abundance.

The diet of ordinary country people was, in fact, predominantly black bread, milk, cheese, eggs and occasionally bacon or fowl. They hadn't suffered too badly during the Wars of the Roses – in fact, it was a period when wages for most were relatively high. By the middle of Henry VIII's reign, the white meats – that is, dairy products – were considered common fare and people from all classes would eat meat whenever they could get it.

One other addition to the diet was the rook. The rook population must have increased over the centuries, for in 1533 an Act was passed commanding every parish to keep nets to catch them. The preamble stated:

> For as much as innumerable numbers of rooks, crows, and choughs do daily breed and increase throughout this Realm . . . and do yearly devour and consume a wonderful and marvellous quantity of corn and grain of all kinds . . . so that if the said crows, rooks and choughs should be suffered to breed and continue they will undoubtedly be the cause of great destruction and consumption of grain . . .

Anyone was entitled to enter another person's land without the landowner's permission in order to destroy rooks, and if permission had been asked and refused they could still proceed without being liable for damage and trespass. At a certain time of year the young rooks, having fledged, come to the edge of the nest, preparing to fly, and it is still commonplace to harvest them then, knocking them down from the trees either with sticks, slingshots or even with a shotgun in order to reduce their number. I have eaten rook meat. The trick apparently is to remove the backbone, which makes the meat bitter, and just to eat the breast. It is not unpalatable and is a surprisingly pale meat.

As in medieval times, poaching remained a potential though risky source of additional meat. Interestingly, among the game laws enacted at this period a clear distinction was made between poaching by day and poaching by night. Poaching by day was punishable with fines, and poaching by night was punishable with mutilation or death.

In towns, food was regularly brought in from the countryside and sold at market. This could cause problems when the food in question was meat. Livestock was slaughtered on site by butchers, and this could be a messy business. In London during Henry VII's reign the people who lived in the parish of St Faith's and St Gregory's near St Paul's Cathedral objected to the slaughtering of animals and the scalding of swine that was carried out in the butchery of St Nicholas. The canons of St Paul's also repeatedly complained about this. Eventually the king was petitioned about the 'corrupt airs engendered in the said parishes, by occasion of blood, and other fouler things' that flowed through the streets from the slaughterhouse. In fact, the stench was so bad that even he noticed it on state occasions at St Paul's and in 1489, four years after he had come to the throne, Parliament passed an Act prohibiting the slaughter of animals within the walls of the City of London and also within the confines of any walled town in England, except for Berwick and Carlisle. This was a ban that remained in force for forty-three years, finally being repealed when steps were taken by butchers to provide, in the case of London, underground sewers to remove the blood and filth.

Henry VII died in 1509. He could go to his maker well

pleased with his reign, knowing that he was leaving behind him a country at peace. It was also prosperous. I remember learning at school about Henry's skill at raising funds and, in particular, about Morton's fork, which was a double-pronged attack on people with money. If they were ostentatious in their entertainment of the monarch, Cardinal Morton would take them aside and say, 'Obviously you've got a surplus of money, so we'd be very grateful to receive some' – and woe betide the noble who didn't pay up. If they were economic in their entertainment, they were deemed to be saving their money and therefore had a nest egg they could afford to part with.

Henry's son Henry VIII, who succeeded him at the tender age of eighteen, thus found himself with a lot of money. At this time he was not the gross, corpulent tyrant of popular imagination, but handsome, athletic, musical (he is popularly supposed to have written the song 'Greensleeves'), and a devout Roman Catholic who was awarded the title 'Defender of the Faith' by the Pope for his defence of the Catholic Church against the up-and-coming Protestant religion, a title the sovereign still bears to this day. And Henry VIII was also uxorious – not something one would think of a man who is now remembered for the fact that he had six wives more than almost anything else.

Henry's court at this time was a young court. All those men who, thanks to Hollywood, we think of as old and fat and debauched were young and fit and energetic and full of life. Henry VIII, apart from being a superb athlete, was a great huntsman and thought nothing of getting up at four in the morning and going out to hunt deer, following points – that is, the spots to which a straight run was made – of thirty miles at a time. Presumably horses were changed in between, but this is in anybody's estimation a lot of exercise and a lot of riding – and Henry would have come home to look through his papers and then dine and dance into the night.

Henry VIII was always keen on the table, but let me give you this as an example of the youth and energy of the court. In July 1517 a great banquet was held at Greenwich on the feast of St Thomas of Canterbury. Foreign dignitaries were there, along with Henry himself, Wolsey, Queen Catherine and Henry's sister Mary, who was by now married to Charles Brandon, Duke of Suffolk. The guests were served with ten courses and sat at table for seven hours, for the banquet did not end until two o'clock in the morning. Henry's musicians played throughout the meal. A Venetian guest was more than a little impressed, writing later to the Marchioness of Mantua:

There was a buffet set out, 30 feet in length, and 20 feet high, with silver gilt vases, and vases of gold, worth vast treasure, none of which were touched. All the small platters used for the table-service, namely 'seyphi', dishes, basins, plates, salt cellars and goblets were all of pure gold . . . The removal and replacing of dishes the whole time was incessant, the hall in every direction being full of fresh viands on their way to table. Every imaginable sort of meat known in the kingdom was served, and fish in like manner, even down to prawn pasties, but the jellies, of some twenty sorts perhaps, surpassed everything; they were made in the shape of castles and animals of various descriptions, as beautiful and as admirable as can be imagined.

In short, the wealth and civilization of the world are here; and those who call the English barbarians appear to me to render themselves such.

It is not so much the ten courses that impress me, but the fact that they sat so long at table, presumably with dancing as well as music, well into the small hours of the morning, when they had probably started their day at seven o'clock the previous morning and, in Henry's case, possibly even earlier. (Henry was a deeply religious man: he attended Mass several times in a busy day and religiously kept the fast days as well as the holy days of the Church.)

A fine example of the sort of extravagant display one could find at Henry's court is the use of marchpane (which may date back to medieval times, but which I associate much more with Henry VIII's time). Marchpane could come in amazing forms. On one occasion, for example, it was modelled into a stag with an arrow sticking out of its side. This was offered to the first lady at the high table, who pulled out the arrow. Red wine, supposed to emulate the heart's blood, then flowed from the wound and was caught up by the server and taken to the top table. This would most probably have been spiced wine or sweet wine of some sort.

Another dazzling exhibit was the four and twenty blackbirds baked in a pie of the nursery rhyme. It was a false pie case which had been baked blind. When it was cool, the base was removed and the blackbirds were inserted into the pie just before serving, with another base installed to keep them in. The pie was then brought into the hall and cut open. Out flew the blackbirds singing merrily and presumably making the most horrible mess. Similar pies were also made with frogs and suchlike in them. They would get out and crawl all over the table, causing the ladies to scream. Everybody would be much amused.

There are also records of sailing ships made out of sugar and marchpane. These would be brought in and all the cannons on the boats would then fire. As I say, marchpane might be medieval in origin, but I can't find any mention of it in *The Forme of Cury* while it does appear in Tudor works as late as 1584. The best recipe I have found is in a book called *A Booke of Cookrye, Very Necessary for all Such as Delight Therein*, gathered by someone called A. W. and printed as an enlarged volume by John Allde in 1584. This obviously refers to an earlier edition, which may have been around in Henry VIII's time.

Making marchpane, let alone turning it into some sort of sculptured edifice, is a very complicated process. Here, for example, is a recipe for it from *A Booke of Cookrye*:

First take a pound of long small almonds and blanch them in cold water, and dry them as drye as you can, then grinde them small, and put no licour to them but as you must needs to keepe them from oyling, and that licour that you put in must be rosewater, in manner as you shall think good, but wet your Pestel therin, when ye have beaten them fine, take halfe a pound of Sugar and more, and see that it be beaten small in pouder, it must be fine sugar, then put it to your Almonds and beate them altogither, when they be beaten, take your wafers and cut them compasse round, and of the bignes you will have your Marchpaine, and then as soone as you can after the tempering of your stuffe, let it be put in your paste, and strike it abroad with a flat stick as even as you can, and pinch the very stuffe as it were an edge set upon, and then put a paper under it, and set it upon a faire boord, and lay lattin Basin over it the bottome upwarde, and then lay burning coles upon the bottom of the basin. To see how it baketh, if it happen to bren too fast in some place, folde papers as broad as the place is & lay it upon that place, and thus with attending ye shal bake it a little more then a quarter of an houre, and when it is wel baked, put on your gold and biskets, and stick in Comfits, and so you shall make a good Marchpaine. Or ever that you bake it you must cast on it fine Sugar and Rosewater that will make it look like Ice.

You will by now have realised what marchpane is: it is marzipan, and marzipan can be worked very dextrously into all sorts of shapes and sizes, although I think that the making of a very large piece must have been a work of art. If you look at the illustrated books from Candis-Verlag in Switzerland you will find that they are still making marzipan and sugar figures, although perhaps not quite as large as the ones made for the Tudor dining hall.

Henry was not the only man to enjoy an extravagant life-style. His reign saw the rise of careerists – new men often from fairly humble backgrounds who achieved power and prosperity – and they were equally keen to show off and to indulge in the pleasures of the table. And of the various ambitious people who fell into this category, none rose faster or went further than Cardinal Thomas Wolsey. Born in 1471 to a butcher and grazier who fought for Henry VII at the Battle of Bosworth, and educated at Ipswich School and Magdalen College School before studying theology at Magdalen College, Oxford, Wolsey rose swiftly in his chosen profession and came into the employ-ment of Henry VIII. His energy and ability made him the perfect candidate to succeed Bishop Wareham as Lord Chan-cellor in 1515, and he became Henry's right-hand man. In fact, he was probably more powerful than any other single individual in English history who was not actually the monarch.

New men needed grand houses to live in. But the restoring

of castles or the building anew of castles was not favoured by the Tudors, as it was regarded as a threat. Wolsey therefore – who clearly saw himself as a major European figure, possibly even a future pope – set out to build himself a grand house. There's no doubt that he succeeded. At a cost of 200,000 gold crowns, he created Hampton Court Palace, at that time the finest palace in England.

The original property that he acquired had been a manor house belonging to the Order of St John of Jerusalem. The new palace took Wolsey seven years to build. The base court contained lodgings for forty honoured guests, each en suite with a garderobe, and an outer and inner room. The second court contained the very best rooms: Wolsey's own private chambers and a suite each for Henry VIII, Catherine of Aragon and their daughter Mary. It has been suggested that Wolsey was inspired by Paolo Cortese's *Manual for Cardinals*, which included advice on palatial architecture and had been published in 1510.

With a palace of such grandeur, the kitchens had to be built to match. As later transformed by Henry VIII, they occupied fifty-five rooms, covering an area of 3,000 square feet, staffed by 200 people, providing meals for 600 to 800 people twice a day. Sited on the north side of the palace – the coolest side – they were reached through three separate gatehouses grouped around three separate court houses. The gatehouse was occupied by the cofferer (the kitchen accountant) and his assistants, and the clerks of the green cloth, who monitored the arrival of supplies and staff for the kitchens. Then there was the spice room, which was situated on the Western Court and filled with spices imported from Europe and the Orient as well as English mustard and herbs grown in the palace's substantial herb garden. This office was also responsible for the huge quantities of fruit grown in the palace gardens, including apples and pears from the two orchards.

Next to the spice room was the chandlery, where wax for candles and tapers were kept, and a coal house, where the charcoal was stored. Charcoal was then being used more and more in cookery.

At the eastern end of the courtroom was the great kitchen, with six great fireplaces (one with the spit racks, the other five with similar cooking apparatus). At the end of the great kitchen were hatches from which the serving men could collect the completed dishes and take them into the hall. For the first time there was a confectionary, where delicate sweet dishes were prepared for the more important members of the court. It was here that the only woman known to have been employed in a kitchen complex at this time made the puddings. I can't help wondering if this helps to explain why the English have always been rather better at puddings and desserts than their Continental cousins.

Other rooms associated with the kitchen were a pastry house where sweet and savoury pies and pasties were prepared in four ovens (the largest measuring twelve foot six inches across), a boiling house for making meat stock and boiling meats, with a great boiling copper on the east wall of the building with a capacity of about seventy-five imperial gallons (341 litres), and three larders. Meat was hung in the flesh larder; sea-fish from the coast and freshwater fish from the palace ponds were stored in the wet larder for consumption on Fridays and during Lent; and pulses and nuts and suchlike were kept in the dry larder.

The living larder was also crucial to life at Hampton Court: as in medieval times you would have found pigeon houses, rabbit warrens, stew ponds (for fish) and a deer park. One interesting fact that I've come across in this period of history is that where deer parks were used mostly as living larders rather than for hunting, there is reference to 'gelt deer' – that is, gelded deer. If you think about it, it makes total sense: you castrate cattle and sheep to enhance meat growth, so why not castrate deer? Anyone who has ever eaten meat or, particularly, offal from a rutting stag will know that it is pretty horrible: testosterone levels during the autumn rut cause the stags to fight and so toughen the meat and impair the flavour. The Tudors logically regarded the deer in the deer parks as merely another source of food to be farmed, and it would have been quite easy to catch a fawn when it came in for extra feeding, put it in a crush and castrate it and then let it run loose again with the rest of the herd. I don't know why the practice didn't continue. When I asked John Fletcher, the well-known deer vet and deer farmer, he said that he had never heard of it.

Once slaughtered, the venison culled from the royal parks was hung in the flesh larder for as long as six weeks before consumption. Meat was also supplied from the palace's pheasant yard. The quantities of meat cooked annually in the royal kitchen are truly eye-opening. In Elizabeth's reign, for example, we know that the kitchens got through 1,240 oxen, 8,200 sheep, 2,330 deer, 760 calves, 1,870 pigs and 53 wild boar in one year.

There was also substantial cellarage. A wine cellar stored the 300 casks of wine drunk by the court each year, with a drinking house attached for wine tastings. Wine and ale for the monarch – a regular visitor – were kept in the privy cellar, while the majority of ale drunk by the court, around 600,000 gallons a year, was stored in the great cellar. These two cellars both had double locks on the doors with keys held by two different officials.

All in all, this is catering on a huge scale, and when you

remember that the largest banqueting venue in London, the ballroom at the Grosvenor House Hotel in Park Lane, seats a maximum of 2,000 people, and they don't fill it twice a day, it makes you realise the amount of effort that the cooking staff must have put in to keep Wolsey and his guests fed and happy. Certainly, Wolsey lived high on the hog and entertained on a lavish scale. His high living and ostentatious display were legendary, and made his downfall, when it came, all the more spectacular. Infuriated that Wolsey had failed to secure him the divorce from Catherine of Aragon he so wanted when it became clear that she would never bear him a son, Henry VIII stripped his chancellor of his titles and his palaces – including Hampton Court. Like so many have learnt before and since, Wolsey came to grief because, having set himself up as the provider of all good things to his sovereign lord, at the final hurdle he failed. There is always a final hurdle, I suspect.

Wolsey died in York a broken man, his final recorded words being the poignant: 'If I had served my God as diligently as I have done my king, he would not have given me over in my grey hairs.' Henry, on the other hand, swiftly took over Hampton Court. It was an ideal palace for him since, by river, it was within easy reach of Westminster but also sufficiently far away from London to be safe from the periodic summer outbreaks of plague. Henry enlarged the palace quite considerably and transformed the kitchens. Even today they retain their Tudor magnificence, and I do recommend a visit, particularly as there is always a standing display of the sort of food that Henry's court might have known. You can also admire the great vine, which has been there since the eighteenth century and which, until not long before I was born, was, I believe, periodically adorned with the blood of a freshly killed animal to keep it going. Now I suspect they use dried blood.

Given the extravagance of Hampton Court, it is perhaps to be expected that Wolsey should have become rather stout in his later years. And, by the same token, it's not that surprising that the once young and athletic Henry VIII should have become a bloated middle-aged man: by the time he was forty-five he was enormously fat, his waist measuring fifty-four inches. He was now no longer able to take the sort of exercise he had enjoyed when young because ulcers – possibly syphilitic – in his leg prevented him from riding or walking without great difficulty. He had a special device made that would lift him on to his horse and carry him from room to room in the palace. One feels rather sad at the thought of Henry, who still loved the outdoor life, being lifted on to his horse the last winter before he died at the age of fifty-five and going out into the coldest weather. Whereas once he could chase stags for thirty miles a day, now he would sit on his horse, wrapped up against the cold, watching his hawk pursue its prey or watching a number of stags being killed in an enclosure. He died a sad, sick old man after thirty-seven years on the throne.

Wolsey and Henry VIII, it has to be said, were not exceptional in their love of the table. The English of Tudor times had a reputation throughout Europe for gluttony. Indeed, overeating was regarded as the English vice in the same way that lust was the French one and drunkenness that of the Germans (although looking at the amount of alcohol consumed in England, I expect the English probably ran a close second to the Germans). The wealthy ate enormous meals and were noted for eating much larger quantities of meat than any of their Continental neighbours. Even in winter, when most meat was in shorter supply, certain types could be secured by falcons – since there were no leaves on the trees it was easier to see the game you were pursuing and you were less likely to lose your hawk.

Andrew Boorde in his *Compendyous Regyment or a Dyetary of Health* of 1542 went through a fairly exhaustive list of the types of meat available to English people, noting for example:

Of all nacycons and countres, England is best servyd of Fysshe, not only of al maner of see-fysshe, but also of fresshe-water fysshe, and of al maner of sortes of salte-fysshe . . . Beefe is a good meate for an Englysshe man, so be it the beest be yonge, & that it be not kowe-flesshe; for old beefe and kowe-flesshe doth ingender melancholye and leporouse humoures. Yf it be moderately powderyd, that the grosse blode by salte may be exhaustyd, it doth make an Englysshe man stronge . . . Veale is a nutrytyve meate, and it doeth nowrysshe moche a man, for it is soone dygestyd . . . Bacon is good for carters and plowmen, the whiche be ever labourynge in the earth of dunge . . . I do say that collopes [slices of bacon] and egges is as holsome for them, as a talowe candell is good for a horse mouth . . . Brawne is an usual meate in wynter amonges Englysshe men . . .

There's an awful lot of meat and fish here, though Boorde does go on to advise his readers to eat vegetables such as turnips, parsnips, carrots, onions, leeks, garlic and radishes and fruit in the form of mellow red apples. You can, however, sense in his work that suspicion of raw vegetables and fruits that was to be found a little earlier in *The Boke of Keruynge*. Virtually every fruit and vegetable that Boorde mentions has some less than admirable quality, and the frequent injunction is to cook it before eating. So for example:

Apples be good . . . they shuld be eaten with suger or comfettes, or with fennell-sede, or anys-sede, bycause of theyr ventostyte [causing wind]; they doth comforte than the stomache, and doth make good dygestyon, specyally yf they be rostyd or baken.

That doesn't mean, though, that fruit and vegetables were regarded as unimportant in the early sixteenth century. Dried fruit continued to be important in cooking, and large quantities of raisins, currants, prunes, dried figs and dates, together with almonds and walnuts, were imported. Luxuries for the nobility of medieval times, these were now becoming ever more widely distributed through society and reaching the tables of the emerging middle classes. What's more, the Tudor age was a great age for gardening and an increasingly wide variety of fruits was grown. As one might expect, apples, pears, plums, cherries and wood strawberries were popular, but we can also trace an influx of fruit from southern Europe into the gardens of the rich. Quinces, apricots and raspberries now make an appearance, as do melons, pomegranates and even oranges and lemons (not that the English climate was particularly kind to citrus fruits, which tended still to be imported). Meat may have taken a central place on the English table, but it was by no means the only thing to be consumed avidly.

Details of a feast served to Henry VIII and his court by the Marquess of Exeter at Horsley in Surrey in the summer of 1533 demonstrate this nicely. The first course consisted of salads of damsons, artichokes, cabbage, lettuce, purslane and cucumbers, which were served with stewed sparrow, carp, capons in lemon, larded pheasant, duck, gulls, forced rabbit, pasties of venison from fallow deer and a pear pasty. This was followed by a stork, gannet, heron, pullets, quail, partridge, fresh sturgeon, another pasty of venison (this time from red deer), chicken and fritters. The third and final course consisted of jelly, blancmange, apples with pistachios, pears with caraway seeds, filberts, scraped cheese with sugar, clotted cream with sugar, quince pie and marchpane. The meal was rounded off with the customary wafers and hippocras. There may have been a strong meat motif here, but there was also plenty of other fare to enjoy.

Elizabeth I was a keen hunter, and this illustration from George Gascoigne's
Noble Art of Venerie or Hunting (1575) shows her enjoying a picnic in a forest
glade. Her ladies-in-waiting stand respectfully behind her while one attendant
proffers food and another a drink.

CHAPTER 4

Orange Carrots and White Bread

England in the Age of Gloriana

Small events can have dramatic and unintended consequences. Had Catherine of Aragon borne Henry VIII a son, the course of Tudor history might have taken a very different turn. As it was, because she failed in her allotted duty, and because Pope Clement VII then refused to grant Henry a divorce (scarcely surprising given that Clement was, at that time, a virtual prisoner of Catherine's nephew, Charles V), a series of events was set in train that led to Cardinal Wolsey's fall and culminated in England's split from Rome. It also led, indirectly, to changes in England's food. Indeed, several developments in the national diet over the next few decades can ultimately be linked to the religious upheavals that Henry VIII set in motion.

The crisis really began in the mid 1520s when Henry finally came to the conclusion that Catherine of Aragon was unlikely to bear him a male heir and when he also encountered Anne

Boleyn: young and attractive in his eyes; a 'common stewed [professional] whore' in the eyes of the less than impressed Abbot of Whitby. He went on to marry Anne in 1533, precipitating his excommunication by the Pope. From then on the screws tightened inexorably on the traditions and institutions of the Church of Rome. In 1534 Henry was made Supreme Head of the Church of England and the authority of the Pope in England was abolished. In the same year Cardinal Wolsey's successor and former right-hand man Thomas Cromwell was authorised to inspect all the country's monasteries. Major landholders who paid money and allegiance to the Pope, they were a tempting target for Henry. Cromwell was able to seize the lands and indeed the buildings of the abbeys, monasteries and priories throughout the country and either sell them or grant them to the 'new men' who were seeking to increase their social standing.

The great symbolic break with the past was the abolition of the feast of St Thomas à Becket of Canterbury held on 7 July, along with the lesser feast day of the anniversary of his martyrdom on 29 December. These Henry did away with in 1537. He did not like the thought that an archbishop of Canterbury had been made a saint for his defiance of the king (in this case Henry II), and he ordered the clergy to denounce Becket from their pulpits as a traitor. Becket's bones were dug up following a commission of inquiry. They were publicly burnt and his shrine at Canterbury Cathedral was closed. All the treasures at the tomb were forfeited under the usual treason laws; it took twenty carts to carry the treasures from Canterbury to London.

In religious terms, England's Reformation was not immediately as earth-shaking as might be supposed. Henry was no radical

Protestant: the format of church services changed little in the years straight after the break with Rome, and Henry continued to observe the principal traditional holy days and fasting days even after he had repudiated the Pope's authority. His Archbishop of Canterbury, Thomas Cranmer, behaved likewise. Technically, as the Archbishop of Canterbury, he and the Archbishop of York were actually allowed to eat more than other bishops and lower clergy under the sumptuary laws that limited personal expenditure on food and possessions; nevertheless, on many evenings he would sit at the supper table wearing gloves to show that he did not wish to be served anything. As late as 1540, when the architect of the dissolution of the monasteries, Thomas Cromwell, eventually fell from grace, the Lord Mayor of London, William Roche, was actually told to enforce the fasting laws, and several prominent Protestants suffered terms of imprisonment for eating meat on fast days. In 1543, when persecution of strict Protestants was stepped up a notch, the authorities in London sent officers to enter the houses of prominent Protestants at dinner time to see what they were eating.

Nevertheless, the nature and frequency of fasting did change. The number of days involved was substantially reduced, and practical rather than religious reasons for their observance constantly stressed (Elizabeth I put out numerous proclamations to encourage people to eat fish on fast days in order to sustain England's fishing fleet). Moreover, what people ate on these days started to alter. The consumption of eggs, cheese and milk had traditionally been frowned on; hence Shrove Tuesday is celebrated with pancakes, which use up milk and eggs before the Lenten fast begins. Now the rules were slackened, and were finally abolished in 1541. With dairy now firmly back on the menu, the almond milk that had been so widely used in medieval times was no longer so necessary, and its use started to dwindle.

A more indirect and haphazard food-related consequence of England's Reformation and the abolition of the monasteries was the appearance in the countryside of wild rabbits. As I mentioned before, rabbits, the favoured, pampered dish of the nobility and the rich, were introduced to England by the Normans, and throughout the Middle Ages they were kept in carefully tended warrens both by the wealthy and by the Church. At some point before the eighteenth century they became established in the wild, and it seems likely that when the monasteries and therefore the monastic warrens were abandoned, some escaped and then bred and thrived in the wild, providing country dwellers a few generations later with a new source of meat.

Not, I hasten to add, that warrens disappeared with the Tudors. They remained an important part of the countryside. When I recently visited the village of Quenington in Gloucestershire, for example, I noticed that one of the main streets was called Coneygar Road and there was also a Coneygar Farm, even though there was no longer sign of the original warren. The great houses kept their warrens, too, sometimes on a lavish scale. Today you can still visit the curious lodge at Rushton, built in the shape of a triangle by Thomas Tresham between 1594 and 1597 to celebrate the Holy Trinity (Tresham was a Roman Catholic who was often fined for his beliefs; a few years later his family was involved in the Gunpowder Plot). It looks like a folly but was actually built to house Tresham's chief warrener. Remains of the warren can still be seen nearby.

The link between the dissolution of the monasteries and the

rise of the rabbit may ultimately be impossible to prove; the link between the dissolution and the increase in the number of roadside inns is easier to establish. Rich travellers had always been able to stay with relatives when moving around the country, especially the nobility, who were almost invariably related to each other by marriage or by some form of shared landowner-ship. Other travellers, however, had tended to rely on the monasteries for hospitality. With these gone, inns became ever more necessary as providers of food and lodging. They were often set in what had previously been a monastic guest house. A good example is the very good hostelry just by the gates of the old abbey in Battle in Sussex, which was clearly once the abbey guest house.

Tudor inns cannot have been very comfortable. In most instances travellers were expected to share rooms with total strangers and were frequently expected to share beds as well. These were often very large, sleeping six people, probably lying head to toe. The great bed of Ware, now in the Victoria and Albert Museum, which was probably constructed in around 1590 as a publicity stunt for the White Hart Inn at Ware, was supposed to have accommodated twenty couples at once. Even those travellers who could afford better sleeping arrangements and better food cannot have enjoyed a particularly restful stay: you never knew who was going to steal your purse in the middle of the night, or indeed your horse. As for the quality of the food served in such establishments, this depended on the vari-able cooking skills of the landlord and his wife. Nor did landlords and landladies always have a very edifying reputation. One popular story, *The Pleasant Historie of Thomas of Reading*, written around 1597 by the Norwich silk-weaver Thomas

Deloney, claimed that a former hostess of the Ostrich Inn at Colnbrook in Buckinghamshire constructed a bed above a trap-door in one of the rooms, releasing rich visitors into a boiling cauldron while they were fast asleep.

Bakers in those areas frequented by travellers developed a nice sideline in small pies and pasties to be carried and eaten en route. Previously, pie cases had tended to be 'coffyns': large pastry vessels designed for cooking and serving the food but not intended to be eaten, except perhaps by the servants after the meal. Now there was a great increase in pastry that was designed to be eaten. The ever-growing wool trade, and the plethora of mutton that inevitably accompanied it, led to the development of what were to be known in Scotland as 'tuppeny struggles': little mutton pies that were easy to put in your bag and carry on your journey.

It wasn't just those passing through the countryside who were affected by the dissolution of the monasteries. Country dwellers were, too. The monasteries may have been guilty on occasion of corruption and even sexual debauchery (though the charges may have been exaggerated by their opponents), but they did at least have a sense of a wider social responsibility than those who now bought up the old monastic properties. To make things considerably worse, the dissolution of the monasteries coincided with the first real major wave of enclosures whereby aggressive landowners took over common land that had been farmed by villagers for generations, causing genuine hardship that sometimes broke out in civil unrest. For all its glamour, the Tudor era is also the era of the 'sturdy beggar': the unemployed wanderer who might be one of those lay brothers thrown out of work when the monasteries were forced to close their doors; or the victim of land enclosure; or the victim of the price inflation that dogged the century. Once those down on their luck could turn to the Church for help; now they looked to local charity – or turned to crime.

Over time, enclosure, particularly in the south of England, made it harder and harder for country people to keep their own livestock, but in Tudor times many still kept a family cow, while those new landowners who gained from the dissolution of the monasteries often turned over pasturage to newly acquired herds. The net result seems to have been a gradual increase in the consumption of cow's milk and a complementary decline in the popularity of sheep and goat's milk. As for town dwellers, they looked to the country for the provision of butter and cheese, but to a growing number of urban dairies, where cows were kept in stalls and fed on bean pods and other greenery, for their milk. Both milk and cream were increasingly used in cooking as the century wore on, especially in the making of fancy desserts – syllabubs, junkets set with rennet, and trifles, although, as this recipe from Thomas Dawson's *The Good Huswife's Iewell* of 1596 shows, the Elizabethan trifle is not quite what we would expect to see today:

> Take a pinte of thicke Creame, and season it with Sugar and Ginger, and Rosewater, so stirre it as you would then have it, and make it luke warme in a dish on a Chafingdish and coals, and after put it into a silver piece or bowle, and so serve it to the boorde.

The ripples that spread out from the dissolution of the monasteries affected medical care, too. Up until now, although there had been physicians, especially in the towns, most people had been treated by the herbalists in the various monasteries. Herbs were grown extensively in monastic gardens; there was a huge degree of knowledge and expertise surrounding the herbariums of the various religious institutions.

After the dissolution of the monasteries this form of medical treatment ceased to be available and so people had to look elsewhere for help. It's quite possible that some of the monks who had been working in the herbariums set up as practitioners in the towns; certainly urban practitioners became increasingly significant. Henry VIII had always been interested in medical matters and as early as 1511 – the second year of his reign – had enacted a charter stipulating that anybody practising medicine within seven miles of the City of London had to be examined on their training and expertise by the Bishop of London and a panel of experts; similar provisions had been made for other towns. That these provisions were in place when the dissolution of the monasteries came was no doubt a huge help in registering people who were licensed to practise. Later in his reign Henry also gave a charter to barber-surgeons, who were considered much lowlier than physicians, which regulated their practice and what they were allowed to do when operating on and treating patients. Those who didn't have recourse to an expert were thrown back on their own resources. Housewives increasingly found themselves having to master basic herbal cures, and the 'receipt' books they compiled often have more than a sprinkling of home-prepared medicines among the food recipes.

Henry VIII may not have been a fully fledged Protestant, but some of those around him were. Archbishop Cranmer, for example, who helped make the case for Henry's divorce from

Catherine of Aragon, was a somewhat surreptitious Protestant in Henry's lifetime but came into his own when Henry's son, the young, earnest and rather sour Edward VI, succeeded his father in 1547. Over the next few years, Cranmer reformed the English Church, one of his major achievements being the magnificent Book of Common Prayer. More relevant to our story, the archbishop and those around him helped create a climate in which Protestants on the Continent facing persecution and worse were able to flee to England. The flow stopped briefly when Edward died in 1553 and was succeeded by his devoutly Catholic sister Mary, but when she in turn went to meet her maker five years later, to be succeeded by her sister Elizabeth, Protestant asylum-seekers freely made their way to England. By the 1590s there were some 15,000.

Many were highly skilled craftsmen. The German contingent, for example, included iron workers who soon set to work in the Sussex and Kentish Wealds, helping to stimulate industry there to such an extent that in 1584 a law was passed compelling iron workers to resurface roads that had been worn down by the constant toing and froing of consignments of iron ore. And it's tempting to speculate that these may have been among the foreign workers in England who helped encourage the growing English love of pickled food. Cucumbers were certainly being pickled in Elizabethan times, although 'gherkins' don't get a mention until a century later (Samuel Pepys refers to them as 'rare things' in a diary entry in 1661). That love of food with a strong acidic flavour has medieval roots, of course, as has the word 'pickling' in the sense of preserving in brine or vinegar, but I can't help wondering whether the Tudor migrants from central and eastern Europe played a part in all this. It is, after all, a very short hop from the taste of food like sauerkraut to the pickled items that were for so long a staple of English pub food. Over time, these pickles came to be stored in glass containers (much better than earthenware containers, which, unless well glazed, tend to leak when vinegar is left standing in them) and, again, it is tempting to suggest a link with the Continent here since many of the French Huguenots who sought refuge in England from religious persecution were skilled glass workers.

The effects of the dissolution of the monasteries, then, were varied and diffuse and reached into all sorts of corners of Tudor life and the nation's food. But there were more visible consequences, too, which came about as thousands of acres of monastic land were purchased by the ambitious and the upwardly mobile. These new owners – very much a hallmark of Elizabeth I's reign – wanted their wealth to show, and soon the castles and manor houses of the past were giving way to spectacular new houses built by people like William Cecil at Burghley, John Thynne at Longleat, and Bess, Countess of Shrewsbury, at Hardwick. Nor was land the only source of new wealth. Sir Francis Willoughby built Wollaton between 1580 and 1588 using money he had generated from his iron-manufacturing works, from his coal mines and from selling woad to dyers. Similarly Althorp, the Spencer house, was built on the fortune generated by sheep. To me, the great houses of Elizabethan England are the defining image of the age, with their magnificent dining rooms, their long galleries and the ostentatious display of glass in their numerous windows.

William Cecil is a classic example of the new man made

good, and Burghley the classic example of the grand Elizabethan house. Cecil's grandfather David kept the best inn at Stamford, in Lincolnshire, but went on to secure the favour of Henry VII, who made him a Yeoman of the Guard. Cecil's father, Richard, was a Yeoman of the Wardrobe at court. Cecil himself went to Cambridge, which he left after several years without taking a degree, joined Gray's Inn and then rose through the ranks under the Duke of Somerset, uncle and regent to Edward VI. He was canny enough to survive the Catholic reign of Mary, and fortunate enough to became attached to Elizabeth at a time when she was living – essentially under house arrest – at Hatfield House. Once Elizabeth succeeded to the throne in 1558, Cecil's career took off. He was Lord Chancellor throughout much of her reign, a prudent adviser who was prepared to tackle problems that Elizabeth shied away from.

He was also a great builder, in an age of great builders. And to my mind his finest house – which he helped to design – was Burghley House in his native Lincolnshire. Burghley was built on land which had come to Cecil's father after the dissolution of the monasteries and to this day it remains one of the most magnificent Elizabethan houses in England. It has to be said that it wasn't perhaps the most rational of decisions to build a house in a location that was going to take its owner rather a long time to reach from London. Cecil apparently made the journey riding a mule, which was gentler on his gout than a restless thoroughbred (there's an enchanting painting of this in Hatfield House). On the other hand, Cecil's regular journeys on the high road must have kept him in touch with what was going on outside London – unlike modern politicians, who wouldn't dream of travelling with everyone else on the Tube or in second-class carriages. Unlike modern politicians, too, Cecil allowed any traveller of a reasonable degree to call at the house for food, whether he himself was in residence or not. If nothing else, this must have allowed him to pick up interesting information from passers-by.

Burghley, like the other grand houses of the period, was built for entertainment and would have been able to receive Elizabeth I on one of her regular progresses around the country as she checked up on the loyalty of her subjects and ate them out of house and home (it is recorded that another of William Cecil's houses, Theobalds, near Cheshunt in Hertfordshire, was visited by the queen on ten separate occasions – the staff must have been exhausted by the end). The kitchen at Burghley, therefore, is suitably lavish. It has two open fireplaces, three bread ovens and also a stove – a new innovation – comprising a long metal trough set on a brick base which contained charcoal, over which the cooks could prepare sauces and other such things that needed instant heat. Along with the other great Elizabethan houses it also has extensive flat areas on the roof. These were apparently used not only for taking exercise (where you'd be sheltered from the wind though not the rain) but for indulging in confidential conversations. Since Lincolnshire has always been a good area for pork, I'd also like to think of the Elizabethan lords and ladies up on the roof with their tables and stools having a picnic lunch that possibly included Lincolnshire chine, cut from collar of pork and, with its parsley stuffing, England's answer to *jambon persillé*.

As for the house of another of the queen's favourites, Kenilworth, owned by the Earl of Leicester, this was described by one admirer as one of the wonder houses of the time:

. . . every room so spacious, so well belighted, and so high
roofed within: so seemely to sight by due proportion without;
in day time on every side so glittering by glasse, at nights by
continuall brightness of candle, fire and torch-light, transparent
thro' the lightsome windows, as it were the Egyptian Pharos
reluctent [shining] unto all the Alexandrian coast . . .

As at Burghley, food played an important part in life at
Kenilworth. When the queen visited in 1575 she and her courtiers were treated to a banquet that was served in a thousand
dishes of glass or silver by 200 gentlemen. It all proved cripplingly expensive for the earl and was viewed with firm disfavour
by those like the pious zealot Philip Stubbs who were of a more
self-denying nature. 'Nowadays,' he grumbled, 'if the table not
be covered from the one end to the other with delicate meats
of sundry sorts, and to every dish a sauce appropriate to its
kind, it is thought unworthy of the name of a dinner.'

In houses such as Burghley and Kenilworth huge amounts
of money were spent on lavish banquets and on the ingredients
that made them lavish, such as spices and condiments. And
while gluttony was probably a little less prevalent than it had
been in the reign of Henry VIII, excess drinking – or 'large
garaussing' as it was called – which was supposed to have come
back to England with the soldiers who had fought in the Low
Countries, was common. The rich could carouse with dozens
of different types of French wine, not to mention ones from
Italy, Greece and elsewhere. Even poorer people imbibed heavily.
William Harrison in his 1577 description of England noted this
alcoholic tendency with some distaste: 'It is incredible to say
how our maltbugs lug at this liquor, even as pigs should lie in

a row lugging at their dame's teats, till they lie still again and be not able to wag.'

Not surprisingly, Elizabeth I's court was also conceived on a lavish scale, increasingly influenced in later years by the extravagance of Italian culture celebrated by such sixteenth- and seventeenth-century writers as Vincenzo Cervio and Bartolomeo Scappi, the latter serving as chef to the Vatican and responsible for the monumental cookbook *Opera dell'arte del cucinare*, published in 1570. As for Elizabeth's personal tastes, these can be seen in various contemporary accounts and records. It's clear, for example, that she had a very sweet tooth indeed. When Sir William Petre entertained her at Ingatestone Hall in 1561, he spent twenty-eight shillings and sixpence on 'comfits of sundry sorts' – in other words, sweets made from fruit or roots preserved in sugar. New Year presents given to her on 1 January 1585 included a box of foreign sweetmeats from her physician, a box of lozenges and a pot of conserves from her apothecary, and 'a fayre marchepayne' (marzipan) from her master cook.

Records of Elizabeth's visit to Ingatestone in 1561 also provide a more general picture of grand eating in court circles. She arrived on Saturday, a fish day, and was duly presented with sturgeon, a royal fish. On other days she was treated to two main courses of meat and game, followed by the 'banquet' – that is, the course of sweetmeats that was served after the main meal had been consumed. The range of meat, fish and game on offer was astonishing: rabbits, sole, flounders, conger eels, cygnets, herons, quails, geese, chickens, oxen, and so on. Unfortunately, we don't know precisely how the food was prepared, but judging from the quantities of herbs, spices, cream, butter and eggs purchased, many dishes must have been accompanied with rich sauces. There is also a reference to 200 oranges, at a total cost of 19¼d.

Elizabeth, like her father, was also addicted to hunting, though not as obsessively. Henry would get up at four o'clock in the morning and hunt all day; Elizabeth, by contrast, might well indulge in an alfresco breakfast first. An engraving from George Gascoigne's 1575 work *The Noble Arte of Venerie or Hunting* shows her in the midst of a lavish picnic, surrounded by courtiers and servants. When she visited Viscount Montague on one occasion, a dancer dressed as a nymph presented her with a crossbow with which she was to dispatch the deer driven across her view, while a butler set up the feast, placing bottles and barrels of beer and wine into the spring to keep them cool. George Gascoigne describes what was on offer:

That doone: he spreades his cloth, upon the grassye banke,
And sets to shewe his deintie drinkes, to winne his Princes thanke.
Then comes the captaine Cooke, with many a warlike wight
    [person],
Which armor bring and weapons both, with hunger for to fight
[. . .]
For whiles colde loynes of Veale, colde Capon, Beefe and
    Goose,
With Pygeon pyes, and Mutton colde, are set on hunger loose . . .
First Neates [cows'] tongs poudred well, and Gambones
    [haunch] of the Hogge,
Then Saulsages and savery knackes [delicacies], to set mens
    myndes on gogge [excite]
[. . .]
Then King or comely Queene, then Lorde and Lady looke,

To see which side will beare the bell, the Butler or the Cooke.
At last the Cooke takes flight, but Butlers still abyde,
And sound their Drummes and make retreate, with bottles by
their syde.

The queen was presented with the fewmets, the deer droppings that had been located when they selected the quarry for
the day. And so the hunt commenced with the scent-tracking
dogs, or lymers, which at this time would have been blood-
hounds, who drove the deer from cover in the deer park as the
hunt commenced.

However, Elizabeth's real passion lay with coursing. The hare
became the most sought after of quarries and was hunted on
horseback with greyhounds. Thomas Howard, Duke of Norfolk,
was appointed by Elizabeth to draw up the rules of coursing.
It seems to have been, rather as today, about the thrill of the
chase rather than the thrill of the kill: certainly the growing
popularity of coursing doesn't seem to have led to a corresponding increase in the number of recipes for hare in Elizabethan
cookery books.

Those who mixed in royal circles and possessed grand houses
liked to have grand gardens, too. The tendency until Elizabethan
times had been to take exercise in the long gallery of a stately
home or in the sporting field. Now well-stocked gardens, the
smell of herbs fragrantly wafting through the air, became
splendid places for ladies, and indeed ladies and gentlemen, to
take their exercise and perhaps indulge in clandestine meetings
in the garden's various hidden nooks and crannies. Herb
and fruit gardens were generally positioned close to the house,

and grapes, plums, apples, pears, walnuts, apricots, almonds, peaches, figs, oranges and lemons were all grown. Vegetable gardens, by contrast, tended to be hidden away behind beech or whitebeam hedges.

William Cecil's son Robert, an enthusiastic gardener himself, employed the botanist and gardener John Tradescant the Elder to travel abroad to bring back rare and wonderful plants. He was later joined by his son, also called John, who voyaged as far as Virginia in his hunt for new species. I've always liked the story that all the horse chestnuts in England are descended from one chestnut that was given to John Tradescant the Elder by a Turkish sea captain; he planted it at Theobalds, so starting a craze for the tree. Long avenues of horse chestnuts are still to be found near many grand houses, perhaps the descendants of Elizabethan trees. One of the most successful of the Tradescants' discoveries proved to be the scarlet runner bean from Central America, presumably brought back originally for its pretty red flowers.

Not all new vegetables had to travel so far. Carrots in one form or another had probably been grown in England for a while, but it wasn't until the sixteenth century that the familiar orange carrot made an appearance, introduced to this country by Protestant refugees fleeing from the savage war being fought in the Low Countries by the Flemish against Spanish occupation. Richard Gardiner writing in 1599 in *Profitable Instructions for the Manuring, Sowing and Planting of Kitchen Gardens* duly celebrates the vegetable: 'Sow carrots in your garden and humbly praise God for them as for a singular and great blessing.'

The Flemish vegetable growers who accompanied the orange carrot mostly landed in Sandwich and Deal in Kent and soon found that the sandy soils here proved perfect for the production of the root crop that they had grown in their own homeland. In fact they set up market gardens all over the South-East, including ones that stretched from Battersea to Wimbledon where a great variety of vegetables and indeed fruits were grown for the London markets.

One of the predominant vegetables of the Elizabethan age was the bean in all its varieties. Elizabeth herself was supposed to favour the white haricot bean, originally from Central America; given the gas-inducing reputation of beans it's perhaps not surprising that her favourite herb was anti-flatulent winter savory. The area beyond Chelsea was noted for its bean fields and it was commonplace among the poor inhabitants of London in later years to take romantic trips out when the bean fields were in flower, to walk around them hand in hand and to smell the sweet fragrance of their flowers. If you've ever smelt a bean flower, you'll know that it has a particularly lovely smell.

The South-East was also helped by the attentions of Richard Harris, who held the title of royal fruiterer to King Henry VIII. He is believed to have planted the first orchards of cherries, apples and other fruit trees around Tonbridge in Kent on the king's instructions. By Elizabeth's time these fruit trees would have come well into their own, just in time to be tended by the Flemish gardeners who were flooding into the county.

Thanks to Walter Raleigh, the new vegetable that the Elizabethan age is most associated with is the potato. Unfortunately, most of the popular wisdom about it turns out to be wrong. In the first place, it was not an overnight success (though potato flowers sometimes adorned the clothes of the fashionable). In fact, it was not until the late eighteenth century that it became popular in England. To that extent it was rather like the tomato (or love apple, as it was called), which arrived from South America at a similar time, was welcomed enthusiastically by the Italians and the Spanish, but regarded with suspicion by the English.

What's more, Raleigh's own place in the history of the potato is, in my view, somewhat suspect. For as long as I can remember, we've been taught that he came across it in the colony he established in Virginia and then presented it with a great flourish at Elizabeth's court. It's far more likely, however, that if he brought the potato back at all, it was to his Irish estates at Youghal, near Cork. Here they flourished, creating a staple of the Irish diet for several centuries to come, until the terrible blight of the nineteenth century brought famine to the country.

Some rather elaborate Elizabethan propaganda may have been involved here. When the herbalist John Gerard published his *Generall History of Plantes* in 1597 he was quick to claim that the potato came from Virginia, writing:

It groweth naturally in America where it was first discovered . . . since which time I have received rootes hereof from Virginia, otherwise called Norembega, which growe and prosper in my garden, as in their owne native countrie . . . The Indians do call this plant *Papus* (meaning the rootes) . . .

He describes the potato plant in some detail:

. . . whereon do grow very faire and pleasant flowers, made of one entire whole leafe, which is folded or plaited in such strange sort . . . The colour whereof it is hard to expresse. The whole flower is of a light purple color, stripped down the middle of every folde or welt, with a light shew of yellownes, as though purple and yellow were mixed togither . . . The roote is thicke, fat, and tuberous; not much differing either in shape, colour or taste from the common [sweet] Potatoes, saving that the rootes hereof are not so great nor long; some of them round as a ball, some ovall or egge fashion, some longer, and others shorter: which knobbie rootes are fastened unto the stalkes with an infinite number of threddie strings.

Leaving aside accusations that John Gerard actually plagiarised his book (and the illustrations) from the work of a Dr Priest, who had written a herbal or general history of plants complete with woodcuts but died before he could publish it, the mention of Virginia as the source of the potato is unconvincing. As far as we know, potatoes were not grown in Virginia until long after Raleigh's time. It's possible that Gerard made a genuine mistake and did not realise that the potatoes he was describing came from South America on ships that may have sailed via Virginia. But it's also possible that Gerard was endeavouring to ingratiate himself with Elizabeth I by claiming that this new food was the first fruit from a colony that had been named in honour of the Virgin Queen by Sir Walter Raleigh.

We're told that Walter Raleigh staged a banquet to introduce Queen Elizabeth to the wonders of the new American colony, at which a dish of potato tops was supposedly served. It's a nice story, but it has long been regarded by food pundits as suspect because potato leaves are actually poisonous (the potato is part of the deadly nightshade family). I do recall, though, that when the city of Sydney decided to recreate this banquet and gave the menu to a renowned chef of Chinese origin, he promptly served up the tops of sweet potatoes, which are non-toxic and much eaten by the Chinese. I think it's therefore safe to assume that what was served to Elizabeth I on that occasion was sweet potato tops; as I've already mentioned, the sweet potato had been growing in southern Spain since the days of Catherine of Aragon's marriage to Henry VIII.

All this bears out a suspicion that I have had since my school days that Raleigh was a spin merchant whose influence has been massively overstated. Even the popular link between his name and the introduction of tobacco doesn't stand up to scrutiny. Tobacco was actually brought back by John Hawkins from America in the 1560s, when Raleigh was in his teens, and it swiftly became prevalent in the form of pipe smoking. By the end of the century, when Raleigh is supposed to have been popularising it, it had come into general use, though not cheap at three shillings a pound. Innkeepers often provided a common pipe at their establishments, and a visiting foreigner noted, 'At there [their] spectacles [i.e. the London theatres] and everywhere else, the English are constantly smoking Tobacco . . .'

Whoever was responsible for introducing the potato to Europe, it was certainly widely known by the end of the sixteenth century and relatively popular in Spain and Spanish-controlled lands, that is the Low Countries (the modern-day Netherlands and Belgium) and areas of Europe that are now part of Germany but at this time were under the rule of the Habsburgs. In England its uses were medicinal rather than dietary. Signature medicine was popular at this time: plants being used to treat the ailment they most resembled. So, for example, beans, and especially kidney beans, were used for the treatment of kidney diseases. The potato was thought to resemble a rather intimate part of a man's anatomy and so was considered to be an aphrodisiac, promoting male sexual stimulation. Bitter experience clearly demonstrated quite quickly that it didn't work very well and its use in this area of medicine soon lapsed, but for a brief period it attracted quite a high price. The aphrodisiacal potato even made an appearance in literature, in John Fletcher's play *The Loyal Subject* (1618):

2 SOLDIER: Will your Lordship please to taste a fine potatoe?
'Twill advance your withered state.
ANCIENT: Fill your honour of most noble itches,
And make Jack dance in your Lordship's breeches.

As Raleigh's founding of the colony of Virginia demonstrates, the Elizabethan age witnessed a huge expansion in exploration and foreign trade. New companies sprang up: the Muscovy Company, for example, founded in 1555, which traded with Russia; and the Levant Company, founded in 1581, which revitalised trade with Turkish markets and imported a whole range of goods including spices. Some foods came from relatively close at hand: one contemporary writer in ranking cheese of the time puts Italian Parmesan first ('Parmesan is the finest of all cheeses'), then Dutch cheese, then British. Other foods came from rather further afield, some English merchants travelling as far as Persia and even India with a view to setting up new markets. The circumnavigations of the globe by Sir Francis Drake and Sir Thomas Cavendish, between 1577 and 1588, set up new markets with the East Indies. Others established cane plantations in the West Indies to supply sugar. Sugar, as we have seen, had been arriving from the Middle East since the twelfth century, but with the establishment of West Indian plantations, not to mention the growing of sugar in Venetian-controlled Cyprus, it became much more widely available. The Elizabethans loved it.

The courtier Sir Hugh Plat's *Delightes for Ladies*, published at the turn of the seventeenth century, is full of recipes that make considerable use of sugar: marzipan, sugar paste, and so on. He also gives a gingerbread recipe that is a subtle development of the older gingerbread we have already encountered:

Take three stale Manchets [loaves of fine white bread], and grate them: dry them, and sift them thorow a fine sieve: then adde unto them one ounce of Ginger being beaten, and as much Cinamon, one ounce of Liquorice and Anniseeds beeing beaten together, and searced [sieved], halfe a pound of sugar; then boil all these together in a posnet [small metal pot], with a quart of claret wine, till they come to a stiff paste with often stirring of it; and when it is stiffe, mould it on a table, and so drive it thin, and put it in your moulds: dust your moulds with Cinamon, Ginger, and Liquorice, being mixed together in fine powder. This is your Ginger-bread used at the Court, and in all Gentlemens houses at festival times.

The increasing availability of sugar gave rise to the art of sugar plate: elaborate models and sculptures made entirely out of sugar and often highly coloured. Even tableware was sometimes made from sugar, although Wyllyam Warde's translation of *The Secrets of the Reverende Master Alexis of Piedmont* was careful to emphasise that sugar is perhaps not the most durable of materials and that people should 'stand no hot thynge nygh to it'.

The English acquisition of a sweet tooth had a downside, in that that tooth rapidly turned black. By the end of her reign Elizabeth's smile was, apparently, no sight for sore eyes, and some women at court blackened their own teeth to curry favour with her. Foreign visitors were swift to notice the deterioration in the quality of English teeth. The English themselves turned to dental products. Some of these made a bad problem worse; one, for example, involved mixing vinegar with wood ash and rose water. The barber-surgeons' guild became very adept at the pulling of teeth.

Certain aspects of trade, then, may not have made the country particularly healthy, but they did enhance its wealth, and the national coffers were further swelled as a consequence of the letters of marque issued to men like Sir Francis Drake to legitimise their buccaneering raids on foreign ships. (When the *Golden Hind* returned to Plymouth after raiding the Spanish fleet, it was estimated that Drake unloaded plunder to the value of £600,000 on to Plymouth Docks – a stupendous sum at the time.) Elizabethan England was consequently quite an affluent country, and it's tempting to assume that this new-found wealth trickled its way down through society as a whole.

In fact, the picture is rather more complicated. For the poorer members of society, there were periods of real suffering during Elizabeth's reign. The monasteries had gone, and nothing had yet come along to fulfil the social role they had played. The old feudal manors had gone, too. Enclosures were nibbling away at common lands. And the population was growing, reaching around 4 million in 1600. When there were years of poor harvests, as there were in the 1570s and 1590s, the prospect for many was grim. A whole string of laws passed in Elizabeth's reign, culminating in the 1601 Poor Law, recognised the problem, even if they didn't necessarily come up with the answer. For such people, food would have been scarce and of indifferent quality.

Further up the social scale, things were considerably better. Wool remained a major industry; indeed, English wool was deemed the best in the world. And while at one point the land given over to sheep seemed to threaten agricultural productivity, the enclosures that harmed the poor simultaneously helped to stimulate more efficient grain production.

The money generated by trade and by farming in Elizabeth's reign can still be seen in the houses that the gentry and the merchant and yeoman classes now built themselves. It also shows itself in the food they ate. Dinners would commonly consist of four, five or even six dishes. On special occasions, they would be even more lavish, the host attempting to ape the fuller tables of those above him in the social pecking order. Beef still formed the main constituent of the diet of the husbandman, or farmer, and the artisan, along with white meats and bread made from rye or barley.

Wildfowl were also popular, and what you start to see in the Elizabethan period is a more professional and concerted approach to trapping them. In the wetlands in East Anglia and around Glastonbury, for example, decoys were built to entice birds along a system of narrow channels until they became trapped in the nets. Sparrow and pigeon dumplings, where the birds were wrapped in dough and simmered, were widely eaten. Ruffs were trapped in nets and crammed for ten days or so with bread and milk until each was 'a lump of fat' (something

I'll explore more fully when I come to consider the Stuarts); then they were beheaded and eaten roasted and with sauce.

The sauces that accompanied wildfowl and poultry might be quite simple: thinly sliced boiled onions with pepper and the gravy from the bird was considered suitable for capons and turkeys, for example. Others were more complex. Sparrows might be stewed in ale with herbs and served upon triangles of bread. Larks could be cooked in wine with bone marrow, raisins and a little sugar and cinnamon. Fruit sauces were not uncommon: gooseberries or apple with goose, for instance.

Quite a range of food, then, was on offer to the more well-to-do, and it is people such as this that Thomas Churchyard, a soldier and jobbing writer, had in mind when he wrote:

> Here things are cheap and easily had,
> No soil the like can show
> No state nor kingdom at this day
> Doth in such plenty flow.

*

I've already talked about the way in which milk was increasingly used in cooking in the sixteenth century. Now I want to turn to two other very common or garden items – eggs and bread – and consider the changes that occurred in their preparation in the course of Elizabeth's reign.

The sixteenth-century transformation of the egg has long fascinated me. Eggs had always been plentiful in both the town and the countryside in the spring, summer and early autumn. But until Elizabethan times, unless someone wanted to make a custard filling for a tart, they were largely eaten roasted in the ashes, or, occasionally, fried in lard or butter, or poached in water or broth.

Andrew Boorde, writing in the reign of Henry VIII, approves of a newly laid egg, rare roasted and eaten in the mornings with a little salt and sugar, but my own experience is that it's difficult to roast eggs in the embers because they dry out so quickly. Certainly, roasted eggs aren't particularly digestible. Presumably others felt the same way, too, because at some point in the sixteenth century boiling eggs in their shells in water became common practice. Buttered eggs served on buttered slices of toasted bread and garnished with pepper and salt also appeared on Elizabethan menus, especially on fast days. Today we would call this dish scrambled eggs. Sometimes, for a change, musk and ambergris would replace the pepper, or bitter orange juice, sugar and spices added. This was also the period when the word 'omelette' entered the English language, though the basic dish had been around for some time.

One favoured Elizabethan pudding that involved egg was a thick compote of boiled puréed fruit mixed with egg and a little cream and then baked as the filling for a tart or simply as a type of fruit fool. And then there was a 'Dishfull of Snow', which involved numerous eggs and constituted a wonderful centrepiece for a banqueting course. The recipe for it from the mid-sixteenth-century *Proper New Booke of Cookery* reads as follows:

Take a potell of sweete thicke creame and the white of eight egges & beate them al togider with a spone, then put them in your creame, and a saucer full of Rosewater, and a disshe full of Suger with all, than take a sticke & make it cleane, and than cutte it in the ende foure square, and there with heate all the aforesayde thinges togither, & ever as it ryseth take it of and put it into a Collander; this done, take one apple and set it in the myddes of it and a thicke busshe of Rosemary and set it in the middes of the plater; then cast your Snow upon the Rosemary & fyll your platter therewith. And if you have wafers cast some in with all and thus serue them forth.

The last remaining vestige of this dish full of snow is, I suppose, the dish that I remember as a child called 'apple snow'.

As for bread, white (or, to our eyes, yellowish) manchet loaves had been a status symbol for many years and as more people became able to afford them in Tudor times, so they became increasingly sought after. This exacerbated a rivalry between the guilds of brown-bread bakers and white-bread bakers that stretched back to the fourteenth century. Various attempts were made by the increasingly powerful white bakers to unite the two guilds in the sixteenth century, but the brown bakers held their ground, even creating their own coat of arms in 1572. The march of white bread, however, proved inexorable and irresistible. Finally, in 1645, the brown-bread guild reluctantly agreed to unite with their white-bread rival.

Bread remained critical to the English diet, both as a staple in itself and as an ingredient. Breadcrumbs were used for all sorts of dishes in the kitchen and were actually stored alongside the spices. They were used for thickening sauces, for thickening drinks, for sausages and stuffing. Gingerbread was prepared by mixing breadcrumbs into a stiff paste with honey, pepper, saffron, cinnamon and ginger and shaping it into a square, then decorating it with box leaves impaled on cloves. Fancy toasts also started being served for the banqueting courses, a development of the medieval idea of 'Poor Knights' – that is, bread dipped into beaten egg and beaten butter and sprinkled liberally with cinnamon. Now we find dishes such as a thick paste of sugar, spice, sweet wine, quinces, raisins and nuts mixed with a little flour, spread upon toasted white bread, decorated with sugar and cut into lozenges and even gilded. Or cooks might prepare buttered loaves, consisting of dough enriched with sugar, butter, egg yolk and spices, and baked with butter melted in a dish. They would then be strewn with sugar before being served.

The Elizabethans regarded buns made with eggs and spices as a great treat, and in Lent, as a special delight, they added currants and raisins. Some have suggested that the hot cross bun, which we traditionally eat on Good Friday, may have a link with the Reformation. Before then, the argument goes, buns were marked with a cross before they went into the oven in order to ward off evil spirits that might prevent the bread from rising properly. After the Reformation, crosses on bread were regarded as papist and so banned. However, because the cross had a special significance on Good Friday, hot cross buns were allowed to continue. It's a nice story, even if the evidence for it is shaky. Elizabeth David does note, however, that in 1592 Elizabeth I restricted London bakeries from making crossed buns 'except it be at burials, or on Friday before Easter, or at Christmas'.

Wheat was the popular grain for bread, but in some places it was difficult to grow. Whole areas of eastern England, including Norfolk and Suffolk, ate mostly rye or maslin bread – a sort of sourdough bread, leavened with a piece of dough from a former batch which was salted and stored until it turned sour. North-west England, by contrast, favoured barley bread. In Cumberland the bread would have been made of pure barley, baked in unleavened cakes. Barley bread had the advantage that it kept well.

Increasingly, bread was baked at home, perhaps in a Dutch-oven-type pot with hot peat or turf placed around it to keep it hot while the bread baked. In Lancashire and Westmorland, they had a strange bread called 'Clap bread', described here by Celia Fiennes, who travelled around northern England in the late seventeenth century:

> Here it was I saw ye oat Clap bread made. They mix their flour with water, so soft as to rowle it in their hands into a ball, and then they have a board made round and something hollow in the middle riseing by degrees all round to the Edge a little higher, but so little as one would take it be only a board warp'd, this is to Cast out the Cake thinn and so they Clap it round and drive it to ye Edge in a Due proportion till drove as thinn as a paper and still they Clap it and drive round, and then they have a plaite of iron same size wth their Clap board, and so shove off the Cake on it and so set it on Coales and bake it; when Enough on one side they slide it off and put the other side; if their iron plaite is smooth and they take Care their Coales or Embers are not too hot but just to make it Looke yelloe, it will bake and be as Crisp and pleasant to Eate as any thing you can imagine . . .

Flour didn't just go to make bread, of course, and apart from its use in such things as pastry, it was also a crucial ingredient in the fancy biscuits that Elizabethans so loved to munch at the 'banquet' course. Some were prepared with eggs to make 'bisket bread' – or sponge fingers, as we would now call them. Almond biscuits were also widely popular. So important was the 'banquet' that it was often staged in its own, separate venue: perhaps another room in the house or, in summer, in a specially built banqueting house outside. Fine dining in the Middle Ages often concluded with hippocras and sweet wafers, but it was left to the Elizabethans to give such emphasis to this final course. Further proof of that sweet tooth that was such a feature of the age is richly demonstrated in Thomas Dawson's 'names of all things necessary for a banquet' in his *The Good Huswife's Iewell*:

Sugar, cinnamon, liquorice, pepper, nutmegs, all kinds of saffron, sanders [sandalwood], comfits, aniseeds, coriander, oranges, pomegranate seeds, Damask water, turnsole [purple colouring], lemons, prunes, rose water, dates, currants, raisins, cherries conserved, barberries conserved, rye flour, ginger, sweet oranges, pepper white and brown, mace, wafers.

The *Generall Historie of Plantes* by John Gerard (or Gerarde) was dedicated by the author to Lord Burghley, himself a keen gardener, and reflects the Elizabethans' love of horticulture. It also reflects their ever-widening horizons: the title page of this second, expanded edition of 1633 shows Gerard holding the flowers of the newly discovered potato.

CHAPTER 5

Preserved Quince and My Lord of Devonshire's Pudding

The Elizabethan Year

So far I've talked in general terms about different aspects of the Elizabethan table, but I'd like now to focus on one family, the Fettiplace family, to show what everyday food was like in Elizabethan times – at least for the fairly wealthy. I've chosen the Fettiplaces because Elinor Fettiplace compiled a wonderful account, now usually known as *Elinor Fettiplace's Receipt Book*, which provides one of the best and most intimate pictures we have of Elizabethan domestic life. She compiled it in 1604 and it was first published in 1986 by Hilary Spurling, who inherited the manuscript from a great-aunt of her husband.

Elinor Fettiplace was born Elinor Poole, the rich heiress daughter of one of the new men of the Tudor age who had fingers in many pies but derived most of his fortune from wool. The Fettiplace family she married into was an ancient one that could trace its lineage back to the Norman Conquest. In fact, there had been Fettiplaces at just about every battle from Hastings in

1066 through to Crécy in 1346, and a later Fettiplace accompanied Henry VIII to his grand European summit at the Field of the Cloth of Gold in 1520.

The Fettiplaces owned substantial lands in Berkshire and Wiltshire, but by the time Elinor came on the scene they were heavily mortgaged. The marriage, therefore, benefited both parties. The Fettiplaces gained Elinor's dowry, while she got to meet the great and the good of the time. Anyone who was anyone in Elizabethan England seems to have woven their way through her life at some time or other, from Robert, Earl of Leicester, to his stepson the Earl of Essex, to the Cecils, to the Thynnes of Longleat. Many of them contributed recipes or remedies to her book.

Lady Elinor resided at Appleton Park (then in Berkshire, now in Oxfordshire) for most of her married life. Houses such as this were built not just for one generation, but for several at a time. Scattered around the rooms you would have found the senior occupants of the house, along with their children and surviving members of previous generations, relations by marriage and possibly a few poor ones too – not to mention the servants. At least twenty people would have sat down to eat; more at key points in the year. In fact it was not uncommon for such households as the Fettiplaces to extend an invitation fairly widely on important days: richer households often welcomed in the poorer local gentry and tenants who perhaps might not have survived the long winter that extended from November to Candlemas (2 February) without such neighbourly hospitality.

Elinor's receipt book is beautifully presented: copied out by a scribe on fine paper and bound in leather. The cover is stamped in gold with leaves and the fleur-de-lys of the Poole coat of arms. As was so often the case at this time, the binding of the book incorporates scraps torn from monastic manuscripts, which, according to the seventeenth-century antiquarian John Aubrey, 'flew about like butterflies' at the time. The volume is also part of an honourable tradition of books compiled and kept by women in which they noted down everything from favourite recipes to preserving techniques to home cures.

In many ways the sort of recipes in its pages aren't that different from those in printed cookery books of the time (it should be borne in mind that since literacy rates were low, such books would probably have been purchased only by the privileged few). Certainly there are similarities in the sort of flavourings involved – sometimes medieval in feel (rose water, cinnamon and ginger), sometimes more 'modern' (oranges and lemons). A comparable book to Elinor's work in some ways is *A Proper New Booke of Cookery Declaring What Maner of Meates Be Best in Season for al the Yeere, and How They Might Be Dressed, with a New Addition, Very Necessary for All Them That Delight in Cookery.* This was first printed in 1575 and covers a wide range of recipes for meat, broths, pies, tarts, jellies, and so on. As the title suggests, it also has a strong sense of what should be eaten when ('A fat Pigge is ever in season. A gose is worst in midsommer moone, and best in stubble time'). Many of the recipes still exert an appeal today, but occasionally in such books you come across truly strange ones, such as a bizarre vegetarian recipe for making a pudding in a turnip root. Here you take a turnip root, wash it, scrape it and hollow it out; then you fill it with a mixture of sugar, cinnamon, ginger, hard egg yolks, claret wine, butter, vinegar, rosemary, mace and dates. Once cooked, you serve it up: a dish to frighten off the most stubborn vegetarian.

A Proper New Booke of Cookery also serves to highlight the main meals of the day: dinner (here in two courses, in which savoury and sweet are, as usual, mixed) and the evening supper. Dinner would have been eaten at midday; supper between five and six o'clock. The book doesn't specifically mention breakfast, but most people at this time would, as in medieval times, have broken their fast with cold meat (or fish on fish days), bread and cheese.

Where Elinor's book differs from *A Proper New Booke of Cookery* is in its inclusion of remedies, a common feature of 'receipt' books and indeed of many other cookery books of the period: people were fully aware of the close connections between food and health. The year she appears to have stopped compiling it, 1604, plague broke out, and not surprisingly she includes several remedies. These are not the sort of brutal purgings and bleedings that medical experts of the time might have proposed, but more gentle purges and medicines. One, which she mentions as deriving from Henry VIII, involves a brew of marigolds, sorrel, burnet, rue, feverfew and dragonwort roots, sweetened with sugar candy. She also notes cures for fevers, insomnia, smallpox, nosebleeds, and so on.

Elinor's home cures show us the extent to which care of the sick was left to family members and family knowledge, and remind me of a book that was published a few years before, in 1585, called *The Widowes Treasure*. This earlier work includes all sorts of cures that could be prepared at home, opening rather charmingly with the rhyme:

> This dedoction [*sic*] is good to eat
> Always before and after meat,
> For it will make digestion good,

And turn your meat to pure blood.
Besides all this it doth excell,
All windinesie for to expell.
And all grosse humours cold and raw,
That are in belly, stomack, maw.
It will dissolve without paine,
And keepe ill vapours from the braine.
Besides all this it will restore
Your memory though lost before.
Use it therefore when you please,
Therein resteth mighty ease.

Treatments in *The Widowes Treasure* include potions to make you urinate (take the powder of berries of juniper and drink it with white wine or else with stale ale served hot), to cure sore feet ('Take Plantaine, and stamp it well, and anoint your feet with the juice thereof and the grise [grief] will swage [assuage]'), to stop children wetting the bed (feed them a roasted mouse – I would have thought that just the threat of that would work), to make your hair grow (burnt acorns mixed with bear grease), and even to deal with passions of the heart ('Take red rose leaves, the powder of Saffon [saffron], the Oyle of Mace, and melt them together, quilt the same in a little thin silke, and draw it over with a little thin Civet, and apply it to the region of the heart' – to my mind it's not clear what effect all this is supposed to have on the heart).

The Widowes Treasure also contains remedies for animals, reminding us that people had to be their own vets as well as their own doctors. If your horse has 'drunk' a horse leech, for example, you have to pour 'Sallet [salad] Oyle' into his mouth.

If he has swallowed a bone or eaten chicken droppings, you must drench him with parsley seed, honey and wine and then walk him for at least two hours, otherwise 'hee will voide at his fundament very foule excrements'. Heaven knows what effect the parsley drench would have had, but presumably walking the horse helped.

When it comes to food, the recipes in Elinor's book show that Elizabethan taste is starting to part company from medieval taste. Spices now tend to be used more sparingly. The sweet and sour meat dishes beloved in earlier times are beginning to disappear, sweet and sour flavours now being kept more apart. Meat sometimes follows a new fashion whereby it is part cooked, then sliced so as to extract the juice and make serving easier, and finally finished off by being cooked in a sauce in a lidded pan on a charcoal burner. Citrus fruit is often used, and there are a number of recipes that employ it. Oranges, in particular, notably the bitter orange imported in quantities from Spain, feature frequently. They were all the rage at the beginning of the seventeenth century. Sir Hugh Plat in his *Delightes for Ladies*, published in 1602, gives copious directions for keeping oranges and for managing to store orange juice all year. He also informs his readers that you can buy the pulp of Seville oranges at around All Hallows Tide – that is, Halloween – because the sweet makers were only interested in treating the rind and preserving it.

Among the recipes Elinor includes for orange is one in which the whole fruit is covered in a clear jelly and another (widely popular at the time) for orangeadoes: orange peel, candied, preserved in syrup or stuffed and stuck with herbs, and then added to sweet pies, used to flavour and decorate fruit fools, or dried and crystallised and carried in people's pockets to eat at the theatre. There's also a recipe for a rather curious Spanish marmalade recipe that Hilary Spurling describes as being somewhat like a sweet fudge:

> Take five sponfulls of rose water and seaven sponfulls of suger finely beaten, make yt boyle you must have redy by you two handfulls of almondes blanched and finely grownd, with 15 or 16 dates ye stones and whights taken out, and yor dates cut smale and beaten in a morter, then mix yor dates and almondes well together, then put yt in your Sirrope stirringe yt well together, then take on sponfull of pouder of sinamond, halfe a sponfull of ye pouder of pearles, three sheetes of Golde, stirr all theise well, but you must take yt first from the fire or else yt will bee to stiff that you can-not mingell yt, before yt bee through cold put yt upp into a marmalad boxe.

The recipes I've mentioned mostly use bitter oranges, but it's worth noting in passing that sweet oranges were also starting to arrive in England in the early seventeenth century and that they became popular very quickly – they were, if you like, the sun-dried tomatoes of their day. One recipe of the time that I particularly like involves hollowing out a sweet orange and filling it with a delicious rich buttered cream flavoured with orange juice and candied orange rind. The lid of the orange is then replaced and stuck down with custard so that, to the casual glance, it looks as though it's just an ordinary orange. I have served it at dinner parties and it has always been incredibly popular, though you do need to make sure that all the pith has been removed. Claire MacDonald and I once designed a menu for a banquet at a Scottish museum, and, because the caterers unfortunately did not take out the pith, the end result was very bitter and unpleasant.

One important point needs to be made about the serving of food in Elinor's time. Whereas her ancestors would invariably have dished up each course on a bread trencher, Elinor would have been familiar with something a little closer to what we're used to today: in her case, a thin, square wooden board with a large hollow measuring five or six inches in diameter to hold the meat and gravy and a smaller recess for the diner's own portion of salt. Many dishes were still served with pieces of bread under the meat and poultry – much as they are under a woodcock or grouse today – but the idea of a utensil made out of something that could be washed and reused was gaining ground. Simultaneously, while the great salt was still part of the Elizabethan table, it was now much more for decoration and show; small, readily accessible trencher salts were provided for less important dinners.

Glazed earthenware pottery was also making an appearance. In 1567 Dutchmen Jasper Andries and Jacob Jansen came to England from Antwerp to establish a pottery in Norwich and subsequently another in London which produced a smooth glossy white surface capable of being painted with metallic oxide glazes to give permanent decorations. Earthenware cups started to take over from wooden ones, though silver and gold remained the choice of the wealthy, and horn beakers and black leather jugs continued to be used by the less rich. These earthenware cups were made in vast quantities in the Surrey and Hampshire kilns in a fashionable Tudor green, a brilliant copper green glaze with a creamy base. In the North-East they tended to be fired with a dark red glaze and would often be decorated with flowers or stags' heads.

Glass was similarly becoming increasingly widespread by Elinor's time. In 1577 a description of England by William Harrison notes:

> It is a world to see in these our days, how our gentility . . . do now generally chose rather the Venice glasses, both for our wine and beer . . . The poorest also will have glass if they may; but sith [since] the Venetian is somewhat too dear for them, they content themselves with such as are made at home . . .

The Venetian Jacopo Verzelini set up a glass house in London with a Protestant refugee from the Netherlands and began to produce bowls and glasses of the highest quality, elaborately engraved with armorial arms and initials. Glassware factories also existed in Surrey and Sussex, the Bristol Channel area, in Staffordshire, Cheshire and Lancashire and North Yorkshire. They produced distilling equipment as well as goblets and bottles, and Sir Hugh Platt in his *Jewell House of Art and Nature* (1594) describes 'a beer glass of six or eight inches in height and being of one equal bigness from the bottom to the top', much the same as the type of beer glass found today.

As I say, such changes would have been familiar to Elinor. But what emerges most strongly from her book is something that never changes: the rhythm of the seasons. Much of Elinor's book, as indeed much of her life, was taken up with making the most of the good weather and preparing for the bad; enjoying food when it was in season but also making sure that, where possible, it could also be stored for later use. Inevitably, therefore, the book constantly mentions making preserves and putting things in the storeroom in anticipation of the often very lengthy seasons of entertainment enjoyed by the Elizabethans. (Just how long is demonstrated by the hospitable Elizabethan Sir William Holles, who, according to Hilary Spurling, began his Christmas at All Hallow's Tide (1 November) and kept it up to Candlemas (2 February); his grandson bitterly said of him that the family fortunes might as well have been poured down the privy.) Preparation, then, was everything. After all, the Fettiplaces could expect to entertain fifty people twice daily during the twelve days of Christmas.

Christmas Day itself was a minor feast at the time, so Elinor's main focus was the feast of the Epiphany on Twelfth Night, 6 January. The Fettiplaces entertained lavishly, though not as lavishly as some. Hilary Spurling records, for example, that on 6 January 1552 Sir William Petre of Ingatestone Hall in Essex fed over one hundred people at dinner. Between them they devoured sixteen raised pies, fifteen joints of beef, four of veal and three of pork (including a whole suckling pig), three geese, a brace each of partridge, teal and capons, six coneys (or rabbits), a woodcock and one dozen lark, a whole sheep and quite a lot besides.

Once Epiphany was out of the way, Elinor would have immediately started setting down food stocks again for the following winter, and this is something she would have continued to pay attention to throughout the ensuing year. We know she grew cabbages and herbs; she pickled samphire, cucumbers and artichokes for winter salads, with bright yellow broom buds for decoration. Like so many of us, Elinor would have spent time in the early part of the year making marmalade – though not marmalade as we think of it but a fruit paste or fruit leather rather like membrillo or the fruit leathers that you get in the Middle East. Once early summer arrived, she would have preserved soft fruit and plums. In early autumn she would have set to work on apples, pears, quinces, rosehips and barberries, making sure all was ready before the first frosts of November. In this she was greatly helped by the increasing availability of sugar, the first sugar refineries for cane sugar having opened in London some half-century earlier. Such fruits appeared on her dinner table as part of a last course – a dessert course – at dinner where those conserves, dried candied fruit, jellies, sweetmeats, fruit tarts and, of course, cheese and sweet wine were served to round off the meal.

Elinor's book does not contain many recipes for meat, presumably because the roasting and spit-roasting of meat was the thing that she assumed everybody knew. There is, however, a nice recipe for dressing a shoulder of mutton. The Cotswolds were famous for their mutton as they were the home of the great wool industry, and we must remember that much of Elinor's fortune came from wool. The recipe reads as follows:

Take a showlder of mutton and being halfe Roasted, Cut it in great slices and save the gravie then take Clarret wine and sina-mond [cinnamon] & sugar with a little Cloves and mace beatne and the pill [peel] of an oringe Cut thin and minced very smale. Put the mutton the gravie and these thinges together and boyle yt betweene two dishes, wringe the Juice of an oringe into yt as yt boyleth, when yt is boyled enough lay the bone of the mutton beinge first Broyld in the dish with it then Cut slices of limonds and lay on the mutton and so serve yt in.

Given the horrors of English vegetable cookery that lie ahead of us, it is interesting to see that when cooking spinach she says, 'boyle yt well with as little water as you can for the less water the sweeter your spinage wil bee.' She then proposes draining it, shredding it and adding that medieval staple verjuice (a sour juice usually made from unripe grapes or crab apples), butter and sugar. It's left to stew for a while, after which the yolks of two eggs and the equivalent of cream are beaten together and added. Once this is all heated through, it is served with a sprinkling of sugar.

February sees an attractive recipe for buttered loaves:

Take the top of the mornings milk, warme it, & put therto three or fowre spoonfulls of rose water, then run it [rennet], & when it is hard come take some flower, the yolkes of two eggs, the white of one, & some melted butter, & some sugar & some nutmeg, then temper [mix] all this together with the milk, & mould it up into loaves, then set them on papers, & so bake them, if you make five loaves as big as manchets [fine bread rolls], you must put half a pound of butter to them, when they are baked, straw [sprinkle] some sugar upon them, & so serve them.

Essentially, what you are doing here is making a stiff scone dough which you divide into several pieces and then season. Hilary Spurling suggests that you need a fairly hot oven (190°C/325°F/ gas mark 5) for about twenty-five to thirty minutes, and she points out that the leftovers make very good toast the next day.

The next staging post in the annual calendar was Shrove Tuesday, marking the beginning of Lent. Then, as now, dinner culminated in great mounds of pancakes and apple fritters, here spiced and flavoured with rose water and ale or sherry. Elinor also includes a recipe for a soufflé omelette filled with apple purée, which is quite delicious:

> Take the whites of eggs & beat them very well, then put to them some creame, & a little flower, & some cloves and mace beaten smale, & some sugar, & the pap [pulp] of two or three boiled apples & stir it well alltogether, then fry it in a frying pan with some sweet butter, & when it is half fried, break it in pieces like fritters & so fry it.

She also gives a recipe for straightforward apple fritters but flavours them with a little ground cloves, a little bit of mace and a teaspoon of ground ginger. In determining how thick to make the mixture, she rather charmingly says, 'put in enough flour as will make it thick enough to hang upon your apple'. There's also a reference to a spatula – a 'little wooden sputter' – to be used for turning the fritters.

Elinor was very keen on her garden, and she devotes considerable attention to setting out all manner of herbs and vegetables, then pricking out, earthing up, pruning, cutting and harvesting. She's very careful to note that this needs to be done on a regular basis so that fresh produce is available for as much of the year as possible. The planting year starts in April at the waning of the moon. Then comes midsummer when various pot herbs are planted to ensure a winter harvest. Radishes and artichokes feature, as do cucumbers and lettuce, all of which would have appeared in salads. And then there are mentions of various flowers such as violets which are candied or infused in syrups for decorative or medicinal use.

With the first of the spring milk, cheese makes an appearance, as does cheesecake. Elinor's recipe for the latter resembles to some extent the Yorkshire curd tarts we get today, though the flavouring is rather different. Essentially it comprises a pastry case filled with egg yolks, drained curds, butter, currants and then those characteristically medieval ingredients rose water and a little grated nutmeg. By the time it got to table it would have been richly adorned, probably with candied flower petals: a characteristically Elizabethan touch. Love of decorative food can be traced elsewhere in Elinor's book, particularly in her recipe for the sugar plate that was so loved by the rich of the period. She has two recipes for sugar plate sweets. One is a marbled confection of white, yellow and blue sugar plate; the other is a deep pink quince sugar paste, sweet and crunchy.

May was a month of major significance for the Elizabethans, the month that really marked the beginning of summer. There may have been pagan overtones to May Day and its maypole, but Protestant England still marked the day with feasting and dancing and, judging from the number of babies born nine months later, other things as well. One rather charming tradition was to wash your face in May morning dew to whiten the skin, a custom recorded some time later in Samuel Pepys's diary for May 1667:

After dinner my wife away down with Jane and W. Hewer to Woolwich, in order to a little ayre and to lie there to-night, and so to gather May-dew to-morrow morning, which Mrs Turner hath taught her as the only thing in the world to wash her face with; and I am contented with it.

This was also the time of year when fish started to come into their own. The Fettiplaces' land in Berkshire lay near the River Kennet, affording excellent river trout as well as freshwater crayfish. Elinor cooked her trout with green ginger and ale, which I think might have overpowered little brown trout from the river. However, I find her crayfish recipe for August thoroughly appealing. You take one hundred crayfish, a little water (two or three spoonfuls), the same amount of white wine, a blade of mace or a little nutmeg, a little salt and some lemon peel and let them simmer together. When they are cooked through put in half a pound of butter and keep shaking until the butter is melted, adding in a little more lemon juice to taste.

In May Elinor also started pickling or preserving some of the things I've already talked about: broom buds (yellow, plump and delicious-looking) and samphire, moving on to cucumbers, artichokes and green walnuts in July. I mentioned earlier that pickling became something of a Tudor obsession, and it's a measure of its popularity that Elinor should devote so much attention to it.

June saw the arrival of strawberries, barberries and gooseberries (the latter grown in Britain since at least 1275). One of Elinor's recipes that I thoroughly recommend if you are lucky enough to find a boiling fowl is to make a piquant sauce for it with gooseberries, stock, wine and butter, flavoured with herbs. Elinor also preserved raspberries and carnation cherries – that is, flesh-coloured cherries, as opposed to dark morello cherries – suspending them in sugar preserve, then drying them and putting them into boxes as a delicacy for the dessert course. She also includes a recipe for a cherry marmalade ('Ruf marmalad'), in which stoned cherries are cooked slowly in their own weight of sugar; I can assure you that it's delicious, provided that you don't caramelise the sugar by cooking it too quickly. Cherries and gooseberries, along with apricots, make a further appearance in recipes for fruit wine. Apricots were something of a new adventure for the Elizabethans, who favoured cooking them in pies as well.

Another new and fashionable thing that Elinor Fettiplace lists is a recipe for a cake big enough to be cut into well over one hundred slices. This could have made an appearance at one of the various celebratory feasts that punctuated the year in the countryside – perhaps harvest, haymaking, sheep-shearing or Twelfth Night. In Shakepeare's *The Winter's Tale* the Clown's shopping list suggests that preparations are being made for just such a cake for a sheep-shearing feast. He relates how he has been dispatched to buy three pounds of sugar, five pounds of currants, four pounds each of prunes and raisins, plus mace, dates, nutmeg and ginger. Thirteen pounds of dried fruit and three pounds of sugar and some nutmeg were the correct proportions for such a great cake, heavily spiced and faced up with sweetmeats. Elinor's recipe reads thus:

Take a peck [twelve and a half pounds] of flower, and fower pound of currance, one ounce of Cinamon, half an ounce of ginger, two nutmegs, of cloves and mace two peniworth, of butter one pound, mingle your spice and flowre & fruit together, put as much barme [fresh yeast] as will make it light, then take good Ale, & put your butter in it, all saving a little, which you must put in the milk, & let the milk boyle with the butter, then make a posset [a spiced drink of hot milk mixed with alcohol] with it, & temper the Cake with the posset drink, & curd & all together, & put some sugar in & so bake it.

Here is the recipe again, based on Hilary Spurling's modern and reduced rendering of it. Mix a pound and ten ounces of plain flour with half a pound of currants, two level teaspoons of cinnamon and one of ginger, a generous grating of nutmeg and four ground cloves. Make your posset by warming a glass each of milk and brown ale, about three-quarters of a pint in all, with two ounces of butter and around a teaspoon of sugar. Dissolve one ounce of fresh yeast or half an ounce of dried in a cup of the posset and add this to the mixture. Knead your dough till it comes together and turns springy. Leave it in a bowl with a cloth over the top to rise for an hour or so. When it is doubled, knock the dough down, knead it again and shape into two loaves. (At this point, Elinor would probably have made it into a huge round cake which she put on the floor of her bread oven.) Leave the dough for another forty minutes or so to rise again. Bake in an oven (an Aga is best) at gas mark 6 (200°C/400°F) for twenty-five to thirty minutes, and then bathe them with rose water and sugar when they come out of the oven.

The Petres at Ingatestone Hall, half a century earlier, fed as many as 120 reapers on their three farms – a similar number to those catered for by the Fettiplaces. It is recorded that in one week in August the Petres' workers devoured half a steer sent out ready carved from the kitchen, half an ox, four sheep and 162 gallons of beer. This would all have been taken out to the fields at midday, along with cakes and cheese and leather bottles containing beer. One of the dishes provided might have been the lettuce pie Elinor Fettiplace describes, where the best lettuce of the summer was quartered, boiled, buttered and mixed with hard-boiled egg yolks, raisins, currants, nutmeg, cinnamon, sugar and pepper. This would then be finished off with a syrup of claret, sugar and vinegar thickened with egg yolks. This is a rather medieval dish for Lady Fettiplace, but none the worse for that.

By now it was August and time for harvesting the grapes. Most years these would probably not have ripened fully and so were preserved green and made into a sort of fruit preserve which would have gone very nicely with meat. For September Elinor records three different ways of drying pears, one of which involves peeling and cooking the fruit without sugar in the strong yeast used for brewing beer before hardening it off in a bread oven. The result would have been none too attractive; hence, perhaps, Shakespeare's description of Falstaff at a low ebb as 'crest-fallen as a dried pear'. The playwright would have had rather more time for some of the preserved fruits Elinor took the time to prepare: red and white quinces, pears and apples (though a particular type of apple called the John apple, because it ripened around St John's Day (24 June), was said to keep two years and was thought to taste best when thoroughly shrivelled). Elinor reckoned to be able to cook her white pippins as late as Lent the following year and would have made use of various clever storage ideas of the time, such as sealing them in wax containers or hanging them up in pierced earthenware pots in the branch of a tree all winter. (We followed similar methods when I was young, for example spreading apples out on straw in a dry loft.)

Quite a few of Elinor's recipes involve applying modern techniques to traditional ingredients. Some, however, involve modern techniques and modern ingredients. Take syrup of tobacco, for example, which had a family connection for Elinor as she was related by marriage to Sir Walter Raleigh. Elinor's recipe reads:

> Take a quart of water & three ounces of tobaccho, put the tobaccho in the water, & let it lie a night & a day close covered, then boile it to reduce it from a quart to a pinte, then straine it, & put to everie pinte a pound of sugar, then put in the whites of three or fowre eggs finelie beaten, then set it on the fire, & when it boiles scum [skim] it, then cover it close, & let it boile, till it bee serop [syrup].

This is intended to be a soothing syrup for lung trouble, bad coughs and for loosening phlegm. Tobacco, a disinfectant as well as a narcotic and sedative, was used to deaden pain from toothache, cure worms and heal wounds; it could also be made into an alcoholic cordial. By now tobacco was being grown in England (one famous plantation was at Winchcombe in the Cotswolds where Elinor's brother-in-law Lord Chandos resided), but it remained enormously expensive, worth its weight in silver in West Country markets. Elinor would have smoked her tobacco in a silver pipe; the less well off would have used a walnut shell and a straw.

Another relatively modern ingredient was the sweet potato. Elinor's recipe for buttered sweet potatoes wouldn't be out of place at an American Thanksgiving dinner. However, her preserved sweet potatoes are, certainly to many palates, a rather stranger concoction. She recommends boiling them in water until they are very soft, and then peeling and slicing them before adding them to a syrup made with water, sugar, rose water and oranges. In fact, they taste quite nice prepared in this way.

November in Elinor's world was the month when livestock was butchered. It's clear from Thomas Tusser's *A Hundred Good Pointes of Husbandrie*, which went through many editions following its first publication in 1557, that although some stock had to be killed because the grass was starting to die back, many animals, including, of course, the breeding stock, were kept going on some form of silage so that there would be fresh meat throughout the winter. At this time of year, Elinor made her own sausages, black puddings and boiled haggis from the butcher's scraps. Nothing was wasted. Even a sheep's pluck – or heart, liver and lungs – could be used to provide bags for the boiled puddings, or the guts could be turned into sausage skins. She gives two consecutive, almost identical recipes for boiling calf's head and feet. Calf's feet are not that widely available nowadays and are probably more familiar in the cuisine of the West Indies. I have tried them and actually quite like them: they make a very sticky sort of stew. But I realise that the more squeamish might find them hard to take.

One rather nice recipe that Elinor includes for this season of the year is for My Lord of Devonshire's pudding. The Lord of Devonshire in question was Charles Blount, who was a favourite of the newly crowned King James I and a lover of Penelope Rich, daughter of the first Earl of Essex, Elizabeth's favourite who disgraced himself and was executed. It's worth giving the details here because it's a good recipe – and even nicer the following day. First you need to slice some white bread thinly and remove the crusts (Hilary Spurling recommends six to eight slices for six or more people). Then cut up a generous handful of stoned dates, a handful of raisins, a tablespoonful of currants and a little marrow from a marrow bone (if you can't get marrow, butter the bread instead). Lay some slices of bread in the bottom of your dish, then put a layer of the fruit and more bread on top, adding more fruit and bread in layers until your dish is full. Then take a pint of single cream (I actually prefer double cream for this recipe) and three eggs (yolks and whites), and a pinch each of cinnamon and grated nutmeg and three or four tablespoonfuls of sugar. Beat it all well together and pour it into the dish until it is full, dredge with more sugar and spices and then bake it for about three-quarters of an hour at about gas mark 3 (160°C/325°F).

And so we reach Christmas again and the end of Elinor's year. Hers is a delightful and evocative book, sadly now out of print, but you may still be able to find it in second-hand book-shops. I once sold a copy, complete with a picture of Elinor in her rather elegant late-Elizabethan, early-Jacobean dress, to someone in Papua New Guinea. I have often wondered whether the tribes there now ever feel inspired to recreate that sort of costume out of birds of paradise feathers.

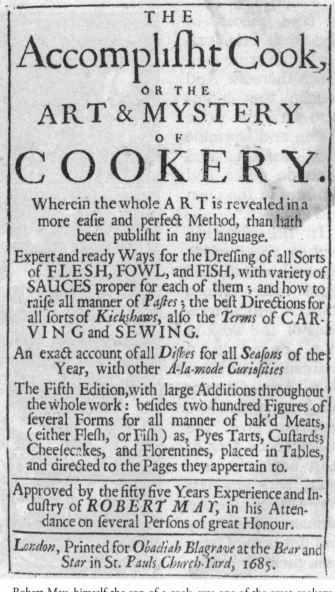

THE
Accomplisht Cook,
OR THE
ART & MYSTERY
OF
COOKERY.

Wherein the whole A R T is revealed in a
more eafie and perfect Method, than hath
been publisht in any language.

Expert and ready Ways for the Dreffing of all Sorts
of FLESH, FOWL, and FISH, with variety of
SAUCES proper for each of them ; and how to
raife all manner of *Paftes* ; the beft Directions for
all forts of *Kickfhaws*, alfo the *Terms* of CAR-
VING and SEWING.

An exact account of all *Difhes* for all *Seafons* of the
Year, with other *A-la-mode Curiofities*

The Fifth Edition, with large Additions throughout
the whole work : befides two hundred Figures of
feveral Forms for all manner of bak'd Meats,
(either Flefh, or Fifh) as, Pyes Tarts, Cuftards;
Cheefecakes, and Florentines, placed in Tables,
and directed to the Pages they appertain to.

Approved by the fifty five Years Experience and In-
duftry of *ROBERT MAY*, in his Attendance on feveral Perfons of great Honour.

London, Printed for *Obadiah Blagrave* at the *Bear* and
Star in St. *Pauls Church-Yard*, 1685.

Robert May, himself the son of a cook, was one of the great cookery
writers of the seventeenth century. His *The Accomplisht Cook*, first
published in 1660 when its author was already seventy-two years old, is
a wonderfully wide-ranging work that, among many other things,
includes no fewer than thirty-eight recipes for sturgeon.

CHAPTER 6

Double Cream and Pastry Galleons

The Early Stuarts

F ood fashions don't suddenly change when a new monarch comes to the throne, but it's nevertheless fascinating how often in English history the arrival of a new king or queen heralds new developments in the national cuisine. As we've seen, this was certainly the case with Eleanor of Aquitaine and Henry VIII, and it's also true of the first of the Stuart kings, James I.

Elizabeth I died, childless, in 1603. She remained a keen hunter almost until her death – only two years earlier she was recorded as hacking ten miles to a meet and then hunting all day. By the end, she had lost her appetite, was prey to melancholy and found it difficult to sleep, but the old imperiousness was still there. When Lord Burghley's son Robert Cecil foolishly suggested one evening that she really must go to bed, she gave him short shrift: 'Must! Is *must* a word to be addressed to princes? Little man, little man! Thy father, if he had been alive, durst not have used that word.' Capricious and vain though she could be (she was famously obsessed with whether her cousin Mary, Queen of Scots, was more beautiful than she was), her achievements were extraordinary, and her long reign was a period of relative stability and growing wealth.

Her successor, James VI of Scotland and I of England, could scarcely have been more different. He was ugly, with a tongue that was too big for his mouth so that he spat and spluttered when he talked and ate. He didn't like to wash much and when he had been hunting, he dabbled his hands in the blood of the killed stag and pulled out the umbles, or guts, himself, a job normally reserved for the huntsman. He would then wipe his hands on a napkin in a rather perfunctory way. He tends to get a poor press from historians, but it has to be admitted that he was a great survivor: when he assumed the English crown he had already managed to keep the throne of Scotland for thirty years during a time of upheaval and civil strife that culminated in the execution of his mother, Mary, Queen of Scots. He also had a reputation for learning, and was an author in his own right.

I have heard it said that James was the originator of the saying 'The golden road the Scotsman needs is the road that leads to London.' That may have been true in his case, but it is the foods that accompanied him on his trek in 1603 that are of interest to us. First and foremost among these were Scottish cattle. James was apparently fond of beef: there's even a story that, impressed with a particular cut that he was served, he knighted it with the words 'I dub you Sir Loin' (unfortunately, as with so many stories of this type, it's not true: sirloin actually derives more prosaically from the French word *surloigne*, 'above the loin'). After his accession to the English throne he established free trade between his new kingdom and the country of his birth, and, as a result, an increasing number of Scottish cattle were driven down south to the Home Counties, some no doubt being fattened up and sold on the way, others ending up in the London markets. These would have been the precursors of today's Highland cattle – considerably smaller but nevertheless very hardy.

It wasn't just meat that the Stuarts liked. The homelands of Clan Stewart around Dumfries and Galloway and Ayrshire were dairy-producing areas, and there seems to have been a passion for double cream which persists to this day among descendants of the Royal Stuart household clan. Cream had been used regularly in English cooking for centuries, but I have a theory (which will probably be shot down in flames) that until James I's time it was rarely eaten uncooked: it was either incorporated into cooked dishes or consumed in the form of clotted cream. It's certainly the case that today the British are very unusual in their love of uncooked cream. The Italians cook theirs, and the nearest the French get to raw cream is when they mix it with alcohol and sugar. I'm convinced that it was the Scottish influence of the Stuarts that changed the English palate.

Whatever the precise truth of the matter, it does seem to be that around this time we start finding more mentions of dishes where cream has simply been added rather than cooked. The now classic strawberries and cream (with sugar) started to make an appearance in Tudor times, but Andrew Boorde for one was wary of the combination, arguing that 'such bankettes [banquets] hath put men in jeopardy of they lyves'. Once the Stuarts were ensconced it seems to have become more common – though the strawberries the Stuarts would have known were more akin to the wild strawberry than the fruit we know today.

Another Scottish tradition that I'm fairly certain came south at this period was pudding, or rather pudding cooked in a pudding cloth in the way that Christmas pudding was prepared until we started using basins. In Scotland there's a traditional fruit pudding known as a cluty or cloutie dumpling (a cluty being a cloth), and this may be one of the ancestors of our modern puddings. Pudding cloths are very useful items, making it possible to convert flour, milk, eggs, butter, sugar, suet, marrow and raisins into a whole series of hot, filling and nutritious dishes with minimal trouble and cost. All you have to do, once you have securely tied the ends of the cloth around the pudding, is to plunge it into a boiling pot. You can even boil it alongside other things, leaving it to simmer for hours without having constantly to check it. Varying in texture and quality from light, moist, custardy-type puddings to substantial masses of heavily fruited oatmeal, boiled puddings became a mainstay of English cookery throughout society. You can understand why a Frenchman, Monsieur Misson, visiting England later in the century should have exclaimed, 'Ah, nothing more excellent than an English pudding.'

A further Scottish influence of the period can be found in the cold smoking of fish. Until Stuart times, the English tended either to hot-smoke their fish or salt it. The Scots, however, had perfected the process of cold-smoking it – in other words, treating the fish at quite a low temperature. I once wrote a rather lengthy article for *Decanter* magazine about the curing of fish and, in the course of my researches, discovered that there were 167 ways of curing fish in Scotland. These included one that must have been as rare as caviar: drying the fish on the rocks in the sun. I live in Scotland and I can just picture the housewife calling out to her son, 'Willy, get out there and bring in the fish: it's raining again.'

It's tempting, too, to attribute a whiff of a Scottish accent to some of the new types of biscuits that were starting to become popular in the early seventeenth century. The traditional biscuit could be a fairly tough affair – as the literal meaning of the word 'biscuit', 'twice baked', suggests, and as sailors often found as they munched their way through ship's biscuits. Gradually, however, it acquired different forms. Elinor Fettiplace, for example, has various recipes for what we would regard as sponge biscuits, involving flour, eggs, butter and sugar. In the early 1600s a new crunchy form of biscuit arrived based on flour, sugar and egg whites. It's generally credited as being a French invention, but given the traditional close contacts between France and Scotland (Mary, Queen of Scots was first married to the French dauphin), it seems quite possible to me that it came to England by way of Scotland. Certainly, Scotland has an honourable place in the history of biscuits, notably in its mastery of shortbread, of which the English Shrewsbury cakes, made from flour, sugar and butter and flavoured with spices, are a relative.

Scotland wasn't the only country to exert an influence on the English table of Stuart times. Italy retained the powerful attraction that it had enjoyed in Elizabeth's reign. And not just in matters of food. It is thanks to the Italians that the humble table fork finally made its way into English hands in the first decades of the seventeenth century.

Up until the early 1600s, English people had made do with spoons and knives. Forks were certainly known – they were used for taking meat out of the boiler and there were two-pronged forks for fishing out pickles – but the idea of using one to eat from a plate was anathema, even though the Italians had been using them since the late Middle Ages. Then in 1611 a young squire from Odcombe in the county of Somerset, Thomas Coryate, published an account of a grand tour that he had made of the Continent. *Coryate's Crudities* includes stories of drinking in Heidelberg and watching women act on the stage in Venice (a shocking notion for English people at this time), and then notes the Italian predilection for the fork:

> I observed a custome in all those Italian Cities and Townes through the which I passed, that is not used in any other country that I saw in my travels, neither doe I thinke that any other nation of Christendome doth use it, but only Italy. The Italian and also most strangers that are commorant [resident] in Italy, doe alwaies at their meales use a little *forke* when they cut their meate. For while with their knife which they hold in one hand they cut the meate out of the dish, they fasten their *forke*, which they hold in the other hand upon the same dish, so that what-soever he be sitting in the company of any others at meale, should unadvisedly touch the dish of meate with his fingers from which all at the table doe cut, he will give occasion of offence unto the company, as having transgressed the lawes of good manners, in so much that for his error he shall be at least brow-beaten, if not reprehended in wordes. This forme of feeding I understand is generally used in all places of Italy, their *forkes* being for the most parte made of yron or steele, and some of silver, but those used only by Gentlemen. The reason of this their curiosity is, because the Italian cannot by any meanes

indure to have his dish touched with fingers, seing all mens fingers are not alike cleane. Hereupon I my selfe thought good to imitate the Italian fashion by this forked cutting of meat, not only while I was in Italy, but also in Germany, and oftentimes in England, since I came home: being much quipped [mocked] for that frequent using of my *forke*, by a certain learned Gentleman, a familiar friend of mine, one M. *Laurence Whitaker*, who in his merry humour doubted not to call me *furcifer* [fork-bearer], only for using a *forke* at feeding, but for no other cause.

Coryate was initially laughed at for his love of this foreign affectation, and was satirised on the stage as the 'Fork-carrying traveller'. However, he was unfazed and the fork gradually gained in popularity.

The earliest known English silver fork, bearing the London hallmark for 1632, now resides in the Victoria and Albert Museum. On the handle are engraved the crests of two naval families, Manners and Montagu of Boughton, so the fork was presumably the property of John Manners, afterwards 8th Earl of Rutland, who in 1628 married Frances, daughter of Edward, Baron Montagu of Boughton. It is very simple in design: a plain bar of silver divided at one end into two prongs. It is not known precisely how it came to be the property of John Manners or what happened to it over the next 250 years. All we know is that in the early twentieth century it was bought from a London dealer and that it may at one time have been kept among the cutlery at Haddon Hall in Derbyshire.

The rise of the fork coincided with a period when kitchen

equipment in general was improving. Cauldrons had existed for a long time, but now larger ones, made of iron or brass, and often lidded, made an appearance, allowing whole meals to be cooked in a single operation. The meat would go in the body of the main cauldron to boil, along with vegetables tied up in net bags and fixed to the side, and puddings either in cloths or in light wooden bowls which remained bobbing around on the surface of the liquid in the cauldron until they were thoroughly cooked. Poultry, game or meat stews were placed in earthenware vessels with butter, herbs and spices, the lid then being sealed in place with strips of pastry and the vessel immersed in a cauldron for several hours to cook. Jugged hare also probably made an appearance around this time: it was cooked in a cauldron within a jug, as the name suggests.

Along with better cauldrons came a wider availability of porringers, similar to saucepans, of iron, bronze, tinned copper or even silver and supported over the fire on a gridiron or a trivet, a small three-legged iron stand. The word 'saucepan' is first recorded in 1686. In larger establishments the coal- or charcoal-heated stove, in addition to a normal fireplace, was also becoming more common – ideal for sauces, preserves and various main dishes. As for ovens, these, in the form of the traditional bread oven, were becoming ever more popular in less grand establishments. Not only did they allow for bread to be baked at home, but they could also accommodate pies and pasties, which required a lower temperature and could therefore be put in after the bread had been removed. A pie might consist of a pastry case filled with a custard of egg and milk poured from a long-handled wooden custard filler. Once placed in the oven, the door would be sealed in place again and the contents left to bake.

Even the spit that we so associate with medieval cooking underwent a transformation. In the Middle Ages the boring and uncomfortable task of turning the spit had been left to some poor greasy youth, known, not surprisingly, as the turn-spit. Then dogs were pressed into action, as described by John Caius, founder of Caius College, Cambridge:

> . . . there is comprehended under the curs of the coarsest kind a certain dog in kitchen service excellent. For when any meat is to be roasted, they go into a wheel where they, turning about with the weight of their bodies, so diligently look to their business, that no drudge nor scullion can do the feat more cunningly.

By the reign of James I, people were going one better and starting to use clockwork jacks to turn the spit before the fire. These jacks were mounted on the sides of the fireplace and could turn the spits at a slow and uniform rate. New shallow dripping pans with sloping bases which conducted the fat into a central well began to become fashionable. Then a long spoon could be taken, a basting ladle, and the fat poured back over the meat to keep it moist and tender.

A further mechanical advance came rather later in the century with the invention of the steam digester, ancestor of the pressure cooker, by the French physicist Denis Papin. He demonstrated the first one in 1679, showing how it could turn the hardest of bones as soft as cheese without the need of water or other liquor. Pigeons, seasoned as if to be baked in a pie, could effectively be stewed in their own juices.

The range of food available continued to expand in early Stuart times, as existing trade routes were consolidated and new merchant ventures, such as the East India Company, embarked upon. Ingredients that we have already encountered – such as sugar and spices – became ever more readily available and ever more affordable. The continuing popularity of that combination of sugar, spice and dried fruit is shown in dishes such as White Pots, which were the precursors of our bread and butter pudding. Banbury cake was often eaten at wedding feasts, its outer layer of plain dough sandwiching a rich filling of dough mingled with currants. The great cakes of the Middle Ages, mentioned later by people like Elinor Fettiplace, were now enclosed in tin rings, which made them much more manageable and easier to prepare for special occasions and wedding feasts. It was around this time, too, that modern gingerbread appeared. Up until the late sixteenth century gingerbread had tended to be a solid paste of highly spiced breadcrumbs and wine with added ginger, but gradually a lighter version became popular, involving flour, treacle, ginger and cinnamon. Regional variations developed, too: it's not that much of a jump from gingerbread to the oatmeal-based parkin that you still find in Yorkshire today.

It's also striking how many types of fruit and vegetable became more widely available. The Dutch market gardeners who had arrived in Tudor times were now opening up gardens in north and north-west London, their wares, such as lettuce and other salad crops, being widely sold in the city's markets. It has been estimated that they were employing around 1,500 people by the middle of the century. Covent Garden market, which was rebuilt by Inigo Jones in 1630 for the fourth Earl of Bedford, started to sell fruit and vegetables in 1656; its rapid success can be gauged from the fact that within ten years people were

Sr John *Tradescant Senr*

A new world of food Various new fruit and vegetables arrived in England in the sixteenth and seventeenth centuries, from tomatoes to potatoes. John Tradescant the Elder (*c.* 1570–1638) played an important role. A keen gardener and plant collector, he worked for the Earls of Salisbury at Hatfield House and for Edward, 1st Baron Wooton, before establishing his own garden in Lambeth. He is now inevitably most associated with the genus of plants named after him, *Tradescantia*, the spiderwort, but he also successfully grew melons, among other exotic fruit and vegetables.

Tudor tableware Pottery became a little more sophisticated in the late sixteenth and seventeenth centuries. This plate shows the Tower of London, painted with considerable artistic licence. An inscription in praise of Elizabeth I encircles it.

Stuart tableware A blue and white tin-glazed earthenware dish, probably made to commemorate the marriage of a shoemaker.

The arrival of the fork Two early examples of English forks, one of them with a handle that could be folded for travelling, along with a spoon dating from the same period. Forks had been used in Italy for some time, but were a novelty in England when the traveller Thomas Coryate described them in his 1611 work *Coryate's Crudities*.

A Tudor kitchen An early-twentieth-century photograph of the kitchen at Canons Ashby in Northamptonshire. The house was built in the 1550s and has been little altered since Georgian times. The dairy stands next to the kitchen; close by is a winter parlour where the family could gather together in cold weather – a reflection of the move away from the communal living of medieval times.

Kitchen improvements A charcoal-burning stove in the kitchens of Henry VIII's palace at Hampton Court.

A city tavern Taverns became increasingly popular in the later sixteenth and seventeenth centuries. One of the drinkers in this rather crude woodcut is indulging in one of the period's other great fads: pipe-smoking.

The marriage feast at Bermondsey Joris Hoefnagel's painting of around 1570 shows how rural Bermondsey still was in Elizabethan times. Note the cooks hard at work in the kitchen.

The nation's capital Although London was a sizable city by the 1570s when this map was prepared, there were still plenty of green spaces, and while much of its food supply had to be brought in from elsewhere, fruit and vegetable gardens abounded, particularly around Kensington to the west and Battersea to the south.

Urban living Things were rather more crowded in the City itself, as this view of the coronation procession of King Edward VI in 1547 suggests. The canons of St Paul's complained on more than one occasion about the stench and filth caused by nearby slaughterhouses, and the food on sale was often far from fresh.

Tudor dining William Brooke, 10th Baron Cobham (1527–97), with his second wife Frances, six of his children and his sister-in-law Johanna. Fresh fruit was regarded with a degree of trepidation by some people in Tudor times, but clearly not here.

Charles I at dinner The king is shown with his wife Queen Henrietta Maria and son Charles, Prince of Wales (later Charles II), attended by courtiers and servants; other servants are carrying dishes in and out of the hall through the arch on the right. In the background, onlookers gather behind a balustrade.

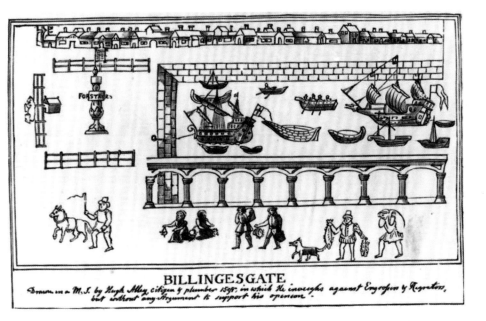

BILLINGESGATE

Drawn in a M.S. by Hugh Alley, citizen & plumber 1598; in which he inveighs against Engrossers & Regrators, but without any Argument to support his opinion.

Elizabethan trade Billingsgate market in London. By Elizabeth I's reign the market sold not only fish but 'victuals and fruit' as well. English ships ventured ever further afield in the last decades of the sixteenth century and by the 1600s were establishing trading posts as far away as India. The earliest reference to tea by an Englishman comes in a letter dated 27 June 1615 from an agent of the East India Company working in Japan.

The arrival of the pineapple John Tradescant's son, also called John, travelled as far as Virginia in his botanical wanderings. He is generally credited with being the first person to cultivate pineapples in England; the stone pineapples that decorate Lambeth Bridge commemorate his achievement.

A Stuart cook Robert May worked for various noble famili and also wrote one of the best cookery books of the seventeent century, *The Accomplisht Cook.* A fascinating snapshot of Stuart taste, it covers a vast range of recipes, from a complicated Spanish Olio Podrida to roast e

A Stuart foodie Sir Kenelm Digby (1603–65), as portrayed in around 1650 (circle of Sir Anthony van Dyck). The recipes he included in *The Closet of the Eminently Learned Sir Kenelme Digbie Kt. Opened* reflect the range of his social contacts: the Countess of Newport's Cherry Wine and the Sweet Drink of My Lady Stuart among them.

complaining about the amount of rubbish it was generating. It remained a focal point for fruit and vegetables in London until the latter part of the twentieth century. What was on offer was impressively diverse. Gervase Markham's *The English Huswife* of 1615 assumes that the housewife of his day will have ready access to everything from asparagus and spinach to a vast array of herbs and edible flowers to oranges, lemons, capers and olives.

Country estates increasingly set up kitchen gardens, with hot beds and glasshouses for the cultivation of exotic fruit and vegetables. These would have been stocked with the sort of items to be found in the apothecary John Parkinson's 600-page book of gardening, *Paradisi in sole paradisus terrestris*, which he dedicated to Charles I's wife Henrietta Maria in 1629: a mix of familiar and the distinctly novel, such as red beetroot (first mentioned in John Gerard's *Generall Historie of Plantes* of a few years before), potatoes and even melons, of which Parkinson notes, 'This Countrey hath not had untill of late yeares the skill to nourse [nurse] them up kindly.' The sheer variety grown by lovers of horticulture in the Stuart era is sensuously celebrated in Andrew Marvell's poem 'The Garden':

> What wond'rous life in this I lead!
> Ripe apples drop about my head;
> The luscious clusters of the vine
> Upon my mouth do crush their wine;
> The nectarine and curious peach
> Into my hands themselves do reach;
> Stumbling on melons as I pass,
> Insnar'd with flow'rs, I fall on grass.

The concluding stanza of the poem reminds us both of the elaborate design of grand seventeenth-century gardens and of the continuing importance of herbs to everyday cooking. Here Marvell describes a sundial made from flowers and herbs, cleverly punning on the word 'time' – or 'thyme':

> How well the skilful gard'ner drew
> Of flowers and herbs this dial new;
> Where from above the milder sun
> Does through a fragrant zodiac run;
> And, as it works, th' industrious bee
> Computes its time as well as we.
> How could such sweet and wholesome hours
> Be reckoned but with herbs and flowers!

*

While the poor as always faced a hand-to-mouth existence, it does seem to be the case that the early Stuart period brought with it greater consumption – and, in particular, greater consumption of meat – across a broader spectrum of society. This, combined with a growing population, placed pressure on farm and grazing land. Something had to be done, and the solution adopted was to increase the acreage available by draining fenland and turning it over to agriculture. English need turned to Dutch expertise, and an engineer by the name of Cornelius Vermuyden, who was born in Zeeland in Holland and, therefore, had unrivalled knowledge of the art of keeping water at bay, was brought to England to drain the marshy Canvey Island and was then employed by James I to drain land in Windsor Park. James's son Charles I subsequently engaged Vermuyden to drain Hatfield

Chase. Payment, as was so often the case with the Stuarts, proved problematic. Vermuyden's fees were always in arrears, although he was fobbed off with a knighthood in 1629.

His major undertaking, however, was the Great Level project, which began in the 1630s and involved draining tens of thousands of acres of land around the Wash. The Earl of Bedford, in partnership with a consortium of Dutch and English investors, backed the venture. Local hunters and fishermen opposed it, and they fought a guerrilla war against the Dutch workforce that had been recruited, sabotaging the windmills, pumps and camps of the would-be drainers. In the end brutal economics won the day: farming was more profitable than eels. There was a hiatus during the Commonwealth period, but draining started again under Charles II. Vermuyden was also involved in an early scheme to drain Sedgemoor in Somerset. In 1685 the newly improved land provided a suitable surface for the battle that saw the defeat of the Duke of Monmouth, the eldest illegitimate son of Charles II.

The greater prosperity enjoyed by some seems to have been accompanied at court by greater spectacle – and greater vulgarity. James lavished affection and largesse on his favourites, such as George 'Steenie' Villiers, the first Duke of Buckingham, and became involved in murky scandals, such as the Overbury affair, which involved adultery, wrongful imprisonment and possible murder. At the height of the case James even sought to bring undue pressure to bear on the Chief Justice of the King's Bench, Lord Coke (pronounced 'cook'). Coke has nothing really to do with this book, but I can't resist repeating the food-related anecdote told about him. It is said that one night when in bed with his wife, Lady Elizabeth Hatton, the humble-born Coke put his hand on her belly and felt the stirring of a baby. 'Flesh in the pot?' he asked. 'Aye,' his wife replied, 'or else I would not have married a cook.'

As well as being a place of intrigue, James's court was a place of display. His wife Anne of Denmark is thought to have brought a love of lavish entertainment with her from her native country, and pageants, masques and play-acting became hugely popular, offering a perfect opportunity for members of the court to appear fairly scantily clad in extremely extravagant set pieces of theatre. The Banqueting House in Whitehall was built to house this type of festivity, and it must have grated on the more puritanically minded people of the age. What I find interesting is the contrast between the lascivious James enjoying the hedonism that he wouldn't have got away with in his native Scotland, and the pragmatic James who supported new colonies and trade routes.

The food served on such occasions took up the theatrical theme. Pastry galleons had cannons that could be fired (afterwards the ladies were given eggs filled with rose water to throw at each other to remove the stench of the gunpowder – shades of the gilded young of the twentieth century throwing bread rolls at each other). Pies could be loaded with frogs that would jump out when the pie was opened, causing the ladies to squeal and scream in mock terror, until they were rescued by their admirers. There was even something called marzipan bacon, which consisted of alternate strips of red and white marzipan. If you want to try this yourself, you need eight ounces of ground almonds, four ounces of caster sugar, two tablespoons of rose water, red food colouring, and cornflour or icing sugar for dusting. Mix the almonds and the sugar with the rose water to make a stiff paste. Divide in two and knead a few drops of the red food colouring into one half. Using either cornflour or icing sugar to dust the paste, roll each piece into a rectangle about three-eighths of an inch (10 mm) in thickness and cut into four strips. Starting with a white slab, the fat, build up alternate red and white layers to form a miniature piece of streaky bacon from which thin slices can be cut lengthwise, allowed to dry and then served – hopefully to the delight of all.

Contemporaries were swift to raise an eyebrow at the extravagant levels eating and drinking could reach. In his play *The City Madam* (1632), for example, Philip Massinger writes:

> Men may talk of country-christmases, and court-gluttony,
> Their thirty-pound butter'd eggs, their pies of carps' tongues,
> Their pheasants drench'd with ambergris, the carcases
> Of three fat wethers bruis'd for gravy to
> Make sauce for a single peacock . . .

The satirical poet George Wither went even further, while also providing us with a fascinating insight into the sheer range of what was on offer:

> The diet they are grown unto of late,
> Excels the feast that men of high estate
> Had in times past; for there's both flesh and fish,
> With many a dainty new-devised dish.
> For bread they can compare with lord and knight,
> They have both ravel'd [wholemeal], manchet [best quality
>   wheat bread], brown and white
> Of finest wheat; their drinks are good and stale [old and
>   strong],
> Of perry, cyder, mead, metheglin, ale,

Of beer, they have abundantly. But then
This must not serve the richer sort of men;
They with all sorts of foreign wine are sped,
Their cellars are oft fraught with white and red . . .
Then if their stomachs do disdain to eat
Beef, mutton, lamb, or such-like butcher's meat;
If that they cannot feed of capon, swan,
Duck, goose, or common household poultry; then
Their store-house will not very often fail
To yield them partridge, pheasant, plover, quail,
Or any dainty fowl that may delight
Their gluttonous and beastly appetite.
So they are pamper'd whilst the poor man starves!
Yet that's not all; for custards, tarts, conserves,
Must follow too, and yet they are no let [hindrance]
For suckets [sweets of candied fruit], march-panes, nor for
   marmalet,
Fruit, florentines, sweet sugar-meats, and spices
(With many other idle fond devices)
Such as I cannot name, nor care to know.
And then besides the taste, 'tis made for show;
For they must have it colour'd, gilded, printed,
With shapes of beasts and fowls, cut, pinch'd, indented
So idly, that in my conceit 'tis plain,
They are both foolish and exceeding vain.
And howsoe'er they of religion boast,
Their '*belly is the god*' they honour most.

Paradoxically, the period that saw all this banqueting and masquerading also witnessed the continuing retreat of the great and the good into their own dining rooms, where they could eat their meals in privacy and peace. This move away from the 'let's all eat together' atmosphere of the large dining hall started in late medieval times. Henry VIII would often dine with just a few invited guests and high-ranking courtiers. His daughter Elizabeth went further, almost invariably eating apart from others and only going to the great hall for the entertainments that followed the meal or on high days and holidays. Yeomen warders would bring the dishes to the hall, they would be tasted for poison, and then while some food was taken to the diners, some was carried through to the queen's private dining room. Nor were royalty the only people to behave in this way. At Ingatestone Hall in the 1550s Sir William Petre had his own private, panelled 'dining parlour' next to the hall. James I, with his love of lavish entertainment, kicked against the trend a little, but his son Charles, who was a more private person, rarely dined in public. A painting of the royal family at table by the artist Gerrit Houckgeest, dating from 1635, shows them dining alone, attended by courtiers and servants, with others admitted to watch them eating having to stand behind a balustrade. Later in the century, Charles's rather more flamboyant son had many of his meals in private, but did condescend to dine in public three days a week.

I can't leave the topic of entertainment in early Stuart times without touching briefly on the world of the theatre. Of course, some plays were performed before the monarch, but the vast majority of the 2,500 or so plays written between 1590 and 1642 (when the theatres were closed by Parliament) were written for ordinary play-goers, who flocked in their thousands to the theatres that sprang up on the south bank of the Thames in London. And we have a very good idea of the 'fast food' they ate. Research into the history of the Globe theatre reveals that the audiences snacked on walnuts, hazelnuts, plums and cherries. They also ate crabs, oysters (a very cheap food at the time), cockles, mussels, winkles, whelks, haddock and possibly even sturgeon. Those who could afford seats in the galleries might, in addition, have munched on such imported foods as dried figs, peaches and raisins. Those standing before the stage might have taken fruit pies in with them. Recent newcomers to England such as tobacco, pumpkin and marrow were consumed, too. Vast quantities of hazelnut shells have been excavated from the site of the Globe, though it's not entirely clear whether they were discarded by theatre-goers or placed there as a sort of absorbent floor for those in the yard to stand on.

Theatricality of a rather different order can be seen in some of the cookery books of the Stuart period, for this era saw the beginning of the rise of the celebrity chef – the curse of the modern age. Up until now, books about food had been either household books compiled by women who wanted to record or share their recipes, or household management books in the manner of *The Forme of Cury*; now we really start to see books written by professional chefs. Later in the century we will encounter Patrick Lamb, master cook to Charles II. But for now, let us meet Robert May, author of *The Accomplisht Cook*.

May was born in 1588, the son of a cook in the household of Sir William and Lady Dormer of Wing in Buckinghamshire. The Dormers had been yeomen farmers in Oxfordshire and Buckinghamshire since the Middle Ages and had gradually made their way up the social ladder. Robert Dormer was raised to the Earldom of Caenarvon in 1628 and died fighting for Charles I in 1643.

Robert May appears to have been born on the estate at Wing and undoubtedly started his apprenticeship there. At the age of ten he was sent to Paris where he remained for five years, studying not just cooking but also the French language, as well as printed books and manuscripts of cookery. On his return he was bound over to Arthur Hollinsworth of Newgate market, a London cook and a member of the Worshipful Company of Cooks (the city livery guild that protected the status and trade within the capital). Owing to the destruction of the Cooks' Company records during the Blitz, all we know about Hollinsworth is that he was cook to the Grocers' Company and to the Star Chamber, both of which jobs must have provided him with experience of fairly lavish and elaborate feasting that he could pass on to May. The Grocers' Company was a wealthy city guild, and the Star Chamber, named after the star-spangled ceiling of the room in which it met, was the most powerful and secret court of the land, which convened twice a week during the legal term at the Palace of Westminster.

After he completed his apprenticeship May returned to Wing to work alongside his father. His new employer was Elizabeth, Baroness Dormer, the daughter of Anthony Browne, 1st Viscount Montagu, who was a staunch Roman Catholic.

After the death of Lady Dormer in 1631 he went to work for the Castlehavens – another Catholic family – possibly briefly serving the unfortunate 2nd Earl, who managed to get himself accused of rape and sodomy by his wife and who wound up being beheaded on Tower Hill. At the outbreak of the Civil War, May was working for Viscount Montagu, and during the Civil War he was in the service of Elizabeth, Countess of Kent, living at Wrest Park in Bedfordshire, with a house at Whitefriars in London. The countess was a philanthropist who fed seventy to eighty poor people a day, as well as ministering to their ills. The fact that May worked for Catholic families gives an interesting slant to his recipes because, although these people would have had quite a lot of money, they would have been constantly fined and excluded from the court scene. May's recipes, then, tend not to be grandiose ones. They are, however, interesting and unusual, and cover a wide variety of subjects that would be less likely to be found from a court chef.

The Accomplisht Cook was first published in 1660 when May was already seventy-two years old, and it ran to several editions, the last being in 1685, just three years before the glorious and bloodless revolution of William and Mary. It's free from the plagiarism that mars so many other cookery books (in part, because few were published during the Commonwealth period), and has a freshness all its own. It's also very revealing of the sort of food that would have been enjoyed by the well-to-do in the mid seventeenth century.

Here's one of May's more ambitious recipes: a dish that was popular at the court of James I and was called an Olio Podrida – basically an incredibly complicated stew imported from Spain. Appropriately enough, May calls this one an 'Olio Royale':

Take a wrack of Mutton, and a Knuckle of Veal, put them a boiling in a Pipkin of a Gallon [a gallon pot], with some fair water, and when it boils, scum [skim] it, and put to it some salt, two or three blades of large Mace, and a Clove or two; boil it to three pints, and strain the meat, save the broth for your use and take off the fat clean.

Then boil twelve Pigeon-Peepers [young pigeons], and eight

Chicken-Peepers, in a Pipkin with fair water, salt, and a piece of interlarded Bacon, scum them clean, and boil them fine, white and quick.

Then have a rost Capon minced, and put to it some Gravy, Nutmegs, and Salt, and stew it together; then put to it the juyce of two or three Oranges, and beaten Butter, &c.

Then have ten sweet breads, and ten pallets [palates] fried, and the same number of lips and noses being first tender boil'd and blanched, cut them like lard, and fry them, put away the butter, and put to them gravy, a little anchove, nutmeg, and a little garlick, or none, the juyce of two or three Oranges, and Marrow fried in Butter with Sage-leaves, and some beaten Butter.

Then again have some boil'd Marrow and twelve Artichocks, Suckers [?], and Peeches finely boil'd and put into beaten Butter, some Pistaches boiled also in some wine and Gravy, eight Sheeps tongues larded and boiled, and one hundred Sparagus boiled, and put into beaten Butter, or Skirrets [a type of water parsnip].

Then have Lemons carved, and some cut like little dice. Again fry some Spinage and Parsley, &c.

These foresaid materials being ready, have some *French* bread in the bottom of your dish.

Then dish on it your Chickens, and Pidgeons, broth it; next your Quaile, then Sweet breads, then your Pullets, then your Artichocks or Sparagus, and Pistaches, then your Lemon, Poungarnet, or Grapes, Spinage, and fryed Marrow; and if yellow Saffron or fried Sage, then round the center of your boiled meat put your minced Capon, then run all over with beaten butter, &c.

Presumably it's the lemons, pomegranates, grapes, saffron and almonds here that give the dish its Spanish aspect. Various national cuisines are evoked in the course of the book, dishes being presented, for example, 'in the French fashion' or 'in the Italian fashion'.

A large number of recipes in *The Accomplisht Cook* deal with venison – a reminder of just how important hunting remained throughout so much of English history. I've already mentioned James I's less than sanitary activities when killing a stag, but it's worth emphasising that the passion for hunting went well beyond the court. Deer can be very destructive, biting away tree bark and nipping out the new shoots. Hunting therefore fulfilled a dual role: preserving crops and vegetation and providing meat for the table. It was also a popular community exercise, not just the preserve of the gentry. Deer remained part of the living larder throughout the seventeenth century, and James's wealthier subjects were able to keep their own deer parks, ranging considerably in size according to status and wealth.

James himself was, as I have indicated, an avid hunter as well as a superb horseman (he was responsible for bringing the first Arab horses to England). Indeed, when his ministers got wind of the Gunpowder Plot to blow up Parliament in 1605 they had to wait until James returned from hunting before they could make any decisions. If he announced his intention to chase after quarry in a particular part of the country the land-owner was required to stop hunting in that area until he arrived, and he alienated many by reinforcing the old forest laws. He became something of a tourist attraction, drawing great crowds of people whenever he set off on the chase. 'God's wounds! I shall pull down my britches and they shall see my arse,' he is said to have threatened on one occasion.

In *The Accomplisht Cook*, May includes recipes for both red deer and fallow deer. Here, for example, is his suggestion for baking a 'fallow-dear':

Take a side of venison, bone and lard it with great lard as big as your little finger, and season it with two ounces of pepper, two ounces of nutmeg, and four ounces of salt; then have a pie made, and lay some butter in the bottom of it, then lay in the flesh, the inside downward, coat it thick with seasoning, and put to it on the top of the meat, with a few cloves, and good store of butter, close it up and bake it, the pye being first basted with eggs, being baked and cold, fill it up with clarified butter, and keep it to eat cold. Make the paste as you do for red deer, course drest through a boulter [sieve], a peck and a pottle of this meal will serve for a side or half hanch of a buck.

Hunting, as in earlier eras, extended beyond deer, and May's book includes mentions of such game birds as herons, gulls and bitterns. What fascinates me is that it's clear from what he writes that it was common not to slaughter a bird as soon as it was captured but to keep it and fatten it. Here is what he has to say about herons:

Herns [*sic*] are nourished for two causes, either for Noblemens sports, to make trains for the entering their hawks, or else to furnish the table at great feasts; the manner of bringing them up with the least charge, is to take them out of their nests before they can flie, and put them into a large high barn, where there is many high cross beams for them to pearch on; then to have on the flour [floor] divers square boards with rings in them, and between every board which should be two yards square, to place round shallow tubs full of water, then to the boards you shall tye great gobbits of dogs flesh, cut from the bones, according to the number which you feed, and be sure to keep the house sweet, and shift [change] the water often, only the house must be made so, that it may rain in now and then, in which the hern will take much delight; but if you feed her for the dish, then you shall feed them with livers, and the entrals of beasts, and such like cut in great gobbits.

In some cases, as with godwits, knots, grey plovers and curlews, the birds were force-fed in the way that the French force-feed geese today for *pâté de foie gras*:

Take fine chilter-wheat, and give them water thrice a day, morning, noon, and night; which will be very effectual; but if you intend to have them extraordinary crammed fowl, then you shall take the finest drest wheat-meal, and mixing it with milk, make it into paste, and ever as you knead it, sprinkle into the grains of small chilter-wheat, till the paste be fully mixt therewith; then make little small crams thereof, and dipping them in water, give to every fowl according to his bigness, and let his gorge be well filled: do thus as oft as you shall find their gorges empty, and in one fortnight they will be fed beyond measure, and with these crams you may feed any fowl of what kind or nature soever.

Clearly, this fattening of wild birds was a regular occurrence and I'm fascinated by the attention that May gives this whole activity – and by the charming details he includes, such as the rather lovely thought that the roof should leak so that the heron can preen itself in the rain. Incidentally, the somewhat gruesome reference to feeding gobbets of dog flesh to captive herons reminds us that at this time it was commonly believed that dogs carried the plague and so they were often killed during the outbreaks that peppered the early part of the seventeenth century. It's ironic when you consider that the dogs might very well have killed the rats whose fleas did carry the plague and therefore might have prevented it.

Another strange thing to be found in Robert May's book is his numerous recipes for sturgeon, that strange prehistoric fish which dates back nearly 200 million years. I found this very surprising until I remembered that even when I was a small child sturgeons could still be found in England – my father was once sent some that had been found in one of the rivers. In the seventeenth century, sturgeon seems to have been quite commonplace in such great rivers as the Severn, the Avon and the Thames, and could be found as far north as Scotland. Indeed sturgeons' remains have been found in middens excavated at Westminster Abbey. Of the twenty-five different types of sturgeon, only one is still found in British waters. Today they're a royal prerogative, but the way that May writes about them suggests that he did not regard them as anything out of the usual.

The Accomplisht Cook contains a total of thirty-eight recipes for sturgeon, including the following one for preserving the fish to keep all year:

Take a Sturgeon, draw it, and part it down the back in equal sides and rands [strips], put it in a tub into water and salt, and wash it from the blood and slime, bind it up with tape or packthred, and boil it in a vessel that will contain it, in water, vinegar, and salt, boil it not too tender; being finely boil'd take it up, and being pretty cold, lay it on a clean flasket [shallow basket] or tray till it be through cold, then pack it up close.

The predominant spices used for cooking sturgeon seem to be ginger, cloves, mace, nutmeg, ginger and pepper, and the accompanying sauces are usually made with white wine or orange juice. The dish is frequently served with lemon, which was very much the flavour of the time. One recipe for marinating sturgeon calls interestingly for four gallons of rape oil – one thinks of rape oil as a very modern phenomenon. In another recipe for making forcemeat of sturgeon, May tells you to mince your sturgeon raw with a good fat eel, a blade of mace, pepper and salt and some sweet herbs, or if you want you could stuff it with carrots or turnips. That suggestion of using carrots and turnips for stuffing must have been considered very recherché at the time. There are also several sturgeon pies of various shapes and sizes to be eaten hot or cold. Given the sheer number of recipes here, I can't help wondering whether May didn't on occasion think, 'Oh, my God! Not sturgeon again. I suppose I'll have to find yet another way of cooking it.'

Salmon features less prominently in *The Accomplisht Cook*, in part perhaps because it was regarded as a very common fish (if you remember, in the Middle Ages, London apprentices refused to eat it more than three times a week). There is, however, one recipe that I particularly like, which I featured on *Two Fat Ladies* and put in the second *Two Fat Ladies* book, where it received much acclaim. In fact, I probably had more letters about this dish than I have had about any other. It is salmon cooked with oranges. For this, you take two pounds of salmon, using a cut, cleaned and skinned, taken from just behind the head. You line your cooking dish with slices from three peeled oranges, place the salmon on top, seasoning it with two teaspoonfuls of grated nutmeg and a little salt, and then pack the remaining orange slices over the top and round the sides. Pour on the juice of one orange and a little red wine, bring to the boil, cover and simmer for fifteen minutes or until the salmon is just cooked. Serve with triangles of toasted bread. It is one of the nicest ways of cooking salmon that I know.

Eels feature prominently in May's book, and it's interesting to see just how much he has to say about them. One particularly appealing dish is roasted eel:

> Cut it three inches long, being first flayed and drawn, split it, put it on a small spit, & roast it, set a dish under it to save the gravy, and roast it fine and brown, then make sauce with the gravy, a little vinegar, salt, pepper, a clove or two, and a little grated parmisan, or old *English* cheese, or a little botargo [salted and dried grey mullet roe]; the eel being roasted, blow the fat off the gravy, and put to it a piece of sweet butter, shaking it well together with some salt, put it in a clean dish, lay the eel on it, and some slices of oranges.

This is effectively an eel kebab, and it really works. There is a particular restaurant in Chinatown in London where they prepare eel in a similar way, and very good it is too.

I've already mentioned pies in the context of May's recipes

for sturgeon, and it is remarkable just how many he includes of all shapes and sizes and with all sorts of different fillings, from game to fish to sweet. Many are accompanied by illustrations that show you how to decorate pies, presumably so that your diners, faced with a whole range of different pies at once, could tell at a glance which was a sweet pie, which had meat, which had fish, and so on. To go with the sweet tarts there are recipes for custards and buttered egg dishes sweetened with various juices and sugar. One rather curious custard contains cream and almonds and the eggs of carp or pike, beaten well into the mixture until it thickens. I can't say I have ever tried making a custard with fish roe – but then this was presumably meant to be a savoury sauce.

It is difficult to distinguish in May's book which dishes come from which part of the long period over which he cooked, but some of them are obviously from earlier in his career and, rather satisfyingly, given what I said earlier about the impact of the Stuarts on English cooking, some of them are clearly influenced by Scottish cuisine. There's even a recipe for haggis. Haggis could be found on medieval menus, but then it was made with pork stuffed into a bladder rather than the fillings we now associate with the dish. May gives quite complicated instructions for making it. He also talks about how to make 'subtleties', including several of the ones I've already mentioned, such as ships that fire cannons, harts with 'wine' blood, and pies with leaping frogs. These clearly date from before the time of the Civil War, since May rather ruefully notes, 'These were formerly the delight of the Nobility, before good House-keeping had left *England*, and the Sword really acted that which was only counterfeited in such honest and laudable Exercises as these.'

These more sophisticated and ambitious recipes appear along-side some very simple ones, for example for porridge or sausage. As May says in his introduction, 'In the contrivance of these my labours, I have so managed them for the general good, that those whose Purses cannot reach to the cost of rich Dishes, I have descended to their meaner Expences.' Regrettably the intro-duction also displays a flash of ego that is all too familiar in the celebrity chef, and there's rather a lot of name-dropping – for example he evokes the names of Lord Montagu, Lord Lumley, Lord Dormer and Sir Kenelm Digby, 'at whose Feet I prostrate these Endeavours'. In fairness, though, this sort of fawning attention was a hallmark of the age.

Little is known about Robert May's last days. He doesn't appear to have married and we assume that he died around 1664. He deserves to be remembered.

By the King.

A PROCLAMATION

FOR THE

Suppreſſion of Coffee-Houſes.

CHARLES R.

Hereas it is moſt apparent, that the Multitude of Coffee-houſes of late yeares ſet up and kept within this Kingdom, the Dominion of Wales, and the Town of Berwick upon Tweed, and the great reſort of Idle and diſaffected perſons to them, have produced very evil and dangerous effects; as well for that many Tradeſmen and others, do therein miſ-ſpend much of their time, which might and probably would otherwiſe be imployed in and about their Lawful Callings and Affairs; but alſo, for that in ſuch Houſes, and by occaſion of the meetings of ſuch perſons therein, divers Falſe, Malicious and Scandalous Reports are deviſed and ſpread abroad, to the Defamation of His Majeſties Government, and to the Diſturbance of the Peace and Quiet of the Realm; His Majeſty hath thought it fit and neceſſary, That the ſaid Coffee-houſes be (for the future) Put down and Suppreſſed, and doth (with the Advice of His Privy Council) by this His Royal Proclamation, Strictly Charge and Command all manner of perſons, that they or any of them do not preſume from and after the tenth day of January next enſuing, to keep any publick Coffee-houſe, or to utter or ſell by retail in his, her, or their houſe or houſes (to be ſpent or conſumed within the ſame) any Coffee, Chocolet, Sherbett or Tea, as they will anſwer the contrary at their utmoſt perils.

And for the better accompliſhment of this his Majeſties Royal Pleaſure, His Majeſty doth hereby will and require the Juſtices of Peace within their ſeveral Counties, and the Chief Magiſtrates in all Cities and Towns Corporate, that they do at their next reſpective General Seſſions of the Peace (to be holden within their ſeveral and reſpective Counties, Diviſions and Precincts) recall and make void all Licenſes at any time heretofore Granted, for the ſetting, or Retailing of any Coffee, Chocolet, Sherbett or Tea. And that they or any of them do not (for the future) make or grant any ſuch Licenſe or Licenſes to any perſon or perſons whatſoever. And His Majeſty doth further hereby declare, That if any perſon or perſons ſhall take upon them, him or her, after his, her or their Licenſe or Licenſes recalled, or otherwiſe without Licenſe, to ſell by Retail (as aforeſaid) any of the Liquors aforeſaid, That then the perſon or perſons ſo offending, ſhall not onely be proceeded againſt upon the Statute made in the fifteenth year of His Majeſties Reign (which gives the Forfeiture of Five pounds for every moneth wherein he, ſhe or they ſhall offend therein) but ſhall (in caſe they perſevere to offend) receive the ſevereſt puniſhments that may by Law be inflicted.

Given at Our Court at *Whitehall* this Nine and twentieth day of *December* 1675. In the Seven and twentieth year of Our Reign.

God ſave the King.

LONDON,

Printed by the Aſſigns of *John Bill* and *Chriſtopher Barker*, Printers to the Kings moſt Excellent Majeſty. 1675.

The first coffee house in England was opened in Oxford in 1650 and the new drink achieved rapid popularity. Charles II, however, clearly regarded coffee houses with great suspicion, and in this proclamation he criticises both those who 'do therein mis-spend much of their time' and those who gather there to spread 'Malitious and Scandalous Reports'. His words had no effect whatsoever, and coffee houses continued to thrive.

CHAPTER 7

Coffee and My Lord Lumley's Pease-Porage

War and Peace in the Seventeenth Century

International trade boomed under the Stuarts. James I came from a dynasty that had always been land-poor and which had sought to compensate for this through the wealth that could be generated by active trade with various European powers – Venice and Russia to name but two. He brought this trading zeal with him when he moved from Edinburgh to London, and his reign saw a corresponding expansion in trading ventures: the establishment of the colonies in North America, the agreement with the city guilds to set up plantations in Ulster, and the further development of the East India Company and the Muscovy Company, established the previous century. He even allowed the disgraced Sir Walter Raleigh out of prison to voyage to South America in search of the gold of El Dorado, executing him on his return when he failed to deliver the goods.

The East India Company played a crucial role in the trade boom. Anxious to compete with the newly established Dutch

East India Company, which was actively trading in spices – in particular, pepper, nutmeg and mace – with the Spice Islands, James instructed Sir Thomas Roe to visit the Mogul emperor Nur-ud-din Salim Jahangir and negotiate a commercial treaty that would give the Company exclusive rights to take up residence and build 'factories' (trading posts) in Surat and other areas. In return the Company offered to provide the emperor with goods and rarities from the European market. The mission was highly successful and a trading post was set up at Surat in 1612, followed by further factories in Madras (1639), Bombay (1668) and Calcutta (1690). By 1647 the Company had twenty-three factories, each under the command of a factor or master merchant and governor. Over time the aggressive East India Company pushed out competition from the Portuguese and the Dutch, laying the foundations of Britain's involvement in India and indeed the early British Empire.

You may ask why I'm devoting quite so much attention to a corporate joint stock company when I should be talking about food, but the point is that while the East India Company brought back everything from raw silk to indigo, much of what it carried was food related: spices and pepper from Java, cloves from the Moluccas, mace and nutmeg from the Banda Islands, and, in time, such strange new items as tea. As a result, for at least the next 200 years the Company and the national diet were to be inextricably linked.

New items of food continued to arrive in England. The first bunch of bananas seen in England arrived from Bermuda in 1633; they were hung up to ripen and be admired in the shop of a herbalist named Thomas Johnson in Snow Hill in London. Pineapples also made an appearance. The stone pineapples on

Lambeth Bridge in London celebrate John Tradescant the Younger, who was said to have been the first person to grow them in England. Some decades later, Charles II's gardener John Rose was also successfully cultivating them.

Foreign trade brought with it the establishment of English settlements and colonies, and, perhaps not surprisingly, there are tantalising glimpses of Stuart English cuisine still found today many thousands of miles away from the mother country. America is the classic example. The reigns of James and Charles I saw the migration of many thousands to the newly formed American colonies, a large proportion of them Puritans seeking religious freedom abroad. These included a significant retinue from East Anglia and Lincolnshire, and I have a strong suspicion that it was these people who introduced to New England such dishes as chowder and cobbler that we now regard as being quintessentially American. The North American clam chowder has much in common with Stuart fish and oyster stews, particularly the use of crushed biscuits (now generally sprinkled on top; once used to thicken the stock) and the occasional use of pork. Cobblers, the sweet or savoury dishes adorned with what are basically lumps of scone dough cut into circles and placed around the edge, were eaten in seventeenth-century England (though not called by that name) and are today popular all over the north-eastern states of America and indeed throughout a lot of the rest of America. (Incidentally, when I was young I was told that it was the Puritan strain in America that explained why so many people got divorced and married again, the argument being that divorce was preferable to adultery. I'm not sure whether that's true and, if it is, I'm not sure whether that's quite what the founding fathers had in mind.)

For the sailors who made all this travel and trade possible, the longer journeys now posed dietary problems. From Stuart times until Nelson's day and beyond, a seaman's diet consisted almost entirely of salt meat (usually salt pork) and hardtack – biscuits made out of flour and water and dipped into the juice of whatever was being boiled up on board. Each seaman was calculated as requiring a daily diet of one pound of biscuits, one pound of salt meat and a gallon of ale. This was hardly wholesome fare. Because salt attracts salt, the salted meat, unless sealed in barrels, became so saline that it needed extensive washing to get rid of the worst of the congealed salt. Rats were another threat to meat storage, and the biscuits were invariably full of weevils. It's true that ships also carried vegetables and kegs of butter, but these were difficult to keep fresh, and such cheese as was carried was usually one of the very hard Suffolk or Essex varieties made from the thinnest of skimmed milk. So tough could it prove that sailors sometimes used it for carving buttons. The ordinary sailor, then, was confronted with salty meat, weevil-infested hardtack, rancid fat, beer that rapidly turned sour, and water that was rarely fresh. In a diary entry for 25 May 1660, Samuel Pepys records talking to the Duke of York about the diet of seamen, and discovering that they ate nothing but peas, pork and boiled beef.

None of this provided much opportunity for the ship's cook to show his skills. Generally the best dish he could muster was lobscouse, made of ship's biscuits crumbled into a stew of salt meat. It became particularly associated with the port of Liverpool, hence the reason why Liverpudlians are often known as 'Scousers'. Or he might cook the similar-sounding loblolly ('lob' is a dialect word for the bubbling of food while it is boiling), a thick oatmeal gruel. Loblolly was later known as burgoo, and it's a reflection of the cosmopolitan nature of the sea that burgoo should be related to the Turkish bulgur (wheat). Somewhat later there was the wonderful-sounding dandyfunk, which sounds like a weed but was actually a sort of cake made from broken sea biscuits baked with fat and molasses. The sailor Edward Barlow records a particularly disgusting meal at Cadiz on Christmas Day 1661, when the crew had to eat beef that had been pickled for at least two years and some stinking oil and butter.

For the officers and perhaps also the warrant officers, things were rather better. Ships had for a long time carried live animals on board to provide meat, milk and eggs for the senior members of the crew, and now we start to see the shipping on board of turkeys. Turkeys, even those of the seventeenth century, provided quite a lot of meat, and in those days they were more robust and less nervous than the ones we know. They survived well at sea on a limited diet of grain, and just one could serve an entire officers' mess.

As a naval official, Samuel Pepys was very concerned about the generally poor quality of the diet on offer, writing:

Englishmen, and more especially seamen, love their bellies above everything else, and therefore it must always be remembered, in the management of the victualling of the navy, that to make any abatement in the quantity or agreeableness of the victuals is to discourage and provoke them in the tenderest point and will sooner render them disgusted with the King's service than any one other hardship that can be put upon them.

He took responsibility for the naval diet, recommending among other things that the standard weekly rations for each man should include a gallon of beer, two pounds of beef and a pound of bread.

Such a limited diet inevitably had an impact on the health of the crew, and scurvy, caused by vitamin C deficiency and characterised by bleeding gums, was rife. It seems curious to me that nobody noticed that French and Spanish seamen of the time, who carried large quantities of onions and garlic with them, were much less afflicted by scurvy that English sailors. There was scurvy grass, which had been known in England since medieval times, but unfortunately this was too fragile to be suited to a long sea voyage.

The power of citrus juice in combating scurvy was recognised by the 1590s, but it was the James Lancaster expedition to the East Indies in 1601 that demonstrated once and for all how effective it could be. One of James Lancaster's captains had brought with him bottles of lemon juice, and three spoonfuls were administered to every man on board one of Lancaster's fleet of four ships each morning, with dramatic results. Those who drank it remained healthy; those on the other three ships succumbed to scurvy. The newly formed East India Company was so impressed that it arranged for supplies of lemon water to be taken on all its ships. Unfortunately the navy didn't follow suit. Lancaster himself remained convinced that scurvy was caused by a diet of salt meat, while one naval physician maintained that it was a consequence of salt beef and pork, an overflowing of black bile, the corruption of unwholesome air – and idleness. Consequently the navy as a whole continued to suffer for many decades to come.

The East India Company's profits soared in the early Stuart period. Its third voyage alone made a return of over 200 per cent. If you want a sense of just how much profit was being generated you should go to the guildhall of the felt makers, Girdlers' Hall in the City of London, and see the carpet that once belonged to Robert Bell. Robert Bell was one of the first investors in the East India Company and rose quickly through its ranks. His carpet, woven in India in 1630 in deep blues and reds, is eight metres long – a truly stunning sight. Bell's rather beautiful house in Wimbledon still stands.

There's a certain irony in all this. It was, as we have seen, James I who was so instrumental in encouraging the expansion of foreign trade. Yet many of those who grew rich on it, and in particular the London merchant class, were devout Puritans who were to be the backbone of opposition to royal authority in the 1630s and 1640s after the death of James and the accession of his son Charles I. Charles's authoritarian approach, his constant need for money to pay for his court and his wars, and his distinctly un-Puritanical attitude to religion were scarcely calculated to appeal to such people. Within years of his accession he was at loggerheads with an increasingly vociferous and disaffected parliamentary opposition. The royal court consumed what the merchant class provided; the merchant class despised them for it.

The English Civil War, when it finally came in 1642 with Charles's raising of the royal standard at Nottingham, was protracted and bloody, resulting in the deaths of tens of thousands of people. It was accompanied and followed by a period of austerity: theatres were closed in the same year the Civil War broke out, and maypoles banned by Parliament two years later.

Food – particularly festive food – suffered as well. The Puritans opposed all forms of public feasting and we know that among other things they banned the eating of plum pudding on Christmas Day (but only then – there's no evidence that it was frowned upon otherwise). The consumption of wine also declined during this period, not in this case because the Puritans disapproved but because the Navigation Act of 1651, which was designed to curb Dutch trade, had the side effect of reducing the importation of French and German wines. Ale or beer or, in the West Country, cider – all very popular drinks – filled the void. Had Charles's nemesis, Oliver Cromwell, gone to America as he once planned to, until prevented at the last minute by writ of *ne exeat regno* for non-payment of taxes, how different history might have been.

One rather curious food book that has come down to us from this period is entitled *The Court and Kitchen of Elizabeth Commonly Called Joan Cromwell the Wife of the Late Usurper, Truly Described and Represented*. It appeared in 1664, just a few years after Oliver Cromwell's death. In fact, there is no evidence that Elizabeth Cromwell, as she was actually called, had anything to do with the book. The daughter of Sir James Bourchier, who was a prosperous fur dealer and leather dresser, she was no author but a loyal and faithful wife to her husband Oliver, in his roles first as a country squire, then as military leader and finally as Lord Protector. She remained very much in the shadows, but we get some idea of what she must have been like from Samuel Cooper's miniature of her painted in the 1650s, which shows a rather fashionable woman with a quirk of amusement in her face and a contented expression. Oliver was devoted to her; in one letter after the battle with the Scots at Dunbar in 1650 he writes to her, 'Thou art dearer to me than any creature.' However, he doesn't seem to have written to her as often as she would have liked, and in the one letter that survives from her she remonstrates mildly with him, showing in the process an approach to spelling that can only be described as cavalier:

I should rejoys to hear your desire in seing me, but I desire to submit to the provedns of God, howping the Lord, houe hath separated us, and heth oftune brought us together agane, wil in heis good time breng us agane, to the prase of heis name. Truly my lif is but half a lif in your abseinse . . .

Inoffensive though Elizabeth clearly was, she seems to have attracted the attention of Royalist pamphleteers, and *The Court and Kitchen of Elizabeth* turns out to be a bit of anti-Cromwellian propaganda. It suggests that she was guilty of bribery and corruption, that she was mean and – rather bizarrely – that she kept cows in St James's Park to make her own butter. Clearly a serious charge.

Indirectly, though, the book does tell us a bit about food during Cromwell's time. Most of the fare is pretty everyday stuff: simple meat dishes, plain sausages and beef olives (thin slices of meat containing stuffing). Some of the dishes are more interesting. One quite ambitious one, for example, is headed 'How to make Scotch Collops of Veal'.

Take a Fillet of Veal, cut it out into very broad slices, fat and lean, not too thick; take eight Eggs, beat them very well with a little salt, grate a whole Nutmeg, take a handful of Thyme

209

and strip it, take a pound of Sawsedges, half a pint of Stewing Oysters, the largest to be had, wash and cleanse them from the Gravel: then half fry your Veal with sweet Butter, then put in your Sawsedges and Oysters, then take a quarter of a pound of Capers, shred them very small; three Anchovis, dissolve them in white Wine and fair water, so put in your Eggs, shred Capers, and Anchovis, Butter and Spice, and mingle them, and strew them in the Pan upon the Veal and Oysters; serve it with Sippets, with a little fresh butter, and vinegar, and Limons sliced, and Barberies, with a little salt. You must have a care to keep the meat stirring, lest the Eggs curdle with the heat of the fire.

It is a curious sort of a dish and, with its anchovies and capers, foreshadows aspects of Georgian cuisine. Another dish, called a marrow pudding, suggests that, if she ever ate it, Elizabeth must have been a fairly formidable woman, because this is intended to be eaten at breakfast:

Take a pound of the best Jordan Almonds, blanch them, beat them fine in a stone or wooden Mortar (not in brasse) with a little Rose-water, take a pound of fine powder Sugar, a penny Loaf grated, grated Nutmeg, a pint of Cream, the Marrow of two Marrow-bones, two grains of Ambergris; mingle them altogether with a little Salt, fill the Skins [pig's intestines], boyl them gently as before.

The only other recipe in this book that I find interesting is one which involves boiling a capon with cardoons, mushrooms, artichokes or oysters – and that's simply because, as anybody who knows me knows, I have a passion for cardoons. This alone would be sufficient to make me view the Cromwells sympathetically, whether or not Elizabeth had anything to do with the book that bears her name. But there is another reason for regarding the couple favourably, too: Cromwell was the man who invited back the Jews, who had been expelled from England in 1290. The Jewish community duly re-established itself, one of its early members, a certain Jacob, opening a coffee shop in Oxford in 1650. In time, they thrived. I have to say that the cardoon did not.

The period of relative austerity under Cromwell came to a sudden end with the restoration of the monarchy in 1660, and in terms of conspicuous consumption the floodgates opened. The theatres reopened, now with women on the stage as well as men. Dress became flamboyant again. High days and holidays were marked with celebration rather than solemnity. And food received a new boost, even if Charles II did spend more of his money on his mistresses than on his stomach. The Stuarts certainly got around: most of the noble families of England are connected in some way either to a mistress of Charles I or a male lover of his father James. Charles II also rarely paid his servants, with the result that on one occasion they resorted to stealing all his linen, leaving him with not a single clean tablecloth or a shirt to his name.

Charles's wife was the Portuguese Catherine of Braganza, and while I can't claim that she left a strong mark on English food, I have a strong suspicion that she may have made a contribution to English drink through her advocacy of an expensive new beverage, tea. Of course, the drink itself predated her by many centuries. The Chinese had drunk tea since time immemorial, although curiously Marco Polo does not appear to have come across it in the course of his travels in the thirteenth century. In the course of the sixteenth century, however, we start finding it mentioned in European literature, as it was encountered first by Portuguese and then Dutch traders in the East Indies. The earliest reference to tea by an Englishman is probably in a letter from a Mr Wickham, an agent of the East India Company, writing from Firando in Japan on 27 June 1615 to a Mr Eaton, an officer of the Company who was residing in Macao, asking for 'a pot of the best sort of Chaw'. In Mr Eaton's subsequent accounts of expenditure he mentions three silver porringers to drink 'chaw' in. Even then supplies didn't really start arriving in significant quantities in England (at first from Java) until the middle of the century. In James I's reign it retailed at anything between £6 and £10 a pound – a princely sum – and the first, very small, teapots were made.

And then in September 1658 the following advertisement appeared in the *Mecurius Politicus*:

> That excellent and by all Physitians approved China Drink called by the Chineans Tcha, by other nations Tay, alias Tee, is sold at the Sultaness Head, a cophee-house in Sweetings Rents, by the Royal Exchange, London.

Around the same time, Thomas Garraway, an English tea dealer and founder of the well-known Garraway's Coffee House, made great claims for the quality and virtue of leaf tea in his *An Exact Description of the Growth, Quality and Vertues of the Leaf Tea*:

> . . . in respect of its former scarceness and dearnesse, it hath been only used as a Regalia in high Treatments and Entertainments, and Presents made thereof to Princes and Grandees.

Garraway offered his teas to the public at prices that ranged, according to the quality of the leaf, from sixteen to fifty shillings a pound.

Tea, then, was very much around when Catherine of Braganza arrived in London with her husband in 1660. But availability and popularity are two very different things, and I suspect that it was Catherine, born into a nation that actively traded with the East, who, having encountered and enjoyed tea in Portugal, popularised it when she arrived in England: we certainly know that she liked it and that she drank it in the Chinese fashion, without milk. I know that people tend to feel sorry for her, married to a husband who was a serial adulterer. But I'm not so sure. There are reports that she danced very high and very prettily and that Charles, who was undoubtedly a licentious adulterer, was actually very fond of her. If it was her advocacy of tea that contributed to its popularity, then it shows that even in the frivolous Restoration court, where all the beautiful women vied for the attentions of the 'Merry Monarch', the queen was still an influence. It is interesting to think that a marriage that is made so little of historically should have had such an impact on the trade in tea and on our national love of it.

I also have a suspicion that, through Catherine of Braganza, English food made a mark on Portuguese cuisine. Some years after Charles II's death in 1685 she returned to her native country to act as regent for the young Pedro II. She then ran the country very efficiently until her own death in 1705. My conjecture is that those delicious little custard tarts you so often find in Portuguese cafes are actually of English origin, that Catherine liked them and that she took them back to Portugal with her. England was famous for its custard and its custard tarts, and very similar ones, known as Maids of Honour, were served to Henry VIII at Hampton Court. The pastry you find in the Portuguese version is, in my opinion, the sweet ruff puff pastry of the Tudor court. I'm sure I'll receive horrified letters about this, but I am fairly convinced that it's true. All I can say is 'lucky old Portuguese' – they kept the recipe and we didn't.

Whatever Catherine of Braganza may or may not have done, there's no doubt that English food itself changed after the Restoration. Numerous contemporary accounts attest to this. And perhaps the most compelling is the diary of Samuel Pepys, which he kept assiduously between 1660 and 1669. The first indication of change comes in February 1660, some months before the Restoration, when Pepys notes street protests against the Rump Parliament, which represented the last gasp of the Commonwealth. Then, as now, parliamentarians when left entirely to their own devices seemed to become pretty corrupt, and the Rump Parliament soon made itself unpopular. By 11 February it was clearly on its way out, and Pepys records that during his walk between St Dunstan's, which is on Fleet Street, and Temple Bar (perhaps a ten-minute walk), he saw fourteen bonfires, while in King Steet he noticed seven or eight with people standing around drinking and cooking rump steaks tied upon sticks. There was a spit turning with a rump tied to it, which was being basted as it cooked. Pepys wrote:

Indeed it was past imagination, both the greatness and the suddenness of it. At one end of the street you would think there was a whole lane of fire, and so hot that we were fain to keep still on the further side merely for heat.

I love the thought that the celebration of a disgraced Parliament took the form of barbecuing rump steaks in the street for all to enjoy.

Shrove Tuesday that year was marked by a very good dinner with friends, at which was served a leg of veal and bacon (presumably the veal was larded with bacon), two capons and sausages and fritters, with an abundance of wine. But fasting in Lent was obviously still the norm because Pepys made a Lenten resolution not to drink any strong drink for at least a week. Yet when we come to Good Friday two years later in 1663, Pepys, while noting that dinner consisted simply of sugar-sops (bread, sugared and spiced) and fish, also confesses that this was 'the only time that we have had a Lenten dinner all this Lent'. Things had clearly become much more relaxed between the dying days of the Commonwealth and the early years of the Restoration. This was the era that witnessed the beginnings of the slow retreat of fish from its former central place in the English diet.

Pepys's diary shines a fascinating light on the age, and Pepys himself is a fascinating and rather appealing figure. Born in 1633 and educated at the grammar school in Huntingdon and St Paul's School in London (he was therefore on hand to witness the execution of Charles I in 1649), he went on to Magdalene College, Cambridge, before becoming secretary and domestic steward to Edward Mountagu in the Palace of Whitehall. For most of his life he served as a secretary of the Admiralty where he prospered, eventually earning some £300 a year. He was very much a man of his age, enjoying cock fighting, bear baiting and that great vice of the Restoration period, wenching. His wife had her own admirers but remained faithful to him, though frequently infuriated by his behaviour. In their verbal jousting, she gave as good as she got, but the marriage lasted until her death in 1669. They never had children.

Food crops up again and again in Pepys's diary, and he clearly loved it. In 1658 he underwent a horrendous operation to remove a bladder stone the size of a tennis ball (only slightly smaller than a modern one), and he chose to celebrate his survival by throwing a dinner party. Given the hazards of the operation he can hardly be blamed. The surgeon who performed the operation managed to operate successfully on thirty people that year, but his first four patients the following year all died. Pepys's 'stone' feast was lavish and expensive. Among the dishes served were braised neat's (cow or ox) tongues of which Pepys was apparently very fond, cooked with cinnamon, cloves and red wine and served with brioche – a new fashion that I suspect had come into the country with Charles I's French wife Henrietta Maria and had then trickled its way down to people of Pepys's standing. He also served a fine lamprey pie. (When I made a lamprey pie to celebrate Pepys's anniversary we had real trouble finding lampreys and eventually had to resort to buying them from a fishing shop where they had been frozen to be used as bait. Even so, they were quite delicious.) A few years later, in 1666, when the Great Fire of London was raging, Pepys not only buried important documents and valuables in his garden to protect them, but also a Parmesan cheese – an interesting display of priorities.

Much of the food that Pepys records in his diary is ordinary, everyday stuff and is interesting to us for precisely that reason. On 1 January 1660, at a time when he wasn't particularly well off, he returned home to find that his wife (surprise, surprise, given the season) had dressed the remains of a turkey, burning her hand in the process. On the 2nd he received a dozen bottles of sack from his employer Lord Mountagu, but ate only bread and cheese. Things got better on the 3rd when he had some friends to dine and they had a piece of beef with cabbage and a collar of brawn. There are various references to offal – sheep's head and brawn and the cheaper cuts of meat. And then, on 6 January, he's back to turkey again, eating it in the form of cold turkey pie. He then went out to a tavern where 'the venison pie was palpable beef which was not handsome.'

Pepys often ate out at taverns. The food he found there might include poached eggs, oysters and various cuts of meat. But taverns didn't just provide ready-cooked food. In August 1660, for example, Pepys records coming home by water from Greenwich, going to Fish Street, buying a lobster, meeting up with a couple of friends who had bought a piece of sturgeon and then going on to the Sun Tavern in Fish Street to eat them. This and other references lead one to assume that there were various taverns where you could turn up with your own food which they would cook for you and, presumably, charge a fee for doing so. I can't quite imagine their equivalents today reacting well if you said, 'Look, I've got a lobster and a piece of sturgeon. Would you cook them for me?' Apart from anything else, in nine out of ten cases they wouldn't know what to do with them.

Taverns thrived in Restoration England. Apart from beer and ale they served sherry, German wines, cider from Kent and all sorts of food: anchovies, scallops, neat's tongue, gherkins, mutton chops, pigeons, hams, puddings and pies. At some of them – for example the Pillars of Hercules Tavern in Fleet Street

– diners would sit at a long table and share the food. The bill was divided up according to what you ate. Somebody in the 1970s and 1980s tried this approach, opening an establishment based on similar principles in Jermyn Street, and it was a huge success. I used to go there often and you would mark the wine bottle at the beginning and the end of your sojourn and eat whatever was on the menu.

Certain standard foods turn up over and over again in entries in Pepys's diary. Oysters, for instance. At the end of November 1660 when everybody was rather downhearted at the office because of problems with money for paying the seamen, he says:

> I having two barrels of oysters at home, I caused one of them and some wine to be brought to the inner room in the office, and there the Principal Officers did go and eat them. So we sat till noon, and then to dinner, and to it again in the afternoon till night. At home I sent for Mr Hater [a friend of his], and broke the other barrel with him, and did afterwards sit down discoursing of sea terms to learn of him.

Clearly oysters were a nice, handy – and cheap – daytime snack. It's recorded that Charles II's contemporary Louis XIV adored them. No wonder he had so many mistresses.

Neat's tongue is another common motif in the early diary entries: Pepys was only twenty-eight at the time and clearly having to live on a budget, and this sort of fare was inexpensive. Nevertheless, on festive occasions he was able to push the boat out a bit. The Christmas period of 1660 sees references to a collar of beef and minced pie and also to a chine of beef which he had sent some friends and was then invited round to eat. In 1662, four years after his stone operation, there is another great celebration:

> I had a pretty dinner for them, viz., a brace of stewed carps, six roasted chickens, and a jowl of salmon, hot, for the first course; a tanzy [tansy, by this period usually a sweet, pancake-like dish] and two neats' tongues, and cheese the second; and were very merry all the afternoon, talking and singing and piping upon the flageolette [a type of flute].

By January 1663 things were obviously looking up in the Pepys household, for the quality of the food rises. Now they serve oysters as a first course and then a hash of rabbit and lamb and 'a rare chine of beef':

> Next a great dish of roasted fowl, cost me about 30s, and a tart, and then fruit and cheese. My dinner was noble and enough. I had my house mighty clean and neat; my room below with a good fire in it; my dining-room above, and my chamber made a withdrawing-chamber, and my wife's a good fire also . . . After dinner the women to cards in my wife's chamber, and the Dr and Mr Pierce in mine, because the dining-room smokes unless I keep a good charcoal fire, which I was not then provided with. At night to supper, had a good sack posset and cold meat, and sent my guests away about ten o'clock at night, both them and myself highly pleased with our management of this day; and indeed their company was very fine, and Mrs Clerke a very witty, fine lady, though a little conceited and proud. So weary, so to bed. I believe this day's feast will cost me near 5l [£5].

April saw the Pepyses entertaining again. This time they had:

> . . . a fricassee of rabbits and chickens, a leg of mutton boiled, three carps in a dish, a great dish of a side of lamb, a dish of roasted pigeons, a dish of four lobsters, three tarts, a lamprey pie (a most rare pie), a dish of anchovies, good wine of several sorts, and all things mighty noble and to my great content.

They then went for a walk in the park where they saw the king and Lady Castlemaine, one of the king's current mistresses, and returned home to find the 'house as clean as if nothing had been done there to-day, from top to bottom which made us give the cook 12d. a piece, each of us'.

This may be food at its slightly more expensive, but it's still fairly common fare. However, dotted through the diary are references to rarer items, such as bloat herrings, presumably bloaters, and a jar of gherkins that someone had bought his wife as a present. And then there are mentions of items that really would have seemed novel to people of the early Restoration period. Among them was tea, which is first recorded in Pepys's diary on 25 September 1660 ('I did send for a cup of tee (a China drink) of which I had never drank before'). And then there was coffee.

Coffee, originally from Ethiopia, arrived in England rather later than tea. In 1637 John Evelyn recorded that a Greek student at Balliol College, Oxford, was drinking it, and the first coffee house in England was, as I have already mentioned, opened by a Jew named Jacob in Oxford in 1650. The first coffee house in London, in St Michael's Alley, was opened in 1652 by a Greek, Pasqua Rosée. It was a smash hit and imitators sprang up all over town, though it has to be said that the coffee on offer was of very variable quality: coffee is difficult to roast and one is forever coming across references in letters and in diaries about people drinking burnt brown coffee. Soon coffee houses were becoming important business centres. The newspapers of the day carried no shipping or business news, so coffee houses were a good place to hear the latest news or gossip. Different coffee houses attracted different clienteles: Lloyd's, for example, started life as a coffee house where people interested in insurance and overseas trade gathered. Pepys himself first walked into a coffee house in 1660, but found the drink itself powerfully unpleasant. He wasn't alone in this. Nor was coffee universally well received. Those with vested interests in other drinks were quick to criticise it, and some health concerns were raised. In 1674, *The Women's Petition Against Coffee* alleged that coffee makes a man 'as unfruitful as those Desarts whence that unhappy Berry is said to be brought.'

Chocolate also made an appearance at this time. The Spanish had encountered it in South America, where the Aztecs mixed it with honey, chilli or vanilla. Frequently sold in coffee houses, it never really caught on at this time in the same way as its rival newcomer. It would then have been a thick liquid that needed constant stirring in specially designed chocolate pots. Inevitably it receives a mention in Pepys's diary, for 24 April 1661:

Waked in the morning with my head in a sad taking through the last night's drink, which I am very sorry for; so rose and went out with Mr Creed to drink our morning draft, which he did give me in chocolate to settle my stomach.

Pepys's endless curiosity often takes us into fascinating little byways of food history. On one occasion, for example, he visits a coffee house and ends up chatting to a Mr Harrington and some merchants about Königsberg in Prussia, where:

> . . . he told us himself that for fish, none there, the poorest body, will buy a dead fish, but must be alive, unless it be in winter; and then they told us the manner of putting their nets into the water. Through holes made in the thick ice, they will spread a net of half a mile long; and he hath known a hundred and thirty and a hundred and seventy barrels of fish taken at one draught. And then the people come with sledges upon the ice, with snow at the bottome, and lay the fish in and cover them with snow, and so carry them to market. And he hath seen when the said fish have been frozen in the sledge, so as that he hath taken a fish and broke a-pieces, so hard it hath been; and yet the same fishes taken out of the snow, and brought into a hot room, will be alive and leap up and down. Swallows are often brought up in their nets out of the mudd from under water, hanging together to some twigg or other, dead in ropes, and brought to the fire will come to life. Fowl killed in December (Alderman Barker said) he did buy, and putting into the box under his sledge, did forget to take them out to eate till Aprill next, and they then were found there, and were through the frost as sweet and fresh and eat as well as at first killed.

The powers of ice to preserve food had first been explored by the polymath Francis Bacon, who stuffed a chicken with it to see how long it would keep. This was in 1626, and it's no coincidence that that was also the year he died. Unfortunately he caught pneumonia and died at his house in Highgate shortly afterwards. The preserving powers of ice, however, were swiftly appreciated by others, and in the latter part of the seventeenth century we start to see the construction of ice houses and the use of ice as a food in itself, a topic I will return to later.

Pepys recorded what he ate. His near contemporary, Sir Kenelm Digby (1603–65), ate what he recorded, and can probably lay claim to being the first true dilettante foodie. He came from a family that played a significant role in English history over several generations and that, in the process, seems to have produced both saints and sinners. One nineteenth-century Digby became a nun. Pamela Digby, by contrast, who at one stage was married to Winston Churchill's son Randolph, was said to have studied every bedroom ceiling in Europe – and not to see whether it was well painted. Sir Kenelm himself was a bit of a mixture: the son of Sir Everard, who went to the scaffold for his part in the Gunpowder Plot, Sir Kenelm was a privateer, a spy, a hypochondriac and also an enthusiastic amateur scientist. His life was so action-packed, and he himself such an intriguing personality, that I can't resist sketching his life story briefly.

Kenelm was only three when his father met his untimely fate, but was fortunate in that the main part of the family wealth came from his mother Mary Mulshaw, who was allowed to retain it. Kenelm grew into an intelligent and good-looking youth and as such attracted the attention of King James – something of a mixed blessing because James's favours could become alarmingly intimate. It was a Protestant cousin of his, Sir John Digby, who, in order to get the fourteen-year-old boy away from court and from the influence of his mother and her Catholic friends, took Kenelm to Madrid, where he was the English ambassador. Kenelm was educated there and then at Oxford for a year, where he fell under the influence of the occultist Thomas Allen. Sent abroad again to further his studies he met Marie de Medici, mother of Henrietta Maria, who fell for him hook, line and sinker. His account of Marie's behaviour was so graphic that it had to be expurgated from his memoirs when they were published in 1827. Fleeing her attentions he went to Florence, where he is supposed to have met a Carmelite friar who shared with him the secret of the so-called 'powder of sympathy', which was thought to cure wounds without contact.

From Florence, Kenelm went back to Spain, just at the time that Charles, Prince of Wales (later Charles I), and his friend the Duke of Buckingham were visiting to probe the possibility of a Spanish marriage for Charles. Charles took to Kenelm and he returned to England as part of Charles's household. In due time King James knighted him, apparently trembling so nervously that Buckingham had to turn the sword's side to prevent James from damaging Sir Kenelm. It's possible that the attraction was still there.

For some time he had been in love with Venetia Stanley but since both families disapproved of the liaison they married secretly, announcing it only after the birth of their first child. Kenelm's thirst for adventure was not quenched by marriage, however, and intent on laying his hands on Venetian trade in the Levant he sought a commission from King James. When that failed to materialise – owing to the influence of the Duke of Buckingham, who was not fond of Kenelm – he set off anyway and became, effectively, a pirate. He fired on French and Venetian ships at Iskenderun, which didn't win him many friends.

In 1633 Venetia died suddenly in somewhat mysterious circumstances. Kenelm himself was convinced that she had been murdered; others thought that he had killed her in a fit of jealousy (she certainly had a fairly juicy reputation, possibly undeserved). Whatever the truth of the matter, her death turned his mind firmly towards religion and he became a devout Catholic. That doesn't mean, though, that he became a recluse. He was active on Charles I's part during the Civil War, went to France, where he fought and killed the Baron Mont le Ros in a duel over the baron's declaration at a dinner party that Charles was a coward, was sent on a mission to the Pope in 1655 and, at the Restoration, was back at court again, in part because of his friendship with Charles I's wife Henrietta Maria.

While all this was going on he pursued his interest in food and compiled what is, essentially, a cookery book, *The Closet of the Eminently Learned Sir Kenelme Digbie Kt. Opened*. Some indication of his many connections is immediately apparent from the titles he gives to the recipes: Lord George's Meathe (mead), the Countess of Newport's Cherry Wine, the Sweet Drink of My Lady Stuart and My Lord Lumley's Pease-Porage. His scientific interests are hinted at in Dr Harvey's Pleasant Water Cider, William Harvey being the man who discovered the circulation of blood. And some indication of his many travels is suggested in such dishes as Pan Cotto, 'as the Cardinals use in Rome'.

There are also charming insights into everyday life. His book tells us, for example, that you should eat morello cherries for pleasure and black cherries for health, and that when you take your pulse you should recite the Miserere psalm in a leisurely way that will equal twenty beats. There are inevitable recipes to guard against the plague, along with comments on milking cows and observations on the cleanliness of servants. He also advises making your chickens drunk on strong ale and then lighting a candle over their coop at night so that they carry on eating and become prodigiously fat in a fortnight. It sounds a bit like contemporary battery farming.

But what is most fascinating about Sir Kenelm's book is the range of food influences we can see at work and the trends that are starting to become apparent. The country's passion for cream is displayed in recipes for syllabub – cream and German wine flavoured with cinnamon, nutmeg or cloves. A taste for lighter and clearer soups than the old pottages suggests a French or Scottish influence (it's impossible to tell which, since, as I've already said, the Stuarts were so closely connected with France that the taste could have come directly from Scotland via James I or from France via Henrietta Maria). These soups are made from both veal and a boiling fowl, strained and then seasoned with pot-herbs and violets and sorrel as well as spinach. There is also a recipe for something called Portugal broth, which Sir Kenelm says was made for the queen. It's basically a clear chicken soup with a little parsley, a clove of garlic, a little thyme, a little mint and some bruised coriander seeds and saffron. He suggests that you could add some parsley roots, leeks, cabbage or endive at the end of the cooking. I have a nasty feeling that what you'd end up with is a clear broth with some greens floating around in it.

More obviously Scottish-sounding are recipes for what is essentially porridge made with oatmeal but then enlivened not just with salt but with added sugar or the yolks of new-laid eggs or some fresh butter, and even – a sacrilege to all Scots – some milk cooked in with it. The Scottish influence also shows in the recipes he gives for smoked fish. And then there's a curious recipe that makes use of that novelty of the seventeenth century, tea. Sir Kenelm says it was given to him by a Jesuit who came from China in 1664 and told his friend Mr Waller that they would sometimes make tea in this manner:

> To near a pint of the infusion, take two yolks of new laid-eggs, and beat them very well with as much fine Sugar as is sufficient for this quantity of Liquor; when they are very well incorporated, pour your Tea upon the Eggs and Sugar, and stir them well together. So drink it hot. This is when you come home from attending business abroad, and are very hungry, and yet have not conveniency to eat presently a competent meal. This presently discusseth [dispels] and satisfieth all rawness and indigence of the stomack, flyeth suddainly over the whole body and into the veins, and strengthneth exceedingly, and preserves one a good while from necessity of eating.

Alongside all this novelty are old favourites together with some recipes that even in Sir Kenelm's time must have seemed rather old-fashioned. Pre-eminent in this latter category are one hundred recipes for those wonderfully medieval drinks mead and metheglin. He notes that he collected these from various of his friends and contemporaries, including the Muscovy ambassador, and many are for as much as six or more gallons of the stuff. Detailed consideration is given to the best types of honey to use:

The Honey of dry open Countries, where there is much Wild-thyme, Rosemary, and Flowers, is best. It is of three sorts, Virgin-honey, Life-honey, and Stock-honey. The first is the best. The Life-honey next. The Virgin-honey is of Bees, that swarmed the Spring before, and are taken up in Autumn; and is made best by chusing the Whitest combs of the Hive, and then letting the Honey run out of them lying upon a Sieve without pressing it, or breaking of the Combs. The Life-honey is of the same Combs broken after the Virgin-honey is run from it; The Merchants of Honey do use to mingle all the sorts together. The first of a swarm is called Virgin-honey. That of the next year, after the Swarm was hatched, is Life-honey. And ever after, it is Honey of Old-stocks. Honey that is forced out of the Combs, will always taste of Wax. Hampshire Honey is most esteemed at London. About Bicester there is excellent good. Some account Norfolk honey the best.

I have visions of Sir Kenelm and his friends, including Queen Henrietta Maria, sitting round, tasting each other's mead and commenting on where the honey came from or whatever, just in the way a modern foodie might discuss the quality of sun-dried or sun-blushed tomatoes. He clearly liked his drink. Alongside recipes for mead are ones for everything from beer and cider to sack possets. One of the very few things in this world I regret never having tasted – and now never will – is his recipe for sack, that is, sherry, flavoured with clove gilly-flowers (carnations or pinks). 'If you drink a Glass or two of this sack at a meal,' he tells us, 'you will find it a great Cordial.'

One recipe I haven't tried, and indeed have no intention of trying, is 'Pease of the seedy buds of Tulips':

In the Spring (about the beginning of May) the flowry-leaves of Tulips do fall away, and there remains within them the end of the stalk, which in time will turn to seed. Take that seedy end (then very tender) and pick from it the little excrescencies about it, and cut it into short pieces, and boil them and dress them as you would do Pease; and they will taste like Pease, and be very savoury.

There's an interesting bit of social history here, in that tulips were the great craze of the seventeenth century, but I have to say that this is the one and only time in my life I have ever heard of anybody eating tulip seeds. Not a good idea, I would have thought.

James II's coronation banquet in Westminster Hall on 23 April 1685 was the occasion for an enormous feast involving nearly 1,500 dishes ranging from puffins to pistachio creams. Note the careful and symmetrical way in which the food has been arranged on the tables. The horseman in the middle of the picture is Sir Charles Dymoke, the Royal Champion.

CHAPTER 8

Roast Beef and Sweet Oranges

The Late Stuarts

C harles II died in 1685 to be succeeded by his brother, James. As Duke of York, James II had proved his worth at the Admiralty, but his Catholicism and lack of diplomatic skills were a lethal combination when it came to assuming the Crown. In fact, he was rather more reminiscent of Charles I than of his brother Charles II. After only three years on the throne James was chased into exile, to be succeeded by his Protestant daughter Mary and son-in-law William of Orange.

James wasn't around long enough to have an impact on the nation's taste buds, but we do have an amazing record of his coronation meal from a book I have been fortunate enough to inspect myself, prepared in 1687 by Francis Sandford, the Lancaster Herald. It evokes all the pomp and circumstance and ceremony of the occasion, and also includes a number of detailed engravings. From these we can piece together a very accurate picture of the scene in Westminster Hall when James II and his queen, Mary of Modena, took their seats there on 23 April 1685, and the Royal Champion, Sir Charles Dymoke, rode his horse up the hall and declared:

> If any person, of what Degree soever, High or Low, shall deny, or gainsay, Our Sovereign Lord King James the Second, King of England, Scotland, France and Ireland, Defender of the Faith, &c. Brother and next Heir to Our Sovereign Lord King Charles the Second, the last King Deceased, to be Right Heir to the Imperial Crown of this Realm of England, or that He ought not to Enjoy the same; Here is His Champion, who saith that he Lyeth, and is a False Traytor, being ready in Person to Combat with him; And in this Quarel will adventure his Life against him, on what Day soever he shall be appointed.

Dymoke, in time-honoured tradition, threw his gauntlet to the floor as a challenge. Fortunately, no one took it up.

Their majesties sat at a table at the top of the hall, furnished by Patrick Lamb, the king's master cook. They were served ninety-nine varieties of cold meat and fish, all carefully dressed and brought to the table. There were also hot dishes, sweetmeats and jellies, blancmanges and salads, each one served in a grand dish. Everything was carefully and symmetrically arranged on the table with plates and glasses to fill every space, and dishes set on stands of varying height to create a dramatic effect. It was, as Francis Sandford describes it, 'most delicate and admirable food'. It was also an almost bewilderingly diverse array, served in two vast courses.

Sandford lists the many officers of the cupboard who attended on their majesties and goes on to describe precisely who sat at the other tables and what they were served. The first table on the west side of the hall was for various of the nation's dukes, duchesses, marchionesses, earls and countesses. The first table on the east side of the hall was for archbishops, bishops, barons of the Cinque Ports, judges and the king's ancient sergeant, attorney and solicitor. Another table was for barons and baronesses, and so on down through the hall to rows of unfortunate souls who do not seem to have been given any food at all.

The food was served in messes, as in medieval times – in other words, several people dined from each dish – and their composition varied according to social rank. The sheer variety and quantity on offer is extraordinary. An army of servants handled some 1,445 dishes. There was cold 'Collar'd Veal', hot 'Lamb Stones' (testicles), hot marrow patties, pigs' feet, bologna sausages, hot 'savaloys' (which I take to be some form of sausage), hot oyster patties, cold ragout of oysters, wild duck, quail, puffin and chicken. There were pies, hot asparagus, cold peas, salad and artichokes. There were lemon jellies, gooseberry tarts, almond puddings, pistachio creams, cheesecakes, sweetmeats, mangoes and great pyramids of fruits in season.

It must have been an enormous feat of organisation both in the cooking and the serving to have fed the assembled company with such a range of hot and cold dishes, and I can't help wondering whether the logistical problems involved in getting dishes like hot oyster pies to the diners might have caused a few cases of food poisoning. Many of the dishes are what one would expect to see at a feast at this time, but even then there are a few surprises. Puffins, for one. There's no clue here, or in the cookery book that Patrick Lamb later published, how they were served up in Stuart times. I like to think that they were tastefully arranged in a sort of stargazy pie with their heads sticking out, but they might just as easily have been roasted. I have never myself eaten puffin, but a friend of mine who has relatives in the Faroe Islands, where they do still eat puffin, says that he is told that they taste like fishy grouse. That suggests that, like bittern, they are a red meat with a closely grained flesh and not white and loose as those birds that follow the chicken type of flavour. They seem too cute to eat, but then, fortunately, I've never been quite that hungry in any case.

You will also notice that quite a lot of vegetables are listed as having been served: yet another reminder of just how wrong people have been to assume 'Oh, they never ate vegetables in the past.' The reference to asparagus particularly intrigues me, since the coronation took place in the spring when asparagus isn't really in season. I suppose it's possible that that particular spring was a warm one (contemporary records suggest that the winter had been very cold but that spring was dry and warm), but it's just as likely that what was on offer was forced asparagus.

The attention to detail paid to the arrangement of the food on the table is also striking. This was very much the French approach, with dishes arranged symmetrically to form intricate patterns. In fact French influence is apparent in many of the dishes as well – for example, in the ragouts ('ragoo' as Patrick Lamb spelt it in his cookery book), with their thick gravies. This was a period when the sophistication of the French court and French cuisine were increasingly being aped by the English – scarcely surprising given that many courtiers, and the royal family themselves, had fled to France during the Commonwealth period. It was also the period when the great cook La Varenne published his *Le Cuisinier françois*, a major landmark in the history of French food, and one that shows just how far French cookery of the time was moving away from the highly spiced world of the medieval kitchen. By Lamb's time a meal served *à la française* would start with soup and fish, followed by removes (so named because the soup was 'removed' to make room for them) that would commonly involve dozens of different dishes set on the table at the same time, with both sweet and savoury mixed and matched.

When I was ten years sober in 1997 I succeeded in purchasing a copy of Lamb's book. Describing himself as the 'complete court cook', he was cook to James II, William and Mary and Queen Anne ('Her Present Majesty' when the book was published in 1710), and I was initially thrilled to have it. Sadly, though, for all the painstaking way in which dear Patrick Lamb describes the recipes – how to prepare this and that, how to make stock and what to do with the bones – it has to be one of the dullest books I have ever had in my collection. It's certainly not a patch on Robert May's, which includes some really exciting recipes like his crab salad with pine kernels and an orange dressing.

The sophisticated nature of much of the food on offer at the coronation banquet and in Patrick Lamb's own cookery book went beyond court circles. When, for example, Pepys dined with a Mr Chichly in Covent Garden on 11 March 1667 he noted that his host 'lives in mighty great fashion, with all things in a most extraordinary manner noble and rich about him, and eats in the French fashion all'. And this French approach to food with all its complexity, its attention to detail, its stocks and its sauces, exerted a powerful influence on English cuisine for the best part of the next 200 years. But it was time-consuming and could be expensive, and what we start seeing in the late seventeenth century and – to run ahead of myself a bit – in

Georgian times, too, is the growth of a gap between meat served with a delicate 'cullis', or sauce, and roast beef; between Robert May's French tarts and boiled puddings: in other words, between grand (French) cuisine and plain (English) cooking.

There was a xenophobic aspect to all this. The patriotically minded claimed that pretentious, tricksy French cuisine was just about what you'd expect from a nation England spent much of its time fighting. They argued the case, instead, for good, honest, straightforward English food. The reception to William Verral's *A Complete System of Cookery*, published in 1759, nicely demonstrates the battle lines that were drawn up. Verral (1715–61) was the master of the White Hart in Lewes, and had trained with an eminent French chef, Pierre Clouet; Verral's book was strongly influenced by French cuisine. But one contemporary reviewer (possibly the novelist Tobias Smollett) was not impressed:

> If you are really ambitious of culinary fame, and desirous of gratifying the palates of your countrymen with variety, we advise you to reject the pernicious slops, sauces, and kickshaws [fancy dishes] of the French, which serve only to irritate the appetite, spoil the digestion, and debilitate the constitution; and rather endeavour to contrive dishes of substantial food, upon true British principles: dishes that may suit the digestive powers, enrich the blood, invigorate the nerves, and brace the sinews of the body.

If Jane Austen is to be believed, entire friendships could be forged – or not – according to individuals' attitudes to French food, Elizabeth Bennet's dinner party companion in *Pride and Prejudice* (1813) rapidly giving up on her when he found out what her culinary tastes were:

Miss Bingley was engrossed by Mr Darcy, her sister scarcely less so; and as for Mr Hurst, by whom Elizabeth sat, he was an indolent man, who lived only to eat, drink, and play at cards; who, when he found her to prefer a plain dish to a ragout, had nothing to say to her.

One of the hallmarks of 'English' food was meat. And part of the reason for this was that it was becoming ever more readily available. Increasingly in the late seventeenth and early eighteenth centuries, rich merchants buying up farming estates with profits they had made from joint stock companies put new energy into livestock rearing. Their efforts received a considerable boost in the early eighteenth century when it was realised that turnips were ideal winter fodder for livestock. Now worries about how to keep animals flourishing through the long winter months were becoming a thing of the past, and meat production rose accordingly. Some was consumed locally; much went to the towns. There it was sold to the big houses that had the facilities required for cooking joints, and to the burgeoning cook shops, which supplied those who did not have the luxury of their own well-appointed kitchen. Smollett vividly evokes a typical cook shop and its clientele in his novel *The Adventures of Roderick Random* (1748):

He accordingly conducted us to a certain lane, where stopping, he bade us observe him, and do as he did, and, walking a few paces, dived into a cellar and disappeared in an instant. I followed his example, and descending very successfully, found myself in the middle of a cook's shop, almost suffocated with the steams of boiled beef, and surrounded by a company of hackney coachmen, chairmen, draymen, and a few footmen out of place or on board-wages; who sat eating shin of beef, tripe, cow-heel, or sausages, at separate boards, covered with cloths which turned my stomach.

Cook shops also operated a takeaway service, which Smollett's characters avail themselves of on another occasion:

We dined together on boiled beef and greens, brought from a cook's shop in the neighbourhood, and, although this meal was served up in a manner little corresponding with the sphere of life in which I had lately lived, I made a virtue of necessity, ate with good appetite, and treated my friends with a bottle of wine . . .

The ultimate elevation of meat to national dish came with the foundation of beefsteak clubs, the first of which appeared around 1705. These all-male concerns had a strongly patriotic and political flavour to them and they flourished throughout the eighteenth century and into Victorian times. Beef was central to their revelries and their sense of national pride; it's worth remembering that the phrase 'the roast beef of old England' actually comes from a ballad written by Henry Fielding in the 1730s.

The most famous of the beefsteak clubs, originally known as the Sublime Society of Beef Steaks, was founded in the same decade that Fielding wrote his patriotic song by the theatre manager John Rich, who had had such a stunning success with John Gay's *The Beggar's Opera* a few years earlier that it was popularly said the enterprise had made 'Gay rich and Rich gay' – gay in the old meaning of the word, of course. Rich lived in Covent Garden and was visited by most men of rank and fashion, who enjoyed his wit and conversation. The most constant of these was the old Earl of Peterborough, a crony of the poet Alexander Pope. On one occasion the earl stayed so late, because his carriage was delayed in picking him up, that Rich decided that he would get on with preparing his own dinner: a beefsteak cooked by himself over his own fire on a gridiron. The steak gave forth such an appetising odour that the old lord was persuaded to stay and share it. He liked this entertainment so well that he proposed a repeat performance every week, at the same time and the same place.

So the Sublime Society of Beef Steaks came into being and was duly celebrated in extremely bad verse:

> First Rich, who this feast of the gridiron planned,
> And formed with a touch of his harlequin's wand
> Out of mighty rude matter, this brotherly band,
> The jolly old Steakers of England.

The society never had more than twenty-four members at any time, and anybody who was anybody wanted to belong to it – including, as the century wore on, an increasing number of titled individuals. The Prince of Wales, later George IV, had to wait a whole year to be elected because the vacancy brought about by an existing member's death or retirement had already been filled.

The society, also known as the Beefsteak Club, was all about politicking, gambling, eating and drinking. In its own peculiar way it was a very English invention. The president sat in a chair above the rest with a beefeater's hat and plume on the right-hand back of his chair and a three-cornered hat on the left. Those brought before him to be reprimanded for whatever offence they might have committed had to do penance wrapped in a white sheet. No one was exempted. Even George III's son, the Duke of Sussex, was punished on one occasion for allegedly stealing from a fellow member – he then sulked for the rest of the evening. When proposing a resolution the president placed the plumed hat on his head and instantly removed it. It was all very exclusive and very expensive. The entrance fee was 10 guineas – a lot of money at a time when a London labourer might expect to earn £24 a year – and the members paid five shillings for their steak and ten shillings if, as they were occasionally allowed to, they brought a guest. First names only was the rule, so guests might be surprised later to discover that the person they had been sitting next to and chatting with in a nice easy manner was in fact the Lord Chancellor or the Lord Chief Justice or even a duke.

Roast beef became so closely associated with the English diet that around the middle of the eighteenth century the French started referring to the English as '*les rosbifs*'. But meat wasn't the only national dish. Boiled puddings, which as we've seen came in with the Stuarts, also became increasingly popular. In both their baked and boiled forms they were a wonderfully versatile way of using up all sorts of ingredients. Recipes exist for suet puddings filled with beefsteak, giblets, pigeons, duck, raw fruit, currants and great pounds of butter. They could be bulked out with rice, oatmeal, vermicelli or sago. Some took considerable flair to make, such as pond puddings, where the fruit is placed in the middle of the pudding; Sussex pond pudding, for example, involves scratching a lemon and then putting it in the centre of the pudding, so that its flavours burst out while it is being cooked. The Sussex shopkeeper Thomas

Turner, who kept a diary in the 1750s and 1760s, records eating dishes such as currant pond pudding, plum suet pudding and butter pudding cake alongside the inevitable pieces of beef. Curds, carrots, spinach and even the unpopular potato are all recorded as being cooked in cereal-based puddings.

This mix of meat and pudding took its toll, and an inevitable corollary of such a heavy diet was an increasing tendency to stoutness among its diehard adherents. Charles Howard, 10th Duke of Norfolk, who was president of the Beefsteak Club for a number of years, ate prodigious quantities of steak in an evening and became rather inflated as a result. Queen Anne also indulged heavily. She loved her racing (she is responsible for the establishment of the Royal Ascot meeting) and her hunting, but eventually became too fat to hunt on a horse. The solution she adopted was to follow across country in a racing carriage which she drove herself, with her lady-in-waiting hanging on the back for grim life as they dashed across country after the hounds. Later in the eighteenth century the maverick politician Charles James Fox became so fat in middle age that he had to have a circle cut out of the table at his club to accommodate his stomach. As for George IV in the following century, contemporary portraits bear witness to what happens if you indulge in a breakfast of 'a pigeon and beef-steak pie of which he ate two pigeons and three beef-steaks'.

Eating to excess could all too easily be accompanied by drinking to excess – and here the late Stuart and early Georgian period had new temptations to offer. The first of these, which was to have devastating social consequences in the eighteenth century, was gin, or 'aqua vitae' as it was also known. First imported from Holland in the mid seventeenth century, it seems to have received a boost in popularity when the Dutch William of Orange assumed the throne in 1688. By the 1730s it was causing such social problems that a Gin Act had to be passed in 1736 in an attempt to restrict and regulate its sale. Brandy also became increasingly widely consumed. William's cousin, Queen Anne (one of whose nicknames was Brandy Nan), is said to have been particularly partial to it, pouring it into a cup from a Cadogan teapot – a teapot that has a cork in the bottom rather than a removable lid. To the casual observer it would have appeared that she was imbibing something entirely harmless.

Wine still remained popular. Pepys regularly reports drinking either several bottles with his friends or a pint of wine in some tavern or other on his own. At this time, it was still stored in casks and drawn off in bottles with wooden stoppers just before serving, but the introduction of the cork stopper and the idea of laying down wine in bottles was just coming in at the end of the seventeenth century. Otherwise there was always beer, which remained very much a national drink, brewed at home and also by innkeepers, who served a range of strengths of beer. 'Small beer' – rather less alcoholic than ordinary beer – was consumed by people of all ages. It could be made at home from virtually anything that people had to hand – perhaps dandelion and burdock, or nettles (popular in Lancashire), or horehound and ginger. Safer than water at the time, more nutritious than the newly popular tea, a few pints of good home-brewed beer a day was a worthwhile part of anyone's diet.

I don't want, however, to imply that this was simply a period of national self-indulgence. There was certainly plenty of heavy food and intoxicating liquor around. But if the late seventeenth and early eighteenth centuries offered culinary temptation, they also witnessed the beginnings of a much more sober and scientific attitude to it. I've already mentioned the introduction of turnips as winter fodder for cattle. This was something that happened in the early eighteenth century, but the new spirit of enquiry goes back before then. In fact, it really dates back to the foundation of the Royal Society, established by Charles II on his restoration to the throne in 1660. The society, which had its roots in informal meetings of natural philosphers during the Civil War, brought together some of the best minds of the time, from William Harvey, the discoverer of the circulation of the blood, to Isaac Newton. From the outset it concerned itself with scientific experimentation, including, very early on, an experiment in double fermentation to produce sparkling wine. More significantly, from our point of view, it also contained a separate committee, the Georgical – or agricultural – Committee, dedicated to discussing farming and farming methods.

The committee was formally set up in 1664, but discussions started a couple of years earlier and one of the first things that these revolved around was the potato. This, as you will recall, had been introduced back in Elizabeth I's reign, but had still not really found favour in England 150 years later. On 20 March 1662, however, the committee met to consider a proposal from Mr Buckland, a gentleman farmer from Somerset, who had written to the society to advocate the cultivation of the potato to provide against famine. Minutes of the meeting reveal that the committee was interested in Buckland's suggestions and there was a proposal that all those members of the society who owned land should begin planting the root and persuade their friends to do the same. Seed potatoes and instructions on cultivation were to be provided by Mr Buckland and the chemist Robert Boyle, who already had land holdings in Ireland where potatoes were being grown, and Boyle was to report back on the outcome of the initiative.

Sadly, yet again, the English resisted the potato. This was not to be a triumph for the fledgling society: the endeavour received no publicity, nor indeed were there any efforts to cultivate the crop. Potatoes were not even mentioned in the society report that was subsequently published.

In 1664, perhaps emboldened by the society's endeavours, John Forster, a Londoner of independent means, published a tract which he entitled *England's Happiness Increased*. This is a verbose period of our history and so it comes as no surprise that the longer subtitle should be a short story in itself:

> Or a sure and easy remedy against all succeeding dear years; by a plantation of the roots called POTATOES, whereof (with the addition of wheat flour) excellent, good and wholesome bread may be made, every year, eight or nine months together, for half the charge as formerly. ALSO by the planting of these roots, ten thousand men in England and Wales, who know not how to live, or what to do to get a maintenance for their families, may of any one acre of ground make thirty pounds per annum. Invented and published for the good of the poorer sort by John Forster, Gent.

Forster claimed to be publishing his tract for the good of the 'poorer sort', but he actually dedicated it to 'the High and Mighty Monarch, Charles II by Grace of God, King of Great Britain', etc. Here an economic motive appears. The poor might have benefited, but Foster also claimed that the potato could produce a healthy supplement to the king's income – something

A hero of the Agricultural Revolution Robert Bakewell (1725–95) revolutionised sheep and cattle breeding and was also responsible for producing a powerful breed of horses that proved invaluable both to the farmer and to the military.

The Georgian country estate Wealthy Georgians paid considerable attention to landscaping and improving their lands. This panoramic view of Charlton Park, dating from around 1745, shows a fine formal garden, a meadow filled with cows, and an extensive kitchen garden.

Improving the country's livestock Thomas Coke (1754–1842) was another pioneer of modern stock breeding. He is shown here with some of his Southdown sheep. Holkham Hall, his country seat in Norfolk, can be glimpsed in the background.

'O the Roast Beef of Old England' Georgian suspicion of the French in general and French food in particular is encapsulated in William Hogarth's 1740s engraving of the Gate of Calais. The artist (shown on the left) sketches various unattractive locals eating their less than attractive food. The fine piece of beef being held in the centre of the picture is addressed to 'Madm Grandsire at Calais' – who catered to English visitors. Eighteenth-century beefsteak clubs elevated the meat to a national dish.

Georgian overindulgence A diet that leant heavily towards meat and puddings could take its toll. The glutton in this satirical watercolour by Thomas Rowlandson (1757–1827) is taking the waters at Bath in an attempt to alleviate his gout, but clearly also takes his dinner very seriously.

The height of elegance The dining room at Kedleston Hall in Derbyshire, complete with a niche that was originally designed to display the family silver. 'Grant me, ye Gods, a pleasant seat,' said Sir Nathaniel Curzon, who commissioned the house in 1758. Robert Adam was the architect.

Fashionable entertainment 'Here they drink, and there they cram / Chicken, pasty, beef and ham,' runs an eighteenth-century ballad about the delights of Vauxhall Gardens in London.

Tea Two fads in one: the Georgians loved their tea and they also loved the newfangled cauliflower. This cream earthenware teapot was produced in the early 1760s in Burslem in Staffordshire.

An elegant tea party A family being served with tea in around 1745.

Coffee The golden age of coffee houses lasted from the 1660s until the 1730s. Popular meeting places, they were much used by lawyers, merchants, politicians and others. Quite why tea ultimately overtook coffee in popularity is not clear; may have something to do with the fact that tea leaves could be reused by the less prosperous while coffee grounds could not.

Sugar Slaves at work at a sugar refinery in the West Indies. Sugar was a valuable and much-used commodity in the eighteenth century, but the human cost of producing it was enormous. Note the overseer brandishing a stick.

Country leisure *The Anglers' Repast*, an engraving after a painting by
George Morland (1763–1804), showing Morland himself, his wife Anne
and others. This was the period when the word 'picnic' changed its
meaning from a meal where everybody paid a share, or contributed some
food, to a meal eaten out of doors.

Country living *The Warrener*, an engraving after a painting by George
Morland and dating from 1806. This is a somewhat idealised view of
country life, but it does show that relatively ubiquitous animal the pig,
which many cottagers still kept. Once fattened up, it would be dispatched
for them by a professional slaughterer and a big celebration would be held.

Country sports *Hare shooting*, an engraving after a painting by George Morland. Hare was quite a popular eighteenth-century dish. Hannah Glasse includes recipes for roasting and jugging them, along with various suggestions for appropriate sauces.

Country work George Stubbs (1724–1806) originally painted *Haymakers* in 1783 and then reworked it in the version shown here as an oval plaque for Wedgwood. Like many artists of the time, he romanticises life in the countryside. In reality, the later decades of the eighteenth century proved difficult for farm labourers as more and more common land was enclosed. English farms, however, were very productive.

The Georgian kitchen The increasingly sophisticated nature of the English kitchen is nicely illustrated in this frontispiece to *The Housekeeper's Instructor* by William Henderson published in the 1790s. The great kitchen fire of previous eras is now being much more efficiently utilised and the room is positively bristling with implements, pots and pans.

Georgian technology It's perhaps cheating to include a photograph of a Scottish kitchen in a book on English food, but the Georgian House in Edinburgh, dating from 1796, offers quite simply one of the most outstanding surviving examples of a late Georgian kitchen. It boasts many contemporary refinements, such as a sophisticated jack for turning the spit, and pots and pans on levers that can be swung over the fire.

Charles was always keen on. Forster declares that if the right to grow potatoes is controlled by the king, who then grants monopolies and licences for a price, the Crown could gain an annual income of some £40,000 to £50,000 each year, generated by 10,000 licencees paying £5 each a year. If that wasn't persuasion enough, Forster goes on to argue that if people eat more potatoes, they'll eat less wheat, and that consequently:

> . . . abundance of grain, of all sorts, may every plentiful year be spared to be transported beyond the sea into other countries which will be a great benefit both to His Majesty and to his subjects, for these reasons: First, His Majesty's revenue of Customs will be increased by the often coming in of ships for corn with foreign goods and merchandise. Also a league and amity will be continued with those people to whom it is transported so that from them His Majesty (if need require) may have aid and help against foreign invasions and domestic disturbances . . .

Tempting though this was clearly meant to be, there is nothing to suggest that Charles ever considered John Forster's proposal, and the potato languished in obscurity for a while longer.

In other respects, though, the Royal Society did begin to have an impact on food; or, at least, it would certainly be true to say that one of those who sat on the Georgical Committee made a direct contribution to its study and appreciation. This was the diarist and scholar John Evelyn. The author of such works as *Fumifugium, or The Inconveniencie of the aer and smoak of London dissipated* and *Sylva, or A Discource of Forest Trees*, his interests were many and varied. And when it came to food, his obsession was salad. His book *Aceteria: A Discource of Sallats* displays all the scholarship, all the curiosity and – dare I say it – all the obsessiveness one would expect from someone associated with the Royal Society, and to my mind it remains the ultimate book on the subject.

Salads had been around in varying forms since medieval times. Gerard, among other herbalists, had extolled their health-giving properties, recommending the inclusion of such ingredients as Spanish nuts (almonds), onions, leeks, chives, garlic, winter cress, rocket, tarragon, dandelion leaves, endives and spinach. But it was left to John Evelyn to deal with salads in an encyclopedic way, from a consideration of the best soil in which to grow them to a discussion of the garden implements that should be employed in their cultivation. In so doing, he brought to bear not only his own expertise but the wisdom of a vast range of different authorities, ancient and modern.

Salad, Evelyn tells us, is 'a particular Composition of certain *crude* and fresh Herbs, such as usually are, or may safely be, eaten with some *acetous* [i.e. lemon] Juice, Oyl, Salt &c., to give them a grateful Gust [taste] and Vehicle [one thing being mixed with another to make it more palatable]'. He is adamant that the flavours should be carefully balanced; that, like music, they should contain nothing grating, 'Altho' admitting some *Discords* (to distinguish and illustrate the rest) striking in the more sprightly, and sometimes gentler Notes, reconcile all Dissonancies, and melt them into an agreeable Composition'. Vegetables for salads should never be cooked or boiled, as these processes deprive them utterly of their distinguishing attributes. Fruit should virtually never be included, except as a curious addition. Quite what John Evelyn thought about the tomato – which was, after all, around in his day – I don't know. And, despite his involvement with the

Georgical Committee, he doesn't have much to say about potatoes, beyond mentioning that they are about the size of a wild cherry and are an 'agreeable' salad if pickled.

Salad dressings also go under the microscope. The perfect one in Evelyn's opinion is an artful mixture of mustard, oil and vinegar, with or without the addition of the hard-boiled yolks of new-laid eggs which have been rubbed through a sieve into the dressing. He is also very precise as to the sort of receptacles that could be used, arguing:

> That the *Saladiere* (Sallet-Dishes) be of *Porcelane*, or of the *Holland-Delft-Ware*; neither too deep nor shallow, according to the quantity of the *Sallet* Ingredients; *Pewter*, or even *Silver*, not at all so well agreeing with *Oyl* and *Vinegar*, which leave their several Tinctures, whether silver or pewter, as this would be an outrage.

Aceteria is to my mind a rather pompous and verbose book, but it opens a fascinating window on the times. Like Kenelm Digby, Evelyn is passionate about his subject – not just about the culinary aspects of a salad but also its medicinal qualities (radishes, he tells us, have sometimes been condemned for causing rotten teeth and vomiting; parsley is a diuretic). He even ventures into a consideration of the best way to feed horses: dried food, he says, shortens their lives. He may not have the *joie de vivre* of his friend and fellow diarist Pepys, but he is a fascinating figure nevertheless.

I've already touched on improvements in the production of food – something that I'll return to when considering the Georgians

– but it's worth emphasising just how much started to be done in the closing decades of the Stuart era. As Royalists returned from exile, they brought new ideas from abroad to improve their country estates. In particular, since many had been in Holland and had witnessed at first hand what the draining of potentially very fertile land could achieve, they reinvigorated schemes to drain the Fens. Dutch engineers were once again brought to England and set to work. The fine growing lands of Lincolnshire were established then and the port of King's Lynn, always a thriving port for east-coast trade, became ever busier as it shipped crops from the newly drained lands to London, up the coast to York, or across the sea to the Continent. One lesson that the gentlemen who had fled with Charles had learnt, not to mention Charles himself, was that they could no longer take wealth for granted, and that trade was not a dirty word.

One technological improvement made in the seventeenth century also had an impact on food, though that was certainly not the original intention. Guns in this period underwent a transformation. Whereas once you had had to light the wick of your arquebus and balance it on a stand in order to fire it, now the flintlock did the same job much more quickly and efficiently. Portable guns therefore became the norm, and so for the first time we see the development of shooting birds both for sport and, of course, for the table. Wild birds had always been a feature of the English table, but previously they had been hawked for by the gentry, or shot at with bird-bolts (a kind of blunt arrow), or netted by professional wild-fowlers in places such as the North Kent marshes or the Isle of Grain. Netted fowl would be sent, sometimes by boat, from the marshes to the big towns and cities. The Kent marshes, for example, supplied London, and because the migratory season coincides with the colder months of the year, birds were unlikely to deteriorate while they were being transported.

With the arrival of guns for game shooting came a new zest for breeding hunting dogs, from the pointer and the setter to the spaniel in all its forms. Charles II, for one, loved his dogs – Pepys describes him playing with them when he should have been concentrating on state business – and Charles was infuriated if, as happened on occasion, they were stolen (one advertisement he placed in the *Mercurius Publicus* in 1660 reads, 'We must call upon you again for a Black Dog between a greyhound and a spaniel, no white about him, onely a streak on his brest, and his tayl a little bobbed'). The newly drained fenlands of East Anglia were perfect for game shooting, and we know that Charles went there regularly (while there he would also have been able to indulge his passion for horse racing at Newmarket, which he visited twice a year).

Charles's other great passion was women, including the famous Nell Gwyn. My favourite story about her is that on one occasion, when Charles was visiting her at Lauderdale House in Highgate, she hung her bastard son by him out of the window, saying that she would drop him unless Charles ennobled him. 'God save the Earl of Burford,' Charles is supposed to have cried out in an admirable demonstration of quick thinking. Now I admit that this has nothing to do with the history of food at all, but Nell herself does, if only in a very oblique way. She famously started out as an orange-girl, selling her wares outside the Theatre Royal, Drury Lane. And the oranges she sold were sweet oranges. This is historically significant. The bitter, or Seville, orange had been around for some time, but it would not have been a very appetising prospect at the theatre.

However, the sweet orange – ideal as a refreshing snack – was a recent arrival, only really making its presence felt in England in the reign of James I when the East India Company started to import it. Its appeal to theatre-goers must have been greatly increased by the fact that it was proffered by attractive young women like Nell and by the fact that this was not the only thing most of them – including Nell – were proffering.

If nothing else, Nell serves as a reminder of just how important foreign trade continued to be to the development of English food throughout the latter decades of the seventeenth century. Commodities from all around the world continued to flood into English ports, and new foods were constantly being discovered. But there was a darker side to this international food trade as, increasingly, the cultivation of some of the important staples – in particular, sugar, coffee, cocoa and rice – became dependent on slave labour. The English slave trade actually had its roots in Elizabethan times, but it received a boost when, in 1655, Oliver Cromwell seized the island of Jamaica from Spain. Jamaica was the source of 'white gold' – sugar – grown in plantations tended by slaves. Upon his restoration, Charles II founded a company called the Company of Royal Adventurers Trading to Africa, to which he gave a monopoly. It counted among its members numerous aristocrats and several members of the royal family. In the following twenty years, under its new name, the Royal African Company, it captured 90,000 slaves who were taken across the Atlantic, many of them to work on the sugar plantations in Jamaica.

Slaves were paid for, not with cash, but in kind with cowry shells, textiles, copper, pewter, cutlery, alcohol or guns. For African chieftains the slave trade was an excuse to get rid of possibly dangerous adversaries or rival tribesmen for a profit.

For the white traders, who acted with staggering cruelty, and who regarded their human cargo as less than human, it was the road to huge wealth. It even had its own coin, the guinea, first struck in 1663 by the Royal Adventurers and named after the African coast where they 'mined' their raw material. Torrents of bright new guineas splashed into London's mercantile coffers.

The slave trade transformed the West Indies and America. As for England, the effects of the slave trade went beyond the wealth it generated for merchants. Sugar, rum and molasses became ever more widespread. There was also the beginnings of a black population in England as black boys and girls were taken on as domestic household servants and slaves. Pepys records visiting Swakeleys House, the home built by one of my direct ancestors, where the owner 'showed me a black boy that he had, that died of a consumption, and being dead, he caused him to be dried in an oven, and lies there entire in a box'. The story in my family was that he was put in the bread oven to warm him up because he was complaining of the cold; the oven proved too hot and he died.

The western parts of the United Kingdom also became increasingly prosperous as a result of the trade. At this time the main slave port for trading to the West Indies was at Whitehaven, where it remained until larger ships caused the deeper water port of Liverpool to prosper. The merchant class were obviously the main people to benefit. But they weren't the only ones, and a striking feature of contemporary accounts of everyday life in the late seventeenth and early eighteenth centuries is the extent to which the population at large started to benefit from what international trade – and, in particular, the slave trade – was bringing to England.

Sarah Fell at Swarthmoor Hall in the Furness district of Cumbria provides a good example of this. One of the stepdaughters of the famous Quaker George Fox, she kept house for him and her account book covering the years 1673 to 1678 still survives (a reprint exists from Cambridge University Press). It shows a well-to-do family living a little bit off the beaten track, but able nevertheless to get more unusual or exotic goods relatively easily. Horse messengers could be sent to Kendal and Kirkby Lonsdale to buy brown sugar and oranges. Wine and brandy also came from Kendal, as did such medicinal aids as cinnamon water, juniper berries, saffron and treacle. Holland cheese came via Newcastle. Goods (oranges, for example) could even come from far-away London, the extra cost involved often being split between a group of wealthier families who would club together to keep the costs of carriage down. In fact, even potatoes weren't unknown at Swarthmoor Hall, possibly because Ireland, where we know they were being cultivated by now, was only a short trip away by sea. Tobacco also made an appearance: one entry in the account book, which refers to tobacco pipes for her sister Susanna, suggests that smoking was not entirely a male prerogative.

That said, Sarah's account book also reminds us just how heavily dependent people still were on what was close at hand. Most food came from the fields and gardens around Swarthmoor. Shopping was done at Ulverstone and Dalton on weekly market days, but the fact that more unusual items had to come from Lancaster some twenty miles away, across the treacherous river estuaries, shows that the wares in these markets would have been fairly basic. Like Elinor Fettiplace over 50 years before, Sarah would have had to rely heavily on preserving and pickling food when it was in season to eat at other times of the year. Interestingly,

Cumbria, which houses the port of Whitehaven, has a long reputation for pickling and preserving foods. This, I think, is because the sailors returning from the West Indies would have brought back a little store of spices and perhaps even sugar with them. I remember there was once a Lord Mayor of London who came from Cumbria who served at his mayoral banquet a dish referred to as 'red-spiced beef' which was, as far as I can understand, entirely flavoured with West Indian spices and possibly even something a bit like jerk beef today.

Judging from the money paid to local workers, most people living around Swarthmoor would have lived on a pretty rudimentary diet. Wages, then as now, were lower as you moved away from London, but even so the domestic help Ann Standish only received £1 17s 6d for a year's work, compared with the £4 a year that Pepys paid his maid. What's more, she was fined eight shillings for losing a silver spoon and sixpence for breaking a pot. Outdoor workers received even less. In the hayfield women received only a penny a day and boys harrowing for thirty days received only half a penny each. The women in charge of marketing the dairy produce had a wage of £2 a year. Wages were set by the justices at quarter sessions and it was an offence to ask for more. One must remember that many servants lived in entailed estate cottages and so were provided with meat and drink, the value of which was often greater than the penny or two that they received for their hire. At this level of society, the new foods and dishes being experienced by those further up the social scale would have seemed very alien indeed.

The Georgian era witnessed a transformation in cooking and an explosion in the number of cookery books. This is the frontispiece to Eliza Smith's *The Compleat Housewife*, which went through many editions after its first publication in 1727 and was the first cookery book to be published in North America. We know very little about Eliza Smith, beyond her statement in the preface to her book that she spent over thirty years working for 'fashionable and noble Families'.

CHAPTER 9

Turtle Soup and Plum Pudding

The Georgian Age

The Stuarts had style and flair. They brought us beautiful architecture from the likes of Inigo Jones and Christopher Wren, and beautiful objects from craftsmen like Grinling Gibbons the woodcarver and Jean Tijou the iron worker. I don't think, however, that they were that interested in food – or, at least, put it this way, I don't think that the later seventeenth century represents a high point in the history of English food. So far as the reigning monarchs were concerned, neither James II nor William and Mary seem to have had a particular impact on the nation's diet, nor did Queen Anne and her husband and consort, George of Denmark. In fact, apart from her liking for brandy, the only food-related claim about Queen Anne that I have heard is that she is responsible for the fashion I can remember from childhood of people drinking tea with their little finger crooked and held outwards. Apparently, so the story goes, Anne broke her little finger out hunting, it never set properly, she was therefore compelled to drink her tea with her finger stuck out at an angle, and others followed suit. Like so many fashions it moved down the social scale over the following generations.

The death of Queen Anne in 1714, however, ushered in the one period of history I would really have liked to have lived in, given the option: the Georgian age. The Georgians had an enormous impact on our food, our way of cooking it, our way of consuming it, our way of serving it, and even the times of day when we eat it. And it's an impact that even at the time went beyond the very privileged and wealthy. Every part of society was affected, from the increasingly upwardly mobile middle class in the towns to agricultural workers in the countryside.

Georgian taste and know-how also reached most parts of people's lives. This was a period when the look of houses as well as the way they were arranged internally changed enormously. Perhaps the most famous architects of the period were the Adam family – father William and sons Robert and John – born and raised in Edinburgh, who between them were responsible for such masterpieces as Hopetoun House near Edinburgh, Kedleston Hall in Derbyshire and Pulteney Bridge in Bath. If you were a client with deep enough pockets, you could ask the two Adam brothers to design a house down to the lamp brackets and then put together a team who could build it and furnish it for you – from the murals and plaster ceilings to the smallest items of furniture. Catalogues of the time gave you all sorts of choices – you might want a few carved acanthus leaves here, a little more gilding there. You might want to go further and get somebody like Capability Brown in to design your garden and landscape your park for you. Brown might well recommend which of the newly developed breeds of cattle you should have to graze your parkland. If you went the whole hog, you might even move an entire village to improve the view from the house or to make way for artificial lakes and trees that wouldn't come to maturity until your grandchildren's time.

This attention to design and innovation extended to the kitchen and the dining room. By the eighteenth century the kitchen had moved a long way from the room that would have been familiar to people in the Middle Ages, with an open wood fire on the floor and a smoke hole above. In grand houses – such as Kedleston Hall – it would be situated far from the dining room so that its smells wouldn't penetrate; otherwise it might be tucked out of the way in the basement or on a mezzanine floor. The fireplace remained the focal point, containing a grate which, by 1700, generally took the form of a large oblong basket on four legs fastened to the chimney back with iron bars – ideal for roasting large joints of meat. Gradually it acquired cast-iron plates attached to the front, with metal supports for pans. Above these would be spits turned by a clockwork spin jack or – an innovation in Georgian times – a smoke jack, which was located inside the chimney and was operated by the heat of the fire. The more fiercely your fire roared, the more smoke went up the chimney and the faster the smoke jack turned. It was an ingenious invention and saved a lot of labour.

Other clever fireplace accessories allowed pots to be swung into the fire and winched to the correct height, and you could also reduce the size or the spread of the fire by winding iron 'cheeks' (metal sides) by a rack-and-pinion mechanism. In the latter part of the century in more prosperous houses you might find such ingenious devices as L-shaped boilers that made use of the space around the grate, and very large boilers at the back, fed from a cistern with a ballcock. In front of the fire you could sometimes find metal screens with highly polished surfaces that would reflect heat back into the fire and so help meats, puddings and, indeed, breads and cakes to cook better. The fancier ones occasionally had sliding doors through which the cook could tend to the meal, or shelves on which to keep things warm. I have a little screen from this period with hooks from which to hang your birds, and if you put it in front of the fire it does actually cook them very well. This was also the period of the Dutch oven, or 'hastener', a large metal box with a polished interior in which roast meat and batter puddings – the Yorkshire puddings of their day – could be cooked together, the flavours of the former infusing the latter.

Roasting was the favourite method of cooking meat, followed by boiling done in large pots over the fire. Previously, stewing and sauce-making, which required a gentler heat, had been done over charcoal-powered chafing dishes on the floor of the hearth. By Georgian times, however, some smart houses had separate stoves designed for these very purposes built into a corner of the kitchen. They made life much easier for the cook, who no longer had to bend into the flames to stir a sauce.

Baking, likewise, was turned into a considerably less laborious process in the eighteenth century. The old beehive oven that was built into the kitchen wall had required the cook to build a raging fire, essentially guess when it was hot enough for baking, and then sweep out the hot ashes and hope for the best. It was impossible to regulate the heat once the dough was inside. By the mid eighteenth century, however, this was being replaced by an iron oven with a grate underneath – a perpetual oven – a great labour-saving device that was preferably situated near the fireplace so it could share the flue and chimney. The logical next step, made possible by advances in the iron industry in the north, was for the oven to be incorporated into the central fireplace.

We're clearly moving towards the kitchen range familiar to us from Victorian times, and the first of these, made out of cast iron, was invented in 1780 by Thomas Robinson. It had a central grate, a closed oven with a hinged door on one side and a tank for heating water on the other. At the end of the century the British-born American Count Rumford came up with a more elaborate and energy-efficient design that included an early version of the hob.

If you want to see a perfect example of a Georgian kitchen, go to the Georgian House in Charlotte Square in Edinburgh, built by Robert Adam in 1796. When I first moved to Scotland and was very miserable, I used to take myself off there, sit in the kitchen and take it all in, thinking how wonderful these inventions and devices must have seemed when they were new. There was only one drawback. I've cooked in both medieval and Georgian kitchens and there is no doubt in my mind that the meat roasted over or before an open fire is considerably better in flavour than that cooked in an enclosed oven. Technical progress here made life easier, but it didn't necessarily make the food taste better.

In poorer houses, where no spit was available, meat might well be suspended over the fire from the mantelpiece – a technique later recorded in George Eliot's *Silas Marner* (1861):

There was something in front of the fire, too, that would have been inviting to a hungry man, if it had been in a different stage of cooking. It was a small bit of pork suspended from the kettle-hanger by a string passed through a large door-key, in a way known to primitive housekeepers unpossessed of jacks. But the pork had been hung at the farthest extremity of the hanger, apparently to prevent the roasting from proceeding too rapidly during the owner's absence.

As for those who didn't have ovens, they still sent their pies, stamped with their initials, to the local bakery. One is reminded of the nursery rhyme 'Pat-a-Cake, Pat-a-Cake': 'Pat it and prick it and mark it with B, and put it in the oven for baby and me.' These poorer people would still have been cooking most of their food in cauldrons, as they had done for many centuries.

You get a very good idea of the range of kitchen equipment available in mid-Georgian times from William Verral's *A Complete System of Cookery*, published in 1759. Verral (or Verrall), the landlord of the White Hart at Lewes, clearly felt that many of his contemporaries skimped on things, and he was therefore at pains to give an exhaustive list of the equipment he felt was critical to the smooth running of his kitchen. This included two boilers – one big enough to hold a leg of mutton and the other, two fowl – a soup pot, eight small lidded stew pans of different sizes, two very large lidded stew pots, a frying pan ('for frying any little matters, as an amlette [omelette] or pancake'), a couple of copper ladles (which, like other copper implements, should be coated with tin), two or three large copper spoons, a slice or two, a pewter colander, three or four sieves (one of lawn), three copper cups to hold above half a pint, six smaller copper cups, two *etamines* for straining thick soups, three large wooden spoons and several saucepans. In the kitchens of Verral's era spices and peppercorns still had to be ground on site, and pestles and mortars were on hand for this. Toasting forks were much used – ideal for cooking steak or toasting bread over an open fire. Since sugar still came in quite large conical sugar loaves, you would need sugar cutters and graters to break them down in order to have the sugar ready for cooking.

As for the Georgian dining room, this became – in more affluent houses, at least – a place of elegance, beauty and warmth, and of ever-greater privacy: we're a long way now from the semi-public medieval hall. The dining table could well be made from that most elegant of woods, mahogany – rather than oak – a product of England's thriving trade with the West Indies and first mentioned by English writers in the seventeenth century. Crockery became ever more sophisticated. The early part of the eighteenth century had witnessed the importation of porcelain from China, largely designed for drinking the newfangled beverage tea. The English gradually mastered its production, and by the mid century were also making refined bone china (so-called because ground-up bone was added to the clay). And then there was Josiah Wedgwood. The son of a potter from Burslem in Staffordshire, he eventually opened his own pottery and started producing highly fashionable earthenware. His masterstroke was to offer a service of creamware to George III's wife, Queen Charlotte, getting permission from her to call his range Queen's Ware. Commercial success was now guaranteed. Charming though the earlier English majolica and salt- and tin-glaze had been, there's no doubt that refined Georgian pottery and porcelain brought an added degree of finesse to the dining table, particularly when Wedgwood introduced his jasperware in blue and white, or dark green and white, with its evocation of classical elegance.

Alongside the inevitable plates, bowls, cups and glasses, other items of tableware, reflecting new trends in food and drink, started to make an appearance. Prominent among these was the teapot. Porcelain teapots had been brought from China since Stuart times. Now, home-produced teapots sprang up in all sorts of novel shapes and sizes – I have one which is in the form of a rather primitive elephant; Wedgwood came up with one shaped and coloured like a cauliflower, the cauliflower being the new, expensive and fashionable vegetable of the moment. The sheer range and variety of the Georgian teapot demonstrates the extent to which tea really was the modish beverage of the age. It may have been expensive, not least because of the heavy customs duty imposed on it (hence the reason why, along with brandy and tobacco, it was so widely smuggled), but it was finding its way into ever more people's lives. In 1717 Thomas Twining opened the first tea-shop in London for ladies. Three years later, a tea-garden opened in the very popular Vauxhall Gardens by the Thames.

Those who liked their tea would probably buy not only a teapot but a lockable tea-caddy as well – another indication of the beverage's value and expense. Tea was drunk rather weak and sweetened, although at first usually without milk. There is speculation that milk grew in popularity either because it mitigated the power of the caffeine or because it was realised that, by putting it in first and so cooling the tea that followed, you were less likely to cause cracks in fine porcelain cups. And adding milk really took off in the nineteenth century when stronger and less refined teas started arriving from India, because it helped to balance their flavour. The milk you could buy varied greatly in quality in Georgian times: London milk was pretty nasty stuff (often watered down and already turning sour), unless you could buy it direct from someone looking after the cows that grazed in St James's Park.

In terms of dining room utensils, if you were a guest at someone's house cutlery was now provided – long gone were the days when you brought your own knife and spoon. The plates put before you might even be warmed before food was served on to them thanks to the invention of ingenious plate warmers, often beautifully fashioned, that were either placed in front of the fire or contained compartments holding hot charcoal. Surviving examples generally have carrying handles, so that they could be moved around as required.

The other item of furniture that every well-to-do Georgian household would have kept near or in the dining room was a cupboard for chamber pots. One likes to think that these were used by the gentlemen after the ladies had left the room, but I'm never too sure with the Georgians and I do wonder whether sometimes the more desperate were quite happy to whip them out in the middle of dinner. That made me wonder somewhat anxiously how the poor women coped. Most would have retired behind a screen in the drawing room, but perhaps a few used an article called a 'bourdaloue', which was named after a seventeenth-century Jesuit priest. He preached sermons at Versailles that were so popular that the ladies of the court used to go to church hours before kick-off to get a decent seat. The combination of a lengthy wait and a long sermon proved something of a challenge, particularly as it was not the done thing to leave the chapel mid-service, and so help came in the shape of this device, which looks rather like an over-large sauce boat with a long handle, inserted under the ladies' skirts to enable them to relieve themselves. Owing to the voluminous nature of the skirts these were inserted by the lady's maid, who was in church with her, then removed. I've seen these devices at Lennoxlove House in East Lothian, so they may well have been in general use.

While it can't have been much fun for the servants to have to deal with the waste their masters and mistresses produced, lavatorial products were actually part of their perks – a source of a little extra income. Urine went to the fullers for cleaning cloth, and the 'night soil', which was collected by men with a cart every morning, went to make gunpowder.

Servants' perks, incidentally, were an important part of their income – and God help the Georgian employer who didn't provide them. Leftover tea leaves, for example, would be carefully gathered up, dried and sold on to be reused. Sometimes the latest incarnation of used tea leaves would be dyed with lead blacking to make them look more attractive. The results don't bear thinking about. The satirist Jonathan Swift in his *Directions to Servants* (1745) takes a caustic view of what servants might get up to, evoking a world of dishonesty, stubborn obstinacy, sharp practice and constant bickering, where the servants hate each other only a little less than they hate their master or mistress. He suggests that if the cook tells tales about you, you should throw a lump of soot in the pot; if your master or mistress calls for you, you shouldn't answer until the third or fourth time of asking ('none but Dogs will come at the first Whistle'); and if you can pilfer bits and pieces from your employers, do so. As for carrying out a duty that isn't strictly your responsibility:

Never submit to stir a Finger in any Business but that for which you were particularly hired. For Example, if the Groom be drunk or absent, and the Butler be ordered to shut the Stable Door, the Answer is ready, An please your Honour, I don't understand Horses: If a Corner of the Hanging wants a single Nail to fasten it, and the Footman be directed to tack it up, he may say, he doth not understand that Sort of Work, but his Honour may send for the Upholsterer.

One ruse I myself used in my drinking days was to put the clock back if I was running late so that hungry diners incorrectly assumed that it wasn't yet time to eat. It seemed to work.

The actual times that people ate their meals constantly shifted during the Georgian period. The upper and middle classes might breakfast at 9 or 10 a.m. That doesn't mean that they got up and went down to breakfast – breakfast was usually a meal that was taken after people had gone out and been about their business, or gone riding, or done various other things. It became an ever larger meal with various dishes, both hot and cold, laid out on the sideboard, often over little heaters. Contemporary literature shows that in some houses towards the end of the century breakfast remained set out until noon and possibly even later, so that people coming back from somewhere or other could help themselves.

As for dinner, the main meal of the day, an entire very dull book could be written on when precisely it was served in Georgian times. Among the wealthy, the general trend was to serve it later and later as the century went on: at about three o'clock in the afternoon in the early decades of the century; at six or seven o'clock in the evening as we approach 1800. This gradual migration had a lot to do with the increasing availability of artificial light. In the Middle Ages you went to bed when it was dark. By Georgian times you didn't have to, if you could afford lots of candles or if your dining room ran to a chandelier (the word is first recorded by English writers in the 1730s).

Poorer people, by contrast, continued to eat their dinner in the middle of the day, having started work quite early. Supper, eaten just before they went to bed, might – as it had for centuries – consist of cold meat or pie, or just bread and cheese. As tea became an increasingly popular drink and spread further and further down the social scale, working people might also stop for 'tea' in the middle of the afternoon.

For those whose dinner had moved to the evening, there was now a gap to be filled in the middle of the day. Various words already existed for snacks that might be taken at any time, including nuncheon (meaning literally 'noon drink') and luncheon, defined by Dr Johnson in 1755 as 'as much food as one's hand can hold'; and by the early nineteenth century the modern lunch was well on its way. This caused a degree of linguistic confusion that persists to this day. Lunch always means lunch, but for some lunch is actually dinner. And even those for whom lunch is lunch expect their children at school to be supervised by dinner ladies.

When it came to dinner among the rich and powerful, soup, if on offer, came first, followed by removes ('removes' are simply dishes that replace others that have been taken away). As in previous centuries a remove always contained several dishes mixed and matched in a manner that would seem bewildering to us today. A fish and game remove might come first, then the meat, which would have been allowed to rest after roasting. In cold weather the gravy tended to congeal and have fat swimming on top, and this presumably accounts for the inventions of such clever gravy boats as the argyle, which conceals a hot water cylinder to keep the gravy warm. Pickles and biscuits such as oatcakes remained on the table throughout the meal, and other food such as cold beef might be set on a sideboard to be called for as required. Finally, the English sweet tooth was rewarded, as it had been now for a long time, with a dessert of jellies and sweetmeats and perhaps also fruits, nuts and cheese. Servants were on hand to bring each course to the table, and the butler would replenish empty wine glasses.

Even in quite modest households certain rules were observed when deciding who should sit where. At the beginning of the century the hostess often sat at one end of the table with the women guests, while the husband sat at the other end of the table with the male guests. This is certainly the approach recommended in John Trusler's *The Honours of the Table*, first published in 1788, but, interestingly, by his time a sea change was already underway whereby men and women sat alternately around the table. I have to say this seems infinitely preferable to me – who wants to be stuck next to lots of people of their own sex? Trusler, however, was none too impressed by the new fad:

Custom, however, has lately introduced a new mode of seating. A gentleman and a lady sitting alternately round the table, and this, for the better convenience of a lady's being attended to, and served by the gentleman next her. But notwithstanding this promiscuous seating, the ladies, whether above or below, are to be served in order, according to their rank or age . . .

Once the alternating arrangement came in, it is said that people's behaviour improved, because there was rather less boisterous drinking of health and toasts and so forth down the male end of the table. I'm dubious. Given the amount of drinking that went on in Georgian times, I suspect that both sexes happily joined in the toasts.

When it came to serving the food, it tended to be the hostess who did all the carving and dishing out in the earlier part of the century – except, of course, in grander houses where there were servants on hand. I suspect she missed out on the conversation, and she probably missed out on quite a lot of the food, too. By the middle of the century both the master and the mistress had the task of carving the dishes that stood at each end of the table, helping guests to the main meal that was carved and then encouraging them to help themselves from the dishes that were laid out on the table, and in time carving became regarded as something of a necessary male accomplishment. Certain things, though, never alter, and the advice you find being handed out about good table manners in Georgian times is almost exactly the same as it was in the Middle Ages. Personal hygiene is upheld and you're told not to spit, scratch or pick your teeth. One little Georgian refinement is that it is deemed vulgar to smell the meat on your fork or on the plate – such an activity implies that you think the meat might be tainted.

I've talked about the innovations that made their way into the Georgian kitchen. There's also one that appeared in the garden that should be mentioned: the ice house – a small stone outbuilding containing a deep pit in which ice was kept and with food storage space above. Ice's preserving qualities had been noticed in the previous century by the unfortunate Francis Bacon, who died as a direct result of his experiment. By later Stuart times ice houses were beginning to become a feature of more well-to-do houses, and in the course of the eighteenth century they became quite widespread. I have one at home dating from about 1748.

During the winter when the rivers froze, great blocks of ice were sawn from them, transported on sleds and inserted in the pit of the ice house. This pit had suitable drainage in the bottom to allow the melted ice to run away. The food was then hung on racks or on hooks inserted over the ice pit. As late as the 1960s I came across an ice house in Northern Ireland that was still in use, storing salmon from the River Boyne. Situated in cold spots or under a high bank with trees growing on top of it, ice houses could stay cold for months – in fact, mine is still cold on the hottest summer's day and that's without the addition of ice.

Historically, the other way of preserving food was to bottle it in jars sealed with paper and with a leather cover. This method, too, improved in Georgian times as glass jars and pots became more widespread. And this was also the period that witnessed the rise of manufactured conserves and preserves in jars, notably Keiller's Dundee Marmalade. There's a wonderful legend about how this particular conserve came into existence. In 1700, it is said, a terrible storm off the Scottish coast drove a Spanish merchant ship past Leith, where it was originally bound, on to Aberdeen. The cargo was one of Seville oranges, by now damaged by salt water and too bitter to eat. The captain needed to offload his cargo rather speedily and James Keiller bought it at a knock-down price. Then, presumably, having a dark moment of the soul, he thought, 'What on earth am I going to do with hundreds of damaged oranges?' The Keillers had a grocer's shop and so he threw himself upon the mercy of his wife Janet, and it was she who came up with the brilliant idea of producing what was eventually known as Dundee Marmalade. Marmalade at this time was made by pounding oranges into a soft paste in a mortar. Faced with an entire cargo of oranges, this wasn't feasible for Mrs Keiller and so instead she shredded the peel, producing a less solid preserve that easily filled the pots into which it was put. At the end of the century, a new generation of Keillers felt confident enough to offer this conserve to the world at large, and so an empire was launched that made the family fortunes for decades to come.

So far I've talked about the private, domestic life of the Georgians, but that is only half the story. This was, after all, a highly sociable age. People obviously dined and entertained at home, but for the better off, and for men in particular, there were plenty of opportunities to enjoy a public life as well as to indulge in two particular vices of the age: gambling and politics. The coffee houses that Pepys had enjoyed continued to thrive (by Queen Anne's time London boasted at least 500). Now many started to turn into gambling clubs. White's, which today is a pillar of respectability and which started out as a chocolate house, became a notorious gambling den in the early eighteenth century. Along with other venues offering similar thrills, particularly around St James's, it proved a magnet for young men coming up to London keen to sow a few wild oats and prepared to risk fortunes, and indeed their country estates, on the turn of a single card. Gentlemen might not pay their wine merchants, their tailors or any other tradesmen, but not to pay your gambling debts was unthinkable. The games were not necessarily honest ones: there were plenty of vultures who preyed on the naive young to part them from their money. Nor were cards the only things on young gentlemen's minds: other games could be played with ladies of uncertain virtue in a club's private rooms.

Inevitably, such establishments offered plenty of food and drink to their devotees. Rum – a by-product of the sugar coming from the West Indies – was the new popular drink of the time, often served in the form of rum punch: one measure of sour (lime juice), two measures of sweet (sugar), three of strong (rum) and four of weak (water). Elegant punch bowls and ladles have come down to us from Georgian times, some of them with the name of the club to which they belonged. I was once the owner of a rather stylish decanter that had a lime squeezer as its top and a sugar rasp on the side.

Such a heady brew – not to mention all the gambling – may have helped to bring about the downfall of many a titled gentleman, but the clubs which offered such enticements could, I suppose, be said to have made amends through their one immortal contribution to English cuisine: the sandwich. It seems extraordinary that there was ever a time when the sandwich didn't exist – it seems so straightforward and obvious. The fact is, though, that until 1762, if you wanted a bread-based snack, you would hold bread and, say, meat in one hand, a knife in the other, and then cut off slices of each as required. In that year, however, John Montagu, 4th Earl of Sandwich, feeling suddenly rather hungry, sent for two pieces of bread and some slices of meat, clapped them together, and so created the item that still bears his name. There is some controversy over where he was when he had this moment of inspiration. Some, arguing that he never had a reputation for being a gambler during his lifetime, suggest that he was hard at work at the Admiralty, eating with one hand and writing with the other. Others, however, point out that the earliest known mention of 'the sandwich' places him at a gaming table, holding cards in one hand and eating with the other. Either way, he certainly deserves credit for the invention.

Alongside the gambling clubs were the political clubs. I've already talked about the beefsteak clubs, but they were not the only venues where Whigs or Tories gathered to debate and scheme. There was Brooks's, for example, which was set up in Pall Mall in 1764 by a group of high-ranking Whigs (the club also had gambling rooms). And then there were what were known as 'political taverns': drinking establishments where events of the day were vigorously discussed. It's also worth bearing in mind that inns and taverns often formed the focal point for local politics: these were the public buildings where the hustings could be held and results of elections announced, and where liquid bribes could be offered.

William Verral's White Hart at Lewes is a good example of an inn with political connections. An important coaching inn since Elizabethan times, it was acquired in the early eighteenth century by the Duke of Newcastle, initially as a base for Whig supporters. The building was substantial. Downstairs were a bar, buttery, kitchen and parlour, and stables for the coaching inn. Upstairs were the duke's club room, a games room, three large bedrooms and a dormitory for people of lesser importance. At one point Thomas Paine, the revolutionary writer, stayed there, and Thomas Gray of 'Elegy Written in a Country Church-yard' fame had a much-thumbed copy of Verral's *A Complete System of Cookery*. The club room had a large balcony over-looking the street, and it was from here that announcements of election results were made. Eighteenth-century elections were pretty raucous affairs and it's clear that things very quickly got out of hand on occasion. As late as 1807 the White Hart was the scene of a minor riot when local Tory and slave owner 'Mad' Jack Fuller, who had made the inn his campaign head-qurters and whose nickname scarcely invites confidence, was faced by egg-hurling opponents. Fuller bribed his way to victory, paying for 2,000 dinners at the White Hart and as many again at the Dorset Arms.

William Verral himself deserves an honourable footnote in the history of English food. His *Complete System of Cookery* contains all sorts of fascinating information and some rather good recipes. Verral writes very amusingly about the problems of running a hostelry, lamenting how on occasion the housemaid took his finest lawn sieve for refining sauces and used it to sand the floors up to the club room. As a cook trained in the French tradition he is also amused by the attitudes of some of his customers to anything that looks a bit fancy. Here he is, for example, recalling what happened when he was working on his recipe book and a visiting gentleman happened to look over his shoulder:

> While I was writing on he interrupted me, by asking what was meant by apparatus, here, this word says he (holding it to me to read). Why, Sir, says I, it comprehends all necessary and useful things for dressing a dinner fit to serve a gentleman's table, particularly your pretty little made dishes (what are gener-ally called French dishes). Ump, says my old friend, I seldom eat any thing more than a mutton chop, or so; but, however, 'tis all very well for them that like it.

One of my favourites among Verral's 'pretty little made dishes' is one called 'Des oeuffs [*sic*] au miroir' (Eggs on a Mirror). It involves breaking eggs on to a buttered, heatproof dish sprinkled with spring onion, parsley and seasoning, pouring double cream over the top, cooking it all through and then pouring a little extra cream and orange or lemon juice over the top.

There's also a charmingly worded recipe for a side dish involving anchovies and Parmesan cheese:

> Fry some bits of bread about the length of an anchovy in good oil or butter, lay the half of an anchovy with the bone upon each bit, and strew over them some Parmesan cheese grated fine, and colour them nicely in an oven, or with a salamander [a heated piece of metal which you held over the top of whatever you wanted to brown, like putting it under a grill], squeeze the juice of an orange or lemon, and pile them up in your dish and send them to table.

He adds, rather endearingly:

> This seems to be but a trifling thing, but I never saw it come whole from the table.

I've served these myself at my cocktail parties, and they are delicious.

Sadly, in 1757, two years before his book was published, at a time when he was highly successful and the White Hart was doing well, his wife died. Slowly, William fell apart. Whether he turned to drink or not I don't know, but by March 1761 he was bankrupt. He remarried in 1765 and died the same month.

None of what was on offer in the Georgian period would have been possible if there had not been simultaneous changes and improvements to the land and the way in which animals and crops were raised. England had always been prone to periods of bad weather and poor harvests, but, by and large, times of want and famine had been fairly short-lived and the country had been able to feed itself reasonably well. However, as the population of the country continued to rise throughout the seventeenth and eighteenth centuries, and as more people moved to the towns, the pressure on agriculture increased. With the onset of the Industrial Revolution in the late eighteenth century the urban pressure on the countryside became even greater. And here, I can't resist mentioning a food-related piece of trivia about one of the great engineering feats of the new era. When Thomas Telford built his Pontcysyllte aqueduct over the River Dee, he had the joints of the ironwork caulked with Welsh flannel dipped in boiling sugar and then sealed with lead. Over 200 years later, the aqueduct glued together with sugar still stands. Who knows but that Mrs Telford burnt the jam one day, it fell on to the kitchen tiles and young Thomas, ordered to scrape it off, noticed its strongly adhesive qualities? Actually, as he was brought up in Scotland it was probably marmalade that his mother burnt.

Be that as it may, the population of England and Wales rose inexorably from just under 6 million in 1700 to over 9 million by 1800. With ever more mouths to feed and ever larger towns to supply, farming could have buckled under the strain. Instead it transformed itself. Many people had a hand in this trans-formation, but perhaps the best way to appreciate their overall achievement is to look at the lives of just a handful of the principal movers and shakers in what became known as the Agricultural Revolution.

One of the foremost was Viscount Townshend, popularly known as 'Turnip Townshend'. The product of an old Norfolk landowning family who traced their lineage back to the fifteenth century, he was born at Raynham Hall and educated at Eton and King's College, Cambridge. Farming may have been in his blood, but he was also a statesman, serving on Queen Anne's Privy Council and as Ambassador Extraordinary and Plenipotentiary to the States-General (the Netherlands) between 1709 and 1711, when he was involved in the negotiations for the Treaty of Utrecht that brought to an end one of the interminable wars of the eighteenth century. He then went on to be Lord President of the Council.

It was while he was in the Netherlands as Ambassador Extraordinary that he was able to see at first hand the pioneering work done by the farmers in the Waasland region. So impressed was he that on his return he began to make changes to the running of his estates at Raynham, particularly to the way in which fields were managed. English farmers had, since the Middle Ages if not earlier, practised a system of crop rotation whereby the planting of rye or winter wheat would be followed by, say, spring oats or barley. They wouldn't have understood the science of this, but they had worked out through trial and error that rotation of crops is necessary if the build-up of crop-specific pests and diseases is to be avoided and if the soil is to be kept healthy (something that vegetable growers today are fully aware of). Different families of plants have varying nutritional requirements (leguminous crops, for example, help put nitrogen back into the soil) and the soil will receive a further boost if it is left fallow every now and then. What Townshend did at Raynham was to introduce a system of four-field crop rotation, involving a strict order to the succession of crops planted and the timing of each fallow period, thus improving the fertility of the soil and crop production at a stroke.

Townshend's less than flattering nickname 'Turnip' came about through his adoption of another innovation. Turnips had been around in England for some time, but it was Townshend who advocated them as a very convenient fodder crop for cattle during the winter when there was insufficient grass to sustain them. He also championed potatoes in the same way, although, as with so many before him, he met with some resistance from his fellow countrymen. It does seem extraordinary that a crop we now relish should have proved so difficult to establish for such a long time. However, Townshend's advocacy ultimately seems to have helped: the potato was making headway by the middle of the century, and by the end of the Georgian period was being widely cultivated.

Townshend's obsession with the turnip – it was said to be his favourite topic of conversation – led him to be immortalised by Alexander Pope:

> Why, of two brothers, rich and restless one
> Ploughs, burns, manures, and toils from sun to sun;
> The other slights, for women, sports, and wines,
> All Townshend's turnips, and all Grosvenor's mines . . .

Given how rude Pope was about most people, Townshend seems to have got off quite lightly here.

Another of my heroes of the period is Robert Bakewell, who was born at Dishley Grange, near Loughborough in Leicestershire, in 1725. As a young man he travelled around Europe and especially Holland and Flanders, studying the agricultural improvements that were being made. Then at the age of thirty-five he inherited the farm at Dishley and an estate of 440 acres, of which a quarter were ploughed fields and the rest pasture land. Following in the steps of Townshend, Bakewell experimented with plots of land to test irrigation, fertilisation and crop rotation.

But his greatest contribution to the Agricultural Revolution lay in the realm of breeding livestock. I can remember learning as a child that before Bakewell's improvements sheep weren't much bulkier than a modern Labrador dog, and that particular strains of animal came about purely through chance – usually because they were geographically isolated, rather than because there was any planning involved. Bakewell, however, developed a system that he called 'in-and-in', which for the first time isolated male animals from the females with the intention of controlling which traits were passed on to the next generation. Bearing in mind that the science of genetics was many years off, this was an extraordinary piece of intuition that achieved extraordinary results.

His contemporary, the agricultural journalist Arthur Young, was loud in Bakewell's praise, saying that 'his breed of cattle is famous throughout the kingdom' and that they were 'as fat as bears, yet his land is no better than his neighbours'. Certainly, he seems to have been the first to have bred cattle intended primarily for beef production. Until his time, cows were used both for milk and meat, while oxen were primarily used for pulling ploughs. Bakewell crossed Longhorn heifers with a Westmorland bull, and in so doing created a much larger and better quality beast, the Dishley Longhorn. In the course of a single century the average weight of a bull ready for slaughter more than doubled. We should remember that all those thousands upon thousands of cattle that roamed the American prairies, tough enough to stay out all winter surviving the blizzards and the wolves, were Longhorns originally developed by Robert Bakewell.

Work horses were also transformed by Bakewell. Good-sized horses had been bred in England since the Middle Ages – and they had needed to be hefty given the demands placed on them by heavily armed knights and packs and loads. But when it came to pulling ploughs or working the fields, oxen were what were used. Bakewell developed a horse breed he called the 'improved black cart horse', which was then crossbred with other large-breed animals to produce Shire horses. When horses are of the right size and quality, they are much easier to plough with than oxen and so it's not surprising that until only a few years ago breeds such as the Suffolk Punch were still being sold to countries which had few tractors to call on. By the end of the Georgian period virtually no ploughing was done with oxen.

But perhaps Bakewell's greatest success was sheep breeding. Selecting large, fine-boned animals with long lustrous fleeces from the ordinary native stock, he started with the Lincoln Longwool, which he greatly improved, and then developed the New or Dishley Leicester. This was a hornless beast with a square, meaty body and a straight-topped back; it was eventually exported as far afield as Australia and North America – and taken to the Scottish Borders, where it became the Border Leicester. The Leicester is probably our defining sheep, the ancestor of so many of our modern breeds.

Bakewell was a great populariser. He wrote and lectured extensively about his methods, and these were taken up across Europe, being championed by François de la Rochefoucauld of the French *Académie des sciences*, among others. In 1783 Bakewell formed the Dishley Society to promote his ideas and to advance the interests of livestock breeders. His influence lasted long after his death in 1795.

One of the people Bakewell most influenced was Thomas Coke, 1st Earl of Leicester and master of Holkham Hall in Norfolk, who was born in 1754 and died in 1842 at the ripe old age of eighty-eight. Coke's father, who was born Wenham (or Wenman) Roberts and had to change his name to inherit, was a cousin of the ancient family of Norfolk Cokes who traced their ancestry back to Sir Edward Coke, Chief Justice of the King's Bench in the reign of James I. It was Sir Edward who became involved in the Overbury scandal that rocked James I's court. He was a man of principle who fought for the independence of the judiciary, and some of his independent spirit seems to have rubbed off on his descendant Thomas Coke. A Whig politician throughout his adult life, Thomas claimed to have turned down six offers of a peerage. On one occasion, it is said, he annoyed the Prince Regent, who retaliated by threatening to knight him. 'If he tries to knight me, by God, I will break his sword,' Coke is supposed to have retorted. It wasn't until he was an old man that he was persuaded by his second wife, Lady Anne Amelia Keppel, daughter of William Keppel, 4th Earl of Albemarle, into accepting an earldom for his eldest son Thomas, who became the Earl of Leicester.

As the George IV anecdote suggests, Coke was a robust character. He was also a very keen sportsman and hunting man. In fact, a by-product of his family's love of the chase was the invention of what we now think of as the bowler hat – originally known as the Billy Coke hat or Billycock hat because either his nephew or another relative, according to who you believe, was sick of having his top hat knocked off by tree branches when out hunting. Coke himself greatly improved Holkham Hall, planting over a million trees, not just for decoration but to help drainage and serve as windbreaks for the winds that whip off Siberia and the Urals into Norfolk. He was also the first person to grow wheat rather than the traditional rye in west Norfolk. But his principal claim to fame from my point of view is that he worked tirelessly on improving livestock breeds. Foremost among these were the Southdown sheep – rather curiously named, given how far away the South Downs are from Norfolk. He also cultivated Devon cattle, one of the oldest English breeds, and improved the Norfolk breed of pigs. Indeed he is probably the reason why so much pig breeding still goes on in that county.

Like Bakewell, Coke was a great populariser, holding sheep-shearing events that were known as 'Coke's Clippings' at Holkham to which people came not only from all over England but from all over Europe as well. Arguably they are the ancestors of our modern agricultural county shows. He was adept at dealing with any problem that arose. There is a delightful story of how, when a field of cabbages became infested with caterpillars, he turned loose 200 ducks into the field, which ate all the caterpillars quite happily. Sadly when my friend Johnny Scott and I were filming at Holkham in 2000 we discovered they had just taken the last Southdown sheep off the estate. Given all Coke's hard work and his tireless championing of the breed, it seemed rather sad to me – and a sign of just how badly the wool industry, once the pride of England, has declined.

The last of my agricultural reforming heroes is also the earliest of them. Jethro Tull was born in 1674, near Bradfield in Berkshire. He matriculated at St John's College, Oxford, at the age of seventeen but left without taking a degree and went to study law at Gray's Inn – my own Inn of Court. He developed problems with his lungs and went in search of a cure in Europe, where he acquired knowledge of the agricultural improvements that were happening there and then devoted himself to inventing numerous implements. Among the most important of these was a horse-drawn seed drill that sowed seeds effectively and in straight rows. It was initially and inevitably resisted by farm workers who feared that it would throw them out of a job. Tull also improved the design of the plough (his modifications are still visible in ploughs today) and invented a horse-drawn hoe for clearing weeds in the fields. When it came to weed control, he strongly believed that since horse dung contained seeds it was not an unmixed blessing as a fertiliser, and that if the soil was sufficiently pulverised to release its natural nutrition, fertiliser was not, in any case, always the answer.

In later life Tull acquired Prosperous Farm, which lies just outside Hungerford in his native Berkshire. There he established a famous Guernsey dairy herd. The farm still exists and still keeps Guernsey cattle. Guernsey milk is delicious, as is Guernsey cream. It may help soothe asthma and other lung conditions, and I have often wondered whether Tull chose this particular breed because of his own lung complaints. He died in 1741 at the age of sixty-seven. It was not until the Agricultural Revolution was at its height some thirty years later that many of his innovations were taken up. They are now deeply embedded in the foundations of productive modern agriculture.

The ability of Britain's farmers to keep pace with demand meant that – for those with money, at least – the Georgian larder was always full. What's more, because the century also saw major improvements to the nation's transport system with the building of canals and the construction of improved roads (turnpikes, whose upkeep was paid for by a system of tolls, became widespread in the eighteenth century), what was actually in the larder could be quite varied. Town markets not only were able to offer local produce but might well have available such far-flung items as Scottish salmon, Newcastle smoked haddock, and Cheddar, Gloucester, Cheshire and Stilton cheeses (though Daniel Defoe did report that fish brought to the London markets by road often stank by the time they arrived). Even the exotic turtle, which was brought across from the West Indies on wet straw, made its way, in the form of soup, on to the dining tables of the middle and upper classes. Soup is a bit of a misnomer: turtle soup was more a stew really, since it had different cuts of the turtle floating around in it. So fashionable did turtle become that those who could not afford the real thing resorted to recipes for mock turtle soup, made from calf's head. The fashion for turtle soup endured for decades. As late as the 1890s we find Lady Clark of Tillypronie giving instructions for keeping a turtle alive in a Scottish kitchen before it was dispatched to serve some great feast. Great houses and London livery halls still display turtle shells, polished and edged with silver to form very splendid decorations. Tortoiseshell began to adorn many of the artefacts of the day.

The great staples of the English diet – meat, bread, vegetables – were readily available and reasonably affordable throughout the first half of the century. Daniel Defoe, touring England in the 1720s, describes a country where most people had enough to eat. In fact, he seemed to be more concerned with local outbreaks of immorality and fecklessness than with any incidence of hunger, noting, for example, that men living on the east coast had a deplorable tendency to take a large number of wives (one farmer on Canvey Island was on his twenty-fifth), and that the poor of Cambridgeshire were bone idle ('to their scandal'). He was also fascinated by the range of local foods in England: Essex fish, Cheshire cheeses, Norfolk cattle and pheasants, Kentish hops, Wirksworth ale. It was not until later in the century, when a series of bad harvests, a population that was increasing at an ever swifter rate and the beginnings of the Industrial Revolution all conspired together, that we really start to see the poor going short.

Common vegetables, such as cabbages, turnips, carrots, parsnips and onions, which had long been part of the diet, were increasingly being supplemented by more unusual ones, including French beans, asparagus, artichokes and celery (Neat House, the London market garden now covered by Victoria station, became famous for its celery towards the end of the century). Then there were the cauliflowers immortalised by Wedgwood in his teapots, and *petits pois*, encountered by Charles II during his exile in France in the Commonwealth period and then duly popularised on his return. All these would have been lightly cooked – the terrible English tendency to boil vegetables to death came later – and it's interesting to note that Eliza Smith, the earliest of the more successful cookery writers in the Georgian era, is so emphatic on this point. Salads, championed by John Evelyn in the previous century, continued their upward progress, with cress, cucumber and spring onions regularly making an appearance. Late-eighteenth-century recipes even mention tomatoes – known in England for the best part of 200 years but previously regarded with suspicion. However, these would have been cooked, not served raw. By contrast, fruit, which had previously so often been cooked, was now acceptable raw, even though in this state it more often formed part of a diet for invalids. The old worries that it caused colic or even that it carried the plague were starting to subside.

You get a very good sense of what the reasonably prosperous ate from the well-known diary of Parson James Woodforde, which he kept assiduously for some forty-five years until his death in 1803. Woodforde himself was clearly a rather dull man. Educated at Winchester and then New College, Oxford, he was unambitious and intellectually somewhat mediocre. After graduating he failed to obtain the living of his father's old parish, and then he failed in his proposal of marriage to the love of his life. ('She has behaved to me like a mere Jilt,' he confided to his diary.) Thereafter he settled for being a bachelor and took up the living of Weston Longville in Norfolk (which belonged to New College), arriving there in 1774 and staying until his death. Dullness was, to be fair, offset by a basically good nature. He was always ready to tip with a shilling for some trifling service and to help the needy, as this typical diary entry (for 26 November 1790) suggests:

A poor fellow from Windham (who looked exactly as if he had come out of Jail, a young Fellow, short, black hair, a very dirty shirt, a Short kind of brown great Coat and Kitty-boots) came to the back door and begged some Victuals. I gave him a part of a rost Neck of Veal and bread. He might be, and I hope is a very honest Fellow, but his appearance was much against him.

Woodforde's dullness has also, paradoxically, ensured that he is still remembered, for his very ordinary diary records in minute – and therefore, to us, fascinating – detail everyday life in the last decades of the eighteenth century, from what he was paid by farmers in tithes or by parishioners for marriages and burials to how long particular journeys took. There is, for example, a very detailed account of a trip he made to the West Country from Weston, which serves as a useful reminder of just how expensive and time-consuming travel still was, despite the sort of improvements to the roads that I have already described. Woodforde himself had a couple of horses, and the first stage of the journey, from Weston to Norwich, could be done by horse and cart in a couple of hours. The leg of the journey from Norwich to London, however, took seventeen hours, and the London to Salisbury coach, which set off mid-afternoon, didn't arrive until early the next day. One way and another the journey cost him over £10, and then there were food and accommodation bills to be paid on top of that.

More importantly for our purposes, Parson Woodforde's diary tells us a lot about Georgian food. And there's no doubt that he took his food very seriously. Here is the entry for 3 December 1776, when he was entertaining on a grand scale:

> My Frolic [party] for my People to pay Tithe to me was this day. I gave them a good dinner, surloin of Beef rosted, a Leg of Mutton boiled and plumb Puddings in plenty . . . They all broke up about 10 at night. Dinner at 2. Every Person well pleased, and were very happy indeed . . . They drank of wine 6 Bottles, of Rum 1 gallon and half, and I know not what ale . . . Some dined in the Parlour, and some in the Kitchen. 17 dined etc that paid my Tithe . . . We had many droll songs from some of them . . .

Dinner with Mrs Farr on 19 April 1768 consisted of:

. . . a roasted Shoulder of Mutton and a plum Pudding for dinner
– Veal Cutlets, Frill'd Potatoes, cold Tongue, Ham and cold roast
Beef, and eggs in their shells. Punch, Wine, Beer and Cyder for
drinking.

Even less festive meals were pretty substantial. On 29 August 1786,
he records what would have been for him a fairly modest dinner
of ham, fowls, tripe, green peas, a hare and a raspberry tart.

Parson Woodforde didn't just consume food; he went out
and caught it, too. It's clear from his diary that he was a keen
fisherman, sometimes keeping his catch for a while in the pond
in his garden before taking it to the kitchen, sometimes passing
on a few fish from a particularly good day's angling to friends.
He also liked hare coursing – long popular in Norfolk – both
for sport (as previously mentioned, the Romans had introduced
the brown hare to England for this purpose) and for meat.
Again, he would sometimes share his catch with friends if the
hunting had been particularly good, and they, on occasion,
would reciprocate.

A handful of staple items were clearly produced at home – beer,
for example, which was brewed at various different strengths.
Woodforde paid his maltster about £20 a year. I assume that the
household must also have baked its own bread, but, if it did,
Woodforde took this so much for granted that his diary barely
mentions it. That said, he does record that in the terrible winter
of 1794/5, when the milk froze in the dairy, he gave the poor people
of the parish free bread a couple of times a week. The living at
Weston came with a farm attached, and that yielded things like
pork and corn that could be consumed at home or sold at market.

When it came to more exotic items, Woodforde was not

above doing business with the less respectable elements of local society. On 29 March 1777, for instance, just as he was going to bed at eleven o'clock, he was frightened by the sound of whistling coming from under the parlour window. It turned out to be Andrews the smuggler bringing the parson a bag of Hyson tea weighing six pounds. Had Woodforde bought this legally it could have cost him as much as three guineas a pound. As it was, the smuggler was content with some Geneva gin and ten shillings and sixpence per pound. Woodforde obtained gin and brandy by the barrel in the same nefarious way, paying six shillings a gallon for gin (half the shop price) and ten shillings for brandy. He bottled the liquor himself, quickly and in secret, fully aware that the penalty for being caught with a smuggled barrel was a £10 fine. The smuggler was also able to procure such luxuries as 'silk India Handkerchiefs'.

Dealings with the local smuggler may have added a frisson of excitement to Woodforde's life, but daily life at the parsonage was generally quiet and unvarying. Woodforde lived with his niece, who was also his housekeeper. He had a manservant, a head maid and a lower maid. (Interestingly, when he took on a new maid he agreed that she should have five guineas a year and tea twice a day – a sign of how by the late eighteenth century tea was being drunk at all levels of society; previously men such as Woodforde would have agreed to pay 'beer money' to their servants.) The house had at least four permanent bedrooms and a privy in an outside building. Heating was by coal fire but this was clearly of limited effectiveness in very cold weather; Woodforde records of one particularly icy day in the winter of 1785: 'The Frost severer than ever in the night as it even froze the Chamber Pots under the Beds.' Entertainment consisted of activities like card playing (which Woodforde loved) and visits to the theatre or a concert in Norwich.

So far as daily meals were concerned, he would eat snacks for breakfast and supper but then indulge himself when it came to the main meal of the day, which was served at around three o'clock in the afternoon. His diet was a heavy one, with too much meat, too few vegetables and too many puddings, cakes and pies. It's scarcely surprising, therefore, that he suffered from many of the common complaints of the time: heartburn, colic, bleeding piles and gout (the gout can't have been helped by the fact that at one point he was drinking a bottle of port a day).

As I've already said, the eighteenth century was a great time for overindulgence, and not just because so much meat was consumed: among the wealthy, bread seems to have given way in popularity, to a certain extent, to puddings. It's no coincidence therefore that it was also a period when spa towns, such as Bath and Tunbridge Wells, became popular. Taking the waters was regarded as the height of fashion, and, along with some brisk exercise and abstention from heavy meals, no doubt improved the constitution. You might even nibble on a Bath Oliver, the biscuit invented by the Bath physician Dr Oliver. Once your liver was rested you would feel greatly invigorated and so free to indulge all over again.

It's not a coincidence, either, that it should have been a Georgian – Sir Alexander Dick – who pioneered the propagation of that useful laxative, rhubarb, in Britain. A physician by profession and friend of Dr Johnson's biographer James Boswell, he won a gold medal from the Royal Society of Arts in 1774 for 'the best specimen of rhubarb'. If you go to his house just outside the centre of Edinburgh, now a hotel known as

Prestonfield, you will find that it has a restaurant called the Rhubarb Restaurant and that rhubarb is to be found growing in the grounds. Parson Woodforde certainly availed himself of rhubarb powder on occasion. Unfortunately, that only helped with some of his complaints. When his gout became unbearable he sought to quell it with a supper of gruel.

The poor at this time would not have experienced such afflictions – but then they were not in the position of being able to eat so well that they would ever be in danger of suffering them. After all, in the latter years of the Georgian era farm labourers could expect to be paid little more than seven pence a day, and even such relatively skilled workers as carpenters and masons received only one shilling and threepence. London wages were obviously higher, as they always are – a housemaid might get £5 a year, a labourer £24 a year – but then they would have had to cope with a higher cost of living. This sort of earning power would have yielded a breakfast of bread, butter, cold meats and cheese washed down with beer or, increasingly, tea. Dinner, eaten at noon and still the main meal of the day, might consist of shin of beef, perhaps served with vegetables such as potatoes or cabbage, accompanied by bread and beer, and possibly followed by cheese. You might eat this at home, but equally you might stop off at a tavern or buy your meal from a cook shop. If, however, you were not in work, food was a pretty grim affair served in small portions. Those unfortunate enough to end up in the workhouse could expect a monotonous diet of broth, bread and cheese and – perhaps a couple of times a week – boiled beef and suet pudding. In fact, as the consumption of bread declined among wealthier Georgians, so it rose among the poor. By now white bread was becoming more widely available, and so people tended to scorn the rougher, darker bread, even in times of bad harvest. Unfortunately, the desire for white bread led to a decrease in its quality: often inferior flour liberally laced with alum, which helped bulk it up and make it look whiter, was used.

In the Midlands, where the first flowerings of the Industrial Revolution started to lure people away from the countryside, the labouring classes fared very badly indeed. They lived on bought bread and cheese washed down with beer or recycled tea. Beer has its virtues since it contains both calories and vitamins; tea has few such redeeming features. Rickets and scurvy, diseases of deficiency, increased towards the end of the century, especially in northern towns. Nor was life in the countryside idyllic. The enclosure of common lands that had started in the sixteenth century now gathered pace, cutting people off from pasturage and limiting their ability to gather wood for their fires. Villagers would still have their pigs to supplement their diet and raise a bit of spare cash, but often there were lean times, particularly later in the century, and particularly with the onset of the Napoleonic Wars. It's as well to remember that elegant living in Georgian England didn't extend to everyone.

To my mind, Hannah Glasse is one of the great figures in the history of English food. This is the frontispiece to her *The Art of Cookery Made Plain and Easy*, which was first published in 1746 and covers everything from roasting to baking. Her recipe for curry signals the beginning of an English love affair with Indian food that persists to this day.

CHAPTER 10

Roast Hare and Indian Curry

The Era of Hannah Glasse

Various people from medieval times onwards turned their hand to cookery books, Elinor Fettiplace, Robert May and Sir Kenelm Digby among them. Only a relatively small number, however, published their works for a general readership. In Georgian times all that changed. As the number of people who could read increased, so there was a new demand for books of recipes and household hints. In fact, between the years 1700 and 1800 over 300 books on food and cookery were published, some in many editions. It is safe to say that most middle-class households in Georgian times would have possessed a cookery book and that – for the first time – many housewives and at least some of the cooks they employed would have been able to follow a printed recipe: it's been estimated that, at the mid-century mark, nearly four in ten women could read. It was the beginnings of a national appetite for cookery books that persists today.

There are various Georgian cookery writers who deserve credit for their contribution to English food. But, for me, the towering figure is Hannah Glasse (1708–70). Her *The Art of Cookery Made Plain and Easy* was first published in 1746 and ran to no fewer than seventeen editions before the end of the century. It's a masterly summary of the sort of food that would have been served in well-to-do houses in the mid century. It's also beautifully and clearly written, and Hannah herself is a figure who fascinates me.

The record of her christening at St Andrew, Holborn, in March 1708 states that Hannah was the daughter of Hannah Reynolds, a widow, and Isaac Allgood, a Northumbrian squire and 'coal holder' (that is, the owner of several coal seams). Isaac may have been a man of some wealth, but he wasn't actually Hannah Reynolds's husband: in fact, he had recently made a second marriage to a certain Hannah Clark, the daughter of a London merchant. He did, however, take his illegitimate daughter Hannah with him to Simonburn near Hexham, where she was raised alongside his legitimate children Lancelot and Isaac. People at that time were quite tolerant about illegitimacy and it was not uncommon to bring up your husband's children or indeed your wife's children by different liaisons. Hannah's natural mother also followed, but her relationship with her daughter was not a happy one – Hannah describes her as a 'wicked wretch' in some of her letters – and she had little involvement in her daughter's upbringing.

When Hannah was fifteen or sixteen, her adoptive mother died, her father fell ill and Hannah herself was sent to live with her grandmother in London. She clearly found life there narrow and frustrating, and at the age of sixteen, without consulting her family, rushed into marriage with an Irish soldier by the name of John Glasse, who seems to have been considerably older than her. There was a big family row, but Hannah was eventually forgiven and she and her husband moved to New Hall in Broomfield in Essex, where they served the 4th Earl of Donegal and where Hannah had her first child. When the Countess of Donegal died in 1732, Hannah and John moved to London and over the next few years Hannah gave birth at regular intervals, bearing ten children of whom only five survived.

By the mid 1740s Hannah was hard at work on *The Art of Cookery*, and it was published in 1746 by subscription (as many of the books of the time were in order to ensure their financial viability), also being sold through Mrs Ashburn's China Shop in London. The first print run was received with wild enthusiasm and a second edition followed swiftly. Hannah opted to publish anonymously, and this led to some speculation about who the author might be, some suggesting that the well-known writer and botanist John Hill was behind the enterprise. Thirty years later, discussion still raged. In his *Life of Johnson* James Boswell describes a dinner at which John Hill's candidacy as author was discussed. Dr Johnson, he says, dismissed the idea, not because he was anxious to uphold the claims of Hannah Glasse (who he does mention) but because some mistakes in the book were sufficient to convince him that John Hill couldn't be the author. This was, of course, the Dr Johnson who once said of the notion of a woman preaching a sermon that it was 'like a dog's walking on his hinder legs. It is not done well; but you are surprised to find it done at all.'

Hannah may not have received the credit she deserved, but

the book did make her quite a lot of money and she was able to set up a fashionable costumier's in Tavistock Street, patronised by, among others, the Princess of Wales. Unfortunately, things went downhill from then on. John Glasse died in the summer of 1747, leaving behind quite a lot of debt. Hannah went bankrupt in May 1754 and was forced to sell off the shop, keeping only the stock (which was in her daughter Margaret's name). She then had to sell her most prized possession, her copyright in *The Art of Cookery.* That, at least, was enough to provide her with a certificate of discharge from bankruptcy, but things didn't improve and in 1757 Hannah was consigned to the Marshalsea debtors' prison and then transferred to the Fleet prison. She was presumably at liberty again by the winter, as she registered shares in *The Servants' Directory,* a new book she had written on how best to manage a household. Popular in North America in plagiarised editions, it was not a success in the UK and by 1758 the property in Tavistock Street was listed as empty. To add insult to injury Hannah had to endure a sustained attack in print by a woman named Ann Cook, whose *Professed Cookery* of 1760 seems to have been part of an ongoing vendetta against Hannah's brother Lancelot.

The same year in which *Professed Cookery* appeared saw the publication of Hannah's third and final book, *The Compleat Confectioner.* It was not the success that Hannah had hoped for, and is now very rare, though I am fortunate enough to own a copy of it. We don't know that much more about her life, except that she died in 1770 at the age of sixty-two, still fairly destitute. By this time most of her surviving children had died, one in Bombay, one in Pondicherry, one in Jamaica. Only two daughters appear to have outlived their mother.

If you look on the Internet you will find mention of a BBC documentary in which Hannah is declared to be 'the mother of the modern dinner party'. I would go along with that, since I was the one who made the claim and I still stand by it. What she did was to come up with recipes that are so simply and well expressed that women from ordinary middle-class households could give them to their cooks – or read them out loud – and be confident that the end result would be a success. There are frequent little details that make the recipes a delight to follow, for example the observation in one recipe (which I'll come to in a moment) that you should take as much thyme as will cover a sixpence – a brilliantly visual and practical way to put it.

And this was what Hannah was seeking to achieve, as the introduction to her book makes clear:

> To the reader. I believe I have attempted a branch of cookery which nobody has yet thought worth their while to write upon: but as I have both seen, and found by experience, that the generality of servants are greatly wanting in that point, therefore I have taken upon me to instruct them in the best manner I am capable; and, I dare say, that every servant who can but read will be capable of making a tolerable good cook, and those who have the least notion of cookery cannot miss of being very good ones.

She goes on to explain why she is so anxious to keep things simple:

> If I have not wrote in the high polite stile, I hope I shall be forgiven; for my intention is to instruct the lower sort, and

therefore must treat them in their own way. For example: when I bid them lard a fowl if I should bid them lard with large lardoons, they would not know what I meant: but when I say they must lard with little pieces of bacon, they know what I mean. So, in many other things in cookery, the great cooks have such a high way of expressing themselves, that the *poor girls* are at a loss to know what they mean . . .

Not only did she want to keep things simple, she wanted to keep them affordable, too. She'll say when you can leave out a particular ingredient because it might be too expensive for you, suggesting, for example, after a recipe for gravy, 'You may leave out the wine, according to what use you want it for; so that really one might have a genteel entertainment, for the price the sauce of one dish comes to.'

This leads to a characteristic sideswipe at fashionable French cookery:

. . . if gentlemen will have *French* cooks, they must pay for *French* tricks.

A *Frenchman* in his own country would dress a fine dinner of twenty dishes, and all genteel and pretty, for the expence he will put an *English* lord to for dressing one dish. But then there is the little petty profit. I have heard of a cook that used six pounds of butter to fry twelve eggs when every body knows (that understands cooking) that half a pound is full enough, or more than need be used: but then it would not be *French*. So much is the blind folly of this age, that they would rather be imposed on by a *French* booby, than give encouragement to a good *English* cook.

She's very clear about what is and isn't relevant in a cookery book. She's not interested in cures, unlike the authors of previous 'receipt' books (she only mentions two, though there are a number of soothing recipes for convalescents). Nor is she interested in giving lectures on household management, nor on how to lay a table. When she gives a recipe a foreign name, she does so because she reckons that this name is best known. She doesn't do it in a bid to look fashionable. Don't you just love her!

Throughout, her aim is to make the case for good ingredients, unpompous food and easy-to-learn techniques. I remember the fuss there was when Delia Smith told us all how to boil an egg. She was absolutely right, of course. At the time there was hardly a hotel in the country that could prepare eggs well. Hannah, similarly, is concerned with getting people back to the basics of cookery, pointing out in her first chapter on roasting and boiling:

> That professed cooks will find fault with touching upon a branch
> of cookery which they never thought worth their notice, is what
> I expect: however, this I know, it is the most necessary part of
> it; and few servants there are, that know how to roast and boil
> to perfection.

Her instructions here are simple and straightforward. She even tells you how long each type of meat will take to cook. In a similar way, when it comes to preparing vegetables, she emphasises first principles: the importance of rinsing vegetables in different washes of water to make quite sure that all the grit and dirt is taken from them. Since they would usually have come straight from the vegetable garden or certainly from the market, this is good advice. I certainly remember that vegetables in my childhood could be very gritty and dirty.

The recipes themselves are beautifully and lucidly expressed. Here, for example, is her recipe for roasting a hare:

> Take your hare when it is cased [skinned] and make a pudding; take a quarter of a pound of suet, and as much crumbs of bread, a little parsley shred fine, and about as much thyme as will lie on a six-pence, when shred; an anchovy shred small, a very little pepper and salt, some nutmeg, two eggs and a little lemon-peel. Mix all these together, and put it into the hare. Sew up the belly, spit it, and lay it to the fire, which must be a good one. Your dripping-pan must be very clean and nice. Put in two quarts of milk and half a pound of butter into the pan; keep basting it all the while it is roasting, with the butter and milk, till the whole is used, and your hare will be enough. You may mix the liver in the pudding, if you like it. You must first parboil it, and then chop it fine.

I can vouch for this recipe as I cooked it myself for my television programme about Hannah Glasse, and I was impressed that the baste was indeed all used up when the hare was cooked. I can also vouch for the wisdom of Hannah's observations on the broiling of steaks when she says:

> If you love pickles or horse-radish with steaks, never garnish your dish, because both the garnishing will be dry, and the steaks will be cold, but lay those things on little plates, and carry to the table. The great nicety is to have them hot and full of gravy.

I've spent my entire life telling chefs in restaurants to do precisely that. Sadly, most like to pile garnishes on to your steak willy-nilly. I'm with Hannah Glasse all the way on this.

When it comes to vegetables, Hannah advocates boiling most of them, but is at pains to say that you mustn't overcook them. Spinach, for example, should be cooked until it wilts (interestingly, she advocates serving a butter sauce separately – unusual in an era which liked to use butter sauces very liberally). And here's a recipe 'to dress potatoes' which is worth giving in full because not only does it celebrate the previously largely ignored potato but it is, so far as I know, the first mention of fried potatoes in a cookery book:

> . . . put them into a saucepan with some good beef dripping, cover them close, and shake the saucepan often for fear of burning to the bottom. When they are of a fine brown and crisp, take them up in a plate, then put them into another for fear of the fat, and put butter in a cup.

This is not the only potato recipe to make its way into the book. Hannah also tells you how to boil and mash them. And there's a nice recipe for a potato pudding:

> Take two pounds of white potatoes, boil them soft, peel and beat them in a mortar, or strain them through a sieve till they are quite fine; then mix in half a pound of fresh butter melted, then beat up the yolks of eight eggs and three whites, stir them in, and half a pound of white sugar finely pounded, half a pint of sack [sherry], stir it well together, grate in half a large nutmeg, and stir in half a pint of cream, make a puff-paste [pastry], and

lay all over your dish and round the edges; pour in the pudding, and bake it of a fine light brown. For change, put in half a pound of currants . . .

It may sound a rather strange potato pie, but it's actually very good either hot or cold. It demonstrates the potato's progress by the mid century and also betrays Hannah's northern upbringing – at this time potatoes were considerably more popular in the north than in the south.

Many of the recipes are exactly what you would expect to find in a cookery book of this period: lots of meat and fish dishes; plenty of sauces and soups (including 'portable' soups – soups that were boiled until solid and then reconstituted at a later date); good substantial puddings (including bread puddings, fruit puddings, rice puddings, and Yorkshire pudding – another sign of Hannah's northern upbringing); cakes and biscuits; cheesecakes, jellies and syllabubs; whole pages devoted to pickling everything from cauliflower to lemons (and interestingly some recipes for 'Captains of ships', including one 'To make catchup to keep twenty years'). One little passage that amuses me comes in her cheese section when she distinguishes between Scotch rarebit, Welsh rarebit and English rarebit. Scotch rarebit is just cheese on toast and the bread is toasted on both sides; Welsh rarebit is cheese on toast with mustard; English rarebit is made with brown bread toasted on both sides, soaked in red wine and then heavily coated with cheese and put in a tin oven close to the fire until the cheese is melted and browned. Maybe the last variant has something to do with the drinking habits of the English at the time.

Flavours have come a long way since Elinor Fettiplace's era.

Spices are more sparingly used, as are ingredients like rose water. This is food that, for the most part, we would recognise today: fish cooked in butter; beef cooked with wine; rice pudding; drop biscuits. At the same time, there are constant reminders that the Georgian palate was different to our own. A delicious turkey recipe with a red wine sauce also stipulates that, alongside a shallot and thyme, you should place an anchovy in the bird's cavity while it cooks. A side dish of peas comes seasoned with salt and nutmeg and served in cream. Eggs on toast, cooked under a 'red-hot shovel', are sprinkled with orange juice and nutmeg.

Even for the time, there are some surprises and novelties. And the one I am most drawn to is a rather fine curry. This may seem a little out of place in such an 'English' book, but when you consider how important India was to Britain in this period it's perhaps not so remarkable. After all, two of Hannah's own sons made the journey to the subcontinent, and this was when the East India Company was at its zenith: hugely successful, hugely wealthy and hugely corrupt. Some decades after Hannah published the first edition of her book, the former Governor-General of Bengal, Warren Hastings, was impeached before the Commons on a whole range of corruption charges in a trial that extended from 1787 until 1795. His near-contemporary Lord Clive had also made a fortune in India and was similarly accused of all sorts of wrong-doing. I always remember his ringing words of defence when called before Parliament in 1773. Thinking back on the great opportunities he could have seized to have made money and the lesser ones he reckoned he actually settled for, he declared, 'By God, Mr Chairman, at this moment I stand astonished at my own moderation!'

I've already hinted at Hannah's interest in the East in my reference to catchup, since catchup, or ketchup, comes from the Malay 'catsup'. Hannah's recipe involves beer, anchovies, shallots and seasoning. It's the precursor of some of the commercially produced ketchups you find appearing towards the end of the century, the first being 'Lazenby's Anchovy Essence' and 'Harvey's Sauce', the latter of which you can still buy to this day. The East Indies also gave us piccalilli, pilau and pickled mangoes (Jane Austen mentions eating mango in one of her letters), and by 1780 ready-mixed curry powder was available for sale. It's worth remembering when you hear the claim that chicken tikka masala is the nation's favourite dish that the taste for Indian food in England goes back a long way – even if chicken tikka masala itself has only a nodding acquaintance with the subcontinent.

Hannah's famous recipe 'To make a currey the Indian way' reads as follows:

Take two small chickens, skin them and cut them as for a fricasey [i.e. in eight pieces], wash them clean, and stew them in about a quart of water, for about five minutes, then strain off the liquor and put the chickens in a clean dish; take three large onions, chop them small and fry them in about two ounces of butter, then put in the chickens and fry them together till they are brown, take a quarter of an ounce of turmerick, a large spoonful of ginger and beaten pepper together, and a little salt to your palate; strew all these ingredients over the chickens whilst it is still frying, then pour in the liquor, and let it stew about half an hour, then put in a quarter of a pint of cream, and the juice of two lemons, and serve it up. The ginger, pepper, and turmerick must be beat very fine.

To prepare the rice:

> Put two quarts of water to a pint of rice, let it boil till you think it is done enough, then throw in a spoonful of salt, and turn it into a cullender [colander]; then let it stand about five minutes before the fire to dry, and serve it up in a dish by itself.

I have to say that before I cooked this for my Hannah Glasse documentary I was a bit sceptical: it seemed to have few of the spices that we consider part and parcel of a curry. Nevertheless, I was pleasantly surprised by the end result, as were my guests, who included Michelle Berriedale-Johnson and Paul Levy. The dish is perhaps disconcertingly white, but it has a very good and interesting flavour.

Hannah's last book, *The Compleat Confectioner*, may not have brought her the money she so badly needed, but it still contains some wonderful material. She tells you how to refine your sugars by boiling and skimming, how to preserve various fruits such as oranges and lemons in sugar syrup, and even how to candy them. She also warns about the dangers of cooking acidic food in brass and copper pans (not that she criticises some other less than praiseworthy habits, for example using alum with boiling vinegar to make preserved apples look greener).

She also has much to say about strawberries, and here I would like to think that she was taking advantage of the great eighteenth-century leap forward in the cultivation of a fruit that we now regard as quintessentially English. Historically the only strawberries available had been wild strawberries: sweet but small and quite difficult to find. The seventeenth century saw the introduction of new strawberry varieties from the New

World, but really we owe our modern strawberries to a French spy (and fireworks fanatic), Amédée-François Frézier, who came across a much larger variety of strawberry in Chile and introduced it to France in 1714. This particular strain was rather dull and flavourless, but when crossed with the Virginian strawberries that had arrived in Europe some decades before, the results were impressive. Different varieties of strawberry were soon springing up all over the place – just a few minutes from where I grew up in St John's Wood, for example, a certain William Atkinson was growing a variety known as Grove End Scarlet in the 1820s. Sadly there was no sign of strawberry fields there in my youth, the main strawberry-growing area by that time being Tiptree in Essex.

One great invention that Hannah appears to have come up with on the dessert front is the modern trifle. Trifles are often mentioned in earlier literature, but these recipes tend to be for what we today would call fools. Hannah gave a recipe for what we would broadly identify today as trifle in the first edition of *The Art of Cookery Made Plain and Easy* (though she called it 'Floating Island'), then for a 'Triffle' in the fourth edition, and then this wonderful recipe for 'A grand trifle' in *The Compleat Confectioner*. As ever, the recipe is beautifully written:

> Take a very large china dish or glass, that is deep; first make some very fine rich calves-foot jelly, with which fill the dish about half the depth; when it begins to jelly, have ready some Naples biscuits, macaroons, and the little cakes called matrimony; take an equal quantity of these cakes, break them in pieces, and stick them in the jelly before it be stiff, all over very thick; pour over that a quart of very thick sweet cream, then

lay all round, currant jelly, raspberry jam, and some calves-foot jelly, all cut in little pieces, with which garnish your dish thick all round, intermixing them and on them lay macaroons, and the little cakes, being first dipped in sack.

Then take two quarts of the thickest cream you can get, sweeten it with double-refined sugar, grate into it the rine of three fine large lemons, and whisk it up with a whisk; take off the froth as it rises, and lay it in your dish as high as you can possibly raise it; this is fit to go to the King's table, if well made, and very excellent when it comes to be all mixed together.

In the fifth edition of *The Art of Cookery*, Hannah includes a recipe for another relatively newly fashionable dessert: ice cream. First served in England in the 1670s it seems to have come from Italy via France, its manufacture made possible by successful methods of storing winter ice for summer use. Hannah's recipe runs as follows:

Take two pewter basons, one larger than the other; the inward one must have a close cover, into which you are to put your cream, and mix it with raspberries, or whatever you like best, to give it a flavour and a colour. Sweeten it to your palate; then cover it close, and set it into the larger bason. Fill it with ice, and a handful of salt: let it stand in this ice three quarters of an hour, then uncover it, and stir the cream well together; cover it close again, and let it stand half an hour longer, after that turn it into your plate.

From ice cream it seems logical to move on to jelly, long a feature of English food. Not surprisingly, Hannah includes various recipes for it, recommending isinglass, hartshorn or calf's feet as setting agents. Not surprisingly, either, she doesn't mention that in Georgian times there was often a close connection between jelly and prostitution. Jelly houses, which served jelly in special glasses, were popular haunts for prostitutes and their clients for reasons about which one can only speculate. Hannah's entirely innocent jellies are a delight, particularly her recipe for currant jelly where the glasses are topped with paper soaked in brandy.

As I hope I have made clear, I have a strong affinity for Hannah Glasse. I admire her straightforward, unpretentious approach to cookery. As another cook who is not terribly good at managing money, I also sympathise with the hardships she underwent and am only too glad that modern regulations have spared me debtors' prison. It saddens me that she is virtually unremembered in her native Hexham. When I tried to find out more about her, the county council wasn't particularly helpful, though I was fortunate to come across her letters, which are owned by Mrs Allgood, a descendant of Hannah's father's family. To me, she is one of the greats of English food history.

One striking feature of Georgian cookery writers is just how many of them were women. Alongside Hannah there were, for example, such figures as Elizabeth Raffald (1733–81), author of *The Experienced English Housekeeper*, which was first published in 1769 and ran to numerous editions, both legitimate and pirated; and Maria Rundell (1745–1828), whose *A New System of Domestic Cookery* first appeared in 1805. Elizabeth had been a housekeeper to various families and eventually opened a shop in Manchester selling hot and cold food and confectionery,

A grand Victorian kitchen A painting by Frank Watkins (*fl.* 1859–94).

A grand Victorian dinner party Note the artfully presented dishes. The alternation of male and female guests was a Georgian innovation.

The growth of advertising A children's party of the 1880s, somewhat dominated by Huntley & Palmers.

A celebrity endorsement This Colman's mustard poster from 1890 boasts the great W. G. Grace, proof positive that celebrity endorsements are nothing new. Whether he actually liked mustard is not recorded.

Canning An engraving from the *Illustrated London News* for 31 January 1852, showing the kitchen at Richie & McCall's Cannery in Houndsditch, London. The first tin opener appeared on the scene three years later.

Food on an industrial scale Meredith & Drew were best known as a biscuit and crisp manufacturer, but also turned their hand to things like Dundee cake (this advertisement dates from around 1897). They were later taken over by United Biscuits.

The Victorian shop Wareham & Arscott's in Blandford Forum, complete with advertisement-filled plate-glass windows, is a typical example of a late Victorian food shop. It sold such things as fresh cheese and bacon, but it also offered its customers tinned fruit and that classic product of food industrialisation, Bovril.

The Victorian market Billingsgate in London was transformed by the Industrial Revolution, too. Now that trains could bring fish from the coast swiftly and efficiently, it became busier than ever, its hustle and bustle nicely captured in this 1893 photograph. Only the pipe-smoking man in the middle has time to notice the camera.

Service à la Russe By the 1890s, when this illustration was produced, service *à la Russe* had almost completely superseded the traditional service *à la Française* whereby numerous, often highly contrasting dishes were placed on the table at once. Now that the table was less packed with food at any one moment, there was more room for non-edible ornaments.

Domestic service By 1900 almost ₂ million English women were in service. None of the great houses could have functioned without ₃em, and even humbler establishments would certainly have had ₃ne or two. The very middle-class ₃amily in E. Nesbit's *The Railway ₃hildren* (1906), for example, have a cook and a parlour maid.

The food of the poor Street food was an essential part of the diet of the urban poor in Victorian times. Here people are treating themselves to halfpenny ices in a photograph from around 1876.

Slum living Bread was an all too frequent component of the diet of the Victorian poor, as this late-nineteenth-century photograph of a slum interior shows.

A middle-class Christmas Life was very different for middle-class families, as is demonstrated by this saccharine painting entitled *The Christmas Hamper* by Robert Braithwaite (1826–69), who was associated with the Pre-Raphaelite group of artists. The Victorians invented Christmas as we know it today, and both turkeys and geese featured strongly in their Christmas dinners.

Indian influences Links with India remained strong throughout the nineteenth century, despite the mutiny of 1857 which sought to overthrow British rule. Indian cuisine was very popular, though often not quite in the form that Indians themselves would have recognised.

Proprietor of the first Indian restauran A contemporary portrait of Sake Deen Ma homed, who opened an Indian restaurant the Hindostanee Coffee House, in Portma Square, London, in 1810.

Jewish cuisine Jews returned to England in 1656, but it was only really in the nineteenth century that they arrived in any quantity, fleeing persecution in eastern Europe. Jewish cuisine had a significant impact on English foo not least in the fried fish element of fish and chips. The photograph here shows the Kahn & Botsman kosher salt beef and provisions shop at 183 Brick Lane in around 1910.

along with an employment office for servants. Maria Rundell was the widow of a surgeon from Bath, and her cookery book was a publishing sensation for decades after its first publication. It was, as she explained:

> . . . intended for the conduct of the families of the authoress's own daughters, and for the arrangement of their table, so as to unite a good figure with proper economy . . . This little work would have been a treasure to herself when she first set out in life, and she therefore hopes it may prove useful to others.

The number of women involved in writing such books tells us a lot about the status that most cooking enjoyed in Georgian times. At court and in the great houses, the leading cooks were generally male – as, for example, Patrick Lamb in the early part of the century. Elsewhere, it was all left to women. We're a long way from the medieval hall where squires, anxious to be noticed by their lords, were happy to wait upon them.

Not all cookery writers, though, were women, and not all cookery books were inspired by domestic life. John Farley's *The London Art of Cookery and Domestic Housekeepers' Complete Assistant*, which was first published in 1783, was the work of a man who was head cook at the London Tavern in Bishopsgate, a palatial edifice which boasted elaborately decorated rooms that could hold hundreds of banqueters. Everything was on a grand scale: live turtles were held in vast tanks in the cellar, which was also filled with the finest drink.

Farley's book, however, was very much aimed at the same lucrative market as Hannah Glasse's. In fact, Farley clearly lifted large sections of Hannah's book for his enterprise. Nevertheless, it has a few idiosyncrasies of its own which shine fascinating shafts of light on everyday Georgian life. Like Hannah, he warns of the dangers of poisoning caused by kitchenware reacting with the food prepared in it. But he also makes his way meticulously through the raw ingredients of a well-stocked kitchen, telling the reader how to check them for any signs of contamination before buying them. You are told, for example, not to buy ham if it is 'daubed and smeared, and has a disagreeable smell'. Fish should be avoided if the eyes are sinking or the gills smell. Even straight-forward items like butter need careful attention: 'In buying of butter, you must not trust to the taste the seller gives you, lest they give you a taste of one lump, and sell you another.' It's very clear that the Georgian market was not necessarily the source of particularly fresh – or safe – food.

Farley also has advice on everything from the duties of different categories of servant to how to lay bait for rats and mice ('Mix flour of malt with fresh-butter, and add a few drops of oil of aniseed; make into balls, and with them bait the traps. *This bait has never been known to fail*'). His recipes tend to be fairly catch-all, too. Taking a leaf from Hannah Glasse's book, he is clearly anxious to give recipes that ordinary middle-class people can afford and enjoy. But, in a bid to be all things to all men, he pushes the boat out on occasion. As he explains: 'we have occasionally given the most simple with the most sumptuous dishes, and thereby afforded the means of decorating the Table of the Peer, or the Mechanic.'

What this means is that, on the one hand, he includes a lot of straightforward fare, heavily reliant on meat. This, as I've said elsewhere, was the pattern of much eighteenth-century food, and I suspect that it partly reflects court taste. George I was, of course, from Hanover, and it's interesting to see how similar a lot of German food – with its heavy emphasis on meat – was to English fare. Certainly, we know that George II's court ate very plain roasted meats with no fancy frills, and given the number of Hanoverians living in London at the time (5,000 or 6,000), German influence would have been quite widely disseminated.

On the other hand, Farley does include quite a few more elaborate and rather interesting recipes. Take this very nice soup of chestnuts with pigeons, for example:

Pick half a hundred of chesnuts, put them in an earthen pan, and set them in the oven for half an hour, or roast them gently over a slow fire, but take care they do not burn. Then peel them, and set them to stew in a quart of good beef stock till quite tender. In the meantime, take a piece or slice of ham or bacon, a pound of veal, a pigeon beat to pieces, an onion, a bundle of sweet herbs, a piece of carrot, and a little pepper and mace. Lay the bacon at the bottom of a stewpan, and lay the meat and ingredients on it. Set it over a slow fire till it begins to stick to the pan, and then put in a crust of bread, and pour in two quarts of stock: let it boil softly till one third is wasted, then strain it off, and put in the chesnuts. Season with salt, and let it boil till it be well flavoured: then stew two pigeons in it, and a French roll fried crisp. Lay the roll in the middle of the dish, and the pigeons on each side; pour in the soup, and send it up hot.

There's also a recipe for mackerel with fennel and mint that is very American New Wave, and a nice, rather unusual one for duck with horseradish.

John Farley also has some excellent vegetable dishes: broccoli cooked with eggs and served on toast; asparagus seasoned with pepper, salt, nutmeg and a little onion and topped with yolks of eggs beaten up in some white wine, cream and thick butter and garnished with lemon. As somebody who only likes their asparagus plain with some hollandaise sauce, I find this a very nice variation on a theme. Some vegetables in his book are served rather more simply, though almost invariably with a butter sauce.

One of the striking things about the editions of Farley's book that I have seen is that they open with illustrated suggestions for how you might lay out a dinner on particular months of the year. A first course in February, for example, might include, among other things, soup, turkey, chicken, oyster patties, tongue and mutton. The second course might offer asparagus, duckling, scalloped oysters, prawns, mushrooms, broccoli and ribs of lamb. The dishes would be elegantly arranged – as they had been a hundred years before.

John Farley's era was also Jane Austen's era, when dinners and late suppers were focal points of the social calendar, offering people entertainment, gossip, social advancement and, possibly, an eligible husband or wife at the end of it all. Food also betrayed a lot about people's precise social standing and their personalities. The snobbish Mrs Elton in *Emma* (1816) is shocked at the poor quality of the cakes served at 'routs', or soirées, and at the lack of ice at card parties. The withdrawn hypochondriac Mr Woodhouse in the same novel worries about any dinner party involving more than eight people and eats thin gruel at supper (though he does suggest to a fellow diner that she might push the boat out a bit and eat a soft-boiled egg). As for Emma, the manipulative heroine, dinners provide an excellent opportunity for her hobby of matchmaking. 'Invite him to dinner, Emma,' says her friend Mr Knightley of one individual Emma has plans for, 'and help him to the best of the fish and the chicken, but leave him to chuse his own wife.'

The Victorian rich took entertaining very seriously indeed, lavishing money on extravagant dishes that were served over many courses. This photograph from 1897 shows the dining room at Wickham Hall in Kent, with its carefully decorated table and opulently heavy furniture. Note the tiger-skin rug in the foreground.

CHAPTER II

Pheasant Consommé and Forced Peas

Rich Eating in the Nineteenth Century

O n 14 July 1789 a mob stormed the Bastille in Paris, so signalling the beginning of the French Revolution. Nearly sixty years later the extensive menu for the Reform Club in London for 9 May 1846 included such dishes as *Le Chapon farci de foie gras à la Nelson* and *Le Miroton de homard aux oeufs de pluviers.* A Continental revolution and an English club menu may seem to have little to do with each other. There is, however, a link, as the names of the dishes served at the Reform Club suggest; for, following the law of unintended consequences, one of the stranger effects of social upheaval in France throughout much of the late eighteenth and early nineteenth centuries was an increasing French influence on English cuisine.

In a way this seems rather surprising. After all, the French Revolution, and particularly the Napoleonic Wars that came in its wake, caused waves of anti-French feeling in England. But accompanying this were waves of French chefs either escaping the upheaval in France or trying to find lucrative employment among wealthy English families at a time when there weren't that many opportunities in their homeland. Even the famous Marie-Antoine Carême, author of various cookery books including the magisterial *L'Art de la cuisine française*, was tempted over to England for a while, working as *chef de cuisine* to the Prince Regent (later George IV). In his case, it wasn't a success. Carême hated everything about England, he hated everything about his kitchens, and within a very short space of time he and his ego flounced back to France.

Carême does seem, however, to have introduced one major innovation to the English dining table. As I've already said, dinners in England were traditionally served in two or three big courses, each containing an almost bewildering range of dishes. If you experienced service *à la française* you would arrive in the dining room to find the table elaborately set out with dishes arranged symmetrically. It could look spectacular, but keeping food hot was a real problem and, as at James II's coronation banquet many years before, it can't always have been that safe, either. There was, however, another – more recent – system known as *à la russe*. This involved bringing dishes to the table in sequence, with soup, fish, meat and dessert courses clearly delineated; in other words, the sort of approach with which we're familiar today. Carême worked for the Russian tsar for a while (hence the appearance of that very Russian dish coulibiac in early editions of *Larousse Gastronomique*), and I strongly suspect that he was the one who popularised something that we all now take for granted. Service *à la française* didn't disappear overnight, but over the next few decades it gradually lost ground to its Russian alternative.

Carême may have come and gone; other French chefs, however, came and stayed. In fact a list compiled in 1835 by the *Quarterly Review* of 'The most eminent cooks of the present time in England' is dominated by Gallic names, including Pierre Moret of the royal household; Crépin of the Duchess of Sutherland's household; and Frottier, who worked for the Duke of Cambridge. And pre-eminent among them (though not included in the list since he had only arrived in England relatively recently) was the man who devised that menu at the newly opened Reform Club, Alexis Soyer.

Soyer was a remarkable figure. Born near Paris in 1810 he was sent to the local cathedral with the intention of him becoming a priest, but after rather too enthusiastically ringing the bells at night, and so inadvertently summoning the fire brigade and the town garrison, he was expelled and ended up apprenticed to a cook. For a while he worked for the Prince de Polignac, but when the prince got caught up in yet another French Revolution in 1830, Soyer, finding it impossible to get work in France, moved to England. He then worked for various noble households before, in 1837, becoming chef to the Reform Club in Pall Mall.

His dishes were legendary for their intricacy and flamboyance. One dessert that he served for Ibrahim Pasha in 1846, for example, which he flatteringly called *Crème d'Egypte à l'Ibrahim*, was an almost architectural affair:

> . . . a pyramid about two and a half feet high, made of light meringue cake, in imitation of solid stones, surrounded with grapes and other fruits, but representing only the four angles of the pyramid through sheets of waved sugar, to show, to the

greatest advantage, an elegant cream *à l'ananas*, on the top of which was resting a highly-finished portrait of the illustrious stranger's father, Mehemet Ali . . .

As for his famous 'hundred-guinea dish', which he made in honour of Prince Albert, this included turtles, quails, capons, turkeys, geese, pheasants, partridges, woodcocks, plovers, snipes, pigeons and larks, all garnished with truffles, cockscomb, mushrooms, asparagus, sweetbreads, quenelles, mangoes and a new sauce, 'Soyer's Sauce', which he produced in a lavish bottle especially for the occasion.

Perhaps Soyer's greatest feat of catering, and one which I don't think has been equalled, was for the Great Exhibition of 1851, when he rented Gore House (now replaced by the Albert Hall) to create the 'Gastronomic Symposium of All Nations'. Visitors averaged 1,000 a day and could, according to where they sat, sample the food of countries as different from one another as China, India and France. Unfortunately, while Soyer may have possessed flair he lacked financial acumen and the Symposium lost a fortune. Its architect went on to other ventures but died of a stroke aged only forty-eight. His wife had died after a miscarriage some years before when Soyer was away on business at the Belgian court. Soyer was devastated, blamed himself, and apparently never got over his loss.

Thanks to people like Soyer, French cuisine was increasingly influential in England at this time and its very particular style and demands were widely admired and adopted. Meat could be delicately poached; fish and chicken might be cooked in paper to preserve their moisture. They would be served with sauces that chefs may well have slaved over for hours, reducing pounds of meat to a rich flavourful concoction. Or the chef might be engaged in preparing a newfangled soufflé. Soyer's *Gastronomic Regenerator* of 1846, rather misleadingly subtitled 'A Simplified and Entirely New System of Cookery', demonstrates the complexity of his food in the course of 2,000 recipes, of which the following, for *Turban des filets de perdreaux à la Périgord*, is not untypical (note the references to other recipes):

> Fillet three young partridges, make likewise half a pound of forcemeat from the legs as directed (No. 123), from which make six quenelles . . . make a border of mashed potatoes on your dish, and dress the fillets in crown, alternately with quenelles, put three parts of a pint of demi-glace de gibier (No. 61) in a stewpan, reduce it a third, add four large French truffles chopped very fine, with a little sugar, sauce over and serve.

French cuisine, in other words, moved very much centre stage in wealthier households in the early nineteenth century. Indeed, to be able to serve food in the French style and, ideally, to have a French chef in your employment was a mark of social distinction. Not that everyone appreciated such elaborate meals. The Duke of Wellington, who had a habit of pouring vinegar all over his food, was such a disappointment to his French chef Felix that the cook ultimately gave up on him, dismayed at how uninterested the duke was in what was put in front of him. 'If he were a hundred times a hero, I could not serve such a master and preserve my powers,' he wailed. 'My body might live, my genius would die.'

You might expect to find English monarchs playing their part in promoting this grand French cuisine, just as Eleanor of Aquitaine championed spices or Henry VIII indulged Catherine of Aragon's love of salads. But that doesn't really seem to have been the case. Prinny – or, rather, the Prince Regent (later George IV) – enjoyed his food, as his patronage of Carême and extraordinary stoutness demonstrate, and he staged ludicrously over-the-top banquets at his folly, Brighton Pavilion. However, he was simply going along with the fashions of the time. The same is true of Queen Victoria. She certainly had an impact on other areas of life. As a young woman, her passion for the newly introduced waltz helped make this dangerously provocative dance (men and women together in public in a virtual embrace? Shocking!) respectable. Her enthusiasm for all things Scottish – which she shared with her dissolute uncle George IV – also had an impact on English fashion. But it's harder to point to any clear influence that she might have had on English eating and she certainly never seems to have been an outspoken advocate of the grand French banquet.

In part this may be due to the great tragedy of her life: the death of her husband Albert in 1861. Up until then she ate her meals like everybody else. After that, as she entered her period of prolonged and exaggerated mourning (she wore black for the rest of her life and kept a model of Albert's hand carved in marble beside her on her pillow), she seems to have lost interest in food and had a tendency to eat incredibly quickly. This wasn't good news for fellow diners. Because etiquette demanded that others should stop eating when the queen did, the swift dispatch of her meals must have left others leaving the table feeling rather hungry. She did, however, have a very sweet tooth, so perhaps people had longer to eat their puddings.

That doesn't mean that the food served at Victoria's court

was meagre. The queen may have been increasingly uninterested in it and in grand dining (she didn't even attend the wedding breakfast of her son, the Prince of Wales), but she had a strong sense of duty, and that duty included provisioning the royal household with food on the scale you would expect from the ruler of a mighty empire. At Buckingham Palace we find records of a day's delivery of up to 250 shoulders of ham, 200 necks of mutton and numerous game birds, including pheasant and partridge (these would have been brought in from the royal estates, as would much of the fruit and vegetables). Then there were such delicacies as Italian truffles and hothouse fruits, including particularly large grapes that were mostly used for decoration. Dinner would last an hour and a half, divided into two by the now-fashionable sorbet (usually flavoured with port, brandy or rum), which was designed to cleanse the palate before the roast was served. There might well be nine or ten courses, consisting perhaps of consommé, thick soup, salmon, cutlets of chicken, saddle of lamb, roast pigeons, green salad, asparagus in white sauce, trout mousseline in a champagne sauce, ham mousse and lemon ice cream.

When the queen was at Windsor there was an indoor staff of over 300 servants and a kitchen staff of 45, presided over in the later years of her reign by the royal chef, the inevitably French Monsieur Ménager. At a time when a palace apprentice chef earned £15 a year, Monsieur Ménager commanded a salary of £400 with an additional £200 living allowance. He would arrive at Windsor Castle – or wherever the queen happened to be in residence – in a hansom cab every morning. It was also his duty to provide lavish meals on the royal yacht.

At the queen's Scottish summer retreat Balmoral, where things were slightly less formal, guests might dine on pheasant consommé, cauliflower purée, cod with egg sauce, trout, ham mousse with cucumber, chicken and beef, braised cauliflower, roast turkey, haricot beans, sprouts, a sweet and a savoury. Side tables would be loaded with hot and cold poultry, tongue, beef and salads. You would have thought that there would have been plenty for everyone, but there is a record of the servants – who generally ate very well – complaining on one occasion that the queen's guests had devoured all the beef and poultry, leaving none for them. In general, though, royal entertaining followed the love of excess that was a hallmark of fine dining in the nineteenth century.

I've said that the royal household had little or no perceptible effect on national cuisine – that it reflected the love of all things French rather than created it. It would be true to say, though, that the royal family did have an impact on one food-related institution: Christmas. As is well known, Prince Albert, true to his German roots, placed a Christmas tree in Windsor Castle in 1848. He may not have been the first to do so – we know that, thanks to close links between the British and German royal families, Christmas trees actually started appearing in England in Georgian times – but he was certainly the one to popularise the tradition in this country. He and Victoria were also among the first to send Christmas cards. They weren't alone in their enthusiasm for Christmas, of course. Nostalgia for old traditions was common in early Victorian England, where people, living in a country that was being transformed out of all recognition by the Industrial Revolution, looked back fondly to a never-never time when things had supposedly been simpler and people had been happier. Nevertheless, Victoria and Albert did help fuel and shape a new interest in the festive season. Alexis Soyer played his part, in 1847 sending the queen a ten-foot-high Christmas bouquet, framed with Christmas greens and with twenty-two heads of winged game in its centre. Whether Victoria was amused or not, history does not relate.

Ultimately, the Victorians, spearheaded by Victoria and Albert, gave us the Christmas we recognise today, with its trees, cards and stockings – and food. Christmas had always been a time for lavish eating among those who could afford it, beef, turkey and goose being the traditional meats of choice (Queen Victoria preferred beef, though she did serve turkey on occasion). The Victorians, however, reinforced the idea of a particular Christmas culinary tradition. If we turn to that most famous of all Christmas books – Charles Dickens's *A Christmas Carol* of 1843 – we find both the goose and turkey so familiar to us today very much taking centre stage. The poor Cratchits eat a very small roast goose with mashed potato, apple sauce and gravy for their Christmas lunch, while in the last chapter the repentant Scrooge sends them an enormous turkey. Geese were still being eaten at the end of the century when Conan Doyle wrote a Sherlock Holmes story about a precious stone concealed in a Christmas goose (poorer Victorians often formed 'goose clubs' to save up for Christmas geese), but by this time turkey was more favoured among the middle classes and was well on its way to becoming the Christmas meat of choice. Now, of course, the shoe is on the other foot and we regard goose at Christmas as being more exclusive than turkey.

So far as pudding is concerned, Christmas porridge was what was traditionally eaten, made from chopped beef or mutton and onions, mixed with dried fruit, breadcrumbs, wine, herbs and spices. However, in the Cratchit household of the 1840s it had been displaced by the sort of plum pudding we would recognise today, and Dickens provides a wonderful description of the trepidation and joy that surrounds its unveiling:

> Hallo! A great deal of steam! The pudding was out of the copper. A smell like a washing-day! That was the cloth. A smell like an eating-house, and a pastry cook's, next door to each other, with a laundress's next door to that! That was the pudding. In half a minute Mrs Cratchit entered: flushed, but smiling proudly: with the pudding, like a speckled cannon-ball, so hard and firm, blazing in half of half-a-quartern of ignited brandy, and bedight with Christmas holly stuck into the top.
>
> Oh, a wonderful pudding! Bob Cratchit said, and calmly too, that he regarded it as the greatest success achieved by Mrs Cratchit since their marriage. Mrs Cratchit said that now the weight was off her mind, she would confess she had had her doubts about the quantity of flour. Everybody had something to say about it, but nobody said or thought it was at all a small pudding for a large family.

After pudding, the Cratchit family settle down to apples, oranges and chestnuts, and punch served in 'two tumblers, and a custard-cup without a handle'. Had they had mince pies, these might well still have contained real meat, but the mid nineteenth century saw the gradual replacement of meat by the dried fruit and spices we are familiar with today. Bit by bit, then, we can see Christmas fare being transformed, and by the end of Victoria's reign many of the foods we now associate with the festive season were firmly in place (though not cranberry sauce: it was first recorded in England in 1672 but it only really became popular, thanks to American influence, in the 1970s).

The Cratchits appear to have eaten their 'Christmas dinner' in the afternoon – at any rate, Dickens tells us that it is getting dark when they have finished their punch and chestnuts. For the wealthier members of society, however, dinner was very much an evening affair, and it was during this era that meals for the upper classes settled down into a fairly regular pattern that we would recognise. By the 1830s breakfast might occasionally be a rather elaborate meal served at ten o'clock, but it was more likely to be an informal meal served from about eight o'clock. Gone were the cold meats and cake of Georgian times. Instead there would be various grilled dishes available, sometimes on an ambitious scale. For example, while the older Queen Victoria would usually only have a boiled egg served in a gold egg cup with a gold spoon for her breakfast, others around her would tuck into everything from different types of egg dishes to bacon, grilled trout, grilled turbot, cutlets, chops or beefsteak, roasted woodcock, snipe or even chicken, to say nothing of fancy dishes such as kedgeree or devilled kidneys. Tea and coffee tended to be the drinks of choice, and you would quite often find hot toast and various fancy breads with butter and preserves on offer, too.

One other feature of the grand English breakfast that arrived in Victorian times was the kipper. There are recipes for kippered salmon in earlier books, but it was only in the mid nineteenth century that kippered herrings started to appear on the London market. Kippers are cold-smoked in the Scottish manner, as opposed to bloaters, which are hot-smoked. They are a great way of conserving the herring, of which there were huge stocks in British waters in Victorian times. So popular did they prove both on the breakfast tables of the well-to-do and the supper tables of the poor that they largely displaced the old-fashioned salt herring: the red herring (this now tended to be sent to Africa or to the West Indies). With the advent of the railways, boxes of herrings could be packed in ice and brought down to the English cities from as far afield as Mallaig in Scotland. The best, from Loch Fyne, were known as 'Glasgow Magistrates', so fat and plump were they. The knife-wielding herring wives who prepared them were a pretty determined band of ladies, and woe betide anybody who crossed them. They lived by their own rules, often not bothering to marry the fathers of their children, and they would follow the herring as the shoals moved around the coastal waters of Britain.

With breakfast out of the way, the next meal on the horizon was the Victorian lunch. This varied according to circumstance. It might be a fairly light meal comprising various cold foods, or a more elaborate hot one, much depending on whether the master of the house was at home or not and on whether there were guests staying. Or, of course, people might opt for a picnic lunch, a popular feature of the era for those with large country estates. From a modern point of view, 'picnic' may seem a bit of a misnomer when you see the list of food people champed their way through. Individual items seem perfect picnic food – for example the Melton Mowbray pork pie, which was very popular among fox hunters since it was easy to slip into a pocket. But a 'Bill of Fare for a Picnic for Forty Persons' that appears in the first edition of Mrs Beeton's *Book of Household Management* of 1861 is terrifyingly long. It starts as follows – 'A joint of cold roast beef, a joint of cold boiled beef, 2 ribs of lamb, 2 shoulders of lamb, 4 roast fowls, 2 roast ducks, 1 ham, 1 tongue, 2 veal-and-ham pies, 2 pigeon pies, 6 medium sized lobsters, 1 piece of collared calf's head' – and then makes its way through salads, biscuits, bread and cheese, not to mention 122 bottles of drink (plus champagne). It reminds me of the picnic hamper that Rat prepares in that Edwardian classic *The Wind in the Willows*:

> 'What's inside it?' asked the Mole, wriggling with curiosity.
>
> 'There's cold chicken inside it,' replied the Rat briefly; 'cold-tonguecoldhamcoldbeefpickledgherkinssaladfrenchrollscress-sandwichespottedmeatgingerbeerlemonadesodawater . . .'

Fox hunting, by the way, deserves an honourable mention in the history of English food. Apart from Melton Mowbray pies, which originated in a fashionable hunting county, there is also a very nice dish called Mitten of pork, which is made from chopped pork and sausage meat baked in a lined basin in a bain-marie to form a very firm pudding, and which used to be served on the hunting field. It was named after John 'Mad Jack' Mytton, a famous and eccentric hunting squire. And then there's Sefton of herrings, one of my favourite dishes, made with herring roes and flavoured with nutmeg, and also named after one of my hunting heroes, the 2nd Earl of Sefton. I would also claim that while Stilton cheese may not have been invented for the hunting fraternity, it was certainly taken up by them with gusto and popularised as a result.

For those not bloated by Melton Mowbray pies – or one of Mrs Beeton's killer picnics – the next meal of the day would be 'tea', which earlier in the century may actually have involved cake and wine rather than cake and tea. By Mrs Beeton's time, however, afternoon tea generally meant tea, and she recommends a range of cakes 'both large and fancies'. In the 1874 edition of Mrs Beeton there's a recipe for 'Victoria sandwiches', heralding the arrival of the Victoria sponge cake, named, of course, after the queen and supposedly popular with her. And so to dinner.

When you look at the menus and cookery books of the time you do sometimes wonder how wealthy Victorians didn't simply burst at the dinner table: the number of courses and the range of dishes on offer seem so bewilderingly over the top. But we shouldn't assume that just because the food was there, it was all consumed. Tightly corseted, fashionable women would scarcely have been able to overindulge. Leaving even that aside, though, generous entertaining wasn't really about generous eating; it was about making a grand social statement. You displayed your status by how much you loaded on to the dinner table, and the grander you were, the more you could afford to waste. Wastage from grand meals then became one of the cook's perks, providing him or her with food that they could profit from by selling on. Leftover food could be quite a remunerative business. I remember being told once that in London's Warwick Way market there was actually a stall where you could rent a bone by the hour for making soup, returning it when you'd finished with it. I've also heard that this practice continued in remote areas of Spain in my lifetime. It was, if you think of it, actually a much better way of dealing with leftover food than just throwing it in the bin as we do today.

The wealthy people who generated such waste were basically one of two types: those who had inherited their money and the newly rich who were prospering from Victorian Britain's extraordinary economic success, whether as industrialists or financiers. The latter class blossomed during the nineteenth century, their numbers mushrooming as the century went on. And if you want a sure indication of their rise to affluence, just consider how many etiquette books appeared in Victorian times. They became a virtual mini-industry. As I've already pointed out, an obsession with 'correct' behaviour always seems to go with times of social change. It certainly happened in Richard II's reign. Rather more recently, I experienced it myself, when in the 1980s I used to go up to Leeds once a month to teach a group of rich yuppies how to eat asparagus, which item of cutlery to use for each course, and why it wasn't perhaps a good idea to grip a champagne bottle by the neck and then swig from it. On the other hand, I always remember a remark made by a friend of my mother's who was married to an incredibly rich industrialist. She had a tendency to pick her teeth with her fruit fork at table, and when my mother gently suggested, 'Maybe you shouldn't do that,' she replied, 'Oh, I can do anything I want. I don't have to abide by rules and regulations – and anyway, I may set a new fashion.'

She may or may not have been right, but there's no doubt that her response would have left the Victorian etiquette martinets distinctly unimpressed. They loved rules, setting out page after page of dos and don'ts and potential faux pas: at what time it was acceptable to call for tea, when to leave a visiting card, what to wear for particular occasions, and so on. When it came to table manners, the lists of instructions could be intimidatingly long. You were told which items of cutlery to use for each course (actually a fairly simple piece of knowledge to pick up, since cutlery was often placed in such a way that you would start from the outside and work inwards). You were admonished not to blow on your soup to cool it, and not to eat your food too slowly (which might suggest you didn't like it) or too quickly (which might suggest an overeagerness to be served more). You were advised not to help yourself to food if there were servants around to help. You were counselled not to turn round if a servant happened to drop something. And, if you had survived the meal thus far with your nerves intact and were about to leave the table, you were instructed not to fold your napkin but to lay it beside your plate.

One inevitable consequence of the rise of this new class of well-to-do people was an increase in demand for domestic servants. The 1851 census listed 1 million women as being in service (over one in twenty of the population). By the time of the 1901 census, that figure had doubled. And that posed a problem. Up until Victorian times, many if not most servants came into domestic service via the country estate where they had grown up, and there was a tradition, sometimes stretching back many years, of young girls from a particular family going up to the big house to be trained, then getting married, and so bearing the next generation of servants. Now demand for servants outstripped supply of traditionally trained ones – particularly as more and more middle-class people came to employ them (even people in quite ordinary suburban houses would employ a cook/housekeeper or a maid-of-all-work). Many who now went into domestic service had received no real training for it and struggled as a result. Complaints about servants abounded: if you read Wilkie Collins's novels, the most famous of which were written in the 1860s, there are constant references to servants who are described either as 'sullen' or 'stupid'.

The flip side to that was that many of the people who now employed servants had no idea how to treat them. I discovered this for myself when I was in domestic service. Frankly, it doesn't matter how much money your employer has: if they don't have much experience in employing domestic servants, the chances are that you're not going to be treated very well. That said, the lot of servants in the well-to-do Victorian house generally wasn't too bad. They probably ate fairly well, and certainly better than they would have done at home. Yes, they worked long hours – a maid might work from 6 a.m. to midnight and have only one day off a month – but then this was an era when poorer people did work long hours. Moreover, their clothes were supplied – perhaps including a canvas apron to be worn in the morning when they cleaned the fires, and then a daytime apron to be worn when they were opening the door or serving people upstairs, and so on. In the course of my life I have known a number of people who were in domestic service in Edwardian times, and most said they found it a pleasant experience. Some who had been lady's maids or valets said that service provided them with an opportunity to visit places with their employers that they would otherwise never have seen.

The etiquette that ruled life above stairs had a counterpart that ruled life in the servants' quarters. Precedence was everything. You sat down for a meal according to your place in the pecking order. If you were a valet or lady's maid or nursemaid who had travelled down with visitors to the house, your placement in the servants' hall would depend entirely on the rank of your employer. The servants of a duke or marquess always ranked above those of a rich industrialist, however rich that industrialist might be. And then there were rules that governed the relationship between servants and masters. Quite a considerable part of the dreaded Mrs Beeton's *Book of Household Management*, which I'll come to later, is devoted to instructions on how to treat the cook or the coachman or the various different categories of maid. One injunction to the mistress of the house is not to swear or use bad language in front of the servants. I once cooked for somebody in the country whose natural inclination was to swear. I therefore left a copy of Mrs Beeton open at the appropriate page with an arrow pointing to the relevant paragraph. Fortunately, they were amused.

Mrs Beeton is also careful to lay down rules for when the shoe is on the other foot. As she says, a servant should never embarrass their master:

> Masters as well as servants sometimes make mistakes; but it is not expected that a servant will correct any omissions, even if he should have time to notice them, although with the best intentions: thus it would not be correct, for instance, if he observed that his master took wine with the ladies all round, as some gentlemen still continue to do, but stopped at some one:– to nudge him on the shoulder and say, as was done by the servant of a Scottish gentleman, 'What ails you at her in the green gown?' It will be better to leave the lady unnoticed than for the servant thus to turn his master into ridicule.

This rather reminds me of an experience I had when I was in domestic service. One day the woman for whom I was working invited a rather unpleasant gentleman round for a meal, and when they had finished eating he started to scrape the plates and then stack them. The daughter of the house was horrified, but when she said, 'Oh, Clarissa won't like that!' he merely responded, 'Mrs Thatcher does it at Downing Street.' I couldn't resist myself and retorted, 'Precisely, sir; a grocer's daughter.' My employer gave me a big hug after the meal. When I was a cook and housekeeper I always tried to model myself on the redoubtable Mrs Cadogan in the Irish R. M. books by Somerville and Ross.

I have to say that I do feel a strong sense of affinity for the household servants of Mrs Beeton's time and sympathise with the busy lives they led. Here she is, for example, on the maid-of-all-work:

The general servant, or maid-of-all-work, is perhaps the only one of her class deserving of commiseration: her life is a solitary one, and in some places, her work is never done. She is also subject to rougher treatment than either the house or kitchen-maid, especially in her earlier career: she starts in life, probably a girl of thirteen, with some small tradesman's wife as her mistress, just a step above her in the social scale; and although the class contains among them many excellent, kind-hearted women, it also contains some very rough specimens of the feminine gender, and to some of these it occasionally falls to give our maid-of-all-work her first lessons in her multifarious occupations: the mistress's commands are the measure of the maid-of-all-work's duties. By the time she has become a tolerable servant, she is probably engaged in some respectable tradesman's house, where she has to rise with the lark, for she has to do in her own person all the work which in larger establishments is performed by cook, kitchen-maid, and housemaid, and occasionally the part of a footman's duty, which consists in carrying messages.

The duties of the maid-of-all-work then, as Mrs Beeton outlines them, are alarmingly extensive, from the moment she opens all the shutters of the lower apartments in the house in the morning to the moment she checks that all the bolts are fastened before she retires to bed. Even the short passage that deals with the maid's part in helping with dinner suggests that she must have been well and truly exhausted by the end of the day:

Half an hour before dinner is ready, she should lay the cloth, that everything may be in readiness when she is dishing up the dinner, and take all into the dining-room that is likely to be required, in the way of knives, forks, spoons, bread, salt, water, &c. &c. By exercising a little forethought, much confusion and trouble may be saved both to mistress and servant, by getting everything ready for the dinner in good time. After taking in the dinner, when every one is seated, she removes the covers, hands the plates round, and pours out the beer; and should be careful to hand everything on the left side of the person she is waiting on.

We need scarcely say that a maid-of-all-work cannot stay in the dining-room during the whole of dinner-time, as she must dish up her pudding, or whatever is served after the first course. When she sees every one helped, she should leave the room to make her preparations for the next course; and anything that is required, such as bread, &c., people may assist themselves to in the absence of the servant.

When the dinner things are cleared away, the servant should

sweep up the crumbs in the dining-room, sweep the hearth, and lightly dust the furniture, then sit down to her own dinner.

Populated by wealthy people and their myriad servants, the Victorian age saw a transformation of the country house. Those who had inherited one were often desperate to refashion it in the latest style – perhaps adding a few Gothic battlements, possibly remodelling it completely. Those who had recently acquired money rushed out to build one. Tyntesfield in Somerset is a good example. Rebuilt from 1863 onwards for the guano tycoon William Gibbs, it boasts Gothic windows, a magnificent interior – and even a chapel. Such houses rapidly acquired all the latest mod cons: flushing toilets (Thomas Crapper's toilets, produced from 1861, boasted 'a certain flush with every pull'), and well-equipped kitchens with ranges and possibly even a gas cooker (exhibited at the Great Exhibition of 1851 and increasingly popular from the 1880s). The Victorian age was a great age for gadgets, and endless supposedly labour-saving devices were introduced to the kitchens: special vegetable cutters, elaborate food moulds, tongue presses and fish kettles among them. Alexis Soyer of Reform Club fame came up with various implements, including a 'magic stove' on which food could be prepared at the table – the precursor of the sort of thing you sometimes see in posher restaurants today. *The Times* of the day was impressed:

At the ball given on the evening of her Majesty's departure from Castle Howard, one of the greatest attractions was afforded by M. Soyer's cooking various dishes on the supper tables with his Lilliputian Magic Stove, surrounded by Lords and Ladies not a little surprised to see, for the first time, part of their supper cooked in a ballroom.

Money didn't just go on household items. Much was lavished on the garden, too. During the Napoleonic Wars, early in the century, French prisoners of war were sometimes set to build or enlarge walled gardens (for example at Woodhall Park in Hertfordshire, where Sir Joseph Paxton, who built the Crystal Palace, was apprenticed as a gardener). The more adventurous had their walls heated via a series of flues fed by a small furnace, so that frost damage could be minimised and the fruit on trees espaliered against the wall could be brought to ripeness earlier. Sunlight might be reflected on to specific plants or beds in the garden by adjustable metal plates that were fixed to the top of the walls and could be turned to catch the light from whichever quarter it was coming. Moveable glass screens on wheels might be located in front of a particular tree, whether it be pear or peach or plum, to provide extra heat and light and to force the fruit to ripen in time for a specific date. Greenhouses became ever more common, and many of them were now heated. Paxton's Crystal Palace, erected for the Great Exhibition of 1851, shows what Victorian technology could achieve. So large was it that it could accommodate trees growing in Hyde Park, which attracted sparrows to nest in them. When Queen Victoria asked the Duke of Wellington the best way to get rid of the sparrows, he responded with characteristic brevity, 'Sparrowhawks, Ma'am.' He was right.

All this glass and technology, along with hot beds heated by dung, meant that the Victorians could indulge their passion for out-of-season fruit and vegetables. Greenhouses could grow the delicate Italian white peach. Potatoes were chitted and put into

pots in a heated greenhouse to provide a crop for the Christmas
table. Garden peas were similarly treated, so that petits pois
could be served along with the Christmas goose or turkey. There
were even specialist mushroom houses, in which the fungi could
be cultivated most of the year round. Fruit and vegetables grown
on the estate didn't just feed the big house. If the family
happened to be up in town, hampers of produce would be sent
to them by cart or train.

A very fine example of a kitchen garden of this period can be
found on the outskirts of Liverpool at Croxteth Hall, once owned
by the Earls of Sefton. The second earl was a great sporting
gentleman who, in 1836, co-founded the Waterloo Cup and who
owned the land on which the Grand National at nearby Aintree
was established. When the seventh (and last) earl's wife gave the
house to Liverpool Council in 1972 she specified that the kitchen
garden was to be maintained in its original form, and to this day
it not only provides fruit and vegetables to be sold to help fund
the house, but also collects seeds for Garden Organics. One unusual
sight you will come across there is what's known as a chaliced
pear tree. This is a dwarf pear tree, the centre of which has been
pruned out so that the pears grow on branches forming a chalice
around the outside of the core; the idea is that sunlight can get
directly to the core and help ripen the fruit.

Unsurprisingly, such ambitious gardening required large
numbers of workmen in the garden, and the Victorian era saw
the growth, not only of the servant class as a whole, but particularly of horticulturalists, seedsmen and gardeners. Many of these
enthusiasts became fascinated with cultivating new fruit and
vegetable varieties, and the result was continual experimentation
and an explosion of choice. Where there had once been a handful

of varieties of, say, leek or onion, now there were many, each offering a slightly different taste or appearance. Plums are a perfect example of the flourishing of varieties that occurred during this period. Probably introduced to Britain by the Romans, they were certainly being cultivated in Kent in Henry VIII's time, and over the next century or so new varieties arrived from all over Europe. But it was left to the gardeners and horticulturalists of the nineteenth century to go plum mad. Suddenly, you start getting the Bryanston gage, a pale golden plum bred from the crossing of the greengage and a plum called Coe's Golden Drop. Then there's the Cambridge gage, now grown by the Essex firm Wilkin & Sons for their Tiptree greengage jam. Not to mention Czar, developed by the nurseryman Thomas Rivers in 1874; or Kirke's Blue, grown in what was once the market-gardening area between Hyde Park and the Brompton Road; or, most patriotic of all, the Victoria plum – also known, early on, as the Alderton or Sharpe's Emperor or Denyer's Victoria – with its delicious taste and its short season; or any of literally dozens of other varieties.

It all rather reminds me of that great Kipling poem:

Our England is a garden that is full of stately views,
Of borders, beds and shrubberies and lawns and avenues,
With statues on the terraces and peacocks strutting by;
But the Glory of the Garden lies in more than meets the eye.

For where the old thick laurels grow, along the thin red wall,
You will find the tool- and potting-sheds which are the heart of
    all;
The cold-frames and the hot-houses, the dungpits and the
    tanks:

338

The rollers, carts and drainpipes, with the barrows and the
   planks.

And there you'll see the gardeners, the men and 'prentice boys
Told off to do as they are bid and do it without noise;
For, except when seeds are planted and we shout to scare the
   birds,
The Glory of the Garden it abideth not in words.

By the way, I was always told that the reason why Kipling, the
most public of poets, was not made Poet Laureate was because
he upset Queen Victoria by opening one of his verses with the
lines:

   'Ave you 'eard o' the Widow at Windsor
   With a hairy gold crown on 'er 'ead?

I suspect she can't much have liked the goryness of another of
my favouite poems of his, either:

   When you're wounded and left on Afghanistan's plains,
   And the women come out to cut up what remains,
   Jest roll to your rifle and blow out your brains
   An' go to your Gawd like a soldier.

Not a lot changes.
   But I digress.
   I can't help feeling that there's a certain wonderful vulgarity
about the Victorians, with their Gothic houses, their latest
gadgets, their extravagant meals and their forced green peas and
new potatoes. And there's something vulgar, too, about the way

in which they presented food on grand occasions. They seem to have been obsessed with making everything look garish or resemble something else. If you study the plates in the early editions of Mrs Beeton's *Book of Household Management* you'll come across colourful, slightly ridiculous tableaux of artfully arranged vegetables and fussily constructed desserts. You find this love of artifice elsewhere, too. Right at the beginning of Queen Victoria's reign, for example, Francatelli, the Italian confectioner, gives a recipe for making nosegays out of sugar, instructing you to slice a small melon into rings, candy the melon slices in some sugar syrup and then use them as the holders for a nosegay made from edible sugar flowers. Whether the etiquette of the day would have allowed you to eat them, I don't know, but Francatelli certainly liked his elaborate sugar decorations. He also talks about making pearls, birds and feathers out of sugar to decorate your dessert course. It's all rather reminiscent of one of the meals served in Daisy Ashford's *The Young Visiters*, written in the early 1890s when the author was just nine years old:

> Then they ordered the most splendid refreshments they had tea and coffie and sparkling wines to drink also a lovly wedding cake of great height with a sugar angel at the top holding a sword made of almond paste. They had countless cakes besides also ices jelly merangs jam tarts with plenty of jam on each some cold tongue some ham with salid and a pig's head done up in a wondrous manner. Ethel could hardly contain herself as she gazed at the sumpshious repast and Bernard gave her a glass of rich wine while he imbibed some whiskey before going to bed.

Such fiddly attention to presentation may have looked good. I'm not convinced, though, that it made the food taste any better.

The industrialisation of food really got underway in Victorian times when techniques for canning and bottling were perfected. This engraving comes from one of the numerous editions of Mrs Beeton's *Book of Household Management*, a book that ushered in some of the less attractive traits associated with English food – and a book, consequently, that has a lot to answer for.

CHAPTER 12

Brown Windsor Soup and High Tea

The World of the Victorians

Whon talking about the food of the wealthy in the first decades of the nineteenth century, I mentioned the chef Alexis Soyer. He was exactly what you would have expected of a successful chef of the 1830s and 1840s: flamboyant, ambitious and, above all, French. But there was another side to him. The author of the massive and intimidating *Gastronomic Regenerator* was also the author of *Soyer's Charitable Cookery* (one penny per copy of which went to charity) and *A Shilling Cookery for the People*. During the Irish famine of the late 1840s, when the potato crop was wiped out by blight, he went over to install soup kitchens, including one at the Royal Barracks in Dublin that could feed 1,000 people an hour. On his return he set up soup kitchens for impoverished silk weavers in Spitalfields in the East End of London. He was then asked by the government to find ways to improve methods of preserving food on naval voyages. A few years later, in 1855, hearing of the terrible conditions that British troops faced during the Crimean War, he volunteered to help, and reorganised the catering in the hospitals at Scutari. He also devised improved camp stoves and helped Florence Nightingale in her work at Balaclava and Sebastopol.

Soyer, in other words, saw at first hand both extremes of life in nineteenth-century England, and he serves as a reminder that while for an increasing number the Victorian era was one of plenty, for others life could be very grim indeed. This was, after all, the period when people really felt the full force of the Industrial Revolution. When the first population census was taken in 1801, only a fifth of people in England and Wales lived in towns; by 1851, half did; and by 1901, only a fifth of people in England and Wales lived in the countryside. In the same period London went from being a city of around 1 million to a sprawling urban giant of 7 million, while Manchester was transformed from a town of about 20,000 people in the 1770s to a city of 300,000 and several hundred cotton mills by the 1850s. Men and women thronged to the towns and cities to find employment in the new factories, workshops and mines and so build themselves a better life. As a result they often found themselves living in hastily built houses with appalling sanitation or squashed with many others into old, crumbling buildings. The slum-living of the early decades of the century is well captured by Charles Dickens in his description of Bermondsey's crime-infested Jacob's Island in *Oliver Twist* (1837–9):

> . . . a stranger, looking from one of the wooden bridges thrown across it at Mill Lane, will see the inhabitants of the houses on either side lowering from their back doors and windows, buckets,

pails, domestic utensils of all kinds, in which to haul the water up; and when his eye is turned from these operations to the houses themselves, his utmost astonishment will be excited by the scene before him. Crazy wooden galleries common to the backs of half-a-dozen houses, with holes from which to look upon the slime beneath; windows broken and patched, with poles thrust out on which to dry the linen that is never there; rooms so small, so filthy, so confined, that the air would seem too tainted even for the dirt and squalor which they shelter; wooden chambers thrusting themselves out above the mud, and threatening to fall into it – as some have done; dirt-besmeared walls and decaying foundations; every repulsive lineament of poverty, every loathsome indication of filth, rot, and garbage; all these ornament the banks of Folly Ditch.

One inevitable consequence of people flocking to the towns was that they became ever further removed from the source of their food. Whereas their forebears would have grown some of what they ate, scoured the hedgerows, perhaps kept a pig and possibly have baked their own bread and brewed their own beer, now city dwellers had to rely on food traders and market-stall holders. And since so many women now worked long hours in factories or in service, the temptation was either to buy a quick snack from a cook shop or to prepare food that was as simple as possible.

This was the time when the potato really came into its own. Women would cook potatoes to eke out whatever else they could afford to serve, rather as Mrs Cratchit did for her family's Christmas dinner in *A Christmas Carol*, or people would buy cooked potatoes in the street. Henry Mayhew in his magisterial mid-century *London Labour and the London Poor* devotes an entire section to baked-potato sellers, explaining how they have really come into their own over the previous fifteen years. Theirs, he explains, is a seasonal job, running from the time when the new season's potatoes are large enough to bake – around the middle of August – through to April, when the potatoes start sprouting and going soft and so are unsuitable for baking. They were baked in batches of around seventy-five at a time in the ovens of friendly bakers for a small charge, and then put into a store known as a potato can: essentially a large tin box on four legs with a fire heating a water jacket to keep the potatoes hot and with compartments for salt and butter at one end and charcoal at the other:

> These potato-cans are sometimes brightly polished, sometimes painted red, and occasionally brass-mounted. Some of the handsomest are all brass, and some are highly ornamented with brass mountings. Great pride is taken in the cans. The baked-potato man usually devotes half an hour to polishing them up, and they are mostly kept as bright as silver. The handsomest potato-can is now in Shoreditch. It cost ten guineas, and is of brass mounted with German silver. There are three lamps attached to it, with coloured glass, and of a style to accord with that of the machine . . .

Mayhew then goes on to describe the great range of customers for this fast food:

> The customers consist of all classes. Many gentlefolks buy them in the street, and take them home for supper in their pockets;

but the working-classes are the greatest purchasers. Many boys and girls lay out a halfpenny in a baked potato. Irishmen are particularly fond of them, but they are the worst customers, I am told, as they want the largest potatoes in the can. Women buy a great number of those sold. Some take them home, and some eat them in the street. Three baked potatoes are as much as will satisfy the stoutest appetite.

For wealthier purchasers, the potato was a nice snack and sometimes a convenient hand-warmer (special porcelain potato holders were marketed to encourage this). For poorer people, it was a godsend. And for the potato vendor, who might sell up to 300 potatoes a day, particularly if he had a good stand somewhere, such as Smithfield market, it was a financially worthwhile exercise, yielding perhaps a thirty-shilling profit a week – roughly what a carpenter of the time might expect to earn. I always remember my father – who was born in the Victorian era – telling me that when he went to school in Glasgow he would walk to school to save his bus fare so that he could buy a hot potato.

At some point along the way, the baked potato was joined by the chip. Charles Dickens, for example, mentions 'husky chips of potato, fried with some reluctant drops of oil' in his 1859 novel *A Tale of Two Cities*. And at some other point along the way, the chip in turn was united to fried fish. Some have said this first happened in London. Others say Lancashire deserves the credit. Nobody really knows.

But while we don't know where the marriage took place, we do know it happened in the 1860s, and we do also know a bit about the other partner in the marriage, fish in batter. In *Oliver*

Twist Dickens mentions a 'fried fish warehouse' and it seems that, certainly by the late 1830s, fried fish was commonly being sold with bread as a quick and nutritious snack. Alexis Soyer, for example, is recorded as having bought fried fish and eaten it as he walked through Soho. Many suggest that the inspiration for the dish came from Jewish settlers in London who commonly coated their fish with matzo meal and then fried it before eating it cold. Since fried fish was becoming popular at the time when chip shops were starting to make their presence felt, it's not surprising that someone reckoned the two were worth selling together.

Fish and chips had a lot going for them. Frying fish was a good way to keep it fresh – and from what I remember from my schooldays, it's easier to make cheap fish edible if you fry it in batter than if you try to cook it another way. Chips cooked in dripping and perhaps sprinkled with salt and vinegar constituted perfect fast food. Sadly, health scares in the 1980s led to a decline in the use of beef dripping in fish and chip shops – there's no doubt in my mind that it tastes much better when prepared in the traditional way, particularly as it allows you to cook at a high temperature. At any rate, it's reckoned that by the outbreak of the First World War in 1914, fish and chip shops were selling 800,000 fish dinners every week.

Victorian street food was a huge industry. In the north you would find tripe sellers; I remember the one in Dewsbury market that sold nine different varieties of tripe, including penis and udder (which is remarkably like pease pudding). Another popular street food was pea soup with, according to where you lived, either pig's trotters or bits of ham chopped up into it. Peas boiled in the pod and served with butter were similarly popular. Stalls known in my youth as whelk stalls also sprang up, selling jellied eels, whelks, winkles and prawns, all by the pint or the half-pint. You could splash a bit of vinegar on them and eat them at the stall or take them home with you. However, oysters – so long Everyman's food – started to become scarcer (and so, increasingly, the preserve of the rich) as industrial waste poured into the nation's estuaries, wiping out many of its oyster beds. I remember being told that the reason the Victorian poor had such large families was that they ate so many oysters. The fact that they continued to have large families when oysters had largely vanished from their diet suggests that this theory might not quite hold water.

Alongside potatoes and other street food, poorer town dwellers would have eaten a lot of bread, and a little butter, cheese and bacon, all washed down with weak tea and sugar. When you consider how expensive tea was for much of the Georgian period, and how exclusive white bread was, it seems ironic that the treats of the rich in the eighteenth century should have become the standard fare of the poor in the nineteenth. Neither did much good. As I've already said, white bread and tea are considerably less nutritious than brown bread and beer. The one thing that could be said for tea was that, because the water had to be boiled, it was at least safe to drink.

Tea actually remained relatively expensive in the first half of the nineteenth century and tea drinking declined slightly for a while as a result. But two things changed this. The first was the decision taken by Gladstone in 1853, when he was Chancellor of the Exchequer, to reduce import duties on tea. A confirmed tea drinker himself, he also thought that tea for the working class was infinitely preferable to the alternative: alcohol. The second development was the growth of the tea trade with Britain's most important imperial possession.

Quite how the Indian tea trade started remains shrouded in legend and conjecture. I remember hearing a story that tea seeds were smuggled there from China by an English captain who concealed them in a hollow cane. Others claim that a Scotsman named Robert Fortune was responsible. Born in 1812, he was a botanist who travelled to China disguised as a Chinese merchant, accompanied by a Chinese manservant and, rather curiously, by his wife's sister, who eventually became his mistress and with whom he set up house. No European was allowed into the interior of China in those days, and the Chinese were very protective of anything to do with the tea industry. We know that Fortune managed to make his way into the tea areas and actually observed tea being produced, dried and boxed for the table. Whether he was solely responsible for starting the Indian tea industry is open to question, but there is no doubt that he was instrumental in advising on the running of tea plantations and how tea could be produced for commercial use. By the late 1840s, the Assam Tea Company was thriving. By 1900, half of Britain's tea came from India and nearly 40 per cent from Ceylon; black tea was a firm favourite with British taste buds – and Britons were drinking ten times as much tea a year as they had a century earlier.

Incidentally, in the early days of tea drinking in England, tea was often served in a small handle-less cup, inspired by the Chinese tea bowl; hence the question that would be asked of visitors, 'You'll take a dish of tea?' In Victorian times it was not uncommon to pour tea from the cup into the saucer, allowing you to drink it more or less straightaway because, of course, it would cool more quickly, particularly if milk was added. This habit continued among working-class people well into my youth.

Along with bread and tea, the poor would often eke out their diet with porridge and, if they were lucky, the occasional piece of meat. It was a dull, repetitive and far from balanced diet. When Dr Edward Smith compiled a report for the Privy Council in 1863 about the diet of the poor, he noted again and again how badly they ate. He noted, for example, that a typical daily diet among the poor of Stafford would consist of tea, bread and butter for breakfast; bacon and bread (or meat and vegetables on Sunday and Monday) for 'dinner'; tea, bread and butter for 'tea'; and bread, cheese and beer (or milk and bread for the children) for supper.

If you want to point a finger at when people started to forget how to cook, then the Victorian era has to be the prime candidate. Not that this was the fault of the poor. Living in cramped accommodation as they did, they can't have found it easy to prepare food. Furthermore, fuel tended to be quite expensive, so many couldn't afford to cook a meal more than two or three times a week, even if they had had the money for the ingredients and the time to prepare them. I can't help feeling that, however well intentioned a man like Alexis Soyer may have been with his *A Shilling Cookery for the People*, he was rather missing the point when he gave detailed instructions on how to make a beef pudding or suggested that a hare pie should also contain steak, onions, veal and wine. I also wonder whether the people he was aiming at would have been able to read his book in the first place.

Now that so much food was bought rather than produced

at home, the way was left well and truly open for unscrupulous traders to trick their customers. Fiddling with food to make a bit more money was nothing new: it was something that had been happening since at least medieval times, when bakers had been forced to sit in the stocks with loaves around their necks if they had been found giving short measure. But now the opportunity for fraud was huge. At best, it only affected people's pockets. Adding alum to bread, for example, which was certainly happening in Georgian times, was dishonest but harmless, as was the common practice of bulking out the flour with boiled potatoes. At worst, though, the sort of things that got added to food were highly dangerous. We're concerned today about food additives – E this, and E that – but at least we don't have to worry about copper being added to pickles to make them look greener, red lead being applied to Gloucester cheese to colour the rind, or warehouse floor sweepings being added to pepper. Or at least I hope not.

From time to time, people complained publicly about what was being done to their food. Frederick Accum, for example, published a much-talked-about book in 1820. *The Treatise of Adulterations of Food and Culinary Poisons* revealed many of the tricks of the trade and, appropriately enough, bore a skull and crossbones design. But what is extraordinary is how little changed as a result, although the book did cause a scandal, made Accum lots of powerful enemies, and he ended up having to leave the country. When Mrs Beeton published her *Book of Household Management* some years later, she still felt it necessary to warn people of the potential dangers lurking in the food they were buying. Here she is on the subject of China tea:

Chinese tea has frequently been adulterated in this country, by the admixture of the dried leaves of certain plants. The leaves of the sloe, white thorn, ash, elder, and some others, have been employed for this purpose; such as the leaves of the speedwell, wild germander, black currants, syringa, purple-spiked willow-herb, sweet-brier, and cherry-tree. Some of these are harmless, others are to a certain degree poisonous; as, for example, are the leaves of all the varieties of the plum and cherry tribe, to which the sloe belongs. Adulteration by means of these leaves is by no means a new species of fraud; and several acts of parliament, from the time of George II, have been passed, specifying severe penalties against those guilty of the offence, which, notwith-standing numerous convictions, continues to the present time.

It wasn't until 1875 that a Sale of Food and Drugs Act was finally passed.

Given the generally poor quality and quantity of food for the less well off, it is scarcely surprising that so many of them suffered very bad health. Their teeth were full of cavities. Many had rickets. In Leeds at the turn of the twentieth century, for example, it was reckoned that in the poorer parts of the city, half the children suffered from this condition (rickets sounds a very Victorian condition, but although our modern diet generally has more vitamin D, our indoor, sun-averse lifestyle has recently seen an increase in recorded cases). Infant mortality was high, not only because childbirth was riskier then, but because mothers were often too emaciated to be able to breastfeed their babies. Many took to bottle-feeding, but because they didn't understand hygiene, this could prove a killer. In some areas a quarter of all babies died before they reached their first birthday.

It's tempting to assume that life was rather better for the poor who lived in the countryside, but that wasn't always the case. Indeed, during the years of the Napoleonic Wars when, for various reasons, prices were very high, farm labourers suffered periods of virtual destitution. Once, many of them would have been housed and fed by their employer and so would have been relatively immune to changing economic conditions. Now, as the final pieces of common land were enclosed and rented by tenant farmers, they found themselves reduced to being casual labourers – paid when there was work, left to fend for themselves when there wasn't. And with the arrival of the threshing machine in the 1780s, there was now rather less work than there had been. The writer William Cobbett, touring England in the 1820s, was appalled by what he saw. 'The labourers seem miserably poor,' he wrote on a visit to Cirencester. 'Their dwellings are little better than pig-beds, and their looks indicate that their food is not nearly equal to that of a pig.' Many farm workers moved to the towns in a desperate search for employment. Those who remained struggled to live on their low salaries and, as many traditional cottage industries like weaving were taken over by factories in big towns, found themselves unable to supplement their income from other sources. It's not surprising that many farm workers in the 1830s resorted to arson, machine-breaking and rioting.

William Cobbett was horrified to find that people in the countryside were now eating the same diet as their brethren in the towns: potatoes, bread from the baker's and tea. This wasn't the case everywhere – in the north, especially, you might well still have somewhere to feed a pig or keep a cow. Nor did it hold true throughout the century: some decades were better than others. But our chocolate-box view of Victorian villages, with roses round the door and apple-cheeked villagers, is some way from the truth.

This is quite evident if you read Flora Thompson's *Lark Rise to Candleford* – a book of which I'm very fond – which describes the author's upbringing in a small Oxfordshire village in the 1880s. Although hers is, in some ways, quite a nostalgic account, it contains plenty about the tougher side of rural life. Generally speaking, she says, people had enough to eat and could grow some of their own food: each house had a vegetable garden which supplied potatoes, peas, runner beans, cauliflowers, cabbage, lettuce, and so on; and in the autumn, people foraged for mushrooms and wild fruit. But the diet was still meagre. Breakfast might consist of bread and lard (butter was an expensive luxury). If farm workers were hungry during the day they might munch a turnip or eat some oil cake intended for the cattle, before having some bread and bacon at lunch, washed down with some cold tea. Women tended to have pretty limited diets, saving the best food for their husbands and children. No one starved, but the poorest villagers must have felt hungry much of the time. Flora Thompson describes a mother and daughter who would fry a rasher of bacon each day for their midday meal but take it in turns to eat it, 'the other one dipping her bread in the fat'.

The only times that families enjoyed a richer diet was when they slaughtered one of their pigs. This could be tough for the children: so much attention was lavished on pigs that they became almost part of the family. But for the adults it was one of the highlights of the year. A travelling pork butcher or pig sticker would be dragooned to do the deed and people would then set to work carefully cutting up the carcass and preparing the various cuts that would see the family through the next few months. Then would come the celebration – a 'pig feast' for the extended family:

If the house had no oven, permission was obtained from an old couple in one of the thatched cottages to heat up the big bread-baking oven in their wash-house. This was like a large cupboard with an iron door, lined with brick and going far back into the wall. Faggots of wood were lighted inside and the door was closed upon them until the oven was well heated. Then the ashes were swept out and baking-tins with joints of pork, potatoes, batter puddings, pork pies, and sometimes a cake or two, were popped inside and left to bake without further attention.

Meanwhile, at home, three or four different kinds of vegetables would be cooked, and always a meat pudding, made in a basin. No feast and few Sunday dinners were considered complete without that item, which was eaten alone, without vegetables, when a joint was to follow. On ordinary days the pudding would be a roly-poly containing fruit, currants, or jam; but it still appeared as a first course, the idea being that it took the edge off the appetite. At the pig feast there would be no sweet pudding, for that could be had any day, and who wanted sweet things when there was plenty of meat to be had!

But this glorious plenty only came once or at most twice a year . . .

Lark Rise is full of fascinating little snippets about food. Flora Thompson describes Jerry Parish, who would call round on Mondays with a box of bloaters and a basket of small, sour oranges:

The bloaters were sold at a penny each and the oranges at three a penny. Even at these prices they were luxuries; but, as it was still only Monday and a few coppers might remain in a few purses, the women felt at liberty to crowd round his cart to examine and criticize his wares, even if they bought nothing.

And then there's a charming description of the first time that Flora – or 'Laura' as she calls herself in *Lark Rise* – sees a tomato:

It was on Jerry's cart tomatoes first appeared in the hamlet. They had not long been introduced into this country and were slowly making their way into favour. The fruit was flatter in shape then than now and deeply grooved and indented from the stem, giving it an almost starlike appearance. There were bright yellow ones, too, as well as the scarlet; but, after a few years, the yellow ones disappeared from the market and the red ones became rounder and smoother, as we see them now.

At first sight, the basket of red and yellow fruit attracted Laura's colour-loving eye. 'What are those?' she asked old Jerry.

'Love-apples, me dear. Love-apples, they be; though some hignorant folks be a callin' 'em tommytoes. But you don't want any o' they – nasty sour things, they be, as only gentry can eat. You have a nice sweet orange wi' your penny.' But Laura felt she must taste the love-apples and insisted upon having one.

Such daring created quite a sensation among the onlookers. 'Don't 'ee go tryin' to eat it, now,' one woman urged. 'It'll only make 'ee sick. I know because I had one of the nasty, horrid things at our Minnie's.' And nasty, horrid things tomatoes remained in the popular estimation for years; though most people to-day would prefer them as they were then, with the real tomato flavour pronounced, to the watery insipidity of our larger, smoother tomato.

I'm interested to see that the adult Flora Thompson, writing in the 1930s and early 1940s, should regard contemporary tomatoes as insipid. It's exactly how I feel about today's commercially grown ones. As for the suspicion with which tomatoes were viewed in her day, I remember my sister, who helped the down-and-outs clustered around Westminster Cathedral, telling me that they referred to raw tomatoes as 'cancer balls' and wouldn't eat them. The tomatoes had to be cooked.

Many villagers – no doubt encouraged by the lord of the manor – beautified their gardens by growing flowers among their vegetables, creating that picture-postcard view we tend to have of the Victorian countryside. Many also became obsessed with competitive fruit and vegetable growing, particularly in more industrial areas. Here they were following quite a venerable tradition. Lancashire weavers, back in the pre-industrial days of the 1740s, started holding annual competitions to see who could grow the biggest gooseberry, going to all sorts of lengths to produce the heaviest in show. In the 1830s the poet Robert Southey described how compulsive gooseberry growers would carefully nurture their gooseberry bushes, often only leaving a few fruits on each to give them the best chance of bearing record-breaking berries.

Mining areas produced gardeners particularly adept at growing giant vegetables. One of the most terrifying things I ever did was to judge at a show held in Musselburgh, near where I live, which involved having to weigh up the relative merits of such things as giant Musselburgh leeks and Kelsae onions. I wandered

about in trepidation, convinced that if I got it wrong I'd probably have to move. Until the Thatcher years, the whole area
around Musselburgh was a considerable mining area, as it had
been for centuries.

So far I've talked about the very rich and the very poor of the
nineteenth century. But, of course, there was a huge swathe of
people between those two extremes, from skilled craftsmen to
shopkeepers to successful businessmen. It's also worth bearing in
mind that 'the poor' wasn't a fixed social class. So much depended
on circumstance. You might be earning a reasonable wage at one
moment – sufficient to guarantee you a reasonable standard of
living – but then be plunged into destitution by illness, an
economic downturn that threw you out of work, or, worst of all,
old age. Life was uncertain. The well-paid craftsman in his twen-
ties could very easily become the sixty-year-old pauper.

For those who had a reasonable amount of money – however
fleetingly – there was certainly plenty to eat and increasing
variety. In the early part of the century, Jane Austen records
eating a mango – something that James II would have come
across but that had only recently come within the grasp of the
reasonably well off. Pineapples were becoming common.
Rhubarb, once regarded as a medicine and a laxative, was popularised by Joseph Myatt, who grew it in his market gardens in
Deptford and Brixton in the early decades of the century. Not
to mention plenty of other foods arriving from abroad – from
North and South America, and from the empire, in particular
from India.

I've already talked about Hannah Glasse's championship of
curry in the eighteenth century, but it would be true to say that

it was in Victorian times that it really became popular. Queen Victoria, who was fascinated by all things to do with the subcontinent, had Indian staff on hand to prepare curries for the royal household. She even had an Indian favourite – Abdul Karim – who, later in her reign, occupied the place in her affections once taken by her Scottish servant and former gillie John Brown. Her entourage may have been relieved to see the back of John Brown, but they were none too pleased to find Abdul Karim in his place, and on one occasion threatened to resign.

For her part, Eliza Acton, the best cookery writer of the period, devoted considerable attention to curry in her *Modern Cookery for Private Families* of 1845. I have to say that the British have never really understood curry, tending to add curry powder at the same time as the stock or water, rather than frying it in hot oil to release the flavours; or thickening sauces with a roux of curry powder mixed with flour – as if it were a stew or casserole – rather than adding ground almonds or coconut cream or even a paste of onions. To give her credit, Eliza Acton was aware of the shortcomings of her countrymen. She lamented 'the great superiority of the oriental curries over those generally prepared in England', and suggested that the lack of fresh ingredients was to blame. Acknowledging the superiority of Indian cooks, she tried to come up with ways to improve the English version, suggesting, for example, that coconut could be grated into the gravy to give the curry a more authentic flavour and that people should also try using tamarind, acid apples and cucumber to reproduce that piquancy you get with bitter gourds, mango, and so on. It was a valiant attempt, and certainly better than the lazy alternative of simply adding lemon juice, but I have to say that when I tried this type of curry as a child

I realised straightaway that it bore no resemblance to anything prepared by my grandmother's Indian cook. In fact, I'd go further and say it was really quite unpleasant.

Eliza Acton struggled on with her desire to create something approaching Indian cuisine, while acknowledging that it wouldn't necessarily be to all tastes. She notes, for example, when including an authentically Anglo-Indian curry recipe given to her by a Mr Arnott, that it will probably be somewhat too acidic for English tastes and that the proportion of onion and garlic should therefore be reduced by a half 'for any but well-seasoned Anglo-Indian palates'. She even reproduces Mr Arnott's recipe for curry powder: eight ounces of turmeric, four ounces of coriander seed, two ounces of cumin seed, two ounces of fenugreek seed and half an ounce of cayenne pepper. She recommends that curry enthusiasts should go to Messrs Corbyn and Co., 'druggists' based at 300 High Holborn, for the ingredients.

The sad thing is that there were many around who would have known what a proper curry tasted like. In 1811 *The Times* published an advertisement for the Hindostanee Coffee House in Portman Square, where old India hands could enjoy Indian dishes cooked to perfection under the watchful eye of Sake Deen Mahomed, an Indian restaurateur. The venue boasted bamboo furniture and hookahs. It didn't last that long (perhaps because old India hands tended to bring their Indian servants back with them and so ate at home), but its existence, however fleeting, is indicative of the lure of India. Sake Deen Mahomed, by the way, had more than one string to his bow: he went on to become, by royal warrant, shampooing surgeon to George IV and William IV and opened the magnificent Mahomed's Baths in Brighton – further demonstration of how fascinated the English were by all things Indian. The fascination continued long after Mahomed's death in 1851. Imports of curry powder, prepared in India, rose dramatically throughout the century.

Having said that people were fascinated by Indian culture and Indian food, I should stress, however, that not all English people liked spicy food. In Thackeray's *Vanity Fair* of 1848, Rebecca 'Becky' Sharp certainly finds it all too much for her:

Now we have heard how Mrs Sedley had prepared a fine curry for her son, just as he liked it, and in the course of dinner a portion of this dish was offered to Rebecca. 'What is it?' said she, turning an appealing look to Mr Joseph.

'Capital,' said he. His mouth was full of it: his face quite red with the delightful exercise of gobbling. 'Mother, it's as good as my own curries in India.'

'Oh, I must try some, if it is an Indian dish,' said Miss Rebecca. 'I am sure everything must be good that comes from there.'

'Give Miss Sharp some curry, my dear,' said Mr Sedley, laughing.

Rebecca had never tasted the dish before.

'Do you find it as good as everything else from India?' said Mr Sedley.

'Oh, excellent!' said Rebecca, who was suffering tortures with the cayenne pepper.

'Try a chili with it, Miss Sharp,' said Joseph, really interested.

'A chili,' said Rebecca, gasping. 'Oh yes!' She thought a chili was something cool, as its name imported, and was served with some. 'How fresh and green they look,' she said, and put one into her mouth. It was hotter than the curry; flesh and blood could bear it no longer. She laid down her fork. 'Water, for Heaven's sake, water!' she cried. Mr Sedley burst out laughing (he was a coarse man, from the Stock Exchange, where they love all sorts of practical jokes).

As for the British in India, while there were many serving the Raj who fell in love with Indian food, there were plenty who didn't. One visitor, staying in Bombay with friends in the 1870s, recorded in his diary that their first dinner together consisted of fillets of fish in parsley sauce, roast mutton, chicken pie, Italian eggs and lemon baked custard. Nothing very Indian there. This was the period when the *memsahib* – the English wife in India – was arriving in increasing numbers and bringing her native food with her. Invitations to dinner commonly bore the words 'no hookahs' in the bottom corner by the mid century. Dinner itself would probably involve roast mutton and other such delights, where once upon a time the enterprising Englishman in India would have eaten local food. The one Indian dish that did make its way among the British, albeit with an English accent, was kedgeree, based on *khichari*, a simple recipe of rice and lentils. The English started adding smoked fish to it, along with hard-boiled eggs, curry powder and fried onions, transforming it into a popular breakfast dish. It's still around, if not always made with the inventiveness and flair that it once was. As for Indian curries, these were gradually transformed into a mishmash of curry powder, apples and sultanas.

Indian cuisine was the dominant foreign influence on English food in the nineteenth century, but it wasn't the only one. As previously mentioned, in the first half of the century Jewish fried fish inspired the creation of fish and chips. In the second half, as waves of Jewish immigrants arrived from the 1880s onwards, often escaping persecution in central Europe and, in particular, Russia, so other features of Jewish food started to make their way into England. Settling at first for the most part in the East End of London, these new Ashkenazi Jewish arrivals must have seemed a strange and exotic tribe, the women in their woollen wigs and the men in their dark clothes and large felt hats, with ringlets running down their cheeks and religious tassels hanging down from their waists. They spoke a strange language, Yiddish, and filled the East End with little shops.

I can remember going there as a child with my father and seeing and smelling the barrels of new green or pickled cucumbers and the various types of pickled herrings. I also remember the salt-beef bars, where you could eat your salt beef with bread and pickled cucumber. Very delicious it was, too. Over time salt beef became almost a cockney institution. Because I had Jewish step-cousins, we tended to eat matzo biscuits with our cheese at home, rather than water biscuits. Somehow they seemed crunchier and crisper, and certainly better for breaking up into clam chowder (not that this is something that the shellfish-eschewing Jews would have done).

The other thing these Jewish immigrants brought with them was their own version of smoked salmon, known as London Smoke – much smoother, milder and oilier than the rather harsher smoked salmon of the north. To this day, having been raised as a Londoner, I have to confess that although I've now lived in Scotland for seventeen years, and my fishmonger does beautiful smoked salmon, when I go down to London I'm still delighted to eat the London Smoke. Remarkably, Forman's, who were established in 1905, have only just been moved out of the East End. The founders worked hard and prospered, and their immediate descendants, who over time abandoned the strict kosher precepts of their parents, did well in the catering world. The Jewish contribution to English food can also be traced in the Lyons Corner Houses, popular until the 1970s, which were established by the firm of Salmon & Gluckstein and Joseph Nathaniel Lyons. And it's intriguing to see a family link between Lyons and Nigella Lawson, a famous name in contemporary food. In fact, I find it amazing how a relatively small band of people who arrived in England often virtually destitute could have had such an impact on their new country and have come up with food so much more interesting than the cuisine that surrounded them in Victorian England.

One way and another, then, a rich variety of food became available in nineteenth-century England. And what made it possible for people all round the country to sample it was, of course, the constantly improving nature of transport. From the 1830s, the increased use of steamships allowed a flood of goods to arrive from America and far-flung parts of the empire such as India. The transit of goods around the country was transformed by the arrival of the steam train and the establishment by the 1860s of a national rail network. Suddenly it became possible to send more or less anything to anywhere very cheaply. Romney Marsh sheep could be sent to Smithfield for slaughter (thanks to the combination of trains and ships they even made their way to New Zealand in the 1850s). Stilton could be sent nationwide from Leicestershire. Keiller's marmalade could grow from a cottage industry to a global empire. Even that most temperamental of foods – fish – could now be sent all round the country. Billingsgate fish market had to be refashioned twice – in 1850 and then more elaborately in 1873 – to accommodate increasing stocks arriving from the coast. It's a market I have fond memories of: I can recall getting up early, going to Billingsgate and buying a pack of shrimps to eat on Tower Green. Sadly, it's not the same now that it's been moved to Canary Wharf. Nor, of course, is the railway network what it was. It takes longer to get by public transport from London to Grange-over-Sands today than it took by stagecoach. Queen Victoria would not be pleased: for her the railway allowed her to flee to her beloved Balmoral, where she could admire muscular Highlanders in kilts.

Not only could food be moved more swiftly, it could also be preserved more efficiently. The ice houses that had been so popular with the gentry of the Georgian age gave way to the ice man, who delivered blocks of dripping ice to Victorian middle-class households to be stored in special containers that acted as early refrigerators. Now fish could be transported packed in ice. And with the arrival of refrigeration, meat could be brought in from as far away as Canada, America, Australia and New Zealand, frozen beef and mutton first arriving from Australia in the SS *Strathleven* in 1880.

Also available in the armoury of the food preserver were bottling and canning. It was a Frenchman, Nicolas Appert, who, during the time of the Napoleonic Wars, discovered that food could be preserved by being hermetically sealed in jars with cork and wax. Then an Englishman, Peter Durand, applied the same principles to a tin container, patenting his discovery in 1810. He sold the patent to a Bryan Donkin for £1,000, and Donkin duly set up a canning factory in Bermondsey (his company ultimately became part of Crosse & Blackwell). In the early days it was a laborious process, involving bending lengths of tinplate around a cylinder, and then soldering the edges and the discs that went at the top and bottom. These early cans were unreliable, having a nasty tendency to harbour bacteria, or indeed to burst. I remember hearing of a tin of turkey that exploded so violently that it killed the cook. Nor were the contents necessarily particularly attractive. Tinned meat, for example, tended to come in big coarse-grained chunks with a glutinous mass of fat on one side.

It was the Americans who ultimately perfected canning on an industrial scale, and by the 1880s, as initial scepticism was overcome, England became awash with tinned Pacific salmon, corned beef, sardines, condensed milk, green beans, peas, and heaven knows what else besides. Some idea of its popularity can been gauged from the following picnic passage in Jerome K. Jerome's 1889 comic classic *Three Men in a Boat*, a passage that also identifies one problem that most of us at some time or other have experienced with tinned food:

We are very fond of pine-apple, all three of us. We looked at the picture on the tin; we thought of the juice. We smiled at one another, and Harris got a spoon ready.

Then we looked for the knife to open the tin with. We turned out everything in the hamper. We turned out the bags. We pulled up the boards at the bottom of the boat. We took everything out on to the bank and shook it. There was no tin-opener to be found.

Then Harris tried to open the tin with a pocket-knife, and broke the knife and cut himself badly; and George tried a pair of scissors, and the scissors flew up, and nearly put his eye out. While they were dressing their wounds, I tried to make a hole in the thing with the spiky end of the hitcher, and the hitcher slipped and jerked me out between the boat and the bank into two feet of muddy water, and the tin rolled over, uninjured, and broke a teacup.

In fact the first tin opener had appeared, not a moment too soon, in 1855.

Industrialisation of food brought with it the growth of a market for bottled sauces. Sauces had certainly long been popular in England and you still occasionally find exquisite eighteenth-century silver sauce labels, presumably designed to go on glass sauce bottles. But it was left to the Victorians to industrialise the process on a major scale. Lea & Perrins Worcestershire sauce dates from the year of Victoria's coronation – 1837. With its blend of anchovies, seasoning and vinegar it belongs to a tradition that stretches back to the fermented fish sauce of Roman and Greek times. I rather like the image of Romans in their togas and socks splashing Worcestershire sauce all over their finest recipes.

The related ketchups had also been around for a while, but it was left to the Americans to come up with tomato ketchup in the early years of the nineteenth century. Shortly after the Civil War, a certain Joshua Davenport started to experiment with recipes that settlers had brought over from Europe, using sugar, tomato stock and vinegar flavoured with cinnamon, cayenne and salt; and by 1876 Henry John Heinz was making ketchup in his factory in Pittsburgh. Fortnum & Mason started to stock it a few years later. Similarly it was the Americans who gave us Tabasco sauce, invented in Louisiana in the 1860s.

I myself have a rather nostalgic fondness for brown sauce and can remember trotting down to the cab shelters in St John's Wood as a child in the hope of a bacon sandwich liberally anointed with it. Dorothy Hartley in her *Food in England* recalls a 1950s dark brown spicy sauce, made with chopped shallots, garlic, salt, pepper and mushroom ketchup, which I suspect is the one I sampled. I also once made a batch of sauce myself which essentially consisted of anchovies, garlic, horseradish and various other spices, and which I put in one of those large glass jars that you see in old-fashioned sweet shops. At first it was revolting. After six months it was quite nice. After a year it was delicious. It was based on a recipe devised by the former Duchess of Hamilton; the duke and I had thought of turning it into a commercial venture, but somehow nothing ever came of it.

I also remember reading about a brown sauce invented by some sisters in Yorkshire who put it in a barrel at the bottom of the back stairs for a month, instructing everyone who passed it to give it a shake to keep it properly mixed. Inevitably many brown sauces have gone the way of all flesh – or sauce – but one of the oldest commercially produced ones, HP Sauce, is still going strong over a century after it was launched.

In Victorian times, then, the responsibility for many types of food was handed over from the individual or small shop to the large-scale manufacturer, from meat extract (Bovril, originally with the rather uninviting name Johnston's Fluid Beef, dates from the 1870s) to biscuits (Peek Frean, for example, was set up in Bermondsey in 1857; the Garibaldi biscuit, named after the great Italian hero, was first manufactured by Peek Frean in 1861). It was a great age for promotion and advertisement in newspapers, on billboards and even on the sides of buildings. (I can remember a Victorian advertisement for a product with the delightful name of 'Mazzawattee Tea' that I passed whenever I went to visit some friends in Hertfordshire; it had been placed on the side of a house and not only sported the name but showed an elderly grandmother, in a mob cap, holding out a tin of tea to a small boy, who was presumably her grandson.) Almost overnight, brightly coloured packaging sprang up, and I can still remember the challenge of trying to work out what the contents of some tin or other were long after it had parted company with the printed label it had once borne.

The sheer inventiveness of the Victorians is impressive; unfortunately, it doesn't make me particularly like their food. In the first place, while they came up with many clever time-saving ideas – quick-acting yeast, self-raising flour, custard powder, blancmange powder, concentrated egg powder, gelatine-based jellies – their food didn't necessarily taste any better as a result. If anything, the opposite occurred, the industrialisation of food inevitably leading to a decline in variety and quality. Factory-made cheeses started replacing farm cheeses. Butter was threatened by margarine (originally made from beef fat and milk, later from vegetable oil). Fresh vegetables gave way to bulk-dried vegetables and dried packaged soups.

Moreover, Victorian cookery, in my view, became increasingly dull. You start seeing the danger signs with Eliza Acton – in most respects an admirable cookery writer. In the first edition of *Modern Cookery* she states that garlic should be used, but sparingly. By the third edition, she has decided that garlic is to be avoided. And then there are recipes such as this one for 'Burlington Whimsey':

Set aside until quite cold half a calf's head dressed by the preceding receipt [recipe]. If, on cutting it, the gelatinous part should not appear perfectly tender, pare it off closely from the head, weigh, and mince it; put it into a pint of good gravy, and stew it gently from ten to fifteen minutes. Mince as much more of the head as will make up a pound in weight after the edges are trimmed off, and part of the fat is taken away; add to this three ounces of the lean of a boiled ham finely chopped, the grated rind of a large lemon, three teaspoonsfuls of parsley and one of thyme shred very small, three quarters of a teaspoonful of mace, half a small nutmeg grated, a teaspoonful of salt, and a half-quarter one of cayenne; stir the whole well together, and put it, with half a pint more of gravy, to the portion which has been already simmered. When the whimsey has boiled *softly* from four to five minutes, pour it into moulds or pans, in which slices of the tongue have been evenly arranged, and when quite cold it will turn out very firmly. It may be garnished, before it is sent to table, with branches of parsley, which should, however, be perfectly dry; and when served for supper or luncheon, it may be accompanied by salad dressing.

This is basically a dish of brawn. I'm actually quite fond of brawn. The Victorians, however, seem to have been too fond of it. To my mind this particular recipe is the epitome of dull food dressed up to look whimsical.

And the trouble is that there was far too much dull Victorian food. Brown Windsor soup is a case in point. It's a particularly nasty concoction which owes its colour – of over-varnished wood panels – to the fact that the roux, which is used to thicken the soup, is cooked until it is quite a dark shade of brown. This adds not only an unpleasant colour but also an unpleasant flavour. There were other nasty Victorian soups, too. Mrs Beeton includes a recipe for coconut soup, involving rice flour, mace, cayenne, salt and a pint of cream, which sounds quite revolting.

I also think it was the Victorians who were responsible for

the habit of overcooking vegetables, which cursed English cuisine for the next century. The problem seems to have started in the late Regency period when some writers began to recommend boiling vegetables until they were soft. Thereafter, things got out of hand. Some of the cooking times in Mrs Beeton's *Book of Household Management* look truly alarming, and her suggestion that you should add a little soda when cooking cabbage implies she was more interested in ensuring that the cabbage should look a vivid green than in cooking it well. As in other areas of Victorian cookery, and indeed life in general, appearance seems to have been more important than taste.

It would be unfair to blame any one person or one book for the decline of English cookery, but Isabella Beeton and her ubiquitous book do have quite a lot to answer for. The daughter of a linen merchant who died when she was four, she was brought up by her mother and stepfather at Epsom, where her stepfather was clerk of the course. Her mother was a good cook, and Isabella herself would have seen preparations for the grand meals served at the racecourse, but despite showing an interest in pastry-making in her teens, there aren't otherwise any indications of a devotion to food and cooking. That's not a good sign in a writer of cookery books. If I write a letter or a postcard to a friend, I almost invariably mention some delicious meal I have eaten – or some terrible food experience. Isabella, however, seems to have been more interested in what she was wearing than in what she was eating.

When she was twenty, Isabella married the entrepreneurial publisher Samuel Beeton, responsible for the *English Woman's Domestic Magazine*, a publication that appealed to upwardly mobile Victorians anxious to know the correct way to run their households and to treat their domestic staff. Then came *The Book of Household Management*, which Samuel published in monthly parts between 1859 and 1861. Just four years later Isabella died of peritonitis and puerperal fever, a few days after giving birth to her son Mayson. She was only twenty-eight.

The Book of Household Management, however, started to establish a life of its own. Samuel Beeton was soon out of the picture, forced by bankruptcy to sell his interest in the book to a rival publisher, Ward, Lock & Tyler (I remember coming across his bankruptcy papers in the 1960s when I was in Gray's Inn Library, looking for distraction from my Bar studies, and it seems that, among other things, he'd advertised for people to send him recipes and then not paid them). Ward, Lock & Tyler, however, recognising publishing gold when they saw it, went on to produce endless editions of the book, ever further removed from the original and packed with over-the-top plates illustrating various elaborate dishes.

As I've hinted, a lot of the recipes in the book are very far from appealing and some make you wonder whether all were tested before being consigned to print. I do wonder, for example, how many people trying to prepare the dinner for twelve persons recommended for January struggled to find two of the key ingredients – lobster and peas – at that time of year. Or how many people fell ill after mishandling a recipe for reheated turbot with oyster sauce. And I'm not too keen on the mock turtle soup recipe, based on calf's head, ham and a pound of butter. However, it's not hard to see why the book should have been such a success. For the aspiring Victorian housekeeper with an inexperienced cook, it seemed to cover everything. What's more, it offered very precise instructions to reassure the novice. Gone are Hannah Glasse's 'as much thyme as will lie on a six-pence' or a 'walnut of butter'. Instead, thanks to the more widespread use of kitchen scales, precise measurements can be given. For white stock, for example, you need: '4 lbs. of knuckle of veal, any poultry trimmings, 4 slices of lean ham, 1 carrot, 2 onions, 1 head of celery, 12 white peppercorns, 1 oz. of salt, 1 blade of mace, 1 oz. butter, 4 quarts of water.'

And there's no doubt, from a social history point of view, that Mrs Beeton is a fascinating source of information. She gives us a very good idea as to what great swathes of the population would have eaten from the 1860s onwards, and also offers fascinating glimpses of other areas of daily life. Here, for example, is Mrs Beeton on the subject of what mothers should and shouldn't do after childbirth:

> As regards exercise and amusement, we would certainly neither prohibit a mother's dancing, going to a theatre, nor even from attending an assembly. The first, however, is the best indoor recreation she can take, and a young mother will do well to often amuse herself in the nursery with this most excellent means of healthful circulation. The only precaution necessary is to avoid letting the child suck the milk that has lain long in the breast, or is heated by excessive action.

I like that – 'heated by excessive action'.

There's also plenty of practical advice on family medical matters (though I'm not sure I would use antimony to help cure measles), on dealing with servants, and so on. When it comes to food, we get a very vivid sense of what middle-class people with different budgets would have gone for, because Mrs Beeton was anxious to appeal to as wide a readership as possible. At the more modest end, for example, we get various 'bills of fare' for a 'plain family'. One of the January suggestions reads as follows:

Sunday. 1. Codfish and oyster sauce, potatoes. 2. Joint of roast mutton, either leg, haunch, or saddle; broccoli and potatoes, red-currant jelly. 3. Apple tart and custards, cheese.

Monday. 1. The remains of codfish picked from the bone, and warmed through in the oyster sauce; if there is no sauce left, order a few oysters and make a little fresh; and do not let the fish boil, or it will be watery. 2. Curried rabbit, with boiled rice served separately, cold mutton, mashed potatoes. 3. Somerset-shire dumplings with wine sauce.

Tuesday. 1. Boiled fowls, parsley-and-butter; bacon garnished with Brussels sprouts, minced or hashed mutton. 2. Baroness pudding.

Wednesday. 1. The remains of the fowls cut up into joints and fricasseed; joint of roast pork and apple sauce, and, if liked, sage-and-onion, served on a dish by itself; turnips and potatoes. 2. Lemon pudding, either baked or boiled.

Thursday. 1. Cold pork and jugged hare, red-currant jelly, mashed potatoes. 2. Apple pudding.

Friday. 1. Boiled beef, either the aitchbone or the silver side of the round; carrots, turnips, suet dumplings, and potatoes: if there is a marrowbone, serve the marrow on toast at the same time. 2. Rice snowballs.

Saturday. 1. Pea-soup made from liquor in which beef was boiled; cold beef, mashed potatoes. 2. Baked batter fruit pudding.

By contrast a July dinner party for twelve for, presumably, a rather better-off household offers rather more variety:

FIRST COURSE
Soup à la Jardinière
Chicken Soup
Crimped Salmon and Parsley-and-Butter
Trout aux fines herbes, in cases

ENTRÉES
Tendrons de Veau and Peas
Lamb Cutlets and Cucumbers

SECOND COURSE
Loin of Veal à la Béchamel
Roast Fore-quarter of Lamb
Salad
Braised Ham, garnished with Broad Beans
Vegetables

THIRD COURSE
Roast Ducks
Turkey Poult
Stewed Peas à la Française
Lobster Salad
Cherry Tart
Raspberry-and-Currant Tart
Custards, in glasses
Lemon Creams
Nesselrode Pudding
Marrow Pudding

DESSERT AND ICES

It's interesting to see so many French words strewn around: this was food for the socially aspiring. It's also interesting to note that service *à la française* still holds sway here, rather than the newly modish *à la russe*. The soup would have been ready as the guests came in, and there is a clear progression towards the roast courses. The host would usually have carved the meat, with servants on hand to help and clear away. Elsewhere in Mrs Beeton, it's intriguing to see one or two more unusual items cropping up. Watercress, for example, is quite a popular ingredient. And while Flora Thompson's village may have been highly suspicious of tomatoes, Mrs Beeton uses them frequently, though mostly in their cooked form:

> The Tomato is a native of tropical countries, but is now culti-vated considerably both in France and England. Its skin is of a brilliant red, and its flavour, which is somewhat sour, has become of immense importance in the culinary art. It is used both fresh and preserved. When eaten fresh, it is served as an *entremets* [a dish served after the roast or with the main course]; but its principal use is in sauce and gravy; its flavour stimulates the appetite, and is almost universally approved . . .

As Mrs Beeton's range of menus suggests, Victorian middle-class food covers a very wide spectrum of society, and it would be rash to assume that all these people would have eaten precisely *à la* Mrs Beeton. There was still a lot of regional variation: dishes popular in one part of the country might be completely unknown somewhere else. Even the times at which people ate their meals varied enormously. When it came to dinner, for example, the chances were that the better off you were, the later you ate. In Emily Brontë's *Wuthering Heights*, written in the mid 1840s, Mr Lockwood – a gentleman – wants to dine at five o'clock, but 'the housekeeper, a matronly lady, taken as a fixture along with the house, could not, or would not, comprehend my request', and he ends up eating at midday. At the end of the century, the much-put-upon Mr Pooter in *The Diary of a Nobody* is very much aware of the social niceties of the timing of dinner, as shown in his diary entry for 3 July:

Lupin said: 'I want you both to come and dine with me next Wednesday, and see my new place. Mr and Mrs Murray Posh, Miss Posh (Murray's sister) are coming. Eight o'clock sharp. No one else.'

I said we did not pretend to be fashionable people, and would like the dinner earlier, as it made it so late before we got home.

Afternoon tea also became a complicated occasion in Victorian times. For the wealthy it tended to mean afternoon refreshment, but for many lower-middle and working-class people it was the meal that came next in sequence after the midday 'dinner'. 'High tea', as served particularly in the north of England, could be an ambitious meal: a high tea served in Yorkshire in the 1860s might consist of seed cake, bread and butter, ham sandwiches, a salad, teacakes and muffins, all washed down with tea laced with rum. I associate high tea with visits to Scotland when I was a child, when the question 'Will you have your tea now?' meant that you would end up munching ham or smoked haddock or possibly a boiled egg.

Supper, similarly, was a meal that varied according to place and class. In Arnold Bennett's *Anna of the Five Towns* of 1902, it is a substantial evening meal for a well-to-do family living in the potteries area of Staffordshire and is eaten at eight o'clock. In George Gissing's *New Grub Street* of 1891, it's a snack of coffee and biscuits taken by a literary man at 9.30. In Mrs Beeton's *Book of Household Management*, it's a late-evening meal that might be served at a ball and could consist of:

> Beef, ham, and tongue sandwiches, lobster and oyster patties, sausage rolls, meat rolls, lobster salad, dishes of fowls, the latter *all cut up*; dishes of sliced ham, sliced tongue, sliced beef, and galantine of veal; various jellies, blancmanges, and creams; custards in glasses, compôtes of fruit, tartlets of jam, and several dishes of small fancy pastry; dishes of fresh fruit, bonbons, sweetmeats, two or three sponge cakes, a few plates of biscuits, and the buffet ornamented with vases of fresh or artificial flowers. The above dishes are quite sufficient for a standing supper; where more are desired, a supper must then be laid and arranged in the usual manner.

It serves as a reminder of just how lavish Victorian food could be – if you had the money to pay for it.

The Edwardian era marked the high point of the country-house weekend, when the rich could indulge their passions for hunting, fishing, shooting and extramarital affairs. This photograph, taken in around 1910, shows the meet before the hunt. Substantial picnics would be served on such occasions, just one of various heavy meals of a day that would commence with a cooked breakfast and end with a dinner involving up to twelve courses.

CHAPTER 13

Omelette *Arnold Bennett*
and Bully Beef

From the Edwardians to the Eve of War

The ultimate expression of Victorian overindulgence was Victoria's son, Albert Edward, Prince of Wales, husband of Princess Alexandra of Schleswig-Holstein-Sonderburg-Glücksburg, later to be King Edward VII, and known to many (though not to his face) as Tum Tum. While his mother led her secluded life at Windsor, Osborne and Balmoral, the prince enjoyed himself in town, at his estate in Sandringham, on the Riviera, and at all the venues visited by the rich and the fashionable during the season, from Cowes (he was an enthusiastic sailor) to Newmarket (he owned a stud at Sandringham). While his mother mourned the death of her husband, he conducted a string of affairs with actresses and titled ladies. And while Queen Victoria nibbled her food, Edward devoured his in platefuls.

Edward was a real epicure. He loved unusual and rare food – out-of-season strawberries, early asparagus, caviar and foie gras. He ate enormous meals. Breakfast might consist of poached eggs, bacon, chicken, woodcock and haddock. Lunch and dinner might each involve twelve courses. As for Edward's coronation banquet in 1902 – which had to be postponed while the new king underwent an operation for appendicitis – this would have run, had it been served, to fourteen courses. The cooks saved what they could and sent the rest to feed the poor of the East End. For people used to bread and dripping, the sudden arrival of 2,500 quails must have been quite a surprise.

It was in Edward's lifetime that the country-house weekend really came into its own. It sounds very refined, but I suspect that it simply offered the gentry the opportunity to visit each other's country estates and indulge in a bit of bed hopping. Not only did the hostess have to make sure that all was in order before visitors descended, she also needed to be au fait with who was interested in whom at the time, so that bedrooms could be suitably allocated for night-time visitations. In fact, I sometimes think that a late-Victorian or Edwardian country house at night must have been rather like a railway station, with everybody endlessly passing each other on their way to find their lovers' rooms. Many well-known names had exhausting love lives. Edward's mistress Lillie Langtry, for example, was twice married and had an affair with Prince Louis of Battenberg after her relationship with Edward came to an end. Another one of his amours, Lady Brooke (known as Babbling Brooke for her indiscretion), was even more active. All this lust must have engendered a hearty appetite for food.

Ostensibly, though, the raison d'être for the country-house weekend was to enjoy hunting, fishing and shooting. Hunting was a pursuit enjoyed by both men and women – Lady Brooke, for example, was a keen hunter, as was the Prince of Wales (on his first day tiger hunting in India, he shot six tigers). Fly-fishing, popular since medieval times, was transformed in the nineteenth century by improvements to fishing reels and fishing line. And hunting had become increasingly popular thanks largely to the invention of the percussion cap in the 1830s, which made guns much easier and quicker to use, and by the growing accuracy of sports guns. As outdoor leisure became ever more valued and ever more fashionable, fanatical hunters would decamp by train to visit their friends or shoot grouse on the moors of northern England, Wales and elsewhere. Today, there still exist innumerable photographs of country-house parties in front of various grand houses, the participants sitting there looking rather stiff and uncomfortable (no doubt because of the photographer's injunction to stay perfectly still), and the foreground often littered with large quantities of shot game.

A whole ritual attached itself to days largely spent outdoors. First would come breakfast, laid out in great state in the dining room, the dishes constantly being replenished by the servants as you helped yourself to anything you felt like, from devilled kidneys to little cold game birds, cold pheasant to ham. Also on the sideboard would be one of those wonderful devices for boiling eggs to your liking, complete with a methylated spirit lamp. You might cook your own, or, in a grand house, get a footman to do it for you. Then there would be regional specialities: laverbread in Wales, cockles in cream sauce in Cumbria, potted Morecambe Bay shrimps in Lancashire.

Once you had staggered away from the breakfast table, you'd set off to shoot, the guns perhaps being taken on ahead in one of those newfangled motorised vehicles. If you were a lady you would probably rise a little later and, after breakfast, make your way to the butts or wherever lunch was being served. As the sportsmen wandered over from the morning shoot, footmen would appear, carrying tables and chairs and laying out the napery and the drapery that went with a formal meal, and everyone would sit down to soup and game pies, jellies, trifles and everything else that made up an Edwardian luncheon. It sounds rather wonderful. In fact, it must have been intensely uncomfortable. During the grouse season you would either have been hot and midge-ridden or cold and damp; by the time pheasant shooting came round in the autumn, you must have had your fingers crossed that your host would have some sort of building nearby where lunch would be served.

With lunch out of the way, the guests and the guns would return to the house for afternoon tea, complete with cake, thinly sliced bread and butter, and delicate little sandwiches. These were a culinary art form in themselves, and I always remember being taught how to make proper teatime sandwiches, or boudoir sandwiches, by a wonderful woman called Lillian Fox. The eldest of thirteen children of a farm labourer, she had gone into service in the great house in Somerset where her father worked. Eventually she became a lady's maid and was even sent to Paris to perfect her skills: how to mend fine lace lingerie, how to do her mistress's hair, how to iron with the rather primitive irons of the day, how to look after furs and other items in her mistress's wardrobe, and so on. One skill she passed on to me was how to cut bread really thin. You take yesterday's bread, cut off the crust, butter the end and dip your bread knife (a sharpened steel knife in those days, not a serrated one) in a jug of boiling water until it is hot. Then you wipe it on a cloth and carefully cut your bread very, very thinly, repeating the process until you have sufficient slices to make sandwiches. If you're making tomato sandwiches, you have to remember to peel and deseed the tomatoes before mashing them up with salt and pepper. If you're preparing cucumber sandwiches, you slice the cucumber very finely, leave it to stand with some salt on it, then rinse the salt off and add a little oil and pepper. If it's egg sandwiches you want, you must remember to mash the egg with a little mayonnaise. You might also want to make a more elaborate sandwich, such as the one named after Edward VII's wife Queen Alexandra, made with finely sliced tongue and mashed hard-boiled eggs; it's actually quite delicious.

Once guests at a Victorian or Edwardian house party had finished their tea, they would retire to their rooms to bathe and change for dinner. This meal would be a very formal occasion, with a name card at each place setting and a strict dress code. By Edwardian times there might be little hors d'oeuvres or oysters or caviar served first, before the soup (two types: one thick, one clear), fish (one boiled, one fried), entrée (perhaps escalopes of sweetbread *à la Marne* or something else that didn't need to be carved), a joint with vegetables and potatoes, a sorbet, a roast, and then puddings, ices, savouries and desserts. A different wine would accompany each course, and when the last of the dessert had been eaten the ladies would withdraw to the drawing room while the men drank coffee and liqueurs, smoked and probably told risqué stories. And so to bed and late-night visiting.

As for the game that the country-house guests shot, most of this would be consumed on the estate, though some might make its way to towns. Pheasants were taken to the game larder and hung by the neck, in their full plumage and with their innards still intact, until their heads dropped off. I've heard very off-putting tales of kitchen maids being dispatched to pluck and prepare a pheasant only to find it moving – its flesh alive with maggots. This was less likely to happen with grouse and partridge since they weren't hung for as long as pheasants. But there's no doubt that the Edwardians liked strong flavours. This was, after all, the age when people liked their Stilton to have maggots in it, which you would scrape out before helping yourself to the cheese. I tried Stilton in this state once and found it far too pungent.

Once back in town you might dine out at one of the grand restaurants or hotels that sprang up in England in the later part of the nineteenth century. Traditionally, eating out had been restricted to inns and clubs, and tended to be the preserve of men. Now, as women started to become more emancipated and as the love of public show and social ostentation grew, so dining out by both sexes achieved a new popularity, and venues grew up to accommodate their demands. The Savoy Hotel, opened in 1889, is a case in point. The brainchild of Sir Richard D'Oyly Carte, who had made his money by staging Gilbert and Sullivan operettas and had been much taken by the hotels he'd seen in America, the Savoy was the last word in contemporary luxury: it boasted electric lights, lifts (known as 'ascending rooms') and hot and cold running water. Guest rooms were connected by speaking tubes to the maid or the valet. Not surprisingly, therefore, it was an immediate social – if not, in the short term, financial – success, and attracted the inevitable Prince of Wales, not to mention Oscar Wilde and his lover Lord Alfred Douglas. For Edward VII's birthday in 1905, the forecourt of the Savoy

Hotel was flooded and Edward's birthday cake was brought out on the back of a baby elephant. In *Foie Gras and Trumpets*, Charles Gattey describes the scene:

> Into the water had been released salmon, trout and whitebait, whilst on it floated swans, ducks, and a white, silk-lined gondola adorned with 31,000 carnations, roses and 5,000 yards of smilax. In the air above fluttered a hundred white doves.
>
> Waiters costumed as gondoliers served twelve courses to twice that number of diners seated on gold chairs . . . Three impressive lions carved out of ice bore trays of peaches and glacé fruits . . . Throughout the banquet an orchestra stationed in a smaller gondola played music. Then came a *coup de théâtre*. The lights dimmed as a melon-like moon, suspended overhead, was turned on and Caruso emerged through brocade curtains at the raised end of the gondola to sing – for a *douceur* of £450.

From the start, food was integral to the Savoy's success, and the hotel's manager, Jean César Ritz, was canny enough to employ Georges Auguste Escoffier to manage the kitchens. Escoffier already had a reputation as a fine chef and cookery writer. He believed strongly that *haute cuisine* didn't need to be heavy and loaded down with overpowering sauces: '*Faites simple*' was his watchword as he strode across the kitchen floor in his built-up shoes (he was very short). His *Guide culinaire* is a brilliant and very precise account of French cooking and is still invaluable to cooks today (though you need to read it in French; the standard English version from 1907 does rather terrible things to some of the recipes). However, although he espoused simplicity, there's no doubt that he also loved the theatrical touch. One of his most famous dinners was pink and white themed, at which all the table decorations consisted of pink and white roses, their leaves painted silver, and the food served included the very pink soup borscht, chicken fillets coloured with paprika, and lamb served rare in the French manner. He also knew how to flatter guests, naming dishes after them at the drop of a hat. I can't help wondering, though, how flattered the rather vulgar Australian singer Nellie Melba should have been to have peach Melba named in her honour: after all, with its mixture of peaches, raspberry sauce and vanilla ice cream, it's hardly very ambitious. My grandmother was once at the Savoy when she saw the great opera singer Chaliapin pick up Dame Nellie Melba, who like all the sopranos of her day was not small of figure, and twirl her round like a small child. My grandmother thought it was incredibly exciting.

The book of Escoffier's that I really like best is *Ma cuisine*, a much less formal book than his *Guide culinaire*. Throughout the days of my drinking, and when I worked for mistresses who were into low-fat cooking, yoghurt and salads, I would pore over it and weep gently into my pillow for what had been lost. It's intended for the housewife rather than the chef, though the inclusion of such things as truffles, cockscombs and caviar does sometimes make you wonder. And its delightful asides reveal aspects of Escoffier's rather charming personality. Here, for example, is an extract from the introduction:

The extremely active existence we lead does not leave us leisure to devote the necessary care to the upkeep of our bodies. We are apt to forget that, like a clock, the body will stop if it is not oiled or wound up from time to time. Nature supplies the raw materials in their simplest forms, so we must know how to make the best use of them, otherwise we invite a mass of minor ailments.

And then there's a nice section on coffee where Escoffier remarks, 'Coffee, carefully prepared and taken some time after the meal, in the drawing-room, helps the digestion. Its delicate aroma rises to the head, revives the mind – and then conversation sparkles.' True, Escoffier is guilty of including a recipe for that Victorian horror, brown Windsor soup, but he can be forgiven when he also includes recipes for hors d'oeuvres like anchovies with sweet peppers, eels *à la provençale*, partridge purée, and beetroots in cream salad dressing. You get an idea of the light touch he liked to adopt when he argues that caviar served with thin slices of buttered rye bread should not be accompanied, as it often is, by chopped onions and lemon juice, but be left plain since any additional flavouring simply gets in the way of its exquisite taste.

Appropriately enough for the period, the book contains quite an extensive section on game. Escoffier rightly points out that 'the English eat their grouse rare, but then only the English really eat grouse'; other game birds he mentions range from partridges to great bustards (presumably imported, since by Escoffier's time they would have been extinct in England), dotterel, woodcock, lapwing and, that particularly popular Edwardian bird, the golden plover – now heavily protected, though I still remember plovers' eggs from childhood. There is even a recipe for lark pie. I'm not sure that there's much of a desire for lark in England, but, as the song *'Alouette, gentille alouette'* suggests, the French seem to have no qualms about eating it.

Escoffier's relationship with the Savoy wasn't, in the long term, a very happy one. In 1897 both he and Ritz were dismissed, accused of fraud and financial mismanagement (Escoffier was accused, among other things, of taking kick-backs from suppliers). Escoffier therefore decamped to the new Carlton Hotel, and his fan the Prince of Wales soon joined him there. It was at the Carlton on 26 June 1902, the very day that Edward's coronation had to be postponed due to his ill health, that Ritz suffered a terrible nervous breakdown, tipped over the edge by the knowledge that the festivities he had planned for the hotel would have to be abandoned. He went on to found the Ritz, but otherwise largely withdrew from hotel life. Escoffier, however, remained 'the chef of kings and the king of chefs'.

The Savoy and the Ritz were not the only grand hotels to spring up at this time. Every major city boasted at least one or two, and many existing hotels underwent dramatic facelifts. Claridge's, for example, was transformed by Richard D'Oyly Carte in the 1890s to become the popular stopping-off point for many visiting European crowned heads and, in the 1940s, the popular resting place for many exiled European crowned heads. Luxury hotels also became a magnet for domestic servants looking to improve their prospects by joining the hotel staff. The one hotel that, in my view, maintains the standard and excellence one associates with the Edwardian era is the Goring, which opened its doors in 1910.

Grand hotels and restaurants proved popular places of assignation for the fashionable. Kettner's Restaurant in Soho, for example, which was opened in 1867 by the chef to Napoleon III, was yet another venue to be frequented by Edward VII and Lillie Langtry, and by Oscar Wilde and his male friends.

And if they weren't there, they might be at the Cadogan Hotel – where Oscar Wilde was eventually arrested for gross indecency in 1895. Whereas the scope for adventurous living was relatively limited if you were attending a dinner at a friend's house, the sky was the limit if you opted for a hotel or restaurant with their bedrooms or private rooms and their – usually – discreet staff. Certainly the Victorians and Edwardians had their share of peccadilloes. It was the glamour of the big hotels and their potential for all types of nefarious goings-on that appealed to Arnold Bennett when he wrote *Grand Babylon Hotel* in 1902, in which American millionaires, European princes and English waiters, adopting French names to appear more the part, are all mixed up together in dodgy dealings. Bennett was a devotee of the Savoy, which came up with the Omelette Arnold Bennett, involving smoked haddock, Parmesan and cream, in his honour.

For the more conventionally minded, there were very strict rules in place about hotel conduct: the chaperones of young women were specifically told which hotels their debutante charges could and could not go to, at which times of the day, and on which days. It was, for instance, considered unsuitable for young ladies of debutante age to lunch at the Ritz or dine at the Savoy, unless they were planning a visit to the theatre. Even then, they were expected to dine in the main restaurant, certainly not the Grill Room (now renamed the Savoy Grill).

Not all the new hotels and restaurants were intended only for the wealthy: there was something for every budget, from the luxury meal costing several pounds to an 8d lunch at the Restaurant Lyonnais in Soho. More expensive restaurants tended to scatter French across their menus. The Café Royal, where Wilde was confronted by Lord Alfred Douglas's furious father in 1894 (Wilde managed to charm him on that occasion), offered a sophisticated menu that included foie gras, caviar and champagne, and various elaborate French dishes. Less expensive restaurants offered more obviously 'English' fare. The Lyons chain, which started with one shop in Piccadilly in 1894 and grew to some 250, is perhaps the most famous example. One of their bills of fare for 1912 offered a cup of tea for 1d and various buns for the same price. If you wanted something a little more substantial, you could get roast beef or veal and ham pie or curried mutton and rice for 6d, and perhaps follow these with marmalade pudding or bread and butter pudding at 3d. You would be served by a waitress in a distinctive maid's uniform, known originally as a 'Gladys' and later as a 'Nippy'.

For the town and country poor, there was little sign of improvement in the years leading up to the First World War. However, there was at least a growing awareness of the problems that they faced. From the late 1880s onwards, an increasing number of social investigators took it upon themselves to study the lives and diets of the poor and try to establish, more or less scientifically, how well or badly they were doing. The shipowner Charles Booth embarked on a vast survey of the London poor, published in seventeen volumes in 1902. Not only did he go to the trouble of trying to divide 'the poor' into different categories (class A, for example, was 'savages and criminals'), but he also sought to work out what lay behind their poverty, whether drink or unemployment or illness or any of a number of other factors. His alarming conclusion was that a third of the capital's population was living in poverty. A few years later, Seebohm Rowntree, the son of the founding father of the chocolate company that bore his name, undertook a similar study in York. His findings were similar to those of Booth; he also demonstrated that many people were living in what he called 'primary poverty' – that is, they could not afford the bare minimum daily diet that would keep them relatively healthy.

What gave the work of such people growing publicity was a sense in late-Victorian and Edwardian times that the great British Empire was beginning to falter. In mid-Victorian times, Britannia really did rule the waves. By the end of the century, however, she faced stiff competition from America and from various European powers, notably Germany. People may once have worried about the moral evils of poverty; now they were beginning also to wonder whether a nation containing so many poor people could actually continue to sustain the greatest empire the world had ever seen. The outbreak of the Boer War in 1899 brought this home with a vengeance. When the army reported that it was having to reject up to six out of ten volunteers because they simply weren't physically fit enough, there was consternation in Whitehall. The laissez-faire attitude of the past now looked more than unsatisfactory. The government felt it was time to take action. In the next few years various pieces of legislation were passed that started to put in place what was to become the welfare state. In 1906, for example, local authorities were permitted to offer poorer primary-school children free meals, and by the outbreak of war in 1914 some 200,000 children were taking advantage of this service.

This is really the period when people started to understand how nutrition works. Of course, the physical evidence for the consequences of malnutrition was there in front of them. Faced with a bad diet, poor people fell ill more and they died younger.

What's more, they tended to be much shorter than their better-fed countrymen. During the Boer War the army had to reduce the minimum height requirement for new recruits from five foot three inches to five foot. During the same period it was discovered that boys at private schools were, on average, five inches taller than those in council-run schools. Scientists were becoming increasingly aware of what different types of food did and what the lack of certain types of nutrition might lead to. The word 'protein' was coined in 1838. By the 1900s, people were beginning to understand how vitamins worked; Sir Frederick Hopkins, for example, demonstrated in 1912 that even if someone was eating sufficient proteins, fat, carbohydrate and mineral salts they might still be unhealthy if 'accessory factors of the diet', as he called them, were missing. In the same year Casimir Funk came up with the word 'vitamin'.

The new spirit of scientific enquiry being applied to food was also applied to food production. The Royal Agricultural Society, with its motto 'practice with science', was established in 1838 and devoted itself not only to modernising methods of keeping livestock but to improving pasture and arable lands. Barns were made more draughtproof: that way, animals did not require so much food because they were not having to expend energy on keeping warm. Drainage was improved (often by running clay pipes under the soil), allowing animals to be grazed on areas of land previously regarded as unsuitable and liable to cause bloat in cattle and horses. Farm implements became more sophisticated, allowing more efficient ploughing, especially of heavy clay soil, and steam-driven machines – particularly threshing machines – became more widely used after 1850.

The other major improvement made was to the soil itself. Traditionally the only fertiliser applied to the fields had been animal muck, usually supplied by the sheep or cows that happened to be grazing in a particular field. In Victorian times, however, this started to be supplemented by other fertilisers. William Gibbs, who was responsible for the grand house at Tyntesfield, built his fortune on importing thousands of tons of phosphorus-rich guano from Peru from the 1840s onwards. Bones, hooves and horns were also ground up and sprinkled over the fields, while the German scientist Justus von Liebig (who also gave us the concentrated meat extract that was ultimately to become the Oxo cube) started to research the use of nitrogen-based fertilisers. You can see the beginnings of the chemical farming that in later decades was to bring its own set of problems.

Farm animals continued to grow larger as selective breeding became ever more skilful. The number of Escoffier's recipes that involve veal suggests that cows of the period were very fertile. As for pigs, I can remember seeing a picture of a small girl riding a Lincolnshire curly coat pig as though it were a pony – this one looked as if it weighed forty stone. Bred essentially for tallow, the Lincolnshire curly coat pig was also perfect for the dish known as Lincolnshire chine because its neck was so thick that you had to split it on either side of the backbone, yielding an extra cut of meat that could then be salted, before ultimately being stuffed with parsley and cooked. It's all rather reminiscent of P. G. Wodehouse's giant pig the Empress of Blandings, winner of the fat pig award at the Shropshire Agricultural Show, and rival of Sir Gregory Parsloe-Parsloe's Pride of Matchingham.

The overall state of agriculture fluctuated considerably during the later nineteenth century. There were the usual problems: the occasional poor harvest due to bad weather, outbreaks of disease among the livestock. But what became ever more apparent in the last decades of Victoria's reign and the early years of Edward VII's was that foreign imports were increasingly competing with home-grown produce and that English farming was in decline. Wheat flooded in from America. Supplies of meat arrived from Australia. By 1914, Britain was importing more than 60 per cent of its food supplies and 80 per cent of its wheat.

The effects of this became apparent during the First World War. Because Britain was so dependent on imported food, any threats to supplies had an immediate knock-on effect. At first, most foodstuffs were reasonably plentiful, but as the German U-boats gained a stranglehold on shipping – and embarked on indiscriminate attacks in 1917 – so imports became ever more problematic. Panic-buying started the day war broke out, even though Sainsbury's, for example, posted notices in their shops promising that regular customers would be kept supplied. The government ran propaganda campaigns to encourage people to save food. 'Waste is at all times folly,' one proclaimed, 'but in such a time as this it is unpatriotic.' In fact, sugar had to be rationed from 1916. By 1917, people in some areas were running short of potatoes. In February 1918 the government was forced to bring in general rationing, and meat was among the first items to be controlled.

Not that all suffered alike. In his war memoir *Goodbye to All That*, Robert Graves recalls a meal with Siegfried Sassoon in December 1916 at a rather exclusive golf club:

Siegfried and I went to the club-house for lunch on the day before Christmas, and found a cold-buffet in the club dining-room, offering hams, barons of beef, jellied tongues, cold roast turkey, and chicken. A large, meaty-faced waiter presided. Siegfried asked him sarcastically: 'Is that all? There doesn't seem to be quite such a good spread as in previous years.' The waiter blushed. 'No, sir, this isn't quite up to the usual mark, sir, but we are expecting a more satisfactory consignment of meat on Boxing Day.'

If most people on the home front suffered from the conse-quences of England's dependence on imported food, those on the front line benefited to some extent from its increasingly indus-trial nature. Tinned food, dried vegetables and packaged biscuits formed the core of trench rations. Tinned meat, in particular, or 'bully beef' as it was called (from the French *bouilli*, boiled), was central to most meals. The daily ration of a soldier in the trenches was, theoretically at least, very precise: twenty ounces of bread (or sixteen ounces of flour, or four ounces of oatmeal), three ounces of cheese, four ounces of jam or dried fruit, eight ounces of fresh vegetables (or, if none was available, half a gill of lime juice), two ounces of dried vegetables, four ounces of butter or margarine, half an ounce of salt, a thirty-sixth of an ounce of pepper and a twentieth of an ounce of mustard. The drink ration was six to eight ounces of tea and half a gill of rum or a pint of porter (dark beer). There was also some chocolate and the ever-present tobacco – some twenty ounces of it.

This was hardly exciting food, but it was filling and relatively nutritious, as was the food prepared for those not on the front line or brought to the front when things were relatively quiet.

(There was a tacit understanding between the troops of the two sides that there would be a temporary ceasefire while such wagons were delivering the food, especially at breakfast time, and, generally, an unofficial truce was observed at breakfast.) One soldier in the catering corps recorded a fairly typical day's eating: bacon, tomatoes, bread, jam and cocoa for breakfast; shepherd's pie, made with tinned meat and potato, and bread and jam for lunch; bread and jam for tea; oxtail soup, roast beef, leeks and rice pudding for supper.

In soldiers' letters from the front line there are occasional complaints about the food (particularly the biscuits, which were so hard that, in order to break them up, you had to put them on a board and bash them with something heavy). However, the diet generally seems to have been a reasonable one, and soldiers were very ingenious when it came to preparing meals with whatever happened to be at hand. The Kelly Kettle was invaluable – a very simple device that allowed one to boil water very easily even in filthy trench conditions. I remember hearing of one officer whose batman invariably carried his Kelly Kettle into battle with him on the off chance that they might be able to brew up a cup of tea in a foxhole. On one occasion the officer was injured. His servant managed to carry him back to the lines, and even received a medal for gallantry, but when he got him to the hospital the first question the officer asked was, 'And the Kelly Kettle, is it safe?'

Soldiers may not have complained much about their food in their letters home, but they constantly asked their family to send them food parcels. My father was eighteen at the outbreak of war and served at the front, and I can remember seeing letters from him to my grandmother in which he would say things like, 'That tea from Twinings was particularly good, perhaps you could send some more,' or, 'Perhaps you could ask Fortnum & Mason to send me out another of those excellent fruitcakes.' Officers from prosperous families did particularly well in this regard, but food parcels were received by other ranks as well, and the delivery of parcels from home became something of a logistical challenge.

Trench war consisted of long periods of boredom and squalor interspersed with moments of terror. During periods of inactivity, soldiers might produce bits of trench art, and I've quite often come across spoons, knives and sometimes even forks that they made, along with folding cutlery and one device that had a fork at one end and a corkscrew at the other. Or they might go to the local French or Belgian *estaminet*, where many would have their first experience of 'foreign' food and their first sip of wine. The rest of the time, they endured the filth of the trenches and the constant risk of trench foot. One of my father's abiding memories of the war was the rats which fattened themselves on corpses and discarded tins of bully beef. Even years later, he could not bear the sight of one.

Those returning from the war in 1918 came back to a country that had been profoundly shaken and transformed by it. Nearly a million young men had died at the front. A further quarter of a million people died in the flu pandemic that swept through a weakened nation between 1918 and 1920. The social certainties of the past no longer seemed so certain when so many people had perished. Groups that had previously largely been ignored – particularly women – started to make their voices heard. There was more questioning of authority. Industrial unrest grew, culminating in the General Strike of 1926.

For those with money, however, this was a time to forget and to indulge yourself: the age of flappers, debutantes, cocktail parties, dancing, and imitation of all things American – inspired in part by contact with American soldiers towards the end of the war but also by England's love of Hollywood and jazz. When final wartime restrictions were removed in 1921, restaurant and hotel life really got underway again, the more fashionable ones, like the Savoy, responding to the American-inspired craze for eating and dining by installing dance floors. Clubs became popular, too. I can remember Wilde's club on St James's Place, where I first cooked commercially, in a minuscule kitchen. By the time I came to it in the 1980s it was rather on its last legs, but in the 1920s and 1930s it would have been one of the places to go, to meet people, to eat and to dance. Others in the 1920s included the Embassy Club in Bond Street, popular with Edward VIII when he was Prince of Wales, the Kit-Kat Club in Haymarket and the celebrity-strewn Murray's a little further afield in Maidenhead.

Such clubs allowed people to enjoy everything from lobster pâté and caviar mousse to twice-baked soufflés made with truffles, and little baby lamb chops cooked pink and served cold in aspic. They also allowed their patrons to indulge extensively in two less fattening vices: drink and drugs. Cocktails became immensely fashionable in the 1920s and 1930s; drugs were ubiquitous. I remember commenting to my mother in the 1960s about the amount of drug-taking going on in London among the young, and receiving the response, 'Darling, it's nothing compared to what it was when I was young in the '20s and '30s. All your generation is doing is smoking pot or taking LSD,' she went on. 'When I was young it was heroin, morphine, cocaine, anything you can think of.' It's certainly the case that my mother lost more of her friends to drug-taking when she was a young woman than I did those few decades later. If you read Agatha Christie you'll spot various references to drug-taking alongside the crime-solving. It's perhaps not surprising that the authorities took a dim view of nightclubs, and launched police raids on them from time to time.

Cocktails were served not just in clubs but at home, and the cocktail party became a new fixture of the social diary, held between the hours of six and eight to enable people to go on to dinner afterwards and then to a nightclub. Champagne cocktails, crème de menthe *frappé*, Manhattans (bourbon whisky, sweet vermouth and a dash of Angostura bitters) and more complicated combinations were all popular. In the drinking club I ran I remember serving a concoction of gin, parfait d'amour, blue curaçao and orange curaçao. If you got the proportions right you ended up with a vivid emerald-green drink that looked very dramatic. You couldn't drink very much of it, but the great thing from a business point of view was that those who did imbibe went on to champagne afterwards. To mop up the drink and prolong the party, hostesses also started to serve canapés: little cheese Parmentiers, asparagus rolled in thin brown bread and butter, delicate crab patties and, of course, the ubiquitous vol-au-vents – puff pastry cases with prawns, chicken in white sauce, or anything else that the hostess had to hand. Smoked salmon continued to be popular, and little slivers on pumpernickel or rye bread were offered round much as they are today. Since vol-au-vents can be rather messy, some hostesses would serve filled pastry boats instead.

In other respects, though, the writing was on the wall for

many of the wealthy of pre-war days. Those who drew their wealth from mineral deposits, such as coal, found their earnings declining. Those who depended on agriculture fared even worse. Death duties, introduced in 1894, rose to 40 per cent by 1919 and to 50 per cent in 1930, making it ever harder for the next generation to keep the great estates going. What's more, even if they did have money it became increasingly difficult to find servants. While the men had been away fighting in the war, women – including many who were in service – had moved in to do their jobs, and they didn't abandon them when the men returned. In the next few years they moved into even more spheres previously regarded as male preserves: the number of women in the Civil Service, for example, exceeded 100,000 by the early 1920s. Faced with more interesting jobs, higher salaries and better conditions, fewer and fewer women wanted to go back into service. The result of all this was that the big house increasingly became a large millstone around its owner's neck. Over 200 country houses were pulled down between 1918 and the outbreak of the Second World War in 1939, while others began to look distinctly the worse for wear as they became ever more expensive to maintain. I'm reminded of the grand Victorian pile Evelyn Waugh describes in *A Handful of Dust* (1934), where the beds are damp, the rooms are cold and the whole edifice is slowly falling apart.

Of course, it would be wrong to think that there were suddenly no rich landed gentry left, but there was certainly less opulence than there had been before the war, and also a reaction against the grand eating of Edwardian times. People might have been out to enjoy themselves, but enjoyment did not have to involve vast banquets and course-strewn dinners. You only have to think of the slim, boy-like figure of the gay young thing of the 1920s and compare her with her matronly mother to realise how much things had changed. For such a person lunch might consist of just three or four courses and dinner would be similarly modest. Even grand meals for grand occasions were not what they had once been. The wedding breakfast of the Duke and Duchess of York in 1923, for example, consisted of eight courses; at the beginning of the century you might have expected twice as many.

If the rich were not perhaps doing quite as well as they once had, for the middle classes the post-war period saw a general lift in living standards. Thanks to ever more efficient methods of producing food, and the ever-growing flood of tinned and fresh goods from abroad, the relative cost of feeding a family dropped. In the mid 1930s, at the height of the economic depression that came in the wake of the Wall Street Crash of 1929, people earning between £250 and £500 a year (about one in five of the population) spent less than a third of their weekly pay packet on food. What's more, the food they consumed was of a pretty good quality – not just the inevitable meat and bread but plenty of fresh fruit, vegetables and dairy produce, too. This was partly down to affordability, but it also had a lot to do with a growing popular understanding of what was good for you. The scientific discoveries made earlier in the century were starting to percolate down to popular level. Various public campaigns helped ram home the message: the National Milk Publicity Council started proclaiming 'Drink More Milk' in 1924; 'Eat More Fruit' was another, equally uninspired slogan of the same decade.

Fresh food – or, at least, relatively fresh food – could now come from anywhere. English farmers still produced meat, butter, eggs, fruit, and so on, but these items could also be imported from abroad. New Zealand lamb arrived in great refrigerated ships, as did Danish bacon. Even eggs were imported. You might eat apples and pears as they were collected from English orchards in the autumn, but then carry on eating ones from refrigerated shipments arriving from the southern hemisphere. The close link between food and seasons that had been there for thousands of years was beginning to weaken.

This was a golden age for the docks, not least the London Docks, which unloaded vast quantities of refrigerated meat between the two world wars (during the 1926 General Strike they found themselves sitting on 750,000 frozen carcasses); the King George V Dock was opened in 1921 to help deal with extra demand. They were a profitable place to work, and offered endless temptations. I can remember as late as the 1970s, when I was representing a docker's wife in a divorce case, hearing her protest vehemently because the settlement she was likely to receive did not take into account the sides of beef, bottles of whisky and various other luxuries that her husband was able to prise from the various shipments he handled. I pointed out that I couldn't really stand up in court and demand more money on the grounds that her husband was augmenting his earnings through theft. She wasn't convinced.

Even the nature of shopping changed after the First World War. Although the modern self-service supermarket was still a few years away, the idea that food might arrive in the shop pre-packaged by the manufacturer was catching on. Once you would have stood there as the shopkeeper blended and weighed

The interwar kitchen A poster produced by the Empire Marketing Board in the late 1920s to encourage British consumers to buy products from the empire. This housewife is preparing her Christmas pudding with, among other ingredients, English beer and Jamaican rum.

The 1950s kitchen The first fitted kitchens appeared in Germany in the 1920s; by the 50s thermostatically controlled ovens were common. They certainly made life much easier for housewives.

Kitchen innovation When this advertisement appeared in 1955, fridges were an expensive luxury: as late as the 1970s only 60 per cent of households possessed one.

Eating in wartime A First World War soldier writes an appreciative letter to Oxo while his comrades indulge in some idyllic cooking.

The realities of war A photograph of a field kitchen on the Somme in 1916. Note the rain and the mud.

The last days of horse power Mr Clark makes his daily milk round in Finsbury Park in London. The day in question here is 17 February 1932.

Shopping 1950s style A typical food shop of the 1950s. Although supermarkets were on the march at this time, the high street was still dominated by small, independent food shops – though they were increasingly selling the sort of products that the supermarkets stocked.

The rise of the nightclub Louche nightclubs proved popular in the 1920s. This photograph shows the infamous club owner and hostess Kate Meyrick at a welcome-back party given at the Silver Slipper Club in London's Soho to celebrate her release from prison in 1928. Meyrick was prosecuted several times for breaches of the licensing laws, and once for bribing a police officer.

The meeting of rich and poor A wealthy young couple watch the Jarrow Marchers arrive in London in 1936. For many living in the industrial areas of England at this time, life was grim and food was in short supply.

Chef to the wealthy Auguste Escoffier (left) ran the kitchens at the Savoy Hotel in the 1880s and 1890s. The high priest of fine French cuisine, he wrote several cookery books, including the brilliant *Guide culinaire*.

High society Cocktail parties were de rigueur among the bright young things of the 1920s, though this 1929 picture from the *Illustrated London News* suggests that they appealed to bright older things, too.

Dig for victory England came close to starvation towards the end of the First World War. Consequently, when the Second World War broke out in 1939, a huge amount of attention was paid to the country's food supply. Increasing domestic production was rightly regarded as critical, and farming and encouraging people to grow their own food were major priorities.

Rationing A woman purchasing goods in a Birmingham shop shortly after the introduction of rationing in January 1940. One of the great ironies of English food history is that the national diet in the Second World War was probably the healthiest it had ever been.

Shopping 1970s style A woman and her baby in Tesco.

Contemporary shopping at its best Food stalls at a farmers' market in Bath. One of the great joys of recent years has been the rediscovery of local, high-quality produce.

An early television star Philip Harben wipes tears from his eyes as he prepares a French onion soup in his kitchen in St John's Wood, London, in October 1953. He was a regular visitor to my parents' house.

Cookery as entertainment Fanny Cradoc dominated cookery programmes on Britis television from the 1950s until well into th 1970s. Johnnie was her regular sidekick, though many of her fans would have been shocked to learn that Fanny didn't marry him until 1977.

One of the greats of modern cookery Delia Smith in around 1970. Her genius has been to know what Middle England wants, and then to nudge things very slightly further.

Two Fat Ladies C D W and Jennife Paterson in festive gear.

your tea or took butter from a tub and shaped it for you. Now, in addition to the inevitable tinned goods, you'd find neatly packaged ones, too, proudly proclaiming the name of the major manufacturer that they came from. And although just after the First World War there were still tens of thousands of little independent shops, chain stores were beginning to make their impact felt. Sainsbury's, which had started out with one shop in Drury Lane in 1869, had well over a hundred by the mid 1920s. Tesco opened its first store, in Edgware, in 1929.

Packaged foods of all varieties caught on. Breakfast cereals were one such. Cornflakes, invented by that eccentric American health-food obsessive and advocate of vibrating machines John Harvey Kellogg, rapidly gained ground in the 1920s. As did Grape-Nuts, another late-Victorian invention. The nutritional value of some of these breakfast cereals was probably a bit suspect, but at least they were served with milk. Of more questionable dietary value were crisps, again a Victorian invention but transformed commercially when ways were found to package them in such a way that they kept their crunch. Over a million packets were sold in 1928. Today the average person eats three packets of crisps a week. This was also the period that really saw the English love affair with chocolate take off. Before the First World War, most chocolate had been available in 'plain' or 'milk' bars. In the decades after the war, a whole new range of chocolate treats made their way on to shop shelves: Milky Ways appeared in 1924; Mars bars arrived in 1932; Maltesers came along in 1936.

Faced with more choice, more money to play with – and now fewer, if any, servants – the middle-class housewife of the 1920s and 1930s increasingly spent more of her time in the kitchen. She also turned her attention to improving what was there. Gas cookers, which had started to appear in Victorian times, were now pretty ubiquitous: by the beginning of the Second World War three-quarters of families had them. Three-quarters of houses also had electricity by then too, and while that didn't necessarily make the electric oven particularly popular, there were other gadgets people could invest in such as electric kettles and fridges, though both remained fairly scarce until the 1950s. The average housewife would now spend hours each day cooking and baking, taking her inspiration from cookery books and the increasing number of women's magazines. As a rule, she would avoid 'foreign muck' and concentrate on fairly straightforward meals. Dinner would probably involve meat and two vegetables – perhaps steak and kidney pie with potatoes, peas or cabbage; the vegetables would still tend to be boiled, though Mrs Martineau in her 1920s book *Cantaloup to Cabbage: How to Cook and Serve Vegetables* does mention that one can finish them off in the French manner by frying them in butter. Sunday would see a full roast – beef was nearly twice as popular as mutton and lamb – followed by, say, apple pie or a sponge pudding. Occasionally, there would be daring forays into such exotic flavours as desiccated coconut for the cook keen to come up with a trayful of coconut macaroons. On the whole, though, the range of what was cooked remained pretty conservative.

As is demonstrated by contemporary attitudes to that great departure from traditional English eating – vegetarianism. George Orwell for one was quite rude about it, associating it with sandal-wearing socialists 'with wilting beards'. And G. K. Chesterton was pretty scathing, too:

You will find me drinking rum,
Like a sailor in a slum,
You will find me drinking beer like a Bavarian.
You will find me drinking gin
In the lowest kind of inn,
Because I am a rigid Vegetarian.

Nevertheless, you do start finding a small number of vegetarians in the interwar period (vegetarianism itself, of course, is much older). George Bernard Shaw is perhaps the most famous example. According to Alice Laden in *The George Bernard Shaw Vegetarian Cookbook*, he was constantly complaining about the cost of a vegetarian diet because he insisted on having the best butter, cream, cheese and nuts available. When he ate out, he tended to eat what was put in front of others, minus the meat. It can't have been very inspiring. However, he never wavered. Of his funeral he said, 'My hearse will be followed not by mourning coaches but by herds of oxen, sheep, swine, flocks of poultry and a small travelling aquarium of live fish, all wearing white scarves in honour of the man who perished rather than eat his fellow creatures.'

When it came to eating out, the average person generally selected the same sort of conservative fare that they consumed at home. They did, however, dine out more often than they had before the war – largely because they could now afford to do so. As a result, restaurants, which had been badly hit during the war by government restrictions, blossomed again after it. The most popular tended inevitably to be the most straightforward, for example the Lyons and ABC restaurants. At the latter in 1932 you could get a three-course meal consisting of thick mock turtle soup, roast ribs of beef with Yorkshire pudding, boiled potatoes and spring greens followed by bread and butter pudding, for a shilling and sixpence – a very affordable sum for the average middle-class diner. Of course, some restaurants did have more unusual menus. Schmidt's in Charlotte Street, for example, which opened its doors in 1901, offered heavy German food: game, jugged hare and *sauerbraten* – a pot roast served, usually, with cabbage and potatoes. It serves as a reminder of the Teutonic nature of our royal family – and of the German Jews who settled in London in the late nineteenth century. It was still around in my youth, and I remember its dark wood and heavy red velvet curtains. So far as Italian food was concerned, there was Soho's Quo Vadis, which opened in 1926. And then there was a small band of Indian and Chinese restaurants, catering mostly to their own communities and, in the case of Chinese restaurants, mostly found in areas around the docks – though there was a clutch in Soho in the 1930s that catered to a wider clientele. Nevertheless, 'ethnic' restaurants were the exception rather than the rule.

Not only did more people eat out in the 1920s and 1930s, but thanks to the motor car the reasonably well off could go further afield to eat, too. Evening and weekend excursions became popular, perhaps to the French Horn at Sonning or the Bell at Aston Clinton or the Skindles Hotel in Maidenhead. Or indeed to the Spread Eagle in Thame, run by John Fothergill. Fothergill was a true eccentric. As a young man, when he had been rather beautiful, he had been a friend of Oscar Wilde. He later published a painted self-portrait of himself as a young man as a frontispiece to one of his books and then included, further on in the book, a photograph of him in raddled middle age with the caption 'The Face that Launched a Thousand Chips'.

He could be astonishingly rude – making one group pay extra, for example, because he thought that they were badly dressed and ugly. But the Spread Eagle proved very popular. Members of Oxford dining and boating clubs were among his clientele, Fothergill later recalling an occasion when he had severely underestimated numbers:

> . . . being 'Eights Week' [the university regatta] we had eighty-eight to dinner, besides our house party, ninety-nine in all. I didn't expect more than forty, so that whilst serving the meal I had to prepare another. People often ask if it isn't difficult to cope when you don't know how many you'll have to feed, and before taking an Inn I used to bother over this problem with hypothetical cases. But in practice it doesn't trouble one. True, sometimes almost all you have is your brains to put in the pots and pans for people to eat.

The Spread Eagle was also popular with the likes of H. G. Wells, George Bernard Shaw, Evelyn Waugh and G. K. Chesterton. In his books *An Innkeeper's Diary* and *My Three Inns* Fothergill recounted various snippets of conversations with guests. On one occasion, for example, he recalled a guest saying that he had been in Westminster Abbey showing a party round when one of the party knelt down and prayed. '"Come along, Sir," commanded the verger. "But mayn't I have a few moments of private devotion?" "No, we can't have that, or we should soon 'ave prayin' all over the place."'

Forthergill's books are full of enticing details about food. On 20 January 1923 he records a farmer's dinner involving 'thirty good men'. He served:

Tomato soup

Fish – brown stew

Venison

Jugged hare

Plum pudding

Toasted cheese

Filberts

4*s*. a head

I prepared for the twenty-five who said they would come and only thirteen came. Two bottles of whiskey were bought, which gave me a profit of *3s*., whilst the meal just paid expenses. They were very pleasant, and perhaps were doing their best to forget that I was an interloper . . .

He loved to play practical jokes on people: mauve soup made using the water from cooking red cabbage; borscht made with white beetroots; parsley sauce made with Hamburg parsley root so that it was pure white. When the Second World War came he struggled, like all innkeepers, and indeed caterers, but the recipes he came up with were rather more appetising than those put forward by the Ministry of Food. Here is his recipe for kippered haddock, which he describes as 'my way of getting round smoked salmon':

Take off the backbone of the raw fish, a careful job. Run a knife along under the ribs which should come away all together. Put the board along the edge of the table and slice the fish off the skin below, as you would smoked salmon, with a very sharp knife, or merely chop it up, and (i) lay it on buttered toast biscuits, fairy bread, pumpernikel [*sic*] or neat with salad mixture or on chopped lettuce. (ii) beat raw smoked haddock or kipper with cream cheese and pepper, and spread on buttered biscuits or pumpernikel.

His swaggering approach to food rather reminds me of G. K. Chesterton's poem against grocers and in favour of inns:

> God made the wicked Grocer
> For a mystery and a sign,
> That men might shun the awful shops
> And go to inns to dine;
> Where the bacon's on the rafter
> And the wine is in the wood,
> And God that made good laughter
> Has seen that they are good.

As for motorists and others looking for refreshment in the middle of the afternoon, there was now a plethora of tea-shops to choose from, offering tea and home-made cakes, or perhaps something a little more substantial like Welsh rarebit or poached eggs on toast. They continued into my childhood, and I can remember going to one in Datchet after I'd been out for my riding lesson and being treated to a 'buck rarebit' – Welsh rarebit with a poached egg on top – along with a very nice cake. Many of these establishments were run by women – a reflection of the growing range of occupations open to women in the years following the First World War. P. G. Wodehouse in his 1919 novel *A Damsel in Distress* makes something of a joke about it:

Ye Cosy Nooke, as its name will immediately suggest to those who know their London, is a tea-shop in Bond Street, conducted by distressed gentlewomen. In London, when a gentlewoman becomes distressed – which she seems to do on the slightest provocation – she collects about her two or three other distressed gentlewomen, forming a quorum, and starts a tea-shop in the West End, which she calls Ye Oak Leaf, Ye Olde Willow-Pattern, Ye Linden-Tree, or Ye Snug Harbour, according to personal taste.

There's even an Agatha Christie novel – *After the Funeral* – whose plot hinges on a woman committing murder to steal a valuable painting that will fund her in her ambition to reopen the beloved tea-shop she lost during the Second World War.

If tea-shops and restaurants flourished in the interwar years, the great English pub took something of a back seat. When Mass Observation conducted a survey of drinking in Bolton in 1939 they found that the vast majority of pub-goers were aged over twenty-five and that women accounted for only about one in six customers. In other words, it was mostly older men who were propping up the bar, and beer consumption nationally declined a little. The shift reflected the changing nature of English society: as more people went into 'middle-class' jobs and more people found other outlets for entertainment – cinema, radio, day excursions, and so on – so the appeal of that traditional bastion of the working class, the pub, slackened. Brewers responded by trying to make the new pubs they built in suburban areas more appealing – with games rooms and even, on occasion, cocktail lounges. They even promoted beer as a health drink: 'Guinness is Good for You', 'Bass gives an edge to your appetite and promotes good digestion'. But, arguably, the heyday of the pub was past.

Generally speaking, the 1920s and 1930s were times of reasonable prosperity for many people. You might well have a newly built house in the suburbs, complete with modern plumbing, a small kitchen and a garden. You might even have a car. But in the years leading up to the Second World War, life for working people in some of the big industrial towns and cities could be very tough indeed. The economic depression that came in the wake of the Wall Street Crash of 1929 hit traditional industries very hard and there was, as a result, widespread unemployment – nearly 3 million people were out of work in the early 1930s. This is the era of George Orwell's *The Road to Wigan Pier*, and his account is perhaps the most vivid of those seeking to explain what life was like for those struggling against poverty. People by now could claim some state assistance, but it was never enough to keep a family well fed and housed. Orwell describes an unemployed miner's family trying to get by on a diet that essentially consisted of white bread and margarine, corned beef, sugared tea and potatoes. He also makes a very telling point about the diet of the poor. Some, he argues, would suggest that rather than waste money on such non-essentials as tea and sugar, it would be healthier for the unemployed to buy fresh oranges and raw carrots:

Yes, it would, but the point is that no ordinary human being is ever going to do such a thing. The ordinary human being would sooner starve than live on brown bread and raw carrots. And the peculiar evil is this, that the less money you have, the less inclined you feel to spend it on wholesome food. A millionaire may enjoy breakfasting off orange juice and Ryvita biscuits; an unemployed man doesn't.

This, he goes on, explains why the poor so often eat junk food: it's easy and it's comforting. 'Let's have a three pennorth of chips! Run out and buy us a twopenny ice-cream! Put the kettle on and we'll all have a nice cup of tea!' To condemn them for this is to misunderstand what poverty is like.

One working-class dish of the time that Orwell devotes some space to is tripe. I happen to love tripe, but the English tradition of tripe and onions cooked in milk is not something that I would wish to eat, and Orwell's description of the tripe shop above which he had lodgings is enough to put you off for life:

> . . . there was a slab upon which lay the great white folds of tripe, and the grey flocculent stuff known as 'black tripe', and the ghostly translucent feet of pigs, ready boiled . . . I heard dreadful stories from the other lodgers about the place where the tripe was kept. Black beetles were said to swarm there . . . We lodgers were never given tripe to eat. At the time I imagined that this was because tripe was too expensive; I have since thought that it was merely because we knew too much about it.

Orwell certainly doesn't hold back when he describes life in the lodging house:

> For breakfast you got two rashers of bacon and a pale fried egg, and bread-and-butter which had often been cut overnight and always had thumb-marks on it. However tactfully I tried, I could never induce Mr Booker to let me cut my own bread-and-butter; he *would* hand it to me slice by slice, each slice gripped firmly under that broad black thumb. For dinner there were generally those threepenny steak puddings which are sold ready-made in

tins . . . and boiled potatoes and rice pudding. For tea there was more bread-and-butter and frayed-looking sweet cakes which were probably bought as 'stales' from the baker. For supper there was the pale flabby Lancashire cheese and biscuits.

The life Orwell evokes here is a world away from the revellers who frequented the nightclubs of 1930s London. It's horrifying to think that a nation could contain such extremes in those strange twilight years before the outbreak of the Second World War in 1939. There was, however, one occasion on which the two groups encountered each other. Here it is, described by Barbara Cartland (and quoted in *London Ritz* by Hugh Montgomery-Massingberd and David Watkin) – she happened to be sitting in the Palm Court of the Ritz when one of the hunger marches from the north of England arrived in London at the end of their long journey to lobby for government help:

The poor things were in rags; they looked tired and exhausted. They didn't make a sound; they just gazed around in disbelief, overwhelmed by the fountain, the opulence, the atmosphere. The people having tea just sat there, still, looking upper-class; nothing was said. There was an uncanny silence. Then the marchers were politely asked to leave, which they did without any fuss or bother.

Although supermarkets existed well before the Second World War, they only really became ubiquitous in the 1960s and 1970s. The idea of serving yourself rather than asking the shopkeeper to do everything for you was something of a novelty when this 1960s Sainsbury's advertisement appeared.

CHAPTER 14

Spam and Coronation Chicken

The Second World War
and the Years of Austerity

Ask people who lived through the Second World War what they remember about wartime food, and they'll probably come up with a list of the things they had to go without (bananas, onions, chocolate) and a list of things they would rather have not had to eat (dried eggs, dried potato, whale meat). They'll also recall the ingenuity that cooks had to employ to make unpromising ingredients into some sort of edible dish. Rationing was introduced in January 1940, and many items, such as meat, butter, sugar, eggs and flour, were in short supply. Consequently, even the most straightforward of meals could prove a real challenge to prepare, and those items, like carrots, that were, as a rule, readily available, had to be used in as many ways as possible. I remember coming across a recipe for Lord Woolton Pie (named, in a less than charitable way, after the head of the Ministry of Food) which involved dicing potatoes, cauliflower, swedes, carrots and spring onions (if available), adding vegetable extract and then cooking it all together in water for about ten minutes. At the end you added some slices of potato and browned it in the oven. I tried it. It was actually worse than it sounds.

Frequently, one type of food had to stand in for another. Since sugar was in such short supply, for example, the ubiquitous carrot was often used instead to provide sweetening. This could yield a recipe like the one for carrot fudge, where some of the concentrated orange juice issued to children on their food vouchers was cooked together with carrots and gelatine and left to set in a baking dish. I can't quite bring myself to experiment with this one, though I'm mildly intrigued to know what the end result is like.

Sometimes, people would carefully store up the 'luxuries' among their rations so that they could enjoy them properly at one go. A friend of mine who was a child during the war told me that she used to save up as much of her personal allowance of butter as possible so that she could have a really good helping on her toast at the end of each week. And sometimes, inevitably, people had to make do with food that we would now throw away. Another friend whose family had a farm in Ireland received a food package from them that had been held up in the post for so long that the chicken it contained had become infested with maggots. Rather than chuck it out, her mother boiled the chicken until the maggots floated to the surface and then skimmed them off. Not to have eaten the chicken would have been unthinkable. My family fared rather better with food parcels. Some of my cousins were sent to relatives in America and posted back things like Hershey bars.

On occasion, the desperation to make do with what was to hand could lead to bizarre meals. One of my favourite Second World War stories involves a friend whose family was sent a food parcel from cousins in the Antipodes that contained a little box of what looked to be spices. They gratefully added them to the cake mixture they were baking. A few days later, the letter that should have arrived at the same time as the parcel finally struggled its way through the post. It was only then that they discovered that the spices were in fact the ashes of Uncle Egbert, whose last request had been to have his mortal remains shipped home and scattered over his favourite spot. Let's hope that he liked cake.

Finding ways to store food was a constant obsession. I've heard of people with wartime larders packed with jars of green beans that had been sliced into strips and salted. Then there were eggs preserved in isinglass. Isinglass is a form of gelatine that comes from fish, in particular from sturgeon, and, believe me, a little goes a long way. I can still recall eggs preserved in isinglass solution from my youth: it was essential to keep them below the surface of the liquid so that air couldn't permeate the shells. It was quite an effective mode of storage, though it did impart a rather unpleasant flavour to the eggs.

When it came to shopping, people expected to have to queue and to be offered a very limited choice when they finally got to the counter. I can recall my mother telling me that because so many Italian shopkeepers in Soho were interned on the Isle of Man early in the war, the one thing you could be guaranteed to obtain was unusual types of pasta because the people care-taking the shops had no idea what they were. At that time macaroni and spaghetti were about the only types of pasta that most English people had heard of.

For those with a little cash to spare, there was always the black market. Food would mysteriously disappear from the docks and turn up in the hands of a spiv reminiscent of George Cole's character in the St Trinian's films. Some farmers would 'forget' to declare everything they had produced. The odd butcher would sell a bit of meat under the counter to favoured customers who were prepared to pay for it. I remember that my mother was vehemently against this practice. Occasionally my father would come home with cuts of meat which had been given to him by patients. Convinced that they were black market goods, she would refuse to eat them. In reality, I suspect that in nine cases out of ten the meat was a thank-you present from his patients' own food rations.

Restaurants stayed open during the war, though what they could offer was inevitably somewhat curtailed. They were not allowed to charge more than five shillings a meal – actually a not inconsiderable sum at the time. Some grander establishments got round this restriction by upping the price of the wine. Luxury items like lobster still occasionally made their way on to the menu at places like Wheeler's in St James's, but in general the sort of culinary ingenuity necessary for the average wartime housewife was necessary for the average wartime chef, too. There's a very good fish and chip shop in North Wales that had to make do with salmon that poachers brought them from the River Dee because they couldn't get sea fish during the war. You can still buy salmon fried in batter there, and very good it is, too. My mother told me that she and a friend – an anaesthetist's wife – paid a wartime visit to one particular Soho restaurant because they had heard that it had steak on the menu. They placed their order and in due course two delicious-looking steaks were put in front of them. My mother scrutinised hers, ate a little and then said, 'Ah, that explains it.' 'What do you mean, Molly?' her friend asked. 'Well, it's horse meat,' was the response. The anaesthetist's wife suddenly decided she wasn't really that hungry, and so my mother got to eat both steaks.

There's a certain strange irony in all this. On the one hand, you can hardly say that this era of horse meat, isinglass and 'make do' marks a high point in the history of English food. On the other hand, it does seem to be the case that the wartime diet constituted a high point in the history of English nutrition. Despite the shortages and often less than appealing food, never before had the nation as a whole eaten so healthily – and, arguably, never since, either. And to pile on the irony, it does seem that for once we had politicians and bureaucrats to thank for this. Quite simply, the success of the national diet during the war really is due to the extraordinary work of the Ministry of Food. Important lessons had been learnt during the First World War, when the nation had come within weeks of starvation, and more or less from the opening of hostilities in 1939 every aspect of the nation's wartime diet was carefully planned and brilliantly thought through.

Rationing perfectly exemplifies the Ministry of Food's pragmatism and skill. Everyone had to register for ration cards: buff for adults; green for pregnant women, nursing mothers and children under five; and blue for children between five and sixteen. If you went to stay with someone you had to take your ration card with you, and they would temporarily register you with their local shop and get the extra rations. If you were a commercial traveller staying in inns and so forth, you again had to take your ration card with you and coupons would be clipped according to the length of your stay and what you ate. It was in general a fair system, and it was also a brilliantly flexible one, made more so by the introduction of the points system in 1941. This applied to foods that were nutritionally valuable but whose supply was erratic – initially tinned meat, fish and fruit; later tapioca, rice, dried peas, and so on. Each of these items was 'worth' a certain number of points, and each week you could spend the points you were allocated on whatever you chose. What was clever here was that the Ministry could, by lowering the points value of certain foods when there was a glut, steer people in their direction. Moreover, they could get people to eat food they might normally shun by giving it a points value that was irresistible. When a whole lot of American pork sausage meat arrived, people initially turned up their noses because they had never come across it before and regarded it with considerable suspicion. When its points value was dropped from sixteen to eight, it was devoured avidly.

The handling of food imports was also impressively efficient. To save space on board ships that were in constant danger from U-boats, any foods that could be dehydrated were, and meat was boned and compressed before it was packed. Tinned Spam was perhaps the ultimate triumph of meat packaging – a pork luncheon meat crammed into tins. Those of you who have never tasted it haven't missed much, though I have a certain fondness for Spam fritters.

When it came to producing food at home, every inch of land

that could be was nudged into production. People were urged to take up allotments or to grow vegetables and keep livestock in their gardens. Even the grounds of Buckingham Palace were dug up to make room for food production. My father opted to raise pigs on a patch of land in St John's Wood just off Hamilton Terrace. Someone once asked him, 'Who butchers them for you, Dickie?' 'I'm a senior surgeon of St Mary's, Paddington. Who do you think butchers them?' was the tart response. Once a pig had been slaughtered the whole family – including, in the 1950s, me – would help wash out the tripes and scald the hair off; we prepared a lot of bacon and ham and tripe chitterlings. Everything was eaten. Many others, I am sure, did the same, and although legislation had long been passed to stop people keeping pigs next to their houses, the authorities seemed prepared to turn a blind eye.

As for farms, acres of land that had been lying idle before the war were ploughed up and turned over to arable crops or to pasturing cows. Farmers were encouraged – occasionally dragooned – to work more efficiently and productively. The number of tractors quadrupled (before the war, only one farmer in six had owned a tractor). Crops that delivered a high yield per acre, such as potatoes, were encouraged. Some of the labour was supplied by German and Italian prisoners of war. More significant was the 80,000-strong Women's Land Army. Many of these young women, used to town life, must have found life in the country a very strange and sometimes rather isolating experience. They were, however, astonishingly effective. By 1944 Britain as a whole was having to import only half the food it had before the war and wheat production had nearly doubled.

All this meant that England never went short during the war.

What's more, because the Ministry of Food included nutritional scientists among its personnel, the national diet was astonishingly well balanced. The Ministry's scientific adviser was Professor Jack Drummond, who understood the importance of, say, fresh milk for children (children under five got a pint of milk a day at the subsidised price of 2d), or the nutritional value of orange juice or cod-liver oil. He also knew that if people were to fight or to work in factories they needed food that would give them energy and keep them alert; hence, among other measures put into force, the decision to establish 'British Restaurants' that served good, hot meals at a shilling a head. Many European countries fared increasingly badly as the war ground on: in France, for example, the majority of workers were only receiving 1,500 calories a day by 1943 (as a very rough rule of thumb, women generally need around 2,000 calories a day and men 2,500). By contrast, in England, the average calorie intake per day by 1944 was closer to 3,000. Jack Drummond, incidentally, was the author of *The Englishman's Food*, first published in 1939, which described the slow steps by which the national diet had improved over the previous 500 years. He was a remarkable man. Tragically, he was murdered on holiday in France after the war. The circumstances remain somewhat mysterious to this day.

The Ministry of Food backed up its work with propaganda campaigns, encouraging people to eat this or to cook that. It even came up with a character called 'Potato Pete', an alarming-looking potato with shoes and a hat. He was supposed to encourage children to eat potatoes. I suspect he actually sent them screaming to bed. I've heard that his features were based on Lord Woolton.

The Ministry also encouraged that waste-not, want-not attitude you still find among people who endured the war years. Even now, many older adults hate to throw things away and will make the best use possible of any leftovers. I recall someone once saying of the war, 'We ate leftovers so often that I don't even remember the original meal.' That must have been a common experience.

Victory in 1945 didn't mean the end of wartime restrictions and rationing. It must have been very tough indeed for people who had gone through years of privation and suffering to find that the shortages didn't suddenly stop. In fact, for a while things actually got worse. In 1946 the sweet ration was halved and bread was rationed for the first time. Then came the bitterly cold winter of 1947 when the economy almost stalled and over 4 million workers were laid idle by power cuts. To add insult to injury, the government bought a job lot of the disgusting tinned South African fish known as snoek and tried to get everyone to eat it – without much success. Had it not been for American help via the Marshall Plan, things would have been grim indeed. I was born in 1947 and can still remember coupons for sugar and for sweets. They both remained rationed until the queen's coronation in 1953, and I remember how excited my siblings were when restrictions were removed. I knew I ought to be thrilled, too, but I was simply too young to understand what was being returned to us.

I still vividly recall the high street of my childhood. Even though I was brought up in London, the area where I lived – St John's Wood – felt like a village. There was a police station where I used to go to say hello to the station sergeant, who would give me a wink and a toffee. There was a proper old-fashioned haberdasher's shop, complete with all sorts of threads, silks, buttons and hooks, run by an old boy who'd been there since time immemorial and could recall how the Finchley Road had looked before it was lined with blocks of flats in the 1930s. In the mews off the high street there was a dairy which, when I was very young, still had its own cows. The milkman with his horse and cart would bring the milk round each day. Then there was an English cafe selling wonderful fry-ups; sometimes my brother would take me there as a treat and we would have bacon and eggs, adorned by HP Sauce and tomato ketchup from the bottles that stood on the table.

And then there was a sweet shop with jar upon jar of sherbet lemons, liquorice allsorts, barley sugars and many others. You went in clutching your halfpenny or penny, chose something and then watched avidly as the sweet lady measured out a portion on the scales and transferred the sweets to a paper bag. You'd clutch this for dear life as you wandered home, feeling the sweets getting stickier and stickier in your grip. One of my favourite treats was Wagon Wheels: giant chocolate-covered biscuits with some sort of marshmallow filling that seemed awfully large and almost impossible to finish – until you embarked on one. I also adored gobstoppers, taking them out of my mouth periodically to see which coloured layer I had reached.

On occasion my mother would send me out with her shopping list to make the rounds of the relevant shopkeepers. Some things came in packets, but many items had to be cut up and weighed in front of you. Butter was scooped out of barrels. Bacon was sliced for you, and you had a choice of streaky, back, green or smoked. Cheese was cut with a wire – something that never failed to fascinate me. Fortunately, I wasn't expected to carry all these purchases home myself. Local traders all had delivery boys who could drop things off by bicycle. Larger orders, particularly from the grocer's, would come by van. I'd ask for help crossing the roads, but otherwise I was very much left to my own devices. If I hadn't returned by the time my mother was expecting me, she would simply ring up the shops on my route and ask, 'Have you seen Clarissa? Please send her home.'

There was a food shop for just about everything. St John's Wood had three greengrocer's shops, one of which was run by a large and voluble Sicilian family who always seemed pleased to see me, called me a 'sweet little girl' and treated me to a plum or some cherries. There was a baker's which sold not just bread but typically English fairy cakes, maca-roons, splits and doughnuts. There were two butcher's and two fishmonger's, one of which, Mac Fisheries, was part of a nationwide chain. The other had a tank of live eels and I can recall going there with my nanny, or with the cook, to purchase a couple of live eels that would then squirm and twist in a bag until we got them home and handed them to the gardener to nail their heads to a post on the wall of the garden shed and skin them. Then they would be cooked, usually in the Belgian manner in a green sauce; sometimes Louise, our cook, would jelly them.

What distinguished the high street in St John's Wood from the average one you'd find in any 1950s town or village were the shops that served the local Jewish community. There was, for example, a kosher butcher that sold very good salt beef. We went there on occasion and I can vividly remember being shushed by my mother when I asked in a rather loud voice, 'Mummy, why don't we buy our sausages here as well?' As for the fishmonger's run by the very English Mr and Mrs Brown and their son, they sold not just eels and ordinary fish, but carp and gefilte fish balls as well. I had a particular fondness for the fish balls, which were delicious when heated through or fried. And then there were two local cafes that sold Viennese-type pastries, laden with cream and chocolate.

We had a delicatessen, too, which sat squarely on my road, Circus Road. It offered vats of different types of pickled cucumber and pickled herring, along with sauerkraut and foreign and English cheeses. Rather surprisingly for a delicatessen in a Jewish area it also sold fresh frankfurter sausages and various types of German wurst. It was a wonderful place to wander. Occasionally, somebody would give me a bit of sausage to taste, or a bit of salami.

I have vivid memories of our home. My parents had been bombed out of their previous house and had lived in rented accommodation until the end of the war. The new house boasted a garden that grew the finest camellias I have ever seen. Apparently the previous owners had kept chickens, and the camellias were the beneficiaries of a soil enriched with chicken manure. There was also a small kitchen garden, with a fig tree and various other fruit trees, including old pear trees presumably left over from when St John's Wood was wooded. These yielded bullet-hard pears, which my father, with that waste-not, want-not mentality born of two world wars, insisted that we gather and cook. They took hours and never seemed to get soft. There was even a 400-year-old mulberry tree. In the coronation year the gardener and I planted a new mulberry tree and I have a photograph of us standing proudly beside it, the gardener scarcely taller than me. Some of the kitchen garden was given over to me to plant radishes, spring onions and exciting things like that.

Our kitchen contained a large and very modern fridge – a Westinghouse. I can remember my mother saying how difficult it had previously been, even with a north-facing larder, to keep things really cold in summer. Those not fortunate enough to own a fridge would sometimes boil their milk in summer to make it keep longer. I even heard of a woman who, when frozen chickens first came in, would place one in a cold oven to defrost and put milk next to it to keep the milk cool.

The fridge wasn't the only newfangled gadget to be found in our kitchen. Along with the sophisticated stove with eye-level grill, we also had a Kenwood mixer, complete with dough hook and whisks. My mother loved devices such as this. She also invested in a hand-beater where you turned a handle to operate the whisks (I've always felt that a balloon whisk does the job better). She bought a patented apple peeler and corer where you put the apple on a prong, turned the handle and gasped in admiration as the peel came off and the core was removed (our cook, however, reckoned it was quicker to do it by hand, and I suspect she was right). And she even had one of those patented egg-slicers that had a wire cage you brought down over the egg to produce immaculate slices (again, the cook argued it was quicker to do this with a knife – and easier to wash up afterwards, too).

Some of my favourite food was simple, nursery food. I loved tinned peaches with evaporated milk, for example, and the various delicious puddings that our cook prepared. On occasion, with the injunction 'Don't tell your mother, dear', she would slip me some toast and beef dripping with a little salt on top (a delicacy regarded as rather lower class at the time). Then there was the treat of a coffee and walnut cake bought from a shop in the Marylebone High Street on cook's day off. Actually, it was considered rather vulgar in the world I grew up in to purchase cake, but we loved it and didn't have the heart to tell Louise that we thought it was better than the ones she cooked. For the adults, or more particularly my father, there was a huge cellar full of wine, most of which had been given to him by his various clients. He drank a very great deal himself, but instructed my mother that if she was ordering alcohol from the grocer, it should be entered on the account as tins of tomatoes or peaches.

We were fortunate enough to have a cook in the 1950s. Other people had Marguerite Patten and Constance Spry, and their cookery books influenced a whole generation of housewives. Marguerite had made her name working as a food adviser to the Ministry of Food and had displayed great ingenuity in coming up with recipes involving unpromising ingredients. In the 1950s she published various cookery books with step-by-step black and white illustrations, and then broke into glorious technicolour with her *Cookery in Colour* of 1960. Superbly practical and reassuring, her books showed the aspiring housewife how to plan everything from a dinner party to an everyday meal. Many of the recipes still stand up well today. Inevitably, though, there are some that fifty years or so later seem period pieces to us, preserved in aspic. And, indeed, aspic (and gelatine) was something of a theme in dishes such as chaud-froid chicken. Elsewhere you can detect that love of moulded food – rice shaped into a ring, for example – that harks back to an earlier age and the recipes of Mrs Beeton. Curiously, I was recently at an event at Michael Heseltine's where his chef produced a jelly ring made with beetroot and flavoured, I think, with blackcurrant. It was quite, quite delicious and made me think that this type of dish is perhaps worth revisiting.

Constance Spry offered cooking on a grander scale, as befitted someone who had made a reputation with her grand floral arrangements (she did the flowers for the queen's coronation) and who, after the war, had set up a domestic science school with her friend Rosemary Hume (who ran the Cordon Bleu Cookery School in London) at Winkfield Place, near Windsor. It doubled as a sort of finishing school; both my sisters went there. *The Constance Spry Cookery Book*, written by both Spry and Hume, is very much aimed at the housewife who has plenty of time to cook and entertain, and the ambitious tone is set straightaway in the introduction:

> Cooking is an art; it demands hard and sometimes distasteful work, but on the whole it is the creative side that prevails. The kitchen should be raised to the status of a studio, as indeed it is in some homes where the mistress is a cook.

As befits a book for the 1950s, considerable space is devoted to various types of cocktail party. In the 1920s they had been de rigueur. For Spry and Hume, however, they are clearly something of a necessary evil and they bemoan the strong cocktails that 'blunt the palate' and the savouries that 'blunt the appetite'. Their cocktail parties fall into three camps: pre-dinner party, fully fledged cocktail party (served between six and eight o'clock) and pre-theatre party, and each demands a different mix of canapés. They're very stern about serving too many similar things: if you have a number of pastry or bread-based canapés, you must balance these with celery stuffed with Stilton (very 1950s), or stuffed grapes or prunes. They're also very keen on after-dinner savouries, a course that has now sadly gone out of fashion. These might consist of devilled soft roes, or perhaps sardines or herring on toast.

The love of moulded food you notice on occasion in Marguerite Patten's recipes is also evident in Spry and Hume's. There is an entire section on the art of aspic making, along with recipes for a rather garishly coloured salmon mousse, for fish cream *suédoise* (set in a charlotte mould, this time with gelatine) and for *oeufs pochés Nantua* (eggs, prawns, béchamel sauce, whipped cream, aspic and the inevitable red food colouring). *Cornet de jambon*, which again strikes me as a characteristically 1950s dish, involves lining a cornet mould with ham, piping in a mixture of pâté, béchamel sauce, mustard, sherry and cream and then – surprise, surprise – topping it all off with aspic. Once you've removed the moulds, you arrange the cornets on a dish with watercress – and chopped aspic.

More appealing, to me at least, is a recipe for Dublin Bay prawns presented in a large bowl filled with crushed ice and served with Alabama sauce – something of a signature dish for Constance Spry. Alabama sauce is a mix of chopped green pepper, celery, garlic, mayonnaise, tomato chilli sauce, grated horseradish and a little cream. It's actually very good and betrays a certain American influence.

There's lots of what we would regard as traditional English fare in the book: roast beef with Yorkshire pudding, apple pie, bread and butter pudding, cakes and biscuits. But as you'd expect from authors with a cordon bleu connection, many recipes have a strong French accent: there are consommés; *sauces blanches*, *brunes* and *mères*; even chicken is *poulet*. Eggs also loom large: *oeufs durs aux champignons*, *omelette fines herbes* and, most striking of all, soufflé. In part, this emphasis on the egg can be seen as a celebration of the end of rationing and the dreaded powdered egg. In part, and certainly so far as soufflés are concerned, it's a practical acknowledgement of the fact that the new 1950s oven was more reliable in terms of desired temperature than previous ones had been, and that people were increasingly living in houses where the distance between the kitchen and the dining room was such that you could reach journey's end with your soufflé still impressively risen.

That said, I can't help thinking that Spry and Hume are probably responsible for terrifying generations of women into thinking that a soufflé is a concoction of fiendish complexity. Under the heading 'Causes of failure' they list nine things that can go wrong – including the dire consequences of not beating the egg whites in the appropriate, preferably copper, bowl. Even in the 1970s I felt obliged to buy one and it hung around for ages. And I remained intimidated by soufflés for years, not helped by the fact that my sister Heather, who had been influenced by Constance Spry and Rosemary Hume at Winkfield, was a dab hand at a cheese soufflé. It was not until I read Robert Carrier's books many years later with their pragmatic American view that if you could make a white sauce, you could make a soufflé, that I tried my hand at anything larger than the small ramekin-dish-type soufflé. Only then did I realise that it is actually a very easy and delicious dish to make.

When it comes to cuisines from countries other than France, Spry and Hume do give these a look, but generally in a highly restricted form. So Italian pasta is certainly present, but largely in the form of spaghetti and to a lesser extent cannelloni, macaroni and ravioli – certainly no lasagne. Moussaka makes it in, but not much other Greek food. Oriental food is passed over. As for curry, given its long-established popularity in English cuisine, it's scarcely surprising to find that the authors devote a lot of attention to it. But this is very much English curry, made with a thing called 'curry-powder' (although, in fairness, they do include a recipe for home-made curry powder, mentioning the Bombay Emporium in London where many of the ingredients such as turmeric and cumin can be bought).

However, I do think that Spry and Hume deserve credit for one curry dish that they came up with. Coronation chicken was created for Queen Elizabeth II's coronation in 1953 and, properly made and served, I reckon it's very good indeed. The recipe in *The Constance Spry Cookery Book* is a fine one, involving two young chickens poached in a light stock and then cut up and mixed with a cream of curry sauce (onion, tomato purée, red wine, seasoning, a little apricot purée, a little lemon juice, mayonnaise, cream – and, of course, curry powder). That touch of apricot is inspired.

At the back of the book, the two authors give the menu for the party served on Coronation Day to 350 people who had been present at the coronation service. In its restraint it makes an interesting contrast to the grand banquets of Victorian and Edwardian days:

Potage de Tomate à l'Estragon
Truite de Rivière en Gelée, Sauce Verte
Poulet Reine Elizabeth [coronation chicken] *or*
Cornets de Jambon Lucullus
Cherry and Walnut Salad
Galette aux Fraises
Mousse au Citron
Coffee, Petits Fours

Suggested dinner-party menus in the book are similarly restrained, generally consisting of no more than three or four courses, as in the following example:

Consommé
Roast Fillet of Beef
Pommes Rissolées, Watercress Salad
Sea-kale or Asparagus au Beurre
White Coffee Ice
Tuiles d'Amandes

Spry and Hume devote quite a lot of attention to presentation, and there's no doubt that this was a great age for decorating your table, for different-coloured tablecloths and different-coloured napkins. Entertaining could be a competitive business, especially when employees were inviting the boss to dinner. And though the old formalities were slowly fading as the 1950s moved into the 1960s, certain things were still expected. Barbara Cartland's *Etiquette Handbook*, for example, first published in 1962, accepts that people no longer wear evening dress when they go out for dinner, but does expect men to wear a dark suit and women to wear a cocktail dress ('Note: it is wise to take a fur stole or scarf when dining in country houses').

So much for life at home in the 1950s. When it came to days out, I have to confess that my own early recollections are scattered. I don't remember much of the Festival of Britain of 1951, for example, but then I would only have been four at the time. On the other hand I do vividly remember going to the Battersea funfair. It had all sorts of exciting rides including one where you were spun round at high speed, held in place by the centrifugal force of the machine. Brave boys would get up and walk around the edge of it. I, on the other hand, just lay there like the crucified Christ, holding my breath and hoping I wouldn't slide down to the floor. The food treat here was candyfloss, which I had never seen before and thought to be totally magical. They made it in front of you, spinning the sugar and then inserting a stick to gather up the sugary cobweb. I managed to get it all over myself.

My first experience of what we would now call fast food came when I went to boarding school at the end of the 1950s and encountered Wimpy Bars. By this time they had come under the management of Lyons, the first 'Wimpy Bar' opening at the Lyons Corner House in Coventry Street in London in 1954. To me they seemed novel and unusual, and I can remember slipping illicitly away from school with my friends to visit one. I suppose they must have remained the dominant hamburger chain until McDonald's arrived in the 1970s.

As I got a little older I caught a glimpse of the exciting new world of coffee bars. This was the age of Bill Haley and the Comets (the very first record I ever owned was Bill Haley's 'Rock around the Clock') and of Elvis Presley, a man who has always seemed to me to be a modern take on a Greek tragic hero: born with every gift the gods could have given him – good-looking, amazing voice, incredibly sexy, wonderfully gyrating hips – but a victim of his own success, prescription drugs and cheeseburgers. I find it almost impossible not to think of coffee bars and rock and roll at the same time. Both were hugely popular with the late-teenage generation, who would spend hours listening to one while experiencing the other in the form of rather unpleasant coffee from newfangled espresso machines. I remember visiting one of the last surviving 1950s coffee bars with Jennifer Paterson in the late 1990s. It was in Swansea and was a world of chrome and linoleum-covered tables. The coffee hadn't improved.

In retrospect every decade can be seen to mark some sort of turning point, but I can't help feeling that the latter part of the 1950s represents a particularly sharp one. Of course, in my case, this may have something to do with the nostalgic gloss I suspect we all bring to the period in which we grew up, but in those few years that saw post-war austerity turn to late-1950s prosperity I do think a lot changed, not least in the world of food. Quite simply, food became cheaper and more accessible. Moreover, the pre-war world of small shops that was still around when I was little began to yield to supermarkets and ever more industrialised ways of producing food. By the mid 1960s we were well on our way to the sort of town centres and shops that surround us today.

When it came to food, increased industrialisation and more 'efficient' ways of making it available was a two-edged sword. New approaches and techniques certainly made it more affordable. On the other hand, they also made it increasingly dull and uniform, and, in this respect, the history of English food over the next few decades is a rather depressing one. The 1947 Agriculture Act nicely exemplifies these two polar extremes. Desperate to encourage farmers to produce more at a time when food was in such short supply, it offered subsidies to those who introduced new technology and who specialised in what they grew or reared. As a result, farms became more productive. It's hard to argue with that. But by encouraging specialisation the Act also opened the way to a reduction in the range of what was produced and, in that respect, the price paid has been a very high one indeed.

The decline of the English pig is a sad example of post-war food planning. Up until the 1950s, there had been a whole range of traditional breeds, from the Lincolnshire curly coat and the Essex curly coat (raised principally for their fat production) to the Gloucester Old Spot and the British Lop. Lurking in the wings, though, was the Landrace pig from Scandinavia, good for bacon but not much else. After the war the Lincolnshire curly coat and the Essex curly coat started to decline, largely because their very fatty meat appealed less to a nation increasingly turning to things like margarine. Even more sadly, so did the Gloucester Old Spot and the British Lop. In fact I suspect that had we not raised the plight of the Gloucester Old Spot on *Two Fat Ladies*, it might have disappeared altogether. As for the British Lop, this breed was saved by stubborn farmers in Cornwall who refused to give their pigs up; but even today there is only one large herd outside Cornwall, at Northfield Farm on the Rutland–Leicestershire border. I recently championed the British Lop in the BBC programme *The Great British Food Revival* and I would urge you to try it: it is an excellent pig and produces very good meat with just the right covering of fat. It may sound paradoxical to urge people to save a rare breed by eating it, but, in farming, that's the only way to secure its long-term future. As for the Lincolnshire curly coat, that seems to have gone for ever. There is still a pig called the Mangalitza which has a curly coat, but it's not related. Now, the Landrace rules supreme.

The same story has repeated itself again and again across just about everything we eat. Before the war, for example, there were literally hundreds of varieties of English apple, each with its own idiosyncrasies and unique taste, from Ashmead's Kernel to the seventeenth-century Nonpareil. After the war, as standardisation and storeability became the watchwords, choice vanished. Around two-thirds of English orchards were grubbed up over the next fifty years and the range of what you could buy severely curtailed. By the late 1970s, Golden Delicious apples from France – reliable, uniform and not very delicious – were dominating supermarket shelves. Today we import almost three-quarters of the apples we consume.

Perhaps the most extreme disappearance has been the rabbit. Before the war most villages had their rabbit man, who made his living going round the hedgerows with his ferrets, taking rabbits and selling them to the local butcher or even to householders. When war came, rabbit was an obvious choice for the pot, and I suspect many people got a bit fed up with it. That, combined with the fact that the rabbit population had, in any case, increased sharply over the previous decades, led to a decision – almost certainly with official sanction – to import the myxomatosis virus from Australia. The effects were devastating. I have vivid memories of going for country walks as a child equipped with a stick so that if I came across one of those poor, myxomatosis-ridden rabbits with their bulging eyes, I could put it out of its misery. The end result was that a useful and flavourful meat that people had been eating for centuries largely vanished from the English diet. You can find plenty of rabbit recipes in *The Constance Spry Cookery Book*, but by the time you get to Delia Smith's *How to Cook* in the late 1990s, they've all gone.

In this drive for uniformity and the loss of variety and traditional foods, the big supermarkets have much to answer for. We too, however, must shoulder some of the blame. Increasingly over the last few decades the word we have tended to associate with food is 'convenience'. Tinned and packaged foods have, of course, been around since Victorian times, but they have become increasingly ubiquitous (we now eat twice as many tinned baked beans per person as any other country). In the 1950s and 1960s they were joined by quick frozen food sold from open-top freezers in supermarkets (and by the 1970s transferred to freezers at home). The next step to food without thinking was the microwave, a post-war invention that now sits in nine out of ten kitchens. Today we munch our way through three times as many ready meals each year as most other European countries. From Vesta meals in the 1960s and 1970s to Pot Noodles and Marks & Spencer ready meals today, we have ceased to be a nation of cooks and have become a nation of food preparers.

There are many reasons for the English love affair with convenience food. The Industrial Revolution, which happened earlier in England than in most other countries, broke the close ties between growing, cooking and eating – and generations have grown up who either don't want to cook or don't know how to, or both. Today they may have well-appointed fitted kitchens with double ovens, but they probably head straight for the microwave. I suspect, too, that quick meals are often popular with people who don't have much money: they may not be particularly cheap, but they have that comfort factor that comes from all the sugar, fat and salt. To quote George Orwell again, 'the less money you have, the less inclined you feel to spend it on wholesome food'.

And there's no doubt that convenience food suits the shifting nature of post-war family lives. In the 1950s around three-quarters of women were housewives; today that figure has dropped to around a third as more women have taken part-time or full-time jobs. In the 1950s six out of ten men returned home for their midday meal. Now most grab a sandwich or a snack at work. Once mealtimes were family affairs. Now the dinner table is an alfresco affair, where members of the family come in at all times, occasionally passing each other en route. There are also more single-person households and more flat-shares than ever before. You need to be quite dedicated to cook yourself a fully fledged meal every day, even if you are the proud possessor of Jocasta Innes's brilliant *The Pauper's Cookbook*, Katharine Whitehorn's *Cooking in a Bedsitter* or Delia Smith's *One is Fun!*

Arguably, the meal that has been most affected by all the rush is breakfast. As we've seen, this was a comparatively late addition to the English roster of meals, but once established the English took it to their hearts. At its most lavish, in Edwardian times, it was a thing of beauty, if possibly a little overwhelming. Even in the late 1950s just over half the population were eating a cooked breakfast during the winter. Today, however, half the population don't eat breakfast at all and those who do are far more likely to eat packaged cereals or toast than to cook themselves anything. What's more, recent surveys show that while older people will tend to sit down to have their breakfast, many younger people will grab something and eat it on the move. It's not hard to conclude that the meal as a family social occasion is in decline.

Peculiarly, while post-war England has shown an ever-diminishing desire to cook, it has displayed an ever-growing appetite for watching other people cook. Cookery programmes date back to the earliest days of television and have been part of my life since childhood, when people like Marguerite Patten ventured on to the BBC to give friendly, no-nonsense demonstrations. I particularly remember Philip Harben, because he was a patient of my father's and regularly used to come to our house, where he'd entertain me with his cookery tricks. One of these involved coming up with unlikely dishes prepared in a frying pan – and indeed he went on to write a book entitled *Imperial Frying* in which he demonstrated that you could even prepare a sponge cake in this none-too-promising way.

But it was probably Fanny Cradock (or Phyllis Nan Sortain Cradock, to give her full and proper name) who can claim credit for turning cookery into entertainment. Absurdly overdressed in an evening outfit, she would cook some dish or other and then emerge from behind the stove or table looking immaculate and declaring, 'There you are, not a stain upon me.' I was deeply impressed by this until years later I met a girl who had worked on the programme and was prepared to reveal Fanny's secret. Apparently, she wore an easily detachable apron and it was this girl's job to remove it before Fanny stepped out in front of the cameras. The apron itself was covered in flour and food. I was so relieved.

Fanny was accompanied by her husband Johnnie, who staggered around in formal evening attire with a monocle and was, I suspect, frequently drunk, and by some poor assistant who had meekly to endure the lashings of Fanny's acid tongue when things weren't done to her satisfaction. I don't think anyone could claim that she was a great cook – her food was garish and over the top. But she did have a sense of humour, and her books are peppered with it. There is, for example, the wonderful instruction in her recipe for prawn cocktail: 'take an unpeeled prawn (that's one with the head on) and lean it against the end of the glass in the way of a reveller on an ocean liner, leaning over the rail preparing to be sick'. It's a wonderful image, perhaps to be expected from someone who also dabbled in writing novels under the pseudonym Frances Dale, including rather bad bodice-rippers that were peppered with interesting historical recipes.

Fanny opened the way for a succession of flamboyant television cooks, not least Graham Kerr, or the Galloping Gourmet as he was known, whose television series of that name straddled the 1960s and 1970s. As for Fanny herself, it was ultimately her flamboyance, or rather her rudeness, that brought her crashing to earth. Invited to give her views on an amateur cook on Esther Rantzen's *The Big Time*, she did precisely that in a performance that was unflinching, unprofessional and unforgivable. She never appeared on television again.

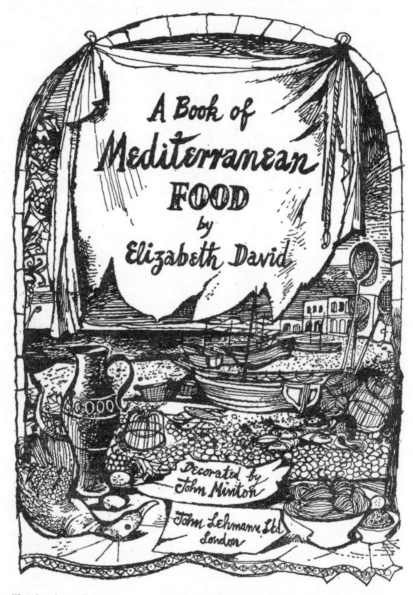

A Book of
Mediterranean
FOOD
by
Elizabeth David

Decorated by
John Minton

John Lehmann, Ltd
London

There's a lot to lament in post-war English cuisine, but there's also a lot to celebrate, and Elizabeth David is definitely a cause for celebration. Her *Book of Mediterranean Food* (1950) was a breath of fresh air in the years of austerity that followed the Second World War, and her espousal of excellent, well-prepared ingredients has become the hallmark of English food at its best.

CHAPTER 15

Prawn Cocktail and Pizza

Modern English Food

Reviewing the state of English food at the end of the 1970s, the eminent food historian John Burnett included two menus that public surveys had suggested were people's idea of a 'perfect meal'. The first was from 1947 and went as follows:

Sherry

Tomato soup

Sole

Roast chicken

Roast potatoes, peas and sprouts

Red or white wine

Trifle and cream

Cheese and biscuits

Coffee

The second was from 1973:

Sherry

Tomato soup

Prawn or shrimp cocktail

Steak

Roast and/or chipped potatoes, peas, sprouts and mushrooms

Red or white wine

Trifle or apple pie and cream

Cheese and biscuits

Coffee

Liqueurs or brandy

Surveys conducted over the past five or so years have come up with a whole range of different answers, few of them involving a complete menu. Some say that pizza is now the nation's favourite dish; others, curry or chow mein; others, such traditional English fare as roast beef and Yorkshire pudding, or fish and chips. All suggest that popular taste has changed quite a lot in the past two or three decades.

It's virtually impossible to spot trends when you're living through them, and yet it's extraordinary how certain dishes and items of food seem in retrospect so typical of a particular time. That mention of prawn cocktail in the 1973 menu comes as no surprise. Nor, from the same decade, would one raise an eyebrow at loving references to Black Forest gateau, duck à l'orange, cheese fondue or wine and cheese parties. The 1980s is the decade of nouvelle cuisine. In the 1990s we embraced sushi.

Even specific items of food can have a period feel to them. Avocados, for instance. They'd actually been known in England for a long time, but they really took off in the 1960s (Sainsbury's started stocking them in 1962). My mother, for some reason, became very keen on them and would serve them as a starter, either with a vinaigrette dressing or filled with prawns mixed with mayonnaise. It's hardly surprising that most of my school friends reckon that they ate their first avocado pear at my parents' house. I myself always thought they were rather tasteless and that it was difficult to get ripe ones – one seemed to spend an awful lot of one's time squeezing avocado pears to see if they were ripe, or putting them in drawers with bananas, which was supposed to ripen them, and then forgetting about them. I suspect that part of the reason my mother thought the avocado pear was wonderful was because somebody had told her that it had slimming properties. (Incidentally, my mother had a rather wobbly understanding of dieting. She seemed to think that if you decided to go on, say, an orange and peanut diet, as she once did, all that meant was that you had to remember to eat the oranges and peanuts before you went on to devour your normal lunch or dinner. Surprisingly, perhaps, she wasn't fat.)

The rather dull-sounding 'basket of goods' that the government uses to calculate the Retail Price Index reflects how the popularity of individual ingredients changes over time. In 1947 wild rabbit was regarded as a typical purchase, along with such things as prunes and condensed milk. Fish fingers had made an appearance by 1962, spaghetti and tinned ravioli by 1987, and pitta bread and muesli – unthinkable in the immediate post-war years – by 2005.

Sometimes you can point to quite specific reasons why particular foods were popular when they were. Chicken was comparatively difficult to find and relatively expensive immediately after the war, so it's not surprising that it made it on to the 1947 menu as something you'd want to have on a night out. By the 1970s it was very common indeed, and steak had replaced it as a treat. Prawn cocktail, scarcely mentioned in 1947 and still very much the taste of a minority in the early 1960s, experienced a meteoric rise in the 1970s when people found themselves able to stock their newly purchased deep freezers with frozen prawns.

Even water is subject to fashion. Back in the Middle Ages very few people would have touched it – ale was a much safer bet. As late as the 1870s, leading lights of the temperance movement seeking to wean people off the demon drink felt uneasy about suggesting cold water that might or might not be contaminated and instead promoted tea. The water supply started to improve, however, and by the 1950s nobody gave a second thought to drinking water from the tap. Still, virtually no one in the 1950s, or indeed as late as the 1970s, would have dreamt of buying bottled water. This was something that foreigners drank because they were foreign and so couldn't get their water supply right. The actor Peter Ustinov recalls in his autobiography how the family nanny filled her suitcase with milk bottles full of London tap water in preparation for a visit to Paris. She certainly wasn't going to risk French tap water.

In the 1980s that all changed. Part of the reason was that an increasing number of English people were taking holidays abroad and acquiring a taste for the bottled water they were served there. Another part was that in a decade that saw a decline in traditional boozy business lunches, bottled water seemed a satisfyingly trendy alternative. Each of us on average now consumes half a glass of mineral water a day.

At some point in the life of most food fashions, a counter-reaction sets in. I'm sure the first person to serve a prawn cocktail did so to rapturous applause. In fact, I have to confess I'm rather fond of it when it's made properly with shredded iceberg lettuce at the bottom of the glass and the prawns mixed with a good Marie Rose sauce (a mayonnaise-based sauce with tomato purée, a dash of Worcestershire sauce and a little seasoning). However, you can have too much of a good thing, and what seemed fresh and exciting in the early 1970s was definitely passé a decade later. To have served a prawn cocktail in 1985 would, I suspect, have been to invite social embarrassment. Similarly with Black Forest gateau, except that here it deserved its fate. As I knew it in the late 1960s and early 1970s it was essentially a rather nasty concoction of chocolate cake made with cheap chocolate, cherries from a jar and UHT cream or, even worse, cream from one of those spray cans, served with soft-scoop ice cream which Margaret Thatcher helped to invent when she worked for Lyons – and yes, I do mean *the* Margaret Thatcher, who started out life as a chemist. As for quiche Lorraine, that mainstay of the late 1970s, I'm sure that properly made with a bubbling filling and good quality lardons it is a delicious thing, but the quiches that were then served, with their cardboard pastry, and congealed and tasteless filling, deserved to fall from favour.

New fashions in English food have rarely taken root simply because a novelty arrived on the scene and everybody rushed forward to try it. After all, this is a nation that took 200 years to adopt the potato, and that still fostered some suspicion of the tomato well into the twentieth century. To create a fashion you need champions – people others are prepared to follow, whether in trying prawn cocktail for the first time or seeing what avocado tastes like. You also need campaigners, people with influence who may often be fighting against some existing fad or institution they can't bear. And the last few decades have certainly had their share of both champions and campaigners.

The first who comes to mind is Elizabeth David. When her first book, *A Book of Mediterranean Food*, was published in 1950, England was still in the grip of austerity, food was dull, vegetables were stewed and olive oil was something you bought at the chemist and was marked 'for external use only'. She, by contrast, evoked a world of sunshine and lavender, of bougainvillea and cannas, and of fresh and simple food beautifully prepared. I suspect the idyllic Mediterranean she described never really existed, but her enthusiasm is intoxicating and her ability to paint a scene in words bewitching. Here she is, for example, in her 1960 book *French Provincial Cooking* talking about the Languedoc area of France:

> You have decided upon your meal, and Madame, in her black dress, has moved majestically towards the kitchen to attend to your wishes. A bottle of cooled white wine is already in front of you, and from the big table in the centre of the restaurant a waiter brings hors-d'oeuvre, to keep you amused and occupied while more serious dishes are being prepared . . . At Nénettes they bring you quantities of little prawns, freshly boiled, with just the right amount of salt, and a most stimulating smell of the sea into the bargain, heaped up in a big yellow bowl; another bowl filled with green olives; good salty bread; and a positive monolith of butter, towering up from a wooden board. These things are put upon the table, and you help yourself, shelling your prawns, biting into your olives, enjoying your first draught

of wine. Gradually you take in your surroundings: the light and sunny dining-room, neither too big nor too small; the comfortably worn flowered wallpaper, the country flowers on the tables, and the shady garden which you can see through the open window at the far end of the dining-room.

Is it any wonder that my generation rushed off looking for this kind of life?

If you haven't read any Elizabeth David, you must. Her recipes are not written in that tight authoritarian way that is typical of so many modern cookery books, but are enjoyable to read and easy to follow. My mother had a set of *A Book of Mediterranean Food, Italian Food, French Provincial Cooking* and *French Country Cooking*, arguably Elizabeth David's greatest works, all written and published by the time she had reached the age of fifty. After that she signed a contract to write some books on English cookery, but English food was never her love and to my mind *Spices, Salt and Aromatics in the English Kitchen* and *English Bread and Yeast Cookery* don't display the same love and passion that her earlier four books possess. She also wrote for newspapers and for magazines. Her last book, *Harvest of the Cold Months: The Social History of Ice and Ices*, was published posthumously and I believe that her editor Jill Norman, who had a major hand in shaping Elizabeth's books, took away carloads of papers from her house as she embarked on completing the book.

I only came to know Elizabeth when I was working at Books for Cooks, by which time she was an old woman. She was apparently very vain, and was clearly difficult and often unhappy. Nevertheless I was so star-struck by her that when she rang the shop on one occasion and announced, 'Elizabeth David here,' I dropped the phone. She died in 1992. At her memorial service person after person got up and talked enthusiastically about how they had sat in her kitchen at the scrubbed pine table with a bottle of wine and a little blue bowl of black olives, and I remember the writer Margaret Visser turning to me and saying, 'Why does nobody mention cooking or food?' Then, at the end, a very old actor, who looked rather like a tortoise, and who had appeared many years before with Elizabeth in *A Midsummer Night's Dream* in the open-air theatre in Regent's Park, stood up to pay his tribute. He described how it had rained so heavily that day that they had been unable to perform, so they'd gone back to Elizabeth's flat where she had made him the best omelette that he had ever eaten. His words moved me to tears.

There is no doubt that Elizabeth helped change the way we eat. With her passion for the food of the Mediterranean, which was taken up in the 1960s and 1970s by the growing number of English tourists who holidayed there, she promoted a love of good, simple ingredients: olive oil, herbs from Provence, French cheeses and meats. She also countered a long-standing English suspicion of such essential ingredients as garlic. This is not the grand French cooking familiar to Edwardians, but more rustic fare – 'unexacting', as Elizabeth David describes it. Her idea of a really enjoyable French country meal is, 'An omelette, perhaps, followed by the sausages which were a speciality of the local butcher, a vegetable dish and some cheese; or perhaps snails and a homely stew . . . or a vegetable soup, a slice or two of country-cured ham and a beautiful big green artichoke.' 'The feeling of our time,' she says, 'is for simpler food, simply presented.'

Over twenty years later, another cookery writer introduced her new book with the observation, 'we may be in danger of losing something very precious, and that is a reverence for simple, natural ingredients and the joy and pleasure they can bring to everyday life.' The writer this time was Delia Smith; the book was *How to Cook*. And Delia's work fascinatingly shows that combination of continuity and change that has always been a hallmark of the best English cooking.

The continuity comes in many of those 'traditional' recipes that people regard as quintessentially English. The one for parsley sauce, for example, is not a million miles removed from the sauce we know that Henry VIII loved. Some of Delia's trifle recipes would not be out of place in Hannah Glasse's *The Compleat Confectioner*. Her shepherd's pie uses fresh minced beef but otherwise continues that baked combination of potato and meat that goes back certainly to Victorian times, when cooks were looking for ways to use up cold mutton and had new and efficient mincing machines to hand (the actual name 'shepherd's pie' seems to date from the 1870s; cottage pie, strictly speaking, is the name of the dish that uses beef). Her cakes follow in the long and honourable tradition of English baking, while her chapter on preserves would receive nods of recognition from every generation of cooks from medieval times onwards.

The change comes in the sheer variety of different cuisines that Delia draws on. As you would expect in an English cookery book, there are curries (no recommendation to use 'curry powder' now), French dishes (soufflés, brioche) and Italian pasta (though many more varieties that you would find in, say, *The Constance Spry Cookery Book*). But Delia is equally at home with Chinese stir-fries, Thai curries, Italian breads and pancetta, Canadian buttermilk pancakes and stuffed Greek vine leaves. She's also happy to intermingle recipes that will appeal to vegetarians with heavily meat-based recipes, and ones aimed at 'waist watchers' with others for steam sponges and suet puddings. In fact there's not much that you find in that eclectic mix of 'favourite' contemporary dishes and meals I mentioned earlier – pizza, curry, roast beef, and so on – that you won't also find in Delia.

Delia's genius is to understand what Middle England wants to eat at any given time, and then nudge it just very slightly forward in a way that seems fresh and exciting rather than strange and intimidating. Her espousal of limes or of capers or of Greek yoghurt has been done in such a reassuring way that people immediately feel that these are worthwhile additions to the store cupboard. They say that we would have lost the Falklands War if Delia Smith had recommended liquid glycerine, rather than liquid glucose, in her Christmas cake icing; we had ample supplies of both but ran out of liquid glucose in two weeks when it featured in Delia's cooking.

Delia's other great skill is in being straightforward and comforting. She's not slightly zany like Philip Harben or a grande dame of the kitchen like Fanny Cradock. What's more, her recipes work – hence the 1980s joke along the lines of 'I danced with a man who danced with a girl who had failed with a Delia Smith recipe'. She has reintroduced an enormous number of people to cooking in an era where this essential skill is under threat.

As for the cosmopolitan nature of Delia Smith's cooking, this reflects a more general cosmopolitan attitude to food that became increasingly apparent from the 1960s onwards. Up until then, restaurants serving non-English food were more the exception than the rule and were regarded with suspicion by many. Now a visit to a trattoria became a regular event – perhaps one of those little restaurants in Sloane Square or in Chelsea with red and white tablecloths and waiters brandishing flamboyant pepper pots. Now I come to think of it, the quality of the food was often such that a lavish grinding of black pepper probably helped considerably, but this was at least an opportunity for people to sample pasta that wasn't macaroni cheese, and to sprinkle a bit of Parmesan (nothing like as good as the Parmesan you can get these days) over everything.

Chinese restaurants also made an increasing impact, thanks in part to an influx of immigrants from Hong Kong in the 1950s and 1960s who came to London, Liverpool, Manchester and other cities whose trading contacts with the Orient had given them long-standing, if small, Chinese communities. Chinese restaurants came in every shape and size. There were grand ones like the Royal Garden near Piccadilly Circus and the Shangri-la on Brompton Road, less grand ones, quite dodgy ones and the increasingly omnipresent takeaway. To someone who had spent part of their youth visiting a grandmother in Singapore, a lot of the food they served didn't seem particularly Chinese to me: the flavour of chop suey with its chicken or pork or prawns, or chow mein, or the omeletty foo yung, never seemed quite right. Things, however, have improved.

Indian restaurants also became far more widespread in the 1960s, although I have to say the experience was not always a very good one in those early days. Unless you went to somewhere like Southall or to a top establishment like Veeraswamy's in Regent Street (which was set up in the 1920s), the food you got wasn't so much Indian food as an Indian cook's idea of an English person's idea of what Indian food was – all liberally heated with chilli powder. One good area to visit in the 1960s and 1970s was Brondesbury Park, just north of Kilburn in north London. Kilburn was, in those days, fairly solidly Irish, since it was where many railway workers and canal builders had settled, and you had to be quite brave – or foolhardy – to talk in too obvious an English accent as you wandered past the men in balaclavas who were collecting funds for the IRA outside the pubs that were dotted along the Kilburn High Road. However, if you kept going you reached Brondesbury Park with its wonderful restaurants selling Indian vegetarian food served with wonderfully crispy rice puffs.

Over time, in fact, just about every national cuisine has come to be represented in a restaurant somewhere in England. Some have been aimed at a general clientele from the start. Others started out life as meeting places for an expat community, for example the Polish restaurants that started to appear in the 1940s; I can remember feeling slightly intimidated the first time I went to Daquise in Thurloe Street, but over time other non-Poles came to brave it as well and fell in love with their very good and cheap pork knuckle with cabbage, or decided that they wanted to dawdle over a glass of black tea. Other cuisines have yet to make the impact I think they deserve to. I happen to love West Indian food, for instance, and I know that there are some wonderful West Indian cafes in places like Brixton, but it seems to me that most people have still to discover the glories of West Indian food.

Given increased immigration to England over the past few

decades, it's scarcely surprising that so many different types of restaurant have sprung up. That in itself, however, doesn't explain their popularity. What has transformed the restaurant scene, in my view, is, quite simply, our growing love affair with the whole idea of going out for a meal. Restaurants are now embedded in our culture in a way that has long been the case in countries such as France but that you wouldn't really have found in the England of, say, the 1930s. And while it's difficult to pinpoint the decade this started, I think the 1960s are a good candidate. That was the decade when eating out, particularly in an informal way, became the thing you did. I can remember vividly when the Stockpot was opened, a small restaurant chain that runs to this day. It was very much aimed at the young, and the founder was cunning enough to get her friends' daughters – the prettier the better – to come and wait tables. This brought in the boys, who came initially to admire the girls and then turned up with their own girlfriends. We all loved the fact that the food was so affordable, and we loved what was on offer. French onion soup or spaghetti bolognese or lasagne were much in demand. Chicken Kiev, which seemed the height of sophistication at a time when garlic seemed dangerously foreign, was particularly popular, its tendency to spurt out sauce when you cut into it with a knife guaranteed to make people giggle.

It all seemed part and parcel of an era in which class barriers were beginning to break down, and in which young men wanted to look like the Beatles and young women went about in mini-skirts and beehive hairdos (I had one myself, which had to be put up three times a week). People of all classes weren't afraid to be seen out enjoying themselves – and what's more, they wanted to be seen. The only moment of embarrassment in the days before cashpoints came if you realised that you had severely under-budgeted for the meal. Wives or girlfriends were constantly left to entertain themselves as the man dashed out to ring a friend who might be able to save the day.

The fascination with new foods and experiences is reflected in the number of books and television series devoted to particular cuisines. The great Claudia Roden is one of the writers who helped show the way with her *A Book of Middle Eastern Food* in 1968, followed by masterpieces such as *The Book of Jewish Food*. Then there's Anna Del Conte, whose books on Italian food – such as her 1976 classic *Portrait of Pasta* – are to my mind the best on the subject. Not forgetting Sri Owen, who has written wonderful works on Indonesian food and on rice.

When it comes to television, I have a particularly soft spot for Keith Floyd, that omnipresent figure of the 1980s and 1990s. While he may not have been a great success as a restaurateur or a publican, opening and closing various establishments and going bankrupt from time to time, and while he may also have had a serious drink problem, he was a brilliant broadcaster. One of his first television series, *Floyd on Food*, was not so much a cookery programme as a programme about food – unusual for the mid 1980s. He then very quickly moved on to filming abroad. In fact, from what I understand he had always wanted to be a travel presenter and had actually approached the BBC with that in mind; however, as they already had people like Alan Whicker, they weren't looking for another travel presenter and so he took up the food mantle instead. Various national cuisines were subject to his enthusiastic and idiosyncratic approach, but for me the highlight was a wonderful moment in one of his programmes about France when he made a piperade for an elderly French lady, who tasted it and told him in no uncertain terms what she thought of it. It was one of those rare moments on television when we were allowed to see something going horribly wrong. What's more, Floyd entered into the spirit of the occasion and happily translated his food taster's less than charitable judgement.

He went on to make programmes all over the world and by the end was running out of steam, unable, it seemed to me, to cook anything that didn't involve lemongrass and ginger. His drinking got so bad that if he was filming one day, he then had to rest for two. Ultimately, he faded from our screens, dying in 2009. Fortunately, others have come along to help fill the void he has left – Anjum Anand, for example, with her series on Indian food, and Thomasina Miers, with her excellent programmes about Mexican cuisine. A measure of the success of such champions is that whereas once you had to search high and low or go to specialist shops for things like lemongrass or jalapeño chillies, now they are fairly readily available and generally of a reasonable quality. I still recall the excitement of someone I met in 1990 at a book launch in Hereford at being able to buy fresh pasta there for the first time.

If food fashion in part involves reacting against what has gone before, one of the most encouraging trends of recent years has been a reaction against the supermarket juggernauts and the rediscovery of locally produced food. Supermarkets by the 1970s and 1980s may have been good sources of cheap food, but there was a high hidden cost to what went into the weekly shopping basket or trolley. English farming was decimated. Those farmers who survived were pressurised into supplying at often cripplingly low prices. Variety disappeared. Instead we were increasingly faced with bland food produced far away in often less-than-ideal circumstances. I remember once asking someone why they had relocated their chicken business abroad and receiving the alarmingly blunt reply, 'No regulations.' What's more, owing to the daftness of the Trade Descriptions Act, it has been quite possible to sell something as 'English' when it has only a nodding acquaintance with this country. Even the traditional English Christmas can be very far from being either traditional or English. In December 2010, for example, various newspapers pointed out that much of the salmon people were consuming was actually 'dog salmon' from China, that much of the frozen turkey on offer was from Chile, Poland and France, and that some of the geese that made their way to the table originally honked with a German or Hungarian accent.

Nor did there seem to be much government interest in farming. It mishandled the disastrous foot-and-mouth outbreak of 2001 and then opted to close the book on it simply by changing one government department – the Ministry of Agriculture, Fisheries and Food (MAFF) – into another – the Department for Environment, Food and Rural Affairs (DEFRA). Four initials became five. I was at the Great Yorkshire Show in 2001 shortly after this happened, and noticed that the DEFRA stand had nothing to say about British farmers or food production. 'Why?' I asked. 'Oh, you can import it cheaper,' was the response. I reported this back to Margaret Beckett on *The Politics Show*. When she asked, 'What idiot said that?' my retort was that it was someone in her department who clearly knew what was going on.

Fortunately, there was a David to the supermarket Goliath and it came in the form of Henrietta Green. One of the first real champions of local produce, she published two seminal books in the late 1980s and early 1990s: *British Food Finds* and *Food Lovers' Guide to Britain*. Then, in the mid 1990s, she began to stage FoodLovers Fairs around the country. I have fond memories of them, and can vividly recall cooking breakfast for Henrietta Green and the Italian cook Valentina Harris one morning as they crawled rather uncomfortably out of the tent they had pitched next to one particular venue. On another occasion, Peter Gott, a rare-breed pig producer from Sillfield Farm in Cumbria, had to shoot a runaway wild boar and we ended up barbecuing it for dinner, smiling in ecstasy at how good it was. And then there was Borough market, officially opened by Jennifer and myself milking a goat. I suspect we all thought it was only going to last a couple of years, but like Topsy in *Uncle Tom's Cabin* it 'growed' until it became one of the great attractions of south London, ultimately drawing in, I suspect, rather more tourists than food lovers.

Henrietta was also instrumental in setting up the National Association of Farmers' Markets in England. The idea actually came from America. On a visit I made to Los Angeles with Jennifer Paterson I can remember being so impressed by a farmers' market I came across that whenever I was asked in an interview what I liked about America, my invariable response was, 'Farmers' markets!' I took up the call when I was back in England and was delighted when Henrietta got it going, and was equally delighted when she asked me to become the patron. Farmers' markets have a sensibly strict rule that produce must come from no further than twenty miles away (forty in the case of London). I can't help feeling that they have been instrumental in reintroducing town dwellers to country life, and to that extent have played a part in bringing together two worlds that had grown increasingly apart. I'm very encouraged by a recent poll that suggests that one in three of us has bought something from a farmers' market in the last year.

The result of this is that, having gone through decades of increasing conformity and dullness, we're starting to rediscover variety and taste. Take cheese, for example. Back in the 1970s the chances are that the Cheddar you bought came heavily wrapped in plastic and that there wasn't that much to choose between the two in terms of flavour. Now we are seeing artisanal cheeses that are better than those produced by most other countries. And the range is truly impressive: the 'B's alone contain such gems as Berkswell, Beenleigh Blue and Blue Vinney. I was talking to a professor from Strathclyde University only recently who said that, given the way the world is going, we'll have to be much more self-sufficient before long. That can only be good news for what is left of the farming industry.

This re-engagement with fresh ingredients has been taken up by some truly inspiring chefs. Sally Clarke is a good example. Inspired by Alice Waters' Chez Panisse restaurant in Berkeley, California, she opened her own restaurant in Kensington Church Street, which continues to this day and remains true to the Chez Panisse tradition of sourcing the best possible produce and basing the menu strictly on what is in season.

Many of the cooks I associate with 'New Wave' cookery operate in this way. New Wave started out in America, where it was championed essentially by four people: Alice Waters at Chez Panisse, Deborah Madison at Greens, Wolfgang Puck and Jeremiah Tower. Its hallmark is a disregard for traditional pairings of food (for example beef with Yorkshire pudding and horseradish sauce, or lamb with mint sauce) and a love of fusing different cuisines – wonderful when it works, still interesting when it doesn't. Alastair Little, at his restaurant in Frith Street, was a great early exponent of the British version. One of the best things I ever ate was his Fiddlehead fern croziers in tempura batter with a soy-based dipping sauce. It was totally delicious and I remember having it as well as a lobster dish simply because I was there with my god-daughter and I was determined that she should taste it.

I've always shared this obsession with good ingredients well cooked, and I'd like to feel that *Two Fat Ladies*, made by Patricia Llewellyn and seen by some 70 million viewers worldwide, played its part. Jennifer and I were determined to celebrate good cooking and fine ingredients. We also wanted to remind people of the rich heritage of our cuisine, from potted shrimps to bubble and squeak to partridges with cabbage to Yorkshire gingerbread, not to mention such traditional staples as eels, tripe and rabbit. And at the same time we wanted to reflect the cosmopolitan side of English cuisine and remind people that it has always been there to a greater or lesser extent. I, for example, elected on one occasion to cook salt-fish cakes with red pepper tapenade, inspired by a trip to Barbados; salt fish, of course, has been one of the mainstays of the island's diet ever since the slave days of the eighteenth century. On another occasion I prepared beef with chestnuts, pears and almonds, inspired by Catalan cuisine but also, with its blend of sweet and savoury and use of almonds, reminiscent of medieval English fare. The range of the recipes we cooked reflected the range of English taste at its best.

And there's no doubt that today, if you have a mind to it, it's possible to eat better and more interestingly than at more or less any other time of our history. Leaving aside the occasional celebrity chef whose restaurants fail to live up to their fame, there are plenty of wonderful cooks producing fantastic food. Antony Worrall Thompson is one who springs to mind. I've always loved his cooking and his innovative approach. I have fond memories of his restaurant Ménage à Trois, which had the very clever idea of serving just starters and puddings, which you could mix and match as you wished to create a three-course meal; hence the name, allegedly. I also have huge admiration for Marco Pierre White, who, for all his eccentricities, is a stunning chef and a good friend. I remember once being pressed by him to have a tarte tatin. 'I hate tarte tatin,' I confessed. He wouldn't take no for an answer, and soon I found myself eating the most delicious dessert you can imagine. I still don't like tarte tatin except when made by Marco.

What's more, you can now eat great food anywhere. Gone are the days when there were no good restaurants outside London. Take Shaun Hill, for example, who turned Ludlow into a gastronomic paradise. Now he runs the Walnut Tree near Abergavenny, serving completely wonderful food. It seems so appropriate that the restaurant he runs in the twenty-first century should have been one that Elizabeth David once visited on a regular basis. There's also a new-found interest in regional dishes – recipes that became popular because they made ingenious use of local ingredients or proved conveniently cheap and filling to earlier generations.

Ultimately, English food is a moveable feast, never standing still, constantly evolving. There are dishes we regard as foreign that turn out, on closer inspection, to have been part of the national cuisine for centuries. There are others we regard as quintessentially English that are, in reality, recent arrivals. All

should be celebrated. Take fish and chips, for example: a reso-
lutely English dish made with potatoes that came from South
America in the sixteenth century and weren't turned into chips
until the nineteenth, combined with the fried fish that originated
with Victorian Jewish migrants. Compare that with curry,
known to English diners for 250 years and more. Or think of
the changing fortunes of garlic, familiar to Anglo-Saxon cooks
(the word derives from Old English and literally means 'spear-
leek'), distrusted by many early-twentieth-century housewives
and now widely popular again. The changeability and adapt-
ability of English food are its great strengths.

Before they come to get me, I hope I will be allowed the
privilege of a final meal, and it will draw very heavily indeed
on English cuisine. Shaun Hill has kindly agreed to cook it,
and the menu I have selected will be as follows:

Oyster beignets made with native oysters

Freshly cut asparagus with hollandaise sauce

Beef consommé with poached bone marrow

Morecambe Bay brown shimps on Matt Jones rye bread

Mint sorbet

Roast wing rib of White Park beef hung for eight weeks and
served with freshly dug new potatoes, cardoons au gratin,
cream made with freshly grated horseradish and beetroot, gravy

Raspberries with pouring cream and clotted cream

It's perhaps a rather rich meal, but in the circumstances I don't
think I will be too concerned.

Appendix of Historical Recipes

Spiced Wine Custard

4 eggs and 2 extra yolks
600 ml (1 pint) red wine
50 g (2 oz) sugar
1 tsp ground cinnamon
1 tsp ground cloves
½ tsp saffron
½ tsp mace
¼ tsp ground galangal (optional)

To serve:
1 pinch ground ginger
1 pinch ground cinnamon
1 tsp ground nutmeg

In a bowl, beat together the eggs and the yolks. Heat the wine to just below simmering point and whisk into the eggs, then stir in the sugar. Pour the mixture back into the saucepan and add the cinnamon, cloves, saffron, mace and galangal (if using). Stir over heat or in a double boiler.

Once the mixture has thickened, pour it into a serving dish, leave to cool, then chill. In a small bowl, mix together a pinch each of ground ginger and cinnamon and a teaspoon of ground nutmeg. Before serving, sprinkle the top of the custard with this spice mixture.

Thirteenth century

Fried Fig Pasties

450 g (1 lb) dried figs
½ tsp saffron threads
1 egg, separated, plus 1 egg white
¼ tsp salt
¼ tsp ground ginger
¼ tsp ground cloves
a generous pinch of pepper
7 sheets filo pastry (puff pastry will work, too)
oil, for deep-frying
125 ml (4 fl oz) clear honey, warmed

Put the dried figs into a bowl and pour over enough boiling water to cover. Leave to soak until softened (20 minutes–1 hour). Drain the figs, reserving enough liquid to cover the saffron threads. Leave to soak for 15–20 minutes. Meanwhile, mince the figs.

In a bowl, beat the egg yolk, then add the minced figs, saffron, salt, ground ginger, ground cloves and pepper, and mix together.

Beat the egg whites until liquid and use to brush each sheet of pastry. Cut the pastry sheets into 7.5 cm (3 in) wide strips. Put a dab of fig mixture at the end of each strip and roll up like a mini Swiss roll, sealing with the egg white.

Heat the oil and deep-fry the rolls until golden all over. Place on sheets of kitchen paper to drain excess oil, then serve with warm honey poured over the top.

Medieval

Sweet and Sour Fish

oil, for frying
3 fillets of lemon sole or plaice, bream, cod or other firm white fish
150 ml (5 fl oz) red wine
150 ml (5 fl oz) white wine vinegar
2 tbsp sugar
2 small onions, chopped
25 g (1 oz) currants
25 g (1 oz) raisins
25 g (1 oz) sultanas
½ tsp cinnamon
½ tsp powdered ginger
½ tsp pepper

Heat the oil in a frying pan. Cut the fillets into smaller pieces and lightly fry them, then transfer to a serving dish and keep warm.

Heat the wine, vinegar and sugar together in a pan until the sugar has dissolved and the mixture becomes syrupy. Add the onions, dried fruit and spices and cook until the onions are tender. Taste and add some water if necessary. Pour the sauce over the fish and serve.

Medieval

Cream Custard Tart

For the pastry:
225 g (8 oz) flour
65 g (2½ oz) butter, diced, at room temperature
40 g (1½ oz) lard, diced, at room temperature

For the filling:
½ tsp saffron strands
6 egg yolks
375 ml (12 fl oz) double cream
85 ml (3 fl oz) milk
65 g (2½ oz) caster sugar
½ tsp salt

Preheat the oven to 200°C/400°F/gas mark 6. Sift the flour into a large bowl and rub in the butter and lard until the mixture resembles breadcrumbs. Add enough water to bind. Roll out the pastry on a lightly floured surface and use it to line a 20 cm (8 in) loose-bottomed cake tin. Line the pastry case with greaseproof paper and fill with baking beans, then bake blind for 15–20 minutes. Remove the tin from the oven and remove the greaseproof paper and baking beans, then reduce the oven temperature to 160°C/325°F/gas mark 3, return the tin to the oven and bake for a further 6–8 minutes to dry out the pastry.

Soak the saffron in a little warm water for 15–20 minutes until it turns golden. In a bowl, beat the egg yolks lightly, then beat in the cream, milk, sugar, saffron water and salt. Pour the mixture into the pastry case and return to the oven and bake for 45 minutes, or until set. Serve warm.

Medieval

Chicken Pasties

350 g (12 oz) shortcrust pastry
2 eggs, beaten
2 tbsp verjuice or lemon juice
pinch of salt
½ tsp ground black pepper
½ tsp ground ginger
450 g (1 lb) raw chicken, cut into strips
3 large rashers streaky bacon, cut in half

Preheat the oven to 220°C/423°F/gas mark 7. Roll out the pastry on a lightly floured surface and cut into 6 large circles.

In a bowl, mix the eggs, verjuice or lemon juice, salt, pepper and ginger together. Dip the chicken strips in this mixture and divide between the pastry circles, laying the strips on one half only and leaving a border around the rim of each. Lay a piece of bacon on top of each mound of chicken strips. Fold over the empty half of each circle, as for a Cornish pasty, then pinch the edges together to seal and prick a few holes in the top of each pasty.

Bake the pasties in the oven for 15 minutes, then reduce the oven temperature to 190°C/375°F/gas mark 5 and bake for a further 20–25 minutes. Serve hot or cold.

Medieval

Game Casserole

25 g (1 oz) butter
75 g (3 oz) onion, chopped
900 g (2 lb) pheasant (or 2 smaller birds)
2 tbsp flour
150 ml (¼ pint) red wine
150 ml (¼ pint) game (or white) stock
2 cinnamon sticks
2 cloves
pinch of saffron
½ tsp salt
1 tsp white pepper
1 tsp sugar
1 tsp ground ginger

Heat the butter in a large pan, add the onions and cook until softened. Dust the pheasant with the flour and fry with the onions, browning it on all sides.

Remove the pheasant and put the onions into a lidded casserole, then place the pheasant on top. Add the wine, stock, cinnamon sticks, cloves, saffron, salt and pepper to the pan and bring to a simmer. Pour this wine mixture over the pheasant, cover the casserole with a lid and simmer gently for 1–1½ hours. (If you are using two smaller birds, you will need to reduce the cooking time.) Add the sugar and ginger 15 minutes before the end of the cooking time.

Once the bird is cooked, remove it to a serving dish and reduce the sauce by boiling it rapidly. Remove the cinnamon sticks and cloves. Rub the onions through a sieve and mix them back into the sauce. Carve the bird and pour over the sauce to serve.

Late fifteenth century

Sweet Cubes of Jellied Milk

600 ml (1 pint) milk
5 tsp unflavoured gelatine
4 oz sugar
1½ tbsp rose water

Pour 4 tablespoons of the milk into a bowl and sprinkle the gelatine on top. Leave to stand for 5 minutes, then place the bowl on top of a small pot of very hot water and stir until the gelatine is dissolved.

Warm the remaining milk in a pan. Add the sugar and the gelatine mixture and stir for 5 minutes. Remove from heat and stir in the rose water. Pour the mixture into a freshly rinsed square dish, leave to set, then cut into cubes with a sharp knife. Arrange in a pyramid or stack to serve.

Sixteenth century, adapted from The Good Huswife's Iewell

Capon with Orange Sauce

1 large chicken
pinch of salt
225 g (8 oz) oranges, divided into segments
50 g (2 oz) currants
4 dates
150 ml (¼ pint) red wine
1 tbsp rose water
3 tbsp sugar
1 tsp mace
½ tsp black peppercorns
225 g (8 oz) bread, cut into large crustless cubes
butter

Put the chicken in a pan, cover with water, add the salt and simmer until tender (about 45 minutes–1 hour). Do not allow the water to boil or the meat will become tough.

Drain 600 ml (1 pint) of stock from the bird and pour into a pan. Add the orange segments, currants and dates and simmer for 5 minutes, then add the red wine, rose water, sugar, mace and peppercorns, and simmer for a further 5–10 minutes.

Fry the bread cubes in butter and place on a dish. Carve the chicken and lay it on top. Pour the sauce over and serve.

Sixteenth century, adapted from The Good Huswife's Iewell

Knott Biscuits

12 egg yolks
5 egg whites
450 g (1 lb) sugar
225 g (8 oz) flour
225 g (8 oz) butter, washed in rose water
20 g (¾ oz) mace, finely grated
15 g (½ oz) caraway seeds
pinch of salt, dissolved in rose water

Preheat the oven to 180°C/350°F/gas mark 4. Put all the ingredients into a bowl and mix together to form a paste. Cut or shape the dough into knots or rings, place on a baking sheet and bake in the oven for 15–20 minutes, or until the biscuits are golden brown.

Sixteenth century

Real Mince Pie

For the filling:
450 g (1 lb) lean beef, minced
50 g (2 oz) suet
½ tsp ground cloves
½ tsp mace
black pepper
pinch saffron
50 g (2 oz) raisins
50 g (2 oz) currants
50 g (2 oz) stoned, chopped prunes

For the pastry:
450 g (1 lb) plain flour
2 tsp salt
50 g (2 oz) lard
4 tbsp milk

For the glaze:
1 tbsp butter
1 tbsp sugar
1 tbsp rose water

Preheat the oven 225°C/425°F/gas mark 7. Put all the ingredients for the filling in a bowl and mix together.

To make the pastry, sift the flour and salt into a large bowl. Put the lard and milk into a pan with 150 ml (¼ pint) of water and bring to a boil. Pour this on to the flour and mix in with a wooden spoon. Turn the warm mixture on to a lightly floured surface and knead to form a soft dough.

Reserve a quarter of the pastry to make the lid, then roll out the remainder and use to line the base and sides of a 20 cm (8 in) pie dish. Fill with the meat mixture. Roll out the remaining pastry and use it to cover the pie. Seal the pastry edges firmly and make a hole in the lid.

Bake the pie in the oven for 15 minutes, then reduce the oven temperature to 180°C/350°F/gas mark 4 and bake for a further 1½ hours.

In a small pan, melt together the butter, sugar and rose water for the glaze and brush over the top of the pie, then return it to the oven for a further 15 minutes. Serve warm or cold.

Mid sixteenth century

Devonshire White Pot

50 g (2 oz) raisins
450 g (1 lb) white bread
25 g (1 oz) butter
3 eggs
600 ml (1 pint) single cream
75 g (3 oz) sugar
¼ tsp grated nutmeg
¼ tsp salt

Soak the raisins in hot water for 10 minutes. While they are soaking, cut the bread into thin slices and cut off the crusts. Butter a 1.2-litre (2-pint) ovenproof dish. Layer the bread and raisins in the dish, adding a few knobs of butter between the layers.

Preheat the oven to 180°C/350°F/gas mark 4. Beat the eggs with the cream in a bowl, then stir in the sugar, nutmeg and salt and pour the mixture over the bread. Let it stand for 15 minutes, then bake in the oven for 40–45 minutes.

Seventeenth century, after Rebecca Price

Apple and Orange Tart

2 oranges
5 medium apples
175 g (6 oz) sugar
2 tbsp flour
1 tsp cinnamon
1 tsp ginger
1 tbsp butter
675 g (1½ lb) shortcrust pastry
sugar, for sprinkling

Preheat the oven to 190°C/375°F/gas mark 5. Peel the oranges and divide them into segments. Peel and core the apples and slice thinly. In a large bowl, stir together the sugar, flour, cinnamon and ginger, then toss the orange segments and apple slices in this mix.

Roll out about three-quarters of the pastry on a lightly floured surface and use to line a pie dish. Pile the coated fruit into the dish and dot with butter. Roll out the remainder of the pastry and use to cover the dish. Knock up the edges and sprinkle sugar on top. Bake in the oven for 40–45 minutes.

Early seventeenth century, after Elinor Fettiplace

Hash of Crabs

3 or 4 artichoke bottoms, diced, or 3 asparagus spears, cut into 1 cm
  (½ in) pieces
2 large dressed crabs
50 g (2 oz) unsalted butter
½ glass red wine
salt
grated nutmeg

Boil the artichoke or asparagus until tender (about 7–8 minutes), then
drain.

Melt the butter in a pan and add the wine, then stir in the crab meat.

To serve, place the artichoke or asparagus on a plate and top with the
crab mixture.

Seventeenth century, after Robert May

Battered Lemons with Greens and Eggs

A couple handfuls of spinach, finely chopped
1 tsp each of chopped thyme, parsley, endive, savory and marjoram
6 hard-boiled eggs, chopped
¼ tsp ground nutmeg
¼ tsp ground ginger
¼ tsp ground cinnamon
¼ tsp salt
1–2 lemons, thinly sliced
flour, for dusting
oil for deep-frying

For the batter:
75 g (3 oz) plain flour
40 g (1½ oz) self-raising flour
½ tsp baking powder
2 tsp white wine vinegar
125 ml (4 fl oz) cold water
salt and pepper

In a bowl, mix together the chopped spinach, herbs and hard-boiled eggs. Stir in the ground nutmeg, ginger, cinnamon and salt.

To make the batter, put all the ingredients in a bowl with half the cold water and whisk. Gradually add the remaining water until the batter has the consistency of double cream.

Dry the lemon slices on kitchen paper, dust lightly with flour, then dip into the batter. Heat the oil in a deep pan and deep-fry the lemon slices until golden. Serve the battered lemon slices with a spoonful of the egg mixture on top of each.

Seventeenth century, after Robert May

Mackerel with Fennel and Mint

1 bunch of mint leaves, chopped
6 fennel stalks, chopped
50 g (2 oz) toasted breadcrumbs
salt
pepper
ground nutmeg
2 mackerel, cleaned
40g (1½ oz) melted butter
2 anchovy fillets, preserved in oil

In a small bowl, mix together the mint, fennel, toasted breadcrumbs and salt, pepper and ground nutmeg to taste. Stuff the mackerel with this mixture. Smear the fish with about a third of the melted butter and grill on both sides until the fish is cooked.

Mash the anchovy fillets in a small bowl and stir in the remainder of the melted butter. Serve the cooked mackerel with this anchovy butter.

Eighteenth century

Eggs on a Mirror

butter
small bunch of spring onions, chopped
small bunch of parsley, chopped
5 eggs
salt
pepper
ground nutmeg
150 ml (¼ pint) double cream
juice of 1 orange

Preheat the oven to 180°C/350°F/gas mark 4. Butter an ovenproof dish. Mix together the chopped spring onions and parsley and sprinkle over the bottom of the dish. Carefully break the eggs into the dish, sprinkle with salt, pepper and ground nutmeg and pour over the cream.

Bake for 7–8 minutes then remove the dish from the oven, spoon the cream over the eggs and pour over the orange juice. Return the eggs to the oven and cook for a further 7–8 minutes until set.

Eighteenth century, after William Verral

Asparagus in French Rolls

225 g (8 oz) asparagus, cut into pieces
300 ml (½ pint) double cream
6 egg yolks, beaten
salt
pepper
ground nutmeg
6 French rolls
50 g (2 oz) butter
6 thin asparagus spears

Cook the asparagus in a saucepan of boiling water until tender (around 7–8 minutes), then remove from the heat and drain.

Heat the cream in a pan and stir in the beaten egg yolks. Season with salt, pepper and nutmeg and allow to simmer without boiling. Stir in the chopped asparagus and heat through.

Hollow out the rolls and fry them in hot butter until crisp. Fill with the asparagus mixture and add a whole spear to each roll. Serve warm.

Eighteenth century, after John Varley

Macaroni à la Reine

225 g (8 oz) macaroni
275 g (10 oz) Stilton (or other rich cheese), crumbled
50 g (2 oz) melted butter
300 ml (½ pint) double cream or thick white sauce
pinch of pepper
pinch of mace
pinch of cayenne pepper
fried breadcrumbs, crushed

Cook the macaroni in boiling salted water until tender (follow packet instructions), then drain.

Preheat the grill. Heat the cream or white sauce in a saucepan. Add the cheese and melted butter and stir until blended and the cheese has melted. Season to taste with pepper, mace and cayenne pepper.

Pour the sauce over the cooked pasta, mix well and put into an ovenproof dish. Sprinkle the breadcrumbs on top and brown under the grill.

Nineteenth century, after Eliza Acton

Bibliography

Acton, Eliza: *Modern Cookery for Private Families* (London, 1845)

Avery, Susanna: *A Plain Plantain* (London, 1688)

Banham, Debby, and Laura Mason: *Confectionery Recipes from a Fifteenth-Century Manuscript* (*Petits propos culinaires*, February 2002)

Beeton, Isabella: *The Book of Household Management* (London, 1861)

Bennett, Richard, and John Elton: *History of Corn Milling*, 4 vols. (Simpkin Marshall, 1898–1904)

Black, J. B.: *Oxford History of England: The Reign of Elizabeth, 1558–1603* (Clarendon Press, 1985)

Black, Maggie: *Medieval Cookery: Recipes and History* (English Heritage, 2003)

Blencowe, Lady Anne: *The Receipt Book of Lady Anne Blencowe* (c. 1694, reprinted by Heartsease Books, 2004, ed. Christina Stapeley)

Book of Fruit and Flowers, Shewing the Nature and Use of Them, Either from Meat or Medicine, A (London, 1653)

Boke of Keruynge, The (London, 1508)

Boorde, Andrew: *A Compendyous Regyment or a Dyetary of Health* (London, 1542)

Braudel, Fernand: *The Wheels of Commerce: Civilisation and Capitalism* (Collins, 1982)

Brears, Peter: *Cooking and Dining in Medieval England* (Prospect Books, 2008)

Bridge, Tom, and Colin Cooper English: *Dr William Kitchener: Regency Eccentric and Author of The Cook's Chronicle* (Southover Press, 1992)

Burnett, John: *Liquid Pleasures* (Routledge, 1999)

——: *Plenty and Want* (Scolar Press, 2nd edition, 1979)

Carter, Charles: *The Complete Practical Cook, or A New System of the Whole Art and Mystery of Cookery* (London, 1730)

Chiquart (trans. Terence Scully): *'On Cookery': A Fifteenth-Century Savoyard Culinary Treatise* (Peter Lang, 1986)

Cooper, Charles: *The English Table in History and Literature* (Sampson Low, 1929)

Coryate, Thomas: *Coryate's Crudities* (London, 1611)

Court and Kitchen of Elizabeth Commonly Called Joan Cromwell, The (London 1664)

Curtis-Bennett, Sir Noel: *The Food of the People: Being the History of Industrial Feeding* (Faber & Faber, 1949)

David, Elizabeth: *A Book of Mediterranean Food* (John Lehmann, 1950)

———: *French Provincial Cooking* (Penguin Books, 1960)

Davidson, Alan: *The Oxford Companion to Food* (OUP, 1999)

Davidson, Alan, and Helen Saberi: *Trifle* (Prospect Books, 2001)

Dawson, Thomas: *The Good Huswife's Iewell* (London, 1596)

Dictionary of National Biography (OUP, various editions)

Digby, Sir Kenelm: *The Closet of the Eminently Learned Sir Kenelme Digbie Kt. Opened* (London, 1669)

Emmison, F. G.: *Tudor Food and Pastimes* (Ernest Benn, 1964)

Encyclopaedia Britannica (Encyclopaedia Britannica Press, 1926)

Evelyn, John: *Acetaria: A Discourse of Sallats* (London, 1699)

Farley, John: *The London Art of Cookery* (London, 1785)

Fell, Sarah: *The Household Account Book of Sarah Fell of Swarthmoor Hall* (ed. N. Penney, CUP, 1920)

Forme of Cury, The (c. 1390, first published by Samuel Pegge, London, 1780)

Fothergill, John: *An Innkeeper's Diary* (Chatto & Windus, 1932)

———: *My Three Inns* (Chatto & Windus, 1949)

Gascoigne, George: *The Noble Art of Venerie or Hunting* (London, 1575)

Gattey, Charles: *Foie Gras and Trumpets* (Constable, 1984)

Gerard, John: *Generall Historie of Plantes* (London, 1597)

Gibbs, Lavinia: *Uncle Hicky: Sir Hickman Bacon: An Edwardian Eccentric* (Lavinia Gibbs, 2001)

Glasse, Hannah: Archive (Northumberland Record Office, Allgood MSS)

———: *The Art of Cookery Made Plain and Easy* (London, 1746)

———: *The Compleat Confectioner* (London, 1760)

Goodman of Paris: A Treatise on Moral and Domestic Economy by a Citizen of Paris, c. 1393, The (trans. Eileen Power, Boydell Press, 2006)

Griffin, Emma: *Blood Sport: Hunting in Britain since 1066* (Yale, 2007)

Hartley, Dorothy: *Food in England* (Macdonald, 1954)

——: *Land of England: English Country Customs through the Ages* (Macdonald, 1979)

——: *Water in England* (Macdonald, 1964)

Hibbert, Christopher: *The Court at Windsor: A Domestic History* (Longmans, 1964)

——: *The English: A Social History* (Guild, 1987)

Hobhouse, Henry: *Seeds of Change: Five Plants that Transformed Mankind* (Sidgwick & Jackson, 1985)

Jarrin, G. A.: *The Italian Confectioner* (John Harding, 1820)

Jones, Philip E.: *Butchers of London* (Secker & Warburg, 1976)

Labarge, Margaret Wade: *A Baronial Household of the Thirteenth Century* (Eyre and Spottiswoode, 1965)

Lamb, Patrick: *Royal Cookery* (London, 1710)

Lindley, Phillip (ed.): *Gainsborough Old Hall* (King's England Press, 1991)

Mallinson, Allan: *The Making of the British Army, from the English Civil War to the War on Terror* (Bantam, 2009)

Markham, Gervase: *Countrey Contentments or The English Huswife* (London, 1615)

May, Robert: *The Accomplisht Cook* (London, 1660)

Mayhew, Henry: *London Labour and the London Poor* (London, 1851)

McNeil, Robina: *Two 12th-Century Wich Houses in Nantwich, Cheshire* (*Medieval Archaeology*, 1983)

Orwell, George: *The Road to Wigan Pier* (Gollancz, 1937)

Osbaldiston, William Augustus: *The British Sportsman, or, Nobleman, Gentleman and Farmer's Dictionary of Recreation and Amusement* (London, 1792)

Oxford English Dictionary (OUP, various editions)

Patten, Marguerite: *Cookery in Colour* (Hamlyn, 1960)

Pepys, Samuel: *Diaries* (Bell & Hyman, 1970–83)

Plat, Sir Hugh: *Delightes for Ladies* (London, 1602)

Priestland, Gerald: *Frying Tonight: The Saga of Fish and Chips* (Gentry Books, 1972)

Proper New Booke of Cookery, A (London, 1575)

Prothero, Rowland E.: *English Farming, Past and Present* (Longmans, 1912)

Reader, John: *Propitious Esculent: The Potato in World History* (Heinemann, 2008)

Ridley, Jasper: *The Tudor Age* (Overlook, 1991)

Robins, Nick: *The Corporation that Changed the World: How the East India Company Shaped the Modern Multinational* (Pluto Press, 2006)

Rose, Sarah: *For All the Tea in China: Espionage, Empire and the Secret Formula for the World's Favourite Drink* (Hutchinson, 2009)

Rundell, Maria: *A New System of Domestic Cookery* (London, 1805)

Russell, John: *Book of Nurture*, in F. J. Furnivall (ed.), *Early English Meals and Manners* (London, 1868)

Sandford, Francis: *The History of the Coronation of the Most High, Most Mighty and Most Excellent Monarch James II* (London, 1687)

Scully, Terrence (ed.): *The Viandier of Taillevent* (University of Ottawa Press, 1988)

Shepard, Sue: *Pickled, Potted and Canned: The Story of Food Preserving* (Headline, 2000)

Sim, Alison: *Pleasures and Pastimes in Tudor England* (Sutton, 1998)

Smith, Delia: *How to Cook*, 3 vols. (BBC Books, 1998–2001)

Smith, Michael: *Afternoon Tea* (Macmillan, 1986)

——: *Fine English Cookery* (Faber & Faber, 1964)

Soyer, Alexis: *The Gastronomic Regenerator* (London, 1846)

Spry, Constance, and Rosemary Hume: *The Constance Spry Cookery Book* (Dent, 1956)

Spufford, Peter: *Power and Profit: The Merchant in Medieval Europe* (Thames & Hudson, 2002)

Spurling, Hilary (ed.): *Elinor Fettiplace's Receipt Book: Elizabethan Country House Cooking* (Viking, 1986)

Stocks, Christopher: *Forgotten Fruits* (Random House Books, 2008)

Thompson, Flora: *Lark Rise to Candleford* (OUP, 1939)

Trusler, John: *The Honours of the Table* (London, 1788)

Turner, Ralph V.: *Eleanor of Aquitaine: Queen of France, Queen of England* (Yale, 2009)

Tusser, Thomas: *A Hundred Good Pointes of Husbandrie* (London, 1557)

Verral, William: *A Complete System of Cookery* (London, 1759)

Vesey-Fitzgerald, Brian Seymour: *Gypsies of Britain* (David & Charles, 1973)

Weinreb, Ben, and Christopher Hibbert: *The London Encyclopaedia* (Macmillan, 1983)

Weir, Alison: *Eleanor of Aquitaine: By the Wrath of God, Queen of England* (Jonathan Cape, 1999)

Widow's Treasure, The (London, 1639)

Wilson, C. Anne: *Banquetting Stuffe: The Fare and Social Background of the Tudor and Stuart Banquet* (Edinburgh UP, 1991)

——: *Food and Drink in Britain: From the Stone Age to the 19th Century* (Barnes and Noble, 1974)

Winder, Robert: *Bloody Foreigners* (Little, Brown, 2004)

Woodforde, James: *Passages from the Five Volumes of The Diary of a Country Parson*, ed. John Beresford (OUP, 1935)

Woolgar, C. M.: *The Great Household in Late Medieval England* (Yale, 1999)

Woolley, Hannah: *The Cook's Guide, or Rare Receipts for Cookery* (London, 1664)

Yarwood, Maureen: *The British Kitchen: Housewifery since Roman Times* (Batsford, 1981)

Picture Acknowledgements

Black and white illustrations are reproduced by kind permission of:

The Advertising Archives: 416; The Bridgeman Art Library: 42 (Private Collection), 76 (Private Collection), 116 (Private Collection/The Stapleton Collection), 148 (Private Collection/ The Stapleton Collection), 200 (Guildhall Library, City of London), 230 (The Stapleton Collection), 254 (Private Collection), 314 (Private Collection), 342 (© British Library Board. All Rights Reserved), 444 (Private Collection/The Stapleton Collection/Royal College of Art); The British Library: xii (©The British Library Board); Mary Evans Picture Library: 170, 380 (Lynne's Collection); Wellcome Library: 292.

Colour illustrations are reproduced by kind permission of:

Inset One
Alamy: Cinnamon merchant (© The Art Gallery Collection), The Burghley Nef (© INTERFOTO); The Art Archive: Harvesting (© The British Library Board), Woman milking (Biblioteca d'Ajuda Lisbon/Gianni Dagli Orti); The Bridgeman Art Library: Beehive (© The British Library Board), Ploughing with oxen (© The British Library Board. All Rights Reserved), The measure and transport of wine (Bibliotheque Historique de la Ville de Paris/Archives Charmet), Roasting meat on a spit (© British Library Board. All Rights Reserved), Gainsborough Old Hall kitchen (John Bethell), Medieval pottery (© Museum of London), Sir Geoffrey Luttrell dining with his family (© British Library Board. All Rights Reserved); The British Library: Calendar scene from the Queen Mary Psalter (© The British Library Board), Watermill (© The British Library Board); Heritage Images: King John hunting (© The British Library), Man hawking (© The British Library), Baking bread (© The British Library).

Inset Two
Alamy: Hampton Court kitchen (© charistoone-images); The Art Archive: William Brooke and family (Marquess of Bath/Eileen Tweedy); The Bridgeman Art Library: *Charles I, Queen Henrietta Maria, and Charles, Prince of Wales, dining in public, 1635* (The Royal Collection/© 2011 Her Majesty Queen Elizabeth II), *Map of London* (Glasgow University Library), *The Coronation Procession of King Edward VI in 1547* (Society of Antiquaries of London), *A Fete at Bermondsey* (Hatfield House, Hertfordshire), The old kitchen at Canons Ashby (© Country Life), Delft plate (Victoria & Albert Museum), Stuart dish (Fitzwilliam Museum, University of Cambridge), 17th-century cutlery (Ashmolean Museum, University of Oxford), *John Tradescant the Elder* (Ashmolean Museum, University of Oxford), Billingsgate Market (Private Collection), Pineapple lithograph (Private Collection), *Portrait of Sir Kenelm Digby* (Private Collection/ Photo © Philip Mould Ltd, London); Mary Evans Picture Library: Woodcut of tavern scene, Frontispiece of *The Accomplisht Cook*.

Inset Three
Alamy: Kitchen of the Georgian House, Edinburgh (© Holmes Garden Photos); The Bridgeman Art Library: *Robert Bakewell on Horseback* (New Walk Museum & Art Gallery/Photo © Leicester Arts Museums), *Panoramic View of Charlton Park* (© Cheltenham Art Gallery & Museums), *Portrait of Thomas William Coke, Esq.* (© Collection of the Earl of Leicester, Holkham Hall), *The Comforts of Bath: Gouty Gourmand at Dinner* (Private Collection/Photo © Agnew's, London), Kedleston Hall (National Trust Photographic Library/Nadia Mackenzie), *A View of the Temple of Comus at Vauxhall Gardens* (Private Collection/The Stapleton Collection), Cauliflower teapot (Fitzwilliam Museum, University of Cambridge), *A Family Being Served with Tea* (Yale Center for British Art, Paul Mellon Collection), *The Coffee House Politicians* (Private Collection), Sugar refinery (Bibliotheque Nationale, Paris/Giraudon), *The Anglers' Repast* (Private Collection), *The Warrener* (Private Collection), *Hare shooting* (Private Collection), *Haymakers* (© Lady Lever Art Gallery, National Museums Liverpool), Frontispiece of *The Housekeeper's Instructor* (Private Collection).

Inset Four

The Advertising Archives: Advertisement for Indian Relish; Alamy: Advertising leaflet for Meredith & Drew Ltd (© Amoret Tanner), 'The Children's Party' advertisement (© Amoret Tanner), Advertisement for Colman's Mustard (© Lordprice Collection); The Bridgeman Art Library: *Billingsgate Market, 1893* (Private Collection/The Stapleton Collection), *Kitchen Interior in a Grand House* (© Gavin Graham Gallery, London), *The Dinner Party* (Private Collection/© Philip Gale Fine Art, Chepstow), Photograph of four domestic maids (Private Collection/The Stapleton Collection); 'Half penny ices' (© Museum of London), Slum interior (© Museum of London), *The Christmas Hamper* (Private Collection); Heritage Images: Richie & McCall's cannery (Ann Ronan Picture Library); Jewish Museum: Photograph of the Kahn & Botsman shop (© Jewish Museum London); Mary Evans Picture Library: Shopfront of Wareham & Arscott Stores (Retrograph Collection), Dinner table *à la Russe*; Wellcome Library: *Sake Deen Mahomed*.

Inset Five

The Advertising Archives: Advertisement for 'English Electric' fridges, Advertisement for OXO, Ministry of Agriculture poster; Alamy: Farmers' market (© Dragomir Misina); The Bridgeman Art Library: *The Arrival of the Jarrow Marchers* (© Geffrye Museum); Corbis: Fifties housewife (© Ocean), August Escoffier (© Hulton–Deutsch Collection), Delia Smith (© David Reed); Getty Images: Purchasing rations (Popperfoto), Silver Slipper Club party (Popperfoto), Milkman in Finsbury Park, Philip Harben; Heritage Images: 'Making the Empire Christmas Pudding' (© The National Archives), Somme field kitchen (Stapleton Historical Collection), Cover of the *Fanny and Johnnie Cradock Cookery Programme* book (© Land of Lost Content); Mary Evans Picture Library: 'The Cocktail Party' (© Illustrated London News Ltd), Bailey's grocery store (The Norman Synge Waller Budd Collection); Optomen Television: Two Fat Ladies (Jason Bell); Topfoto: Tesco photograph.

Index